Russia under Vladimir Putin has proved a prickly partner for the West, a far cry from the democratic ally many hoped for when the Soviet Union collapsed. Abroad, he has used Russia's energy might as a foreign policy weapon, while at home he has cracked down on opponents, adamant that only he has the right vision for his country's future.

Former BBC Moscow correspondent Angus Roxburgh charts the dramatic fight for Russia's future under Vladimir Putin – how the former KGB man changed from reformer to autocrat, how he sought the West's respect but earned its fear, how he cracked down on his rivals at home and burnished a flamboyant personality cult, one day saving snow leopards or horse-back riding bare-chested, the next tongue-lashing Western audiences. Drawing on dozens of exclusive interviews in Russia, where he worked for a time as a Kremlin insider advising Putin on press relations, as well as in the US and Europe, Roxburgh also argues that the West threw away chances to bring Russia in from the cold, by failing to understand its fears and aspirations following the collapse of communism.

'[Written] with admirable even-handedness and insight ... *The Strongman* is not only political history; it is informed by the author's close acquaintance with many of the prime players ... Every chapter of this book is worth reading.' – Mary Dejevsky, *Independent*

'The considerable value of this book lies in [Roxburgh's] painstaking and empathetic effort to understand how Mr Putin came to power, why many Russians still support him today, and how the West's approach to Russia has helped to shape his rule.' – Paul Starobin, *Wall Street Journal*

'[A] lively and absorbing study ... [Roxburgh] is especially well placed to tell the story of how the West's early enthusiasm for Putin turned sour.' – Luke Harding, *Guardian*

'We need an insider to give us some insight into what has really been going on since 1999, when Putin went from unknown to acting president. It is fortunate then that we have Angus Roxburgh ... fair, nuanced and well written ... His account of the complete mutual incomprehension between his employers, Ketchum, and the Russians they worked with is fascinating.' – Oliver Bullough, *Sunday Telegraph*

THE STRONGMAN

VLADIMIR PUTIN
AND THE STRUGGLE FOR
RUSSIA

ANGUS ROXBURGH

I.B. TAURIS

LONDON · NEW YORK

Second Edition, revised and updated, published in 2013
Reprinted 2013 and 2014 by
I.B.Tauris & Co Ltd
6 Salem Road, London W2 4BU
175 Fifth Avenue, New York NY 10010
www.ibtauris.com

Distributed in the United States and Canada Exclusively by
Palgrave Macmillan, 175 Fifth Avenue, New York NY 10010

First published in hardback in 2012 by I.B.Tauris & Co Ltd

ISBN: 978 1 78076 504 4

A full CIP record for this book is available from the British Library
A full CIP record is available from the Library of Congress

Library of Congress Catalog Card Number: available

Typeset in Goudy Old Style by A. & D. Worthington, Newmarket
Printed and bound in Great Britain by
CPI Group (UK) Ltd, Croydon, CR0 4YY

CONTENTS

ABOUT THE AUTHOR

Angus Roxburgh is a respected British foreign correspondent and Russia specialist. He was the *Sunday Times* Moscow correspondent in the mid-1980s and the BBC's Moscow correspondent during the Yeltsin years. He is the author of *The Second Russian Revolution* and *Pravda: Inside the Soviet Press Machine*.

INTRODUCTION

When you shake hands with Vladimir Putin you scarcely notice whether it is a firm or a weak handshake. It is his eyes that consume you. He lowers his head, tilting his eyes upwards towards you, and fixes you for several seconds, as though memorising every detail, or maybe matching your face to a picture he had memorised earlier ... It is a glowering, piercing, highly unsettling look.

Russia's 'national leader' is like no other country's president or prime minister. The former KGB spy was rather reserved and gauche at first, when he was unexpectedly propelled into high office in 1999. But he has grown into a man with no inhibitions – a strongman and a narcissist, who flaunts his physical strength in ever more frequent photo-shoots. In the beginning we saw only a few selected images – Putin the judo champion, Putin at the controls of a fighter jet. Later – particularly after he moved from the president's office to that of the prime minister in 2008 – he began to invite camera crews on expeditions designed solely to project a film-star image. They showed him putting satellite tracking devices on polar bears, tigers, white whales and snow leopards. He took the cameras along to see him swimming the butterfly stroke in an icy Siberian river, and riding a horse through mountains, with bare chest and dark shades. He personally put out wildfires, drove snowmobiles, motorbikes and Formula One cars, went skiing and scuba-diving, played ice hockey, and even crooned 'Blueberry Hill' in English and played the piano in public – unembarrassed by his inability to do either. In August 2011 he had a cameraman on hand when he stripped to the waist for a doctor's examination.

What other world leader acts like this? Having muscular policies is one thing; but no one matches Putin for sheer vanity.

In conversation he is attentive, combative and sometimes explosive, when he touches upon sensitive matters. He is exceedingly well-informed, but also surprisingly ignorant about aspects of Western life. He is courteous, but can also be boorish. As president and then as prime minister he has run Russia with a strong, and tightening, grip. In recent years he has taken to dressing down his ministers in public, creating an atmosphere in which most of his subordinates are terrified of contradicting him, or even of voicing an opinion in case it *might* contradict him. He has created a top-down system – the 'vertical of power' – which instils fear and stifles initiative.

Russia has become a state contemptuous of its people's rights: a country in which the head of the electoral commission says his guiding principle is that whatever Putin says must be correct, and the chairman of parliament describes it as 'no place for discussions'. It is a country in which the most important decision about who will become president is effectively taken in private by two individuals, with no reference to the populace. This was what happened in September 2011, when Putin's protégé and successor as president, Dmitry Medvedev, agreed to retire from the top job after one term to allow Putin to return as president in 2012 for, potentially, another 12 years. The two men cynically admitted what people had suspected but did not know for sure, that this had been the plan ever since Putin had stepped aside from the presidency in 2008: Medvedev's stint in the Kremlin was a mere seat-warming exercise, designed to keep Putin in power for as long as he wished, while paying lip-service to (or, in fact, flouting) the constitutional ban on a president serving more than two consecutive terms.

Putin did not start out like this. Back in 2000 many Western leaders at first welcomed his fresh, new approach, and his willingness to cooperate and seek consensus. It will be the task of this book to try to chronicle and explain how everything changed: why Putin became more and more authoritarian, how he challenged the West and how the West challenged him too; how each side failed to see the other's concerns, causing a spiral of mutual mistrust and lost opportunities. On the one hand there is what the Americans and the West observed: Russia's political crackdown, the brutal war in Chechnya and murders of journalists, the corrupt mafia state and growing bellicosity, culminating in the invasion of Georgia and the gas wars against Ukraine. On the other, there is Russia's view: America's domineering role in the world, its missile defence plans, the invasion of Iraq, the expansion of NATO, Russia's positive gestures that went unanswered, the perceived threat to spread revolutions from Georgia and Ukraine to Russia. And there is each side's failure of vision: Putin's inability to see any connection between his own repressions at home and the hostile reaction abroad; George W. Bush's inability to understand Russia's age-old fear of encirclement or its fury at his high-handed foreign policy adventures.

At the time of writing Putin remains the most popular politician in Russia, perhaps because of the measure of stability and self-esteem he restored to people's lives, and because living standards improved during his rule, due largely to high oil prices which benefit Russia. And yet he has failed in many of his stated goals. Having come to power promising to annihilate terrorism, the number of attacks has grown; corruption has soared, and cripples the economy; the population has slumped under his leadership by 2.2 million people; foreign investment has been far lower, as a percentage of Russia's economic output, than rival fast-growing emerging markets such as Brazil or China; and, despite the massive inflows of energy revenues in the past decade, Russia has failed to create a dynamic, modern economy. This book looks at the struggle for reform inside Russia, and asks whether Dmitry Medvedev as president was (as it often seemed) a frustrated liberal or mere window-dressing.

Politicians are prone to oversimplify complicated issues, especially if it is in their interests to do so. This has been especially true of the discussion in recent years of what is perhaps the trickiest of all international political problems – the right of small nations to self-determination. Kosovo, Chechnya, South Ossetia, Abkhazia, Transnistria ... gallons of ink and roomfuls of hot air have been expended in explaining, usually with categorical assurance, that one small country's independence is or is not a precedent for others. Usually it is the big 'mother country' that insists all other cases are unique (Russia vis-à-vis Chechnya, Georgia vis-à-vis South Ossetia and Abkhazia), while the small nations demand to be treated the same way as those who gained their freedom. It is an issue of exceptional importance in Russia, a multinational state like no other, where dozens of nationalities coexist, some with greater or lesser autonomy, and where the Kremlin has a pathological fear of the state disintegrating if any one of those nations is allowed to set a precedent by gaining independence. The issue runs through the history of the last decade, from the war in Chechnya and the welter of terrorist incidents in Russia, to the short war between Russia and Georgia in 2008. Usually no side is 'right' in any of these conflicts, and it would be simplistic to pretend otherwise – just as it would be simplistic to pretend that the West's decision to recognise Kosovo and NATO's decision on future membership for Georgia and

Ukraine had no bearing on relations between Russia and its neighbours. Perceptions and misperceptions of the other side's intentions often play a greater – and usually more harmful – role than reality.

This is my third book about Russia, and I am aware of the presumptuousness of any foreigner who claims to understand that baffling country. The Russian political scholar Sergei Karaganov wrote of the 'feelings of resentment and rejection that we Russians have when reading unpleasant notes about our country written by foreigners'. There is much that is unpleasant in Russian politics today, and it deserves to be written about. Russia is sometimes its own worst enemy, seeing ill intentions abroad where there are none, and fearing the spread of democracy rather than welcoming it. But there is also a failure on the part of the West to understand the processes going on there or to treat Russia with respect as a country that wants to be part of the world, not shunned by it.

***

This book stems partly from my work as chief consultant on a four-part BBC television documentary titled 'Putin, Russia & the West', made by the Brook Lapping production company. For the series, we conducted hundreds of hours of top-level interviews not only in Russia but also in the US, Britain, France, Germany, Ukraine and Georgia. These original interviews cast fresh light on many of the events covered, and are at the heart of my narrative.

I also draw, particularly for Chapter 9 of the book, on my personal experiences while working for three years as an adviser to President Putin's press secretary, Dmitry Peskov. When the Kremlin decided in 2006 to take on a New York public-relations company, Ketchum, and its Brussels-based partner, GPlus, I found myself making an unexpected detour from my career as a journalist. Neither Ketchum nor GPlus had anyone on their staff who knew much about Russia, and suddenly they needed someone and offered me a job. After eight years covering the European Union, the idea of immersing myself in Russia again was appealing. Most of my career had revolved around it: I had studied and taught Russian, worked as a translator in Moscow and for the BBC Monitoring Service, been Moscow correspondent of the *Sunday Times* and later the BBC.

There was one piquant moment in my biography that made the offer even more tempting. Back in 1989, when Putin was a KGB spy in Dresden, his bosses deported me from Moscow in retaliation for Margaret Thatcher's expulsion of Soviet spies from London. I was then the *Sunday Times* correspondent and was one of three journalists and eight diplomats who were kicked out in the last big spy scandal of the Cold War. How ironic, I thought, to return to Moscow as Putin's adviser! I accepted, and became a Kremlin media consultant, based in Brussels but travelling regularly to Moscow. I was part of a team of some 20–30 people worldwide, but the only full-time consultant. I came to know Peskov and his team very well, and although they always kept up their guard, I was as close as any foreigner in those years to the corridors of power. My personal observations form the basis for much of what I describe during the years 2006–2009.

Our main task as media advisers to the Kremlin was to persuade them to open up to the press, on the rather obvious premise that the more you speak the more your views will be heard. The Russian political class proved remarkably resistant to this idea, and remained so long after I left the PR world and returned to journalism – as I discovered while working on the BBC television series. Persuading senior Russian politicians to give interviews was immensely difficult, and several key figures refused altogether. Others agreed, but only after many months of obstruction by their subordinates who seemed unwilling or afraid even to pass on our request. President Medvedev's spokeswoman, Natalia Timakova, refused point-blank even to speak to us. Ironically it was easier to gain top-level access to the Kremlin in the final years of communism, when I worked on the BBC series *The Second Russian Revolution*, than it is now. Our task became even harder as political uncertainty crept in during the year prior to the 2012 presidential elections. The entire administration was in limbo, as Putin and his president, Dmitry Medvedev, refused to reveal which of them would run for re-election. Suddenly we found that interviews that had been promised were declined. It became clear that canny politicians and functionaries did not dare to stick their necks out in such a time of flux.

Nonetheless we did interview more than a hundred people (either on or off the record) for the TV series and this book. They include heads of government, foreign ministers and senior advisers in eight countries. In Russia we spoke to Lyudmila Alexeyeva, Anatoly Antonov, Stanislav Belkovsky, Vladimir Chizhov, Boris Chochiev, Arkady Dvorkovich, Viktor Gerashchenko, German Gref, Alexei Gromov, Sergei Guriev, Andrei Illarionov, Igor Ivanov, Sergei Ivanov, Grigory Karasin, Mikhail Kasyanov, Viktor Khristenko, Yevgeny Kiselyov, Eduard Kokoity, Andrei Kolesnikov, Konstantin Kosachev, Alexander Kramarenko, Alexei Kudrin, General Marat Kulakhmetov, Sergei Kupriyanov, Sergei Lavrov, Fyodor Lukyanov, Mikhail Margelov, Sergei Markov, Vladimir Milov, Oleg Mitvol, Dmitry Muratov, Gleb Pavlovsky, Dmitry Peskov, Sergei Prikhodko, Yevgeny Primakov, Dmitry Rogozin, Sergei Ryabkov, Vladimir Ryzhkov, Viktor Shenderovich, Dmitry Trenin, Yuri Ushakov, Alexander Voloshin and Igor Yurgens.

In the USA we interviewed Matthew Bryza, Bill Burns, Nicholas Burns, Eric Edelman, Daniel Fata, Daniel Fried, Philip Gordon, Rose Gottemoeller, Thomas Graham, Stephen Hadley, Lt-Col Robert Hamilton, John Herbst, Fiona Hill, General James Jones, David Kramer, Michael McFaul, General Trey Obering, Stephen Pifer, Colin Powell, Condoleezza Rice, Stephen Sestanovich, Dean Wilkening and Damon Wilson.

In Georgia we spoke to Irakli Alasania, David Bakradze, Giga Bokeria, Nino Burjanadze, Vladimer Chachibaia, Raphael Gluckmann, Natalia Kinchela, Erosi Kitsmarishvili, Daniel Kunin, Batu Kutelia, Alexander Lomaia, Vano Merabishvili, Mikheil Saakashvili, Eka Tkeshelashvili, Grigol Vashadze, Temur Yakobashvili and Eka Zguladze.

In the UK we spoke to Tony Brenton, John Browne, Nick Butler, Jonathan Cohen, Michael Davenport, Martha Freeman, David Miliband, Craig Oliphant, Jonathan Powell, George Robertson and Alexander Temerko.

In Ukraine we interviewed Leonid Kuchma, Hrihoriy Nemyria, Oleh Rybachuk and Viktor Yushchenko, and in Poland Alexander Kwaśniewski and Radoslaw Sikorski.

In Germany we interviewed Rolf Nikel, Alexander Rahr, Gerhard Schröder and Frank-Walter Steinmeier, and in France our sources were Jean-David Levitte and Maurice Gourdault-Montagne.

I would like to thank the producer of the Brook Lapping series, Norma Percy, and the executive producer, Brian Lapping, for giving me the opportunity to work on this long but rewarding project. My thanks go to directors Wanda Koscia and David Alter for reading some of the chapters, and to assistant producer Tim Stirzaker for his indefatigable research and organisational help. Above all I am indebted to the series director, Paul Mitchell, and the Moscow producer, Masha Slonim, for their stream of advice and insights. Neil Buckley and Fiona Hill kindly read the manuscript or parts of it and made many sensible suggestions, for which I am very grateful. John Crowfoot and Geoff Bentley spotted a couple of factual errors which I have corrected for this second edition. Lastly, warm thanks to my agent Bill Hamilton, and my excellent editor at I.B.Tauris, Joanna Godfrey.

1

THE SECRET POLICEMAN'S BALL

A new millennium

The Putin era began at midday on the last day of the twentieth century. Taking the entire world by surprise, a wheezing, faltering President Boris Yeltsin appeared on television to announce his resignation, six months ahead of schedule. In a voice breaking with emotion he asked Russians to forgive him for his mistakes and failings, and told his people that Russia should enter the new millennium with 'new politicians, new faces, new intelligent, strong and energetic people'.

Yeltsin had recorded the address in the Kremlin earlier that morning. The first people to know about it, apart from his daughter Tatiana and his closest advisers, were the television technicians who loaded his script into the autocue machine. When he finished he turned away and wiped tears from his eyes, then opened a bottle of champagne, poured a glass for the camera crew and the few presidential staff who were present, clinked glasses and downed his own one in a single go. Even as he did so, his designated successor, Vladimir Putin, was being made up behind a screen in the same room to record his own New Year's address to the people.

It would be broadcast just before midnight. But first he had a few formalities to see to. At two o'clock he was given the 'nuclear briefcase' containing the codes needed to launch a nuclear strike. Then he held a five-minute meeting of his cabinet, followed by a longer session of his Security Council. At six he signed his first presidential decree, granting Yeltsin and the members of his family immunity from prosecution. Then he held a series of quick one-on-one meetings with key ministers. And finally, cancelling a planned trip to St Petersburg, he swept out of the Kremlin in the presidential motorcade and headed for Vnukovo airport. He had plans to bring in the New Year somewhere special.

While billions of people around the globe ushered in the new millennium with parties and fireworks, Russia's new acting president was onboard a military helicopter trying to fly into the rebel republic of Chechnya in hazardous weather conditions that eventually forced the chopper to return to base in neighbouring Dagestan. This was the Putin the world would come to know and fear – the tough guy, the action man, obsessed with combating terrorists and separatists, determined to restore the pride of a country that under Yeltsin had come to look shambolic and sick.

As his helicopter battled with the elements over Chechnya, Russian television aired his pre-recorded address to the nation. It was brief and matter-of-fact, declaring there would be no vacuum of power and paying tribute to his predecessor. It contained only one policy pledge, which in retrospect looks quite remarkable. He said: 'The state will stand firm to protect freedom of speech, freedom of conscience, freedom of the mass media, and property rights, those fundamental elements of a civilised society.'

The freedoms and rights he praised were precisely those that had been obliterated in the communist USSR and then restored under Yeltsin. And yet within a few years Putin would stand accused of flouting them himself, creating a new kind of post-communist authoritarian model, trampling on the free press, and persecuting business tycoons – or indeed anyone – who dared to challenge him.

Why did that happen? The key, or at least one of the keys, to understanding Putin's journey is to look at the Russia he inherited from Yeltsin – a Russia not just economically and militarily weak, but also patronised by the West.

Yeltsin and Clinton

Bill Clinton made his last visit to Russia as American president in June 2000, just two months after Putin's inauguration. Clinton had met Boris Yeltsin some 20 times and built up a close, bantering relationship that came to be described as the 'Bill 'n' Boris Show'. He had also met Putin a couple of times, but like most Western leaders still knew little about him other than his prowess at judo and his past career as a KGB agent – and that was enough to make him wary. Now he found Putin a tough negotiator, who, irritatingly, already regarded Clinton as a lame-duck president with little more than half a year left in office.

Standing a good six inches shorter than the imposing American president, Putin made up for his lack of stature as any judo player does – with agility and skill. He doggedly resisted American plans to abandon (or even amend) the 1972 Anti-Ballistic Missile treaty so as to allow the US to develop a national missile defence programme – the 'Star Wars' system first promoted by Ronald Reagan. The ABM treaty banned both Russia and the United States from deploying defences against nuclear missiles, and for Putin it was a cornerstone of nuclear deterrence: if one side was allowed to develop systems that could shoot down the other's long-range missiles then the delicate balance of power would be destroyed and the side with the shield might be tempted to launch a pre-emptive strike.

Putin dismissed Clinton's criticisms of the brutal new

campaign he was waging in Chechnya and his crackdown against NTV, Russia's leading independent television station. And he revealed his enduring resentment of NATO's bombing of Serbia in 1999 – an event that would inform Putin's foreign-policy thinking throughout the next ten years.

The campaign against Serbia, which was designed to put an end to President Milosevic's ethnic cleansing in Kosovo, was a pivotal moment in Russia's relations with the West. Throughout the Yugoslav wars of the 1990s, Moscow supported Milosevic, at least partly because of traditional Russian affinity with the Serbs, who, like Russians, are Orthodox Christian Slavs.

The 'brotherly ties' between Russians and Serbs may be exaggerated, but the Kremlin certainly saw parallels between Milosevic's attempts to subdue 'terrorism' and separatism in Kosovo and Yeltsin's fight against the same problems in Chechnya. Just as Yeltsin branded the Chechen rebels 'bandits', so Milosevic (and indeed at one point the US government) regarded the Kosovo Liberation Army as a terrorist group. Having launched a bloody war against Chechnya, causing tens of thousands of deaths and a mass exodus of refugees, it was entirely consistent for the Russians to support Milosevic in his efforts to maintain the integrity of what remained of Yugoslavia.

But Yeltsin's pleas not to attack Serbia went unheeded, leaving Moscow feeling that for all the bonhomie of the Bill 'n' Boris Show, and for all the talk of welcoming post-communist Russia into the community of civilised nations, its word counted for nothing. On the eve of NATO's air strikes on Belgrade, Yeltsin would explode with anger during telephone calls with Clinton and sometimes slam down the phone.[1]

Yeltsin's prime minister, Yevgeny Primakov, was flying to Washington on 23 March 1999. He had talks planned with President Clinton, Vice-President Al Gore and the International Monetary Fund. His mission was to secure multi-billion-dollar loans to help stabilise the Russian economy, still reeling from the financial collapse of August 1998. According to Primakov's assistant, Konstantin Kosachev, the prime minister called Gore during a refuelling stop at Shannon in Ireland, and asked: 'Are you going to bomb Yugoslavia?' Gore replied: 'I cannot tell you anything, no decision has been made.'[2]

The government plane took off for the flight across the Atlantic. In the back were Russian business tycoons and officials, drinking vodka and playing dominoes. Suddenly, after four or five hours, Primakov received a call on a crackly, encrypted phone line. It was Gore telling him that NATO air strikes were, in fact, about to begin. Primakov at once called Yeltsin, checked with the pilot whether they had enough fuel to return to Shannon, and then went through to the cabin to inform the businessmen that the trip was abandoned: doing business with the Americans at this moment would be inappropriate.

The reaction was telling. The tycoons, allowing their patriotism to outweigh their business acumen, broke into applause. 'It was very emotional,' says Kosachev. The decision to turn the plane around in mid-flight was meant to send a signal of Russia's profound displeasure. Over the next days the same feelings spilled out onto the streets, as thousands of Russians protested outside the US embassy in Moscow.

On his final presidential visit to Moscow a year later Clinton found the wound was still festering. Putin presented himself as a man who would no longer allow Russia to be ignored or pushed around. For two days he hammered home his criticism of America's plans for a unilateral missile defence shield. Then on the final morning, as they held a farewell meeting in the Kremlin, Putin issued a dark threat that if America went ahead with its plans, Russia's response would be 'appropriate' and 'maybe quite unexpected, probably asymmetrical' – in other words, the Russians would not try to match the sophisticated and costly US system but would take means to render it ineffective. That could mean anything from building huge numbers of nuclear missiles to overwhelm the proposed shield, to destroying the American installations as soon as they were set up.

Clinton heard out Putin's homily, then turned to his aide, Strobe Talbott, and murmured, 'I guess that guy thought I didn't get it the first time. Either he's dense or thinks I am. Anyway, let's get this thing over with so we can go see Ol' Boris.'[3]

With relief, the Americans then drove out of the Kremlin to bid farewell to Clinton's friend, ex-President Yeltsin, now living in retirement in his country dacha. There was a surprise waiting for him. By the time he got there Putin had called Yeltsin and asked him to rub in the message even harder. Russia, he said, would not put up with any American policy that threatened Russian security. When the tirade was over, Clinton steered the conversation back to his own concerns about Russia's future. His parting words, as related by his adviser Strobe Talbott, were quite remarkable – and revealing of the American view of Russia after the fall of communism.

'Boris,' he said, 'you've got democracy in your heart, you've got the trust of the people in your bones, you've got the fire in your belly of a real democrat and a real reformer. I'm not sure Putin has that. You'll have to keep an eye on him and use your influence to make sure that he stays on the right path. Putin needs you, Boris. Russia needs you ... You changed Russia. Russia was lucky to have you. The world was lucky you were where you were. *I* was lucky to have you. We did a lot of stuff together, you and I ... We did some good things. They'll last. It took guts on your part. A lot of that stuff was harder for you than it was for me. I know that.'

As he left Yeltsin's dacha, Clinton turned to Talbott: 'That may be the last time I see Ol' Boris. I think we're going to miss him.'

Clinton's mawkish words clearly suggest he thought that under Yeltsin things had gone very well in Russia and Russia was where America wanted it to be. In fact, things were not going well, and Russia did not want just to go wherever America wanted it to be. In reality, what America was going to miss was a Russian leader who was compliant to the point of submissiveness. Putin would be anything but that.

Yeltsin's Russia

The West's handling of post-Soviet Russia had been just about as insensitive as it could have been. With Western corporations salivating at the prospect of a huge new market, Harvard economists hired by the Russian government urged it to introduce unrestrained capitalism at breakneck speed, with scant regard for the sensitivities of – and consequences for – the Russian people. Their ideas were eagerly taken up by Yeltsin's own reformers, led by the economist Yegor Gaidar, who had been inspired by the 'shock therapy' that had transformed countries like Poland a couple of years earlier. Yeltsin had appointed him to 'give the people economic freedom, and remove all barriers to the freedom of enterprises and entre-preneurship'. Within a few years millions of Russians were reduced to extreme poverty, while a handful of go-getters and former communist officials turned themselves into billionaire oligarchs, snapping up the country's resources for a fraction of their value.

Undoubtedly, under Yeltsin Russians enjoyed Freedom, with a great neon-lit, capital F, such as they had never known in their nation's thousand-year history. The 1990s were riotous years. They saw an explosion of energies that had been pent up for 70 years of communism. Any Russian with a bit of cash and enterprise could set up a small business, if only a little stall selling Snickers bars and vodka. Russians were free to travel abroad, to read whatever they wished, say what they liked and demonstrate against their leaders. There were competitive elections and political parties. National television stations broadcast biting satire and no-holds-barred critiques of Kremlin policies. New private banks sponsored ballets and concerts. Shops quickly filled up with consumer goods and foodstuffs that Soviet citizens had only glimpsed in foreign films. After the dark decades of totalitarian rule, people now felt unafraid. There was optimism and hope. Certainly that's how Russia looked to most Western observers. Evidently, it's how Bill Clinton saw things.

And yet, when I look back at my notebooks and dispatches from the time, I am reminded that most Russians had a very different impression. My reports for the BBC chronicled a decade of shame and humiliation.

Yeltsin's Russia was a country that seemed to be run by thugs. You saw them barrelling down the highways in their cars with darkened windows, or ordering thousand-dollar bottles of wine in the best restaurants and snarling contemptuously at the waitresses, or shopping in horrendously over-priced boutiques, and occasionally gunning each other down in broad daylight. Contract killings were commonplace, as Russia's mafia-style gangs carved up territories and businesses.

The BBC's offices were located in a hotel and business centre part-owned by an American, Paul Tatum. After a dispute with his Chechen business partner, Tatum was riddled with bullets fired from a Kalashnikov rifle – at 5pm as he walked into a metro station near the hotel. His killer was never found. On another occasion I found myself in a traffic jam, and as I slowly edged forward noticed that a little hold-up was going on at the side of the road – again in broad daylight. Several men were pointing their guns at the head of some poor guy lying on the ground. On yet another ordinary day in Moscow a restaurant was raided, and we all threw ourselves to the floor while arrests were made. To get into my local supermarket, you had to walk past guards wearing fatigues and cradling AK-47s. All the early new capitalism was accompanied by violence and threats: whether you managed a five-star hotel or sold souvenirs from a trestle table on the Arbat, you paid protection money to one mafia gang or another.

On the outskirts of the major cities, especially Moscow, the so-called 'New Russians' built mansions with swimming pools, wine cellars and fashionable turrets, all hidden from view behind 15-foot fences. They represented a tiny proportion of the population. Millions meanwhile were impoverished by the economic reforms that started in 1992. The sudden liberalisation of prices led to soaring inflation. Ordinary Russians lined the pavements selling off their belongings. The very centre of Moscow became a huge flea-market. I vividly remember one man in particular – a middle-aged scientist with a PhD – selling old rusting padlocks and other bric-a-brac.

Other scientists emigrated in search of work that would give them a decent wage, many of them taking Russia's strategic knowledge and secrets with them, leaving their country devoid of its best brains just when it needed them.

Railway stations filled with beggars and homeless people. The *Kursky vokzal* – Moscow's main station for southern destinations – became a Dickensian dosshouse full of pickpockets and sick people. Amputees from the first Chechen war (1994–96) began to clump around metro carriages asking for alms.

Business, of sorts, spread everywhere – most visibly in the shape of tiny kiosks selling suspicious-looking alcohols and foodstuffs. Meat, unfit for human consumption, was sold at marketplaces that sprang up spontaneously on pieces of waste ground, which became breeding grounds for rats and disease.

Desperate people sank their savings into pyramid schemes that invariably collapsed, leaving them penniless. In 1992 the government issued privatisation vouchers to every citizen. The idea was that these could be exchanged for shares in enterprises being privatised. In practice millions of people just sold them or gave them away and they ended up largely in the hands of a few shrewd entrepreneurs or state enterprise managers who thereby became Russia's new capitalist owners.

Industry collapsed. Workers were not paid, or were paid several months in arrears, and often with goods – towels or soap or tampons – rather than money. Enterprises themselves traded with each other by barter. A once proud country received shipments of food aid – sugar and margarine from the European Union's surplus stocks and US army rations left over from the Gulf War. A superpower was now holding out a begging bowl.

Flying to Vancouver in April 1993 to ask President Clinton for help, Yeltsin pointed out: 'Remember that East Germany needed $100 billion to get rid of the communist monster.' He returned with the promise of just $1.6 billion, much of it in the form of credits and food aid. Some wondered whether the West lacked imagination. Did Russia not need a 'Marshall Plan' to rebuild its decrepit Soviet-era infrastructure, which was in little better shape than Germany's after the Second World War?

Western consultancies probably profited more from Western aid packages than the Russians did. I remember interviewing the manager of a small Moscow bakery who had been on a month-long management course, paid for by Western governments, with some consultancy in England. 'All I really needed,' she told me, 'was the money to buy some top-class bakery equipment. I know how to manage my company!'

Russian society was truly battered by the abrupt transition from communism. People had literally lost their own country: the Soviet Union, a land of 250 million people in 15 national republics, splintered. Twenty-five million Russians suddenly found themselves residents of foreign countries, stranded in what became known as the 'near abroad'. Inhabitants of Siberia could no longer escape to holiday in the Crimea (now in Ukraine) or even in Moscow, because air fares were beyond their reach. I was astonished, on a trip to Siberia, to hear people calling European Russia the 'mainland', as though they were marooned on a remote island in the middle of an ocean.

There was little sign that the Kremlin's Western advisers understood how to handle this dislocated society. Western governments didn't seem to notice the chaos and squalor – or they didn't care, so obsessed were they with the vision of building capitalism, regardless of its immediate impact. Western corporations only saw a massive new marketplace for their goods. A strange Russian phrase, *Produkt kompanii Prokter end Gembl* (produced by Proctor and Gamble), boomed out at the end of every other TV ad like some new political slogan. I think Russians must have been driven mad by those words. They seemed to replace 'Long live the Communist Party' seamlessly, but instead of promising a radiant future they promised Head & Shoulders and Pampers, which few Russians could yet afford.

American consultants in sharp suits swarmed around, cooing over Nizhny Novgorod's privatisation projects and its pioneering young reformers. The city on the Volga, previously known as Gorky, was the first to sell off major chunks of the state's assets to ordinary people. In many ways it really was inspiring. I remember watching go-ahead Russians, keen to set up their own private businesses, inspecting 195 state-owned trucks and vans, many of them in a dreadful condition, and then bidding for them at an auction. The problem for me, and I suspect for many Russians, was the sight of so many foreigners supervising the process. To all intents and purposes it looked as if America was selling off Russia.

For those who took the leap – 'collectives' of shop-workers who got together to buy and run their own stores, for example – it really worked. As proprietors, desperate to attract customers, they set about transforming their businesses with a zeal that soon swept away the drab Soviet shopping experience. But for those on the other side of the counter, whose savings and pensions were obliterated by hyper-inflation, it was a very different story. Life-expectancy plummeted, alcoholism rose and thousands of quack doctors, psychics and 'white witches' stepped in to take advantage of the general mood of desolation.

And then there was the Chechen war. Yeltsin had encouraged Russia's regions to assert their own powers, but Chechnya, a small Muslim republic in the northern Caucasus, went so far as to declare itself independent. To accept this might have created a precedent which could lead to the break-up of the Russian Federation, so in December 1994 Yeltsin ordered an invasion of the republic. It was an all-round disaster. Thousands of poorly trained Russian troops died, and hundreds of thousands of Chechens were either killed or displaced to neighbouring republics. The capital, Grozny, was reduced to rubble. The Chechens became radicalised and embittered, rekindled their Islamic faith, which had been dormant in the Soviet period, and thousands of men joined the separatist militias – who eventually forced the Russian army out of their country. It was an ignominious defeat, which led to Chechnya's *de facto* independence by the end of 1996. The rebels also took to staging terrorist attacks inside Russia itself: in the summer of 1995 they seized more than a thousand hostages in a hospital in the southern town of Budyonnovsk. The authorities tried to storm the hospital (leading to the deaths of at least 130 people) but then allowed the hostage-takers to escape.

By early 1996 Boris Yeltsin's popularity had slumped to a barely measurable level. Not only were his reforms unpopular and the war in Chechnya a disaster, but the president himself had become an embarrassment on account of his frequent drunken appearances. There is little doubt that the communist leader Gennady Zyuganov could have been elected president in that summer's election if it had been fair. Instead, the country's new oligarchs – billionaire businessmen who feared losing their new-found wealth if the communists came back – banded together to ensure a Yeltsin miracle. These were men who in a 'loans for shares' scheme initiated in 1995 acquired Russia's largest state industries, including most of its oil and gas reserves, for a fraction of their worth, in exchange for bailing out the penniless government. Now they bankrolled Yeltsin's campaign and used the national television stations they owned to skew election coverage entirely in his favour. Yeltsin swept back to power – and the West sighed with relief. For Clinton and other Western leaders, 'democracy' and the 'free market' had been saved in Russia. And that was all that mattered.

What most Western leaders failed to appreciate was the psychological trauma that Russians, as individuals and as a nation, were going through. Vladimir Putin was far more in tune with it.

As the American scholar Stephen F. Cohen wrote, the received wisdom in the US was that 'since the end of the Soviet Union in 1991, Russia has been a nation ready, willing, and able to be transformed into some replica of America'.[4] Leave aside the immense cultural and historical differences that make Russia unlikely ever to become a 'replica' of America. The fact is that Russians were thrown in at the deep end, with no time even to adjust to freedom.

The celebrated Soviet-era poet and singer Vladimir Vysotsky predicted the disorientation way back in 1965, at a time when he could only dream of what it might be like to be released from the communist straitjacket:

They gave me my freedom yesterday,
What on earth am I going to do with it?

The West assumed that Russians would simply know how to use their liberty, as if it was something totally natural – as if Russians were just Americans who had been lumbered with communism for a few years: take away the constraints, give them a free market and everything will be fine. Toby Gati, Clinton's Russia adviser who prepared the first aid package to Russia, admits: 'Perhaps we in the US had a very narrow view of Soviet society and we overestimated the Russians' desire to live by our rules. We started with the assumption that the transformation would be quick and the chaos, which, incidentally, was not seen as chaos but as a transitional period, would soon be replaced by normal life.'[5]

But in the 1990s many Russians found themselves drowning in the tide of capitalism rather than riding it. Moreover there was a deep resentment at the sense of being instructed by outsiders in how to be 'civilised'. It is true that communist ideology was paper-thin, and most Russians jettisoned it easily. But they did not lose certain ways of thinking that predate the communist era and lie deep in the Russian psyche. It was common, and still is, to hear Russians regret the loss of the 'togetherness' they felt under communism. The 'collective' was not a Soviet invention, but had roots in Russian history. But it rubbed against the grain of the individualist Western mores being forced upon them now.

The picture I have described above is a bleak one, perhaps a little bleaker than the overall situation, because undoubtedly there were great joys and advances under Yeltsin too. But it is the darker side of life in the 1990s – so easily overlooked in the West – that provided the fertile soil into which Putin would plant his ideas.

From *kommunalka* to Kremlin

This is a book about Putin in power, not a biography, but a glance at his earlier years is revealing. His background and path to the highest office give clues to the contradictory behaviour he would exhibit as president: the democrat who doesn't trust democracy; the Westerniser whose understanding of the West is flawed and limited; a man who believes in the free market but whose world view was formed in the communist past; a fiery believer in the Russian state, with the icy, ruthless attitude of the ex-KGB man towards its 'enemies'.

Vladimir Vladimirovich Putin was born in 1952 in Leningrad, a city still being rebuilt from the rubble of the Second World War, when it was besieged and bombarded by the Germans for 900 days. His childhood was spent in a *kommunalka*, a communal flat, in which his family had one room and shared the kitchen and toilet with other families – an experience with bitter-sweet memories for many Russians. On the one hand the conditions were awful – there was no bathroom, no hot water, and rats in the stairwell; on the other hand, communal living and the shared experience of post-war reconstruction did much to reinforce the optimistic communist ideology of the day. The young Putin's thinking would have been shaped entirely by crude Soviet propaganda. His was not a dissident or intellectual family which might have listened to foreign radio broadcasts or indulged in subversive discussions. At school he learned that the West was an evil world where capitalists exploited the workers and prepared for war against the USSR; life in his own country, he was told, was immeasurably happier, thanks to the wise leadership of the Communist Party. Even the brief 'Thaw' under Nikita Khrushchev, after Stalin's death, was over by the time Putin was 12, so his secondary school years passed under the aegis of Leonid Brezhnev – a period marked by growing militarism, confrontation with the West, political repression and ideological rigidity. It was during these years that the young Putin showed an interest in joining the party's enforcement machine, the KGB, an ambition he realised only after graduating from Leningrad's law school in 1975.

Putin says he did not even think about the mass terror inflicted by the KGB's predecessor, the NKVD, under Stalin. Indeed, he probably knew next to nothing about it. 'My ideas about the KGB were based on romantic stories about the work of intelligence agents,' he says. 'Without any exaggeration you could say I was the successful product of a Soviet patriotic upbringing.'[6]

He would have known exactly what the KGB got up to, however, when he spent his first decade as an officer in Leningrad during the late 1970s and early 1980s. This was the period when it incarcerated dissidents in labour camps and mental asylums, confiscated foreign literature, jammed foreign broadcasts, controlled all contacts with foreign visitors, vetted the few Soviet citizens allowed to travel abroad and in every possible way helped the Communist Party to exercise total control over society. Abroad, its task was to subvert Western democracies, steal military and industrial secrets, spread communism to developing countries and help the secret services of the 'fraternal socialist states' of Eastern Europe to crack down on dissent. We do not know exactly what Putin did during those years, but one can infer from his work in counter-intelligence and in monitoring foreigners in Leningrad that he was totally committed to the Soviet cause and vigilant to the dangers of Western subversion. To this day he is crushing in his contempt for those who 'betray the motherland' and (as we saw in 2010 when he welcomed home ten Russian spies who were uncovered in the US) full of admiration for those who follow his own career path as a secret agent.

Sergei Roldugin, a family friend, recalls that when he asked the young Putin at the time exactly what he did in the KGB in Leningrad, he replied enigmatically: 'I am a specialist in mingling with people.'

In 1985, promoted to the rank of major, Putin was sent to mingle with the people of communist East Germany. He was based in Dresden, and says his job was 'political intelligence' – recruiting informants and gathering information about political figures and about the plans of 'enemy number one' – NATO. At this stage he must still have been ideologically driven, and still he had no first-hand experience of the West. Neither did he experience at first hand the remarkable awakening of the Soviet Union under Mikhail Gorbachev's policies of *perestroika* (restructuring) and *glasnost* (openness).

While Moscow newspapers and theatres were tearing up the falsified images of the Soviet past and slowly dropping the clichés about Western villainy, Putin was based in one of the communist bloc's most repressive states. The East German leader, Erich Honecker, resisted the winds of change blowing in from Moscow to the last. Putin would have witnessed the gathering unrest in East Germany, however, which culminated in the fall of the Berlin Wall in late 1989. Indeed, in the weeks leading up to the collapse of communist power, it was precisely in Dresden that the peaceful revolution began, with demonstrators taking to the streets to protest – right under Putin's nose.

So Russia's future leader had an unusual vantage point from which to observe the collapse of communism. While missing the Gorbachev revolution at home, he saw at close quarters how East Europeans seized their destiny and wrested themselves free of the Soviet orbit. In his KGB role he was also scrutinising NATO's response, and will have been keenly aware of the verbal promise allegedly given to Gorbachev by the US secretary of state, James Baker, during the German reunification process, that the alliance would not take advantage of the collapse of communism to expand into the former Soviet bloc.

When the game was up for the East German communists – and for the Soviet Union's hegemony over the country – Putin frantically incinerated all the most sensitive files in his Dresden office, and had to brandish a pistol to fend off a rioting crowd that was intent on ransacking the place, having already stormed the offices of the East German secret police, the Stasi. Later Putin claimed he could understand the crowd's reaction to the Stasi: 'They were tired of the Stasi's absolute control. Society was totally intimidated. They saw the Stasi as a monster.' (There is no indication that he recognises that Russians had the same view of the KGB.)

For Putin the most vexing part of the whole episode was

that when the angry crowd was threatening his offices, and he called the Soviet military chief in the Dresden district for help, he was told they could do nothing without a green light from Moscow. 'But Moscow,' says Putin, 'was silent. I had the sense that the country didn't exist any more. It was plain to see that the Soviet Union was sick. And the sickness was a deadly, incurable one called paralysis. The paralysis of power.'

Putin says he understood that Soviet control over half of Europe, based as it was on repression and barbed wire, could not go on for ever. But he admits he resented the loss of influence and regarded it as a national humiliation. 'We just abandoned everything and left.'

It was at this point that Putin made an abrupt life-change that introduced him for the first time to outlooks and influences that would challenge everything he had believed in as a schoolboy, as a student and as a KGB agent. In January 1990 he returned from Germany to his home city, which would soon be renamed St Petersburg. While remaining at first on the KGB's payroll, he found work in the foreign relations department of Leningrad University, and then as assistant to the chairman of Leningrad City Council, a former economics professor named Anatoly Sobchak. One of the leading free thinkers of the *perestroika* period, Sobchak was soon elected mayor of St Petersburg, and in June 1991 he put Putin in charge of the city's foreign relations at a time when it had pretensions of becoming a major financial and investment centre. Sobchak later appointed Putin his deputy.

The former perfect 'product of a Soviet patriotic upbringing' thus became exposed not only to the democratic views of Sobchak but was also plunged into the alien world of Western trade and finance. When communist hardliners (including Putin's KGB chief, General Kryuchkov) staged a coup against Gorbachev in August 1991, Putin says he was at Sobchak's side, drumming up resistance in support of democracy. He said later he believed the plotters' intention, of preventing the disintegration of the USSR, was 'noble', but they in fact achieved the exact opposite. By the end of the year the Communist Party had been swept from power and the Soviet Union broke up. It was a watershed for Putin: 'All the ideals and goals I had when I joined the KGB collapsed.'

Putin's tenure as deputy mayor was not without controversy. Deputies at the city council tried to have him dismissed for corruption following a scandal concerning food imports. He survived, but when Sobchak was voted out of office in 1996 Putin too found himself without a job.

Through a combination of luck and acquaintances, Putin soon found himself in Moscow.[7] His patrons were a group of people who were known as the Family – President Yeltsin's inner circle of advisers. They included Yeltsin's daughter Tatiana, three successive chiefs of staff – Anatoly Chubais, Valentin Yumashev (later Tatiana's husband) and Alexander Voloshin – and the influential business tycoon Boris Berezovsky, who owned 49 per cent of Russia's main state television channel, ORT, and effectively controlled it.

Chubais was a key figure. Back in the early 1990s he had worked in St Petersburg and got to know two of Mayor Sobchak's deputies – one of them Putin, the other a man called Alexei Kudrin, who would later become Putin's finance minister. Chubais then moved to Moscow and became a leading member of the government team that pushed through the controversial privatisation of state assets in Yeltsin's first term. In the summer of 1996 Chubais ran Yeltsin's successful re-election campaign and became his chief of staff. It was he who invited the unemployed Kudrin and Putin to work in the Kremlin – Kudrin as his own deputy, Putin as deputy head of the Kremlin's property department.

Putin quickly worked his way up through the ranks of the Kremlin bureaucracy. He became deputy chief of staff to President Yeltsin in March 1997, director of the KGB's successor organisation, the FSB, in July 1998 and (simultaneously) head of the national Security Council in March 1999.

Just as the Family had arranged Yeltsin's re-election in 1996, so they would soon engineer Putin's appointment as prime minister – with the intention of moving him into the presidency as Yeltsin's successor. They had been impressed by Putin's loyalty. As head of the FSB he effectively stymied criminal investigations into large-scale corruption and money-laundering in which members of Yeltsin's family and senior Kremlin officials were allegedly implicated. (One of the officials, Pavel Borodin, was accused of embezzling fabulous sums during the refurbishment of Kremlin buildings. He happened to have been Putin's first boss in the Kremlin administration.) Putin also helped his former mentor Sobchak evade prosecution on corruption charges. Loyalty would later turn out to be a striking feature in Putin's make-up. Just as he found his own loyalty to the Family repaid, so he as president would richly reward those most loyal to him – and punish those who opposed him. The Family were not let down: Putin's first move on becoming acting president in 2000 would be to sign the decree granting Yeltsin and his family immunity from prosecution.

In the summer of 1999 Yeltsin's coterie dispatched Berezovsky to talk with Putin, who was on holiday with his family in the French resort of Biarritz, and offer him the job of prime minister. Putin demurred, apparently unsure of his abilities, but when he returned to Moscow President Yeltsin would not take no for an answer.[8]

During this dizzy year of his career, Putin found himself dealing with events that would leave a deep impression on his thinking. In March 1999 three former members of the Soviet bloc, Hungary, Poland and the Czech Republic, joined NATO. Whatever the truth about the alleged guarantees given to Gorbachev that NATO would *not* move eastwards (and American officials firmly deny that such a promise was made), this was the first stage of what Russia regarded as an unnecessary and threatening advance of a military alliance towards its own borders. The issue would dog the next decade of Putin's rule.

Just 11 days after NATO's enlargement, the organisation launched its air strikes against Serbia, with all the repercussions described earlier in this chapter. And in August the troubles in Chechnya, which had been smouldering quietly for the past two and a half years, suddenly burst into flames – igniting a visceral fury in Putin that would inform his actions at home and abroad for many years. Fighting terrorism became an obsession.

Since the withdrawal of Russian troops from Chechnya at the end of 1996, the republic had enjoyed *de facto* autonomy and become increasingly lawless. Its relatively moderate elected government was undermined by warlords such as Salman Raduyev and Shamil Basayev, the man who had been behind the hostage-taking in Budyonnovsk. Kidnapping became commonplace. After the murders of six Red Cross workers and four kidnapped telecoms workers, foreigners scarcely dared set foot in the republic. Islamic fundamentalism took hold, and some of the warlords developed links with Middle Eastern extremist groups, including al-Qaeda.

On 7 August 1999 Basayev and a Saudi-born Islamist, Ibn Al-Khattab, launched a well-planned invasion of some 1,500 men into Chechnya's neighbouring republic, Dagestan. Their aim was to establish an Islamic state there – a first step towards the creation of an Islamic superstate throughout Russia's northern Caucasus region. The attack also catapulted Putin to the highest office. The next day Yeltsin appointed his steely security chief as prime minister to tackle the problem.

Putin's sudden emergence from nowhere as the country's future leader was astonishing. He was still virtually unknown in the country, and indeed to most of the political elite. But in the months that followed he became the new face of Russia – tough, energetic and ruthless in responding to ever more audacious Chechen terrorist attacks.

In the space of two weeks in September four bomb explosions destroyed apartment blocks in the cities of Buynaksk, Moscow (twice) and Volgodonsk. Almost 300 people were killed. The attacks were blamed on Chechens and, together with the invasion of Dagestan, provided Putin with the excuse, if he needed one, to launch the second Chechen war. At a meeting with Bill Clinton on 12 September an agitated Putin drew a map of Chechnya and described his plan to annihilate the separatists. 'These people are not human,' he snarled to the press afterwards. 'You can't even call them animals – or if they're animals, they're rabid animals ...'

The apartment bombings were so convenient in providing Putin with the pretext to go to war, and thereby to improve his ratings, that some Russians believe they were carried out by the FSB. Conspiracy theories are so rife – and so outlandish – in Russia that you would have to rewrite history if you believed them all. But real suspicions were raised by a fifth incident, in the city of Ryazan, where police acting on a tip-off foiled an apparent plot after discovering three sacks of white powder, which they identified as explosive, together with detonators, in the basement of a block of flats. Thousands of local residents were evacuated while the sacks were removed and made safe. Putin himself praised the vigilance of the people who had spotted the sacks being carried into the building. When men suspected of planting the bombs were arrested, however, they turned out to be FSB agents. The FSB chief then claimed it had all been an 'exercise' to test responses after the earlier explosions and that the bags only contained sugar. The local FSB in Ryazan knew nothing about such an exercise, however, and issued a statement expressing surprise.

Several other mysterious circumstances surround the apartment bombings. For example, the speaker of the State Duma announced to parliament that he had just received a report of the apartment bombing in Volgodonsk on 13 September – the day of one of the *Moscow* bombings, but three days *before* the

Volgodonsk explosion. Had someone who knew in advance about all the planned attacks got the dates mixed up? But attempts to have the incidents properly investigated in Russia have been thwarted, and the Kremlin reacts with fury to questions on the subject. Moreover, two members of an independent commission that tried to establish the facts were murdered and a third was killed in a car accident, while the commission's investigating lawyer was arrested and jailed for alleged illegal arms possession. The journalist Anna Politkovskaya and the former KGB agent Alexander Litvinenko, both of whom investigated the bombings, were murdered in 2006.

The second Chechen war was intended to avenge the humiliation suffered by Russia in the first, and to put a halt to what Putin apparently regarded as an Islamist threat to the entire country. One of his closest advisers told me on condition of anonymity that Putin feared his tenure as prime minister might last only a few months (like that of his predecessors) and he wanted to use the time to prevent Russia from falling apart. 'The Chechen invasion into Dagestan was a signal from the bandits that they could go further, along the Volga river into some of our Muslim republics – Bashkortostan and Tatarstan.'

I have never heard Putin (or any other Russian leader) speak about the real grievances of the Chechen people – their mass deportation from their homeland to Central Asia under Stalin, the swamping of their culture and language by the Russians during the Soviet period. Nor is there much awareness of the fact that it was the brutal Russian invasion in 1994 that radicalised the Chechen fighters and encouraged Islamic fundamentalism – of which there was not a whiff when I visited the republic before the first war. It was the war, and the atrocities committed by Russian forces, that turned mere separatists into ideologically driven terrorists. Without that understanding, Putin's new war was bound to make matters even worse.

He soon began to reveal the sharp tongue and earthy language that became his trademark. Asked about the ferocity of the Russian campaign, he replied, on 24 September: 'We'll pursue the terrorists wherever they are. If they're in an airport we'll get 'em there. If we catch 'em – excuse the expression – in the toilet ... we'll wipe 'em out right there, in the outhouse. End of story.'

Putin's campaign quickly raised him out of obscurity. But he was not yet the country's most popular politician. One of his predecessors as prime minister, Yevgeny Primakov, had publicly denounced the corruption in Yeltsin's entourage and declared his intention of running for president. Together with the mayor of Moscow, Yuri Luzhkov, he created a political bloc, Fatherland–All Russia, which looked set to do well in parliamentary elections in December, giving him a springboard for the presidential election scheduled for June.

It was at this point that Boris Berezovsky stepped in to ensure the victory of the Family's candidate, Putin. Berezovsky threw the entire weight of his ORT channel behind him, while mounting a sustained smear campaign against Primakov and Luzhkov. He hired a well-known presenter, Sergei Dorenko, who specialised in scandal, sensation and brazenly biased commentary. Berezovsky was delighted to let him take fire at Primakov, who as prime minister had had his companies raided and threatened to jail businessmen like him for economic crimes. Night after night, Russia's main TV channel harped on about Primakov's old age and infirmity and Luzhkov's alleged corruption, while glorifying Putin's heroics in Chechnya.

Meanwhile the inner circle – Berezovsky, Yumashev and Tatiana Dyachenko – met secretly at the dacha of Alexander Voloshin, Yeltsin's chief of staff, to create a political force to support Putin. In September, three months before the Duma election, a new party was born, called Yedinstvo (Unity). It had no roots, no philosophy, practically no policy other than

its support for Putin, but it did have the unabashed endorse-
ment of Berezovsky's ORT and several of his newspapers. On
19 December it won almost twice as many votes as Fatherland–All Russia. The scene was now set for Yeltsin to resign
on New Year's Eve and hand over power to his prime minister
and chosen successor.

The day after the Duma election was 'Chekists Day'.
Continuing a Soviet-era tradition, most professions in Russia
have one day in the calendar in their honour, and this was
the day of homage to the country's present and former secret
police (originally known as the Cheka). In the morning Putin
restored a plaque on the wall of the FSB headquarters, the
Lubyanka, in memory of Yuri Andropov, the KGB chief when
Putin joined up. The plaque had been removed in the de-Sovi-
etising Yeltsin years. At a gala ball in the evening the prime
minister made a speech to his former colleagues, and joked:
'I want to report that a group of FSB operatives, sent to work
undercover in the government, is successfully carrying out the
first stage of its mission.'

The second stage was about to begin. Ten days later, Yeltsin
resigned and Putin assumed supreme power in Russia.

2

COURTING THE WEST

'I want Russia to be part of Europe'

Russia's relations with NATO had been frozen ever since the allied bombing of Yugoslavia in March 1999. 'NATO's representative in Moscow has been told to pack his bags,' announced Russia's foreign minister, Igor Ivanov. 'There will be no contact with NATO, including its secretary general, until the aggression against Yugoslavia stops.'

But at the beginning of 2000, shortly after Vladimir Putin became acting president of Russia, the telephone rang in the secretary general's office at NATO headquarters in Brussels. It was none other than Igor Ivanov, and George Robertson, the new NATO chief, was taken aback. He had arrived in Brussels in October and had decided one of his first tasks should be to get Russia 'back into the security fold', but until now nothing had happened.

'If you were thinking of coming to Moscow,' said Ivanov, coyly warming to his theme, 'I want to say that you might find that this would be welcomed.'[1]

And so it was that Robertson became the first major Western politician to meet the new Russian president. He flew into

Moscow in February on a plane provided by the German air force.

Putin seemed to be tickled by the idea, and the sight of a Luftwaffe jet in Moscow helped to break the ice.

'Why did you come on a German plane?' he asked.

Robertson quickly realised that the word 'Luftwaffe', emblazoned across the side of his plane, evoked a certain sensitivity in Russia in view of the horrors its bombers had inflicted in the Second World War. He explained that NATO itself had no planes, so he had to borrow from the member states.

'Hmm,' said Putin, practising his English. 'Maybe next time, secretary general, you should come in a British plane.'

Robertson had brought a gift for him – a book in English about the tsarist court, which he had found in an antiquarian bookshop. The Russian leader was delighted. It turned out that he was making a serious effort to learn English, now that his profession of 'mingling with people' would include a great many foreign leaders.

'I like to read these English books out loud to practise,' he told Robertson, and then added, 'so now my dog is fluent in English.'

There was substance to the charm offensive as well as jokes. Robertson recalls Putin being quite blunt and to the point: 'He was less confident than he was eventually to be. He was very new to the job. He wasn't even in the job – he was still acting president.'

'I want to sort our relationship out,' said Putin. 'It's not constructive at the moment, and I want to resume relations with NATO. Step by step. It can't happen overnight – and a lot of people disagree with me on this.' Putin gestured at his defence minister, Marshal Sergeyev, and his foreign minister, Igor Ivanov. 'But I know what I want, and I want Russia to be part of Europe. That's where its destiny is. So let us work out how best we can do that.'

The British ambassador told Robertson he was impressed

by such a bold, early foreign-policy decision. The relationship had been so fractious that for him to say 'we are going to resume it' was a big thing. Robertson sensed that Putin wanted to have 'an uncluttered relationship' – to sweep aside the inherited obstacles and talk about the big issues. 'They wanted to be taken seriously as a major player in the world.'

One other world leader was keen to oblige. Prime Minister Tony Blair saw a chance to make Britain Russia's 'partner of choice' in Europe and decided to 'get in early' with a trip to Russia in the first half of March – before Putin was even elected president (the election was due on 26 March). He was more willing at this stage to turn a blind eye to Putin's ruthless campaign against Chechnya than either Chancellor Gerhard Schröder of Germany or President Jacques Chirac of France. The Foreign Office, too, was wary of the ex-KGB man who was apparently presiding over what many considered to be atrocities in Chechnya. But Blair's own advisers in Downing Street argued that he was a new type of leader, someone worth investing with early. 'In my experience,' said Blair's chief of staff, Jonathan Powell, 'KGB officers were the more outward looking members of the old Russian nomenklatura. We decided to reach out to him actually during the election campaign rather than wait till after when there would be a long queue of people wishing to see him. It was risky, but we thought it was the right thing to do, and it did work.' [2]

Powell says Blair scarcely focused on the Chechnya problem until he was on the plane and started reading his briefs. 'The brief produced by the Foreign Office got him increasingly irritated – because even at that stage Tony was concerned about Islamic terrorism, and he could see the danger of it and thought we were being a bit "double standards" in the way we were dealing with the Russian approach to it. So he decided on the plane to cut Putin some slack on Chechnya when we did the press conference.'

Putin was delighted, and laid on a full tour of his home

town, St Petersburg, for the prime minister and his wife, Cherie: the Hermitage art gallery, talks at the tsar's glittering summer palace, Peterhof, and evening at Prokofiev's opera *War and Peace* at the Mariinsky Theatre. The only sour moment came during the talks at Peterhof, when the British ambassador, Sir Roderic Lyne, sat down heavily on a spindly-legged antique chair and shattered it.

'You'll be paying compensation for that, I hope,' quipped Putin – 'not entirely in jest', according to one witness.

The visit achieved everything Blair wanted it to. Powell admits that Britain had felt excluded from the cosy relationship Yeltsin had had with the French and Germans (not to mention Bill Clinton), and now Blair had 'inserted himself'. As soon as the presidential election was out of the way – a mere formality, which Putin won with 53 per cent of the votes – Blair followed up by bringing him to London. There was an uproar in the press as the 'Butcher of Grozny' was invited to meet the Queen at Windsor Castle.[3]

Blair did appear, for a time, to become Putin's chief Western contact. In November, when the American presidential election hung in the balance as ballot papers were recounted in the state of Florida, Putin called Blair for advice about whether he should call George W. Bush to congratulate him. Powell recalls: 'Tony suggested he hold off for the moment until things were clear, and he was very grateful and didn't make the call. It was interesting. It illustrated a sort of relationship you wouldn't normally have had with the Russian president, and it made us feel our investment had been worth it.'

Part of the calculation, of course, was that British business would benefit from closer political ties, so during his April visit to London Putin was taken to meet a group of leading industrialists. Lord John Browne, CEO of BP, was impressed: 'He was a refreshing change.' The businessmen listened to Putin promising laws that would be stuck to, and a crackdown on corruption – and his cold, impassive demeanour made them feel he meant it. Three years later, watched by Putin and Blair at a ceremony in London, BP and a major Russian oil company, TNK, signed a deal for a 50-50 partnership. At the time, BP's $6.75 billion outlay represented the biggest ever foreign investment in Russia. Both sides were happy – though there would be a bumpy road ahead, as Putin began to have second thoughts about selling off his nation's strategic assets to foreigners.

Seeing Putin's soul

As for America, Putin had already decided to sit out the rest of the Clinton term, and started putting out feelers to George W. Bush's team. The Russians had long expected a Bush victory. They even sent a team to the Republican Party Convention in Philadelphia at the end of July 2000. One of its members, Mikhail Margelov, a Russian senator and PR expert who had worked in Putin's election team, said it was part of the new United Russia's outreach to 'conservative parties all over the world', designed to create a right-of-centre 'brand' for Putin's party. They met Condoleezza Rice and other members of the Bush team – not for long, but long enough to get invited back to the inauguration in January.[4]

On the day of the inauguration Rice sought out a Russian diplomat to convey a positive message on behalf of the new administration to Putin. Rice was a Russian-speaker and Soviet specialist, who would be central to Bush's Russia policy over the coming years. Her message held out the prospect of good, friendly relations – but certainly not of a reprise of the Bill 'n' Boris Show. Rice's view was that Clinton's cosy relationship with Yeltsin had become too personalised, and far too soft when it came to calling the Russians to book for their behaviour in Chechnya. In an article that appeared in *The Chicago Tribune* on 31 December 2000 she delivered a scathing denunciation of the Clinton policy:

The problem for US policy is that the Clinton administration's ongoing embrace of Yeltsin and those who were thought to be reformers around him quite simply failed. Clearly the United States was obliged to deal with the head of state, and Yeltsin was Russia's president.

But US support for democracy and economic reform became support for Yeltsin. His agenda became the American agenda.

America certified that reform was taking place in Russia where it was not, continuing to disburse money from the International Monetary Fund in the absence of any evidence of serious change.

Thus, some curious privatization methods were hailed as economic liberalization; the looting of the country's assets by powerful people either went unnoticed or was ignored. The realities in Russia simply did not accord with the administration's script about Russian economic reform.

On top of that, Rice knew there were tough times ahead because Bush was planning to press much harder than Clinton ever did to pursue the goal of building a missile defence shield. She recalled in an interview: 'Bush had been very clear that a reorientation in the offence-defence relationship in arms control was going to be very important to him, and that the ABM treaty was an impediment to missile defence.'[5]

Still, for Putin the change of occupancy in the White House augured well, and the Russians looked forward to getting on with building a new relationship with George W. Bush after his inauguration in January 2001.

The Russians were in for a nasty shock. In March the Americans announced they were expelling 50 Russian diplomats who were working undercover as spies in Washington and New York. What the Russians did not realise – and to this day (judging from our interviews) apparently still do not realise – is that the expulsions also came as a nasty surprise to the incoming Bush administration! The Russians assumed Bush had decided to send a tough signal right from the start of his presidency. But in fact, he was merely clearing out a problem inherited from his predecessor.

The FBI chief, Louis Freeh, had identified the 50 diplomats some time earlier, but the Clinton administration had declined to expel them for fear of spoiling the special relationship with Yeltsin, just at the end of Clinton's term. So now, with a new man in the White House, and knowing that he himself would soon be leaving his job, Freeh decided to get this last piece of business out of the way.

Stephen Hadley, deputy national security adviser to the new president, recalled in an interview: 'Freeh was very strong about the need to take action against this Russian network in the United States. My sense was that it's something he had wanted to do for a long time, but for a lot of reasons in their last year of office, the Clinton administration felt the timing was not right, which meant it was an issue that the new president had to confront. Our judgement was that it could not be ignored. Action needed to be taken and it needed to be swift and early. These were real spies. They were not just diplomats. This was not being done for political purposes, or to send a signal. The decision was made. It was not going to get any easier by kicking a can down the road.'[6]

The task of telling the Russians fell to Bush's secretary of state, Colin Powell. He called in the Russian ambassador, Yuri Ushakov, ostensibly for a courtesy call, a chance to meet the new secretary of state. Powell opened with some banter: 'Do you want the good news or the bad news?'

'Good things are for dessert,' replied Ushakov.

Powell served the hors d'oeuvre. He politely explained that while there was a gentleman's agreement that each side could have a certain number of spies in its embassies, the Russians had gone way over the score. 'We've identified about 50 of them. And you will get notice tomorrow of who they are and they will be asked to leave the country within the next few days. So I need you to go back to the embassy, crank up your fax machine and let Moscow know about this right away.'[7]

Ushakov at once informed his foreign minister, Igor Ivanov, who hit the roof. 'It was completely unprecedented,' he recalls. 'It was a politically motivated action. That was our assessment. And we thought it was done to show who rules the world.'[8]

When the news reached the Kremlin, it could not have hit a sorer spot. This was the job that Putin himself had done for 16 years; these were his fellow Chekists. He called a meeting of his Security Council – the ministers in charge of military, foreign and security matters. They decided to mirror exactly what the Americans had done – but make it worse for them. The head of the Security Council, Sergei Ivanov (also a former Soviet foreign spy), called the US national security adviser, Condoleezza Rice, and told her: 'Our reply will be very cynical. We will expel 50 of your diplomats, but we will not do it immediately. We will spin it out over a period, and we will be very careful to choose not only real spies but "clean" diplomats as well. We will cause chaos in your embassy.'[9]

The tit-for-tat expulsions began. But the Bush team was anxious to move on. This had not been their initiative. Powell called his counterpart, foreign minister Igor Ivanov, to suggest that it was time to close the matter.

'It's not something we can just close,' replied Ivanov. 'We will expel 50. And if you expel more, so will we, soon we'll have no diplomats left and it'll just be you and me handling our bilateral relations.'

They agreed to call a halt. Ivanov flew to Washington on 18 May bearing a letter from Putin. The Russian leader was looking beyond the current tiff, stressing the same things he had spoken of with NATO's Robertson: he wanted to restart the relationship, with a new type of partnership. Powell and Ivanov agreed that the two presidents had to meet. They chose a neutral venue – Slovenia – and a date – 16 June 2001.

It was here, in the sixteenth-century Brdo Castle, just north of the capital Ljubljana, that Bush and Putin had their blind date. Putin has a tremendous ability to mimic his interlocutor and win their confidence – the facility that made him a good KGB 'mingler'. A well-connected Kremlin journalist, Yelena Tregubova, for whom Putin had a soft spot, described being taken out to a sushi restaurant by him when he was director of the FSB: 'He is a brilliant communicator ... a virtuoso ... able to reflect like a mirror the person he is with, to make them believe he is just like them. He does this so cleverly that his counterpart apparently doesn't notice it but just feels great.' [10]

In Brdo Castle Putin worked his magic on Bush. The American brought up an incident in Putin's life that he had been briefed on, concerning a Christian cross which his mother had given him, and he had had blessed in Israel. Putin quickly understood that this resonated with Bush. 'It's true,' he replied, according to Bush's own account to the American journalist Bob Woodward.[11]

Bush says he told Putin he was amazed that a communist, a KGB operative, was willing to wear a cross. (Putin was not wearing the cross at this meeting, though he did bring it to show Bush at Genoa a month later.) 'That speaks volumes to me, Mr President,' Bush said. 'May I call you Vladimir?'

Putin then described how his family dacha had burned down and the only thing he wanted to recover from the ashes was the cross. 'I remember the workman's hand opening, and there was the cross that my mother had given me, as if it was meant to be.' He had Bush hooked.

The two presidents' aides, waiting outside, were getting nervous as the private talks continued. Colin Powell, Bush's secretary of state, chatted with his opposite number Igor Ivanov. Powell recalled later: 'Igor and I and the rest of the delegations were busy sitting round pretending to have a conference and discussing vital issues, but we were all just sitting there tapping our thumbs and our fingers on the table wondering what these fellows were doing.'[12]

Eventually the presidents emerged to hold a press conference. One journalist asked Bush a killer question: 'Is this a man that Americans can trust?' Still under the spell, Bush waxed lyrical: 'I looked the man in the eye. I found him to be very straightforward and trustworthy. We had a very good dialogue. I was able to get a sense of his soul.'

Putin could hardly believe it. He turned to Bush and said in a quiet, boyish voice in English, 'Thank you, mister ...' Bush's aides gasped. Condi Rice murmured to a colleague, 'Oh my goodness, we're going to have some explaining to do over that one.'

Colin Powell later took the president aside and said: 'You know, you may have seen all that but I still look in his eyes and I see K-G-B. Remember there's a reason he's fluent in German, he used to be the *rezident* [agent] in Germany and he is a chief KGB guy.'

Bush's claim to have 'seen into Putin's soul' would haunt him for the rest of his presidency.

Fighting the Taliban together

In less than three months the friendship would be put to the test. When terrorists mounted the world's most devastating attack on the United States on 11 September 2001, Putin was the first world leader to call Bush and offer condolences and help.

Watching the coverage of the planes smashing into the World Trade Center and the Pentagon, Putin was shocked but not entirely surprised. Only the previous day he had called Bush and told him he believed 'something serious' was in the making. This followed the murder of Ahmed Shah Massoud, the leader of the anti-Taliban Northern Alliance in Afghanistan, on 9 September, which Russian intelligence interpreted as a harbinger of worse to come. Russia had supported the

Northern Alliance with arms and cash for several years in an effort to contain the spread of Islamic fundamentalism.

Putin at once called his security chiefs to the Kremlin and asked them what they could do to help. The first thing that occurred to them was to postpone a major naval exercise that was about to get under way in the Pacific, since this could be an unnecessary distraction for the US military. Putin called the White House, but could not speak to President Bush who was still aboard Air Force One, moving to a secure location. Condoleezza Rice took the call. She was in the White House bunker, where a decision had just been taken to put US forces on the highest level of alert, DEFCON 3.

Rice recalled later in an interview: 'I told President Putin our forces were going on highest alert, and I remember him saying, "I know," and it occurred to me, of course they know, they're watching our forces go on alert! He said, "We are bringing ours down, we're cancelling all exercises." And at that moment I thought to myself, you know, the Cold War's really over.' [13]

The Americans soon decided on their response to the attacks, which had been sponsored by Osama bin Laden's al-Qaeda organisation operating out of Afghanistan with the support of the fundamentalist Taliban government there. When Putin asked what else he could do to help, the answer was clear: the only suitable places to launch an assault on Afghanistan, apart from US aircraft carriers in the region, were in former Soviet republics of Central Asia. And those republics – Uzbekistan, Tajikistan, Kyrgyzstan – while nominally independent, were states where Moscow had great influence.

Putin's instinct was to ask the Central Asians to cooperate, and indicated this to the Americans. But then he ran up against unexpected opposition within his own government. The hard-line Sergei Ivanov, now defence minister, was one of Putin's closest allies – like him, a former KGB spy, but more urbane and better versed in Western ways. He was also Condoleezza Rice's main channel of communication in Moscow. When she came to office as Bush's national security adviser, Ivanov was her opposite number, and, even though he had become defence minister in March 2001, Rice liked him and (despite diplomatic protocol, which should have linked her with the new Russian national security adviser, Vladimir Rushailo) she retained the link. At the Ljubljana summit, according to Rice, Bush asked Putin, 'Who should we call if we can't get you and we need a trusted agent?' Putin said, 'That would be Sergei Ivanov.' And Bush said, 'That would be Condi.'

Just three days after the terrorist attacks, Ivanov, the 'trusted agent', suddenly went way off message with regard to Russia's willingness to help. 'I see absolutely no basis,' he said while on a visit to Armenia, 'for even the hypothetical possibility of NATO military operations on the territory of the Central Asian states.'

The Americans were confused by the conflicting signals. Suddenly the presidents of the Central Asian states, not counted among the world's greatest democrats, became everybody's favourites. Putin sent his national security adviser, Vladimir Rushailo, to sound them out. Bush sent his undersecretary of state, John Bolton, to the Uzbek capital Tashkent to win over President Islam Karimov, a man accused of some of the world's most heinous human rights violations. The Americans were in no mood to quibble about such things now. Rice recalled later: 'With Uzbekistan it just became a problem of what would be the price. Karimov needed money and he knew he had us over a barrel.' And indeed, Bolton apparently found him bending over backwards to oblige: 'I [was] all prepared for how hard it will be and he said, "Why aren't you asking for a permanent base?"' [14]

That was precisely what the Russians, and not just Sergei Ivanov, were worried about: the prospect of an American 'presence' – limited access to Central Asian bases for the purposes of their campaign in Afghanistan – turning into something more permanent, something more political.

Ivanov recalls: 'We were concerned that once the Americans had a presence in the region, then "democracy promotion" would start. We know those countries very well – they were part of the same country [the Soviet Union] – and as we say in Russia, "the orient is a very intricate place". We were afraid that political processes that were *not very advantageous to us* could start. And that proved to be true later. The leaders of those countries – Kyrgyzstan, Uzbekistan, Tajikistan – started complaining to us, because they had given the Americans everything they needed, but then they started working with opposition groups, building democracy.' [15]

This was one of the earliest indications that under Putin Russia considered the prospect of democracy on its borders threatening.

On Saturday 22 September Putin called his defence and security chiefs together for six hours of crisis talks at his dacha, hidden in the woods on a cliff-top overlooking the Black Sea at Sochi. Putin argued that it was not only in Russia's interest to help America, but also in Russia's self-interest. For one thing, Moscow had long been disturbed by the rise of Islamic forces in the Central Asian republics, fomented in part from Afghanistan. Russia itself could never again put military boots on the ground in Afghanistan after its catastrophic war there in the 1980s, but if the Americans were going to do it for them why should Russia oppose? Sergei Ivanov recalls: 'We were counting on getting help in return. We knew where the training camps were in Afghanistan. I mean, we knew the exact map coordinates. Those camps trained terrorists – including those from Chechnya and Dagestan, as well as Tajikistan and Uzbekistan ... We were counting on the Americans to liquidate those camps. Or they would capture the terrorists and send them to us.'

Secondly, Putin linked the 9/11 attacks to the same worldwide terrorist threat that he faced in Chechnya. Supporting the Americans could only help garner support for (or at least mute criticism of) his own campaign against terrorism. The Russian leader had already spoken to the Americans about the links between al-Qaeda and the Chechen Islamists – indeed he claimed that Osama bin Laden himself had twice been to Chechnya. Now the Russians had a chance to help the Americans wipe out some of the sources of trouble within Russia itself. 'We all have to understand,' Putin told his team, 'that the situation in the world has changed.'

The hardliners were won over. 'Even the doubters agreed,' Putin said in an interview. 'New circumstances meant we had to help the Americans.'

After four hours, Putin left the meeting to call the American president and inform him of their decision. 'It was a substantive conversation,' Putin recalls. 'We agreed on concrete steps to be taken straight away, and in the long term.' He offered Russian logistical help, intelligence, search-and-rescue missions if American pilots were downed in northern Afghanistan, and even the right to military flights over Russian territory for humanitarian purposes. Most importantly, he told Bush: 'I am prepared to tell the heads of government of the Central Asian states that we have good relations with that we have no objections to a US role in Central Asia as long as it has the object of fighting the war on terror *and is temporary and is not permanent.*' [16] The last words were crucial. Ten years later (despite a Russian attempt to have them evicted in 2009), American forces still operate out of the Manas Air Base in Kyrgyzstan.[17] They were asked to leave their base in Uzbekistan in 2005.

The American campaign was mainly going to involve air strikes, while the Afghans themselves (the anti-Taliban Northern Alliance) would be doing the fighting on the ground. Rice says that she and Sergei Ivanov were given responsibility for getting supplies to the Northern Alliance and preparing them to fight. Even as Putin was calling Bush from Sochi, Russia's chief of staff, General Anatoly Kvashnin, was holding talks with a Northern Alliance leader in Tajikistan.

Russia, it seemed, was now totally aligned with the US in the war on terror. Sergei Ivanov claims that some days after the war began, Russian border guards on the Tajik frontier with Afghanistan were approached by representatives of the Taliban. 'They said they had authority from Mullah Omar to propose that Russia and the Taliban join forces fighting the Americans.' Putin referred to the same incident when the US defence secretary, Donald Rumsfeld, visited Moscow. 'We gave them only one answer,' said Putin in English, showing a crude Russian hand-gesture, a fist with the thumb pushed between the forefinger and middle finger. 'We do it a little differently, but I get the point,' laughed Rumsfeld.[18]

The American assault began on 7 October. It was Putin's birthday. Together with the guests at his party, he watched the news of the first air strikes on television. Defence minister Sergei Ivanov turned to him and raised a glass of vodka: 'Vladimir Vladimirovich, it's a birthday present for you.'

The George 'n' Vladimir show

It seemed that Putin had now answered that journalist's question in Ljubljana: was this a man Americans could trust? Delighted to be seen to be acting in concert with the West rather than against it, Putin now kept up the charm offensive, travelling first to Germany, where he impressed his hosts by making a speech to the Bundestag entirely in German.

He emphasised his country's cooperation in the war on terror, and contrasted this with the slap in the face Russia had felt over the bombing of Serbia – an event now more than two years old but still rankling. 'Decisions are often taken without our participation, and we are only urged afterwards to support them. After that they talk again about loyalty to NATO. They even say that such decisions cannot be implemented without

Russia. Let us ask ourselves: is this normal? Is this true partnership?'

'We cannot have a united Great Europe without an atmosphere of trust,' he said, laying out a grand vision to put an end
finally to the Cold War. 'Today we are obliged to say that we
are renouncing our stereotypes and ambitions and from now
on will jointly ensure the security of the population of Europe
and the world as a whole.'

Chancellor Gerhard Schröder fully supported Putin's idea
of involving Russia in 'jointly' ensuring Europe's security.
Even before this visit they had begun to think the unthink-
able: that Russia might even become a member of NATO.
Schröder recalled later in an interview that they had discussed
what he called a 'fairly visionary' approach to foreign policy: 'I
had discussions with Putin about whether it would make sense
for Russia to join NATO – and I thought that it made perfect
sense, a good prospect for Russia and also for NATO.' [19]

A week later Putin was in Brussels for a meeting with
NATO secretary general George Robertson, ready to push
his luck. Robertson was taken aback when Putin opened the
meeting by asking, 'When are you going to invite Russia to
join NATO?' [20]

Putin's adviser Sergei Prikhodko insists it was just a 'figure
of speech', but Robertson took it seriously.[21] He patiently
explained that this wasn't how things were done. He recalled:
'I said, "Well, Mr President, we don't invite people to join
NATO. You apply for membership. You then have to go
through a process to show that you can be integrated within
NATO, and then an invitation to membership is issued." So
he sort of shrugged and said something to the effect of "Russia
is not going to stand in a queue with a lot of countries that
don't matter." So I said, "Well in that case can we stop this
diplomatic sword dance about membership and actually get
down to building a practical relationship and let's see where
that takes us?" ' [22]

Undeterred, Putin continued to woo the West with concili-atory gestures. On his return from Brussels to Moscow he approved the closure of two Soviet-era military facilities abroad – a naval base at Cam Ranh Bay in Vietnam and a listening post at Lourdes in Cuba. In private, Russian officials admit that these had become expensive white elephants that they were glad to get rid of. But still they hoped they would be seen as goodwill signals that deserved to be reciprocated. Moscow was looking for accommodation on a number of longstanding concerns. An American Soviet-era law, known as the Jackson-Vanik amendment, was introduced in 1974 to restrict trade with the USSR until it lifted restrictions on Jewish emigra-tion. The problem had long since vanished, but Jackson-Vanik was still on the statute books, despite Russian pleading (and American promises to repeal it). Russia also wanted to join the World Trade Organisation to facilitate the growth of its econ-omy, but the US blocked its application and increased tariffs on Russian steel imports. Above all, Putin was still hoping that his good behaviour might earn a reprieve for the ABM treaty and even persuade the Americans not to go ahead with a missile shield.

Such hopes were soon to be dashed. George W. Bush had campaigned for the presidency on a promise to build an Amer-ican national missile defence system, and the ABM treaty stood in his way.

The issue was top of the agenda when Putin made a state visit to the USA in November 2001. The Americans tried to convince the Russians that they had nothing to fear from a missile shield, since its aim was to protect the United States from missiles that might be developed in the future by 'rogue states' such as Iran, Iraq and North Korea (countries he would soon refer to as the 'axis of evil'). As such the defence system would not destabilise the US–Russian strategic balance. Colin Powell recalls: 'The president wanted to convey to President Putin that he, Bush, understood that the Cold War was over and that we had to avoid looking at the Russian Federation through the lens of the Cold War.' [23]

According to deputy national security adviser Stephen Hadley, Bush said, 'My preference would be that we both agree to leave the ABM treaty and we announce cooperation on ballistic missile defence. If it's better for you, Vladimir, for me just to go unilaterally, so that you're not part of it – and maybe even criticise it a bit – that's okay.' [24]

It was the Americans' turn now to try to seduce Putin with some good mood music. He was invited to the Bush family ranch at Crawford, Texas. Putin felt rarely privileged. He explained that he had never been to the home of another world leader. The atmosphere was cosy. While a thunderstorm raged outside, a log fire burned inside. Van Cliburn – a hero in the Soviet Union, where he won the Tchaikovsky Piano Competition back in 1958 – played for the guests. Condoleezza Rice danced and Putin's foreign minister, Igor Ivanov, chatted in Spanish with President Bush. He recalls: 'I speak Spanish because I used to work in Spain, and when Bush found this out he always used to chat to me in Spanish. He called me "Iggy". "Hey, Iggy," he would say, "Como estas?" ' [25]

But nothing could remove the log-jam over the ABM treaty – and Putin certainly did not intend to provide a fig-leaf by agreeing to abandon it jointly with the Americans. The most that could be agreed was that Bush would not embarrass Putin by announcing the withdrawal while he was still in the States.

In December Secretary of State Powell flew to Moscow to bury the treaty. In three days' time, he told Putin, President Bush would publicly announce America's unilateral with-drawal from the ABM. He described the curious reaction he got from Putin. 'Putin looked at me with those steely eyes of his and started to complain: "This is terrible, you are kick-ing out the legs from under the strategic stability, and we will criticise you for this." I said, "I fully understand that, Mr Presi-dent." And then he broke into a smile, and he leaned forward to me and he said: "Good! Now we won't have to talk about this any more. Now you and Igor [Ivanov] get busy on a new strategic framework." And I said. "Yes, sir." ' [26]

Within five months a new strategic arms limitation treaty had been cobbled together. It was rather less imposing than its predecessors, the SALT treaties of the Cold War era and the START treaties signed by Gorbachev and Yeltsin with George Bush Senior. Covering just a couple of sides of A4, it was pretty thin, and though it reduced each side's nuclear arsenals, it lacked any verification provisions or even any obligation to destroy arsenals permanently. But both Bush and Putin needed it for its symbolism. These two leaders were getting on like a house on fire, and they needed a treaty to prove it.

After the signing, Putin and his wife showed George and Laura Bush around the Kremlin, and then took them home to their dacha, where they did some fishing in a pond. Putin was repaying the Crawford experience. The next day they flew to Putin's home town, St Petersburg, where they visited the city's massive war memorial, the Hermitage gallery and the university. Putin then snuck off to attend a judo competition. And in the evening the presidential couples, with ministers and advisers in tow, went to a performance of the *Nutcracker* ballet at the celebrated Mariinsky Theatre.

Here something curious happened. Condoleezza Rice and Sergei Ivanov had struck up a great friendship. And while both were lovers of ballet, neither of them wanted to sit through three hours of the *Nutcracker*. When the lights went down, Ivanov leaned over to Rice and said: 'Condi, do you really want to watch the *Nutcracker*?'

'What do you have in mind?'

'I have an alternative. Have you heard of the Eifman ballet?'

Rice had heard of it. Boris Eifman was an avant-garde choreographer, much more to her taste. 'Let's go,' she said.

Ivanov and Rice slipped out of the Mariinsky and headed for Eifman's studio. They sat side by side in the rehearsal studio, transfixed, sole viewers of a thrilling performance (apart from a somewhat disgruntled looking Vladimir Rushailo, the national security adviser, who had been sent as a chaperone).

'I could see she loved it,' Ivanov recalled later. 'You can't fake that sort of thing.' [27]

They got back to the Mariinsky just before the lights went up, just in time to join the official delegations for a midnight canal trip around St Petersburg.

'Personal relationships do matter,' Rice confided in an interview. 'I came to trust that Sergei Ivanov was someone who was going to deliver on what he said he would do, and I think he believed the same about me.' [28]

It truly seemed like the dawn of a new era. Who could have imagined that it would all soon begin to disintegrate?

3

THE BATTLE FOR
ECONOMIC REFORM

Putting a new team together

It wasn't just Putin's foreign policies that impressed the West. At home, he launched a raft of economic reforms that won plaudits abroad, as they appeared to be aimed at stimulating the economy, entrenching the free market and consigning the last vestiges of communism to the dustbin.

While still prime minister – before he was even acting president – Putin recruited a new team of Western-oriented reformers to draw up a programme. Some, like German Gref and Alexei Kudrin, he knew from his St Petersburg days. Andrei Illarionov was an outspoken liberal economist and Arkady Dvorkovich, a young whizz-kid, was just back from studies at Duke University. Putin himself was still an economic novice, willing to listen and learn, and convinced that things had to change. Kudrin described him in an interview as 'a man of the next generation, who understood modern demands'.[1]

Under Yeltsin major projects had been carried out that had already transformed the economy, particularly mass privatisation and the liberalisation of prices. But the country did not enjoy sustainable economic growth, inflation was high and the new private sector worked inefficiently. Above all, the country's industrial base remained almost entirely focused on the extraction and sale of raw materials – oil, gas, aluminium, timber – while there was scarcely any modern manufacturing.

At the end of 1999 Putin put Gref, a 35-year-old lawyer-turned-businessman, in charge of a new Centre for Strategic Research, which became the engine room of the reforms. Gref, a bustling man with a pointed beard like Trotsky's, was no economist, but few doubted he was the right man for the task. Deputy finance minister Kudrin described him as 'bright and brave ... he was a tank, an engine, and totally committed to the reforms'.

Gref's Centre was a kind of brains trust. He recalled in an interview later: 'You know, what we were trying to do was to have consensus in society. We wanted to shape the programme with maximum input from intellectuals, academics, researchers, managers, economists. Part of the reason why we wanted public consultation was so nobody would think that it came from nowhere, so everybody would help to implement it. So the first task was to involve as many people as possible.'[2]

Not all the ideas that came flooding in were exactly what he had in mind. Gref smiled wryly as he recalled one contribution. 'We received all sorts of ideas, and some of them were pretty exotic, to be honest. One of the institutes of the Academy of Sciences offered us a set of measures which in effect would have brought back socialism. I remember their idea was to create a national fund for the payment of all salaries and then to standardise them all.'

Over the next six months the team held scores of briefings and brainstorming sessions, gradually sifting through all the proposals and pulling together a plan. Putin would occasionally attend, mainly listening and asking questions, often raising the question of how the reforms would impact upon social welfare. He also had his own economics guru, Andrei

Illarionov, whom he used as a sounding board, and in some regards as a counterbalance to the Gref team.[3]

Gref had invited Illarionov, the director of the Institute of Economic Analysis, to join the Centre, but according to Illarionov it was 'too Keynesian' for his liking, so he declined. Illarionov was, and remains, something of an oddball, a maverick who likes to challenge conventional wisdoms. Today he is a leading climate-change sceptic. In the late 1990s he had been fiercely critical of the policies that led to the country's financial crisis and default in August 1998. Perhaps it was his willingness to speak out that attracted Putin's attention (though some years later it would cost him his job). On 28 February 2000 the acting president called him and asked him to come out to his dacha at Novo-Ogaryovo, just outside Moscow, to 'chat'.

The two men spent all evening discussing the economy – or rather, economics. 'He didn't just want to know about interest rates and so on,' Illarionov said in an interview. 'He wanted to get a general understanding of economic reforms, what kind of economy we needed, what should be done, and how it should be put together. He was clearly learning a lot in a very narrow area that was not his speciality.'[3]

At one point they were interrupted by an officer who handed Putin a piece of paper. The acting president was delighted: it was news that the rebel-held town of Shatoy in Chechnya had just been retaken by Russian forces. Illarionov was quick to pour cold water on Putin's celebration. A long-standing opponent of Russia's intervention in Chechnya, he told him bluntly that what was going on there was 'a crime'. Illarionov says he argued that Chechnya should be allowed to become independent, that it could never be crushed militarily and that the response would be an upsurge in terrorism which would backfire on the Russian people.

They had a furious argument. Putin insisted the rebels had to be annihilated. 'His voice even changed,' said Illarionov, 'from the normal one he'd used when discussing economics. Suddenly some sort of iron, or ice, came across. It was a kind of transformation of the personality in front of your eyes – like seeing a completely different person. It seemed we could fall apart at any moment, without any possibility of reconciliation.'

After about half an hour, when it was clear there could be no meeting of minds, Putin suddenly announced: 'OK, that's enough. We will not talk any more about Chechnya.' Illarionov recalled: 'He just stopped this conversation, and for the rest of our meetings and relations over the next six years, he never mentioned Chechnya in my presence or discussed it with me. And after this, we resumed talking about economic reforms.'

By 10.30 it was time for Illarionov to leave, and after their spat over Chechnya he assumed it would be their last meeting. But Putin asked him to come back again the following day. Their economics tutorials became a regular occurrence, and on 12 April Putin officially appointed Illarionov as his chief economics adviser and later as his 'sherpa', or representative, to the G8 group of leading industrial nations.

By May the Centre's reform plan was almost ready, and it turned out to be, in Gref's words, 'ultra-liberal'. 'If we set the private sector free, we could see good growth,' said Kudrin. As the work neared fruition they produced a thick volume – far too dense to be presented to the acting president. As they had no experience in producing slide presentations they brought in a top consultancy, McKinsey, to help them. 'We spent a week at their Moscow office,' says Gref, 'putting together a short version for public presentation and a more professional version to show to ministries and departments explaining what they would have to do.'

On 5 May, two days before Putin's inauguration, the team went to his Sochi residence to give him a 'full immersion' in the project. The young reformers were buzzing with excitement. 'I was euphoric then,' said Kudrin, 'because it was all going according to plan.' From morning till night they held sessions, interspersed with meals and walks in the warm sunshine. The economists talked through every point with Putin, who requested more work to be done here and there but approved the general thrust. It became known as the 'Gref Plan'. Implementing it was to prove even harder than writing it.

Privatising the people's land

Over the coming years the Gref Plan transformed many aspects of economic life. Personal income tax was reduced from as much as 30 per cent to a flat rate of just 13 per cent. Corporate tax went down from 35 to 24 per cent. A new land code made it possible to buy and sell commercial and residential land – for the first time since the communist revolution of 1917. There was a new legal code, measures to curb money laundering, and an attempt to break up some of the great state monopolies: electricity production was split off from the supply network, for example.

The income tax reform was needed because millions of Russians, whose wages were already miserly, simply avoided paying, as the rates were crippling. The same was true of company taxation: some 80 per cent of businesses were avoiding paying taxes. Gref's proposal of a single, low income tax rate for everyone, and a much-reduced company tax, was audacious. The idea was to lower the rates but increase collection. But if people continued not to pay, the state could find itself with an even bigger hole in its budget. The point was not lost on Putin. Gref recalls a particular meeting that he and Kudrin had with him.

'The president asked us: "Are you sure that our total tax revenue isn't going to decrease if we lower taxes?"'

'We said: "Yes."'

'He asked: "What if you are wrong?"'

'I said: "Then I will resign."

"'I'm sorry," said Putin, "but I am not going to approve your plan on that basis! You haven't thought this through. What makes you think your resignation is somehow going to make up for all the money we are going to lose from the budget? Politically, the one doesn't compensate for the other." ' [4]

Gref and Kudrin went away, did their sums once more and re-presented their plan to Putin. This time he agreed.

The International Monetary Fund was less happy. 'At that time we were still working closely with the IMF mission here, and they refused to approve our plans,' says Gref. 'We had difficult meetings in the residency outside Moscow. Then we said to the IMF, "Thank you very much for your advice, but we are still going to lower taxes." ' The IMF subsequently left the country. But Gref describes the reform as 'the key, correct decision, which allowed our economic growth to take off'.

The proposed land reform was even more contentious – this time because it affronted millions of communists and others who believed that land ought to belong to 'the people'. Yeltsin had never dared to oppose them. As Gref prepared to present his Land Bill to the State Duma thousands took to the streets with red banners and anti-capitalist slogans.

At the last minute the government made a few concessions, tightening the regulations regarding the sale of agricultural land, but it made no difference. There was an uproar in the Duma as Gref was asked by the Speaker to take the floor, to present his bill. Deputies from the Communist Party (who had a quarter of the seats) swarmed around him to prevent him from leaving the government benches and reaching the podium. Some of them tried to grab him physically. The din was so loud that the Speaker could not make himself heard, so he called Gref on his phone and told him just to present his bill from where he was. 'No one can hear you anyway,' he said, 'but you've got to do it, otherwise we can't hold the vote.'

So Gref made his speech, as quickly as he could, while

communist deputies hammered their fists on their desks and drowned him out with their chants. The vote was held, the law was passed ... and the chamber instantly turned into a battlefield. Opposing deputies punched, kicked and head-butted each other.

'It was a historic moment,' Gref reminisced later with a smile. 'That's how we won the right to own land in Russia.'

Hands off Gazprom

The initial effect of the package of reforms was impressive. Russians did start to pay their taxes. Inflation fell from 20 per cent in 2000 to 9 per cent in 2006. The economy grew steadily at around 6–7 per cent a year. With the help of rising world prices for oil and gas (Russia's principal exports) the government did not just balance its books but went into surplus. It began paying off its huge foreign debt, which amounted to 130 per cent of GDP in 1998, reducing it by 2006 to just 18 per cent.

As petrodollars poured into the exchequer, the government faced a dilemma. There was those, including Gref, the economy minister, who wanted to spend the windfall on infrastructure: roads, railways, education and the healthcare system. Kudrin, the finance minister, on the other hand, feared that this could fuel inflation. He proposed instead the creation of a Stabilisation Fund, which would soak up surplus liquidity and build up a substantial cushion to protect the country if the price of oil should slump in the future. Most ministers wanted money straightaway for their industries. Regional governors complained to Putin that Kudrin was depriving the economy of cash. 'We had hot discussions about this,' said Gref. In the end both were satisfied. An Investment Fund was set up, which would plough up to $3 billion into infrastructure each year. 'It was a public–private partnership,' said Gref. 'If there was private money, the state financed it. It allowed big factories, power stations and so on to be built with private money.'

But the big winner was Kudrin with his Stabilisation Fund, which reached 522 billion roubles ($18.5 billion) by the beginning of 2005, allowing Russia's debts to the IMF ($3.3 billion) to be paid back in full. Oil revenues continued to pour in. By August 2006 Russia had also paid back its entire Soviet-era debt of almost $40 billion to the Paris Club of foreign government creditors – saving $7.7 billion in servicing costs. Even with these massive outlays, the Stabilisation Fund continued to accumulate as oil prices soared, giving Russia a healthy cushion to fall back on when prices slumped during the world economic crisis of 2008.

Putin's prime minister for most of his first presidential term was Mikhail Kasyanov, a charming, English-speaking free-marketeer with a booming voice, who oversaw the implementation of the Gref Plan. He has since become one of Putin's fiercest critics and a leader of the opposition. In 2008 he tried to run for president, but the Kremlin machine put paid to his plans by discovering alleged falsifications in the two million signatures collected to back his candidature. Back in the days of the 'Putin spring', however, he and the president saw eye to eye on almost everything. Even today he admits that Putin was at that time fully signed up to liberal reforms: 'It seemed to me that Vladimir Putin and I were allies, building – maybe not without mistakes – a democratic state with a market economy.'[5]

Only in one major endeavour did the reformers fail – and it proved to be highly significant. Asked whether Putin interfered much in the day-to-day work of the government, Kasyanov replied: 'In 90 per cent of cases he didn't interfere. The other 10 per cent concerned Gazprom and almost everything connected with it.'[6]

Gazprom was the country's largest company, and the biggest natural gas producer in the world. Created from the former Soviet Ministry of Gas, it was privatised under Yeltsin, but the state retained 40 per cent of the shares. It was in a parlous state, a hotbed of corruption, asset-stripping and tax-evasion.[7] Putin came to power vowing to sort things out, and appointed two St Petersburg cronies – Dmitry Medvedev and Alexei Miller – as new chairman of the board and CEO respectively. Miller knew next to nothing about the gas industry: according to Kasyanov, he spent his entire first year in the job learning. But that was only half the trouble. For the Gref team, the main problem was that Gazprom was a Soviet-era behemoth whose grip on the entire process of exploration, extraction, distribution and sales stifled competition. The oil industry, by contrast, had been broken up into a large number of competing companies in the 1990s.

Vladimir Milov was the young deputy energy minister who was tasked with reforming the gas sector. The idea, Milov said in an interview, was to 'break up the monopoly, separating distribution companies from production companies, turning them into smaller businesses, which were supposed to be privatised and compete with each other.'[8] Putin supported similar plans for the de-monopolisation of the electricity industry, despite protests from his own adviser, Illarionov. But Gazprom was different.

In the autumn of 2002 Milov drafted a plan for the reform of Gazprom. It won Gref's approval, and Kasyanov's. 'It used to seem to a lot of people,' says Kasyanov, 'that splitting up the production and transport of gas could lead to the disintegration of the whole sector, which was such an important part of the country's life-support system. They still try to frighten people, saying that without Gazprom in its existing form, the whole of Russia would collapse. That was just scare-mongering. In fact, all competent economists and industrialists knew that you could carry out a gas reform safely and painlessly. Everything was ready for that.'

According to Milov, the plan was sent to Gazprom's CEO, Alexei Miller, who at once raised it directly with Putin: 'He wrote Putin a furious memo, saying it would be disastrous and we were threatening national security. Putin then wrote on the letter, "I basically agree with Mr Miller. Mr Kasyanov please take that into account." '

Milov says he expected nothing else. 'Putin had shown a very specific interest in Gazprom since his early days. It was quite clear that he thinks of this company as one of the ultimate attributes and sources of power.'

Kasyanov tried to present the plan three times to his cabinet, but Putin insisted that it needed more work and the prime minister should discuss it further with Miller. 'Listen to Miller, listen to him personally,' he told Kasyanov. 'Don't listen to these people who're egging you on.'

Finally, in 2003, Putin simply ordered Kasyanov to drop the subject. 'Literally five minutes before the start of the cabinet meeting he called me and told me to remove the item from the agenda.' Gazprom, as we will see in later chapters, would become one of Putin's most effective levers of power – in the media, economy and foreign policy.

The good life

Putin's first term as president, largely thanks to the economic reform package, saw the first signs of growing foreign investor confidence. On the consumer side, giant multinationals, such as the French supermarket chain Auchan and the Swedish furniture outlet IKEA, pioneered huge retail parks in the Moscow suburbs. Each new IKEA store cost $50 million to open – but they hoped to recoup the investment quickly because, astonishingly, Muscovites seemed to have the cash to spend in them. The only thing that held back even greater investment was the vast amount of red tape and corruption that all entrepreneurs still faced in Russia – and few foreigners had the stamina or knowhow to overcome. (Chapter 12 will look at the crushing effect of corruption in Russia.) Still,

IKEA's huge blue and yellow furniture stores were like flags of modern life, fluttering all around the Moscow suburbs – and soon in other cities too.

In terms of Russian psychology – to the extent that this can be gauged – the shock of the 1990s seemed to be wearing off. I had the feeling (totally subjective, I admit) that people felt less patronised by the West than they had in the Yeltsin era. The foreign advisers were gone, and much of the new growth had a home-grown feel to it. Supermarkets filled up with Russian produce – but not the substandard Russian produce that used to be sold, packaged in identical brown bags; now it came in shiny packaging to match Western products. Russians went back to their old preferences – Vologda butter instead of Lurpak; *molochnaya kolbasa* ('dairy sausage') instead of imported German *wurst*. Wages were being paid again. The tens of thousands who lined the streets in the early 1990s selling their possessions had vanished. Moscow was brash and vulgar, but it had a vibrancy too, with new buildings going up everywhere and businesses opening up every day.

There were causes for optimism. The reason people were shopping at IKEA, after all, was because they were refurbishing their apartments, finally throwing out those ancient cracked tiles and Soviet-era fittings. Only now were many people (at least in the big cities) seeing the real break with communism, after a decade of uncertainty and poverty.

By the summer of 2002 things were looking relatively good. Vladimir Putin and George W. Bush were best friends, and Putin's team was turning Russia into a booming market economy.

But there were darker forces at work too. They threatened both Russia and its relations with the West.

4

THE DARKER SIDE

Muzzling the media

Boris Yeltsin is rocking a baby Vladimir Putin in a cradle. The baby is wailing. Yeltsin tries to sing him to sleep.

'Oh, oh,' sighs Yeltsin. 'You're so ugly. And – God forgive me – your origins are so dark ... and your looks so ... murky ... Oh, Lord, why did I – a democrat to the marrow – give birth to *this*?'

A fairy appears above him. It is Boris Berezovsky, the oligarch who helped bring Putin to power at the end of the 1990s. 'Yes,' he says, 'your first-born were prettier.'

Yeltsin yawns and puts his head down, saying, 'Oh, I am so exhausted. I am going to take a well-earned rest.' He falls asleep.

'Poor man,' says Berezovsky. 'He's worn himself out.'

Suddenly the baby starts crying out loud: 'Wipe 'em out in the outhouse,' he shouts. 'All of 'em ... wipe 'em out in the toilet!'

'Sssh,' says Berezovsky. 'Not all of them ... Calm down, lad. We'll make a human out of you.'

The scene is based on a fairy tale, *Little Zaches*, by the

German writer E.T.A. Hoffmann, the story of an ugly dwarf who has a spell cast on him by a fairy so that others find him beautiful. It was just one episode in the brilliant satirical puppet show *Kukly* (Puppets) which used to be shown on the independent television channel NTV.

Putin had to endure such mockery week in week out at the start of his presidency. He hated it. The 'wipe 'em out in the toilet' line was, of course, a reference to his notorious threat to annihilate Chechen terrorists. Berezovsky was the oligarch who used his television channel to 'beautify' Putin and paper over his KGB past to make him electable. And the dwarf? Well, every Russian viewer understood the reference to Putin's lack of inches.

The scriptwriter of *Kukly* was Viktor Shenderovich, an impish, bearded writer with an irrepressible sense of humour and disdain for authority. He is sure Putin never forgave them for *Little Zaches*. 'Several people told me independently that Putin went mad after this programme.'[1]

But *Kukly* was not the only thing on NTV that offended Putin. When the channel started up under Yeltsin it quickly gained a reputation as a free-thinking outlet, which broadcast unvarnished reports about the war in Chechnya (including the shocking truth about Russian atrocities and the demoralised state of Russian conscripts). Sunday evening's *Itogi*, a political chat-show hosted by the channel's leading journalist, Yevgeny Kiselyov, was unmissable viewing for every thinking Russian.

Russian broadcasting was still in its infancy. Western traditions of balance and independence had not taken root. NTV was used quite openly by its owner Vladimir Gusinsky to further his own interests, as was the main channel, ORT, by its prime shareholder Boris Berezovsky. They had both helped to get Yeltsin elected in 1996, when their business interests could have been threatened by a communist comeback. But in the December 1999 Duma elections, while Berezovsky's ORT had thrown its weight behind Putin's Unity Party, NTV had campaigned for his rivals.

Now, two days before the presidential election in March 2000, NTV broadcast a programme that caused apoplexy in the Kremlin: an investigation into the murky circumstances surrounding the apparent failed apartment bombing in Ryazan the previous summer and a discussion of the possible involvement of the FSB (see Chapter 1). Gusinsky's deputy, Igor Malashenko, was told by the information minister, Mikhail Lesin, that NTV had now 'crossed the line and were outlaws in their eyes'.

From this moment, it seems, NTV was doomed. Gusinsky's business empire, Media-Most, which owned NTV, was in deep financial trouble. In the 1990s it had borrowed hundreds of millions of dollars to implement extravagant plans to extend its reach. It had even launched its own satellite, at huge expense, hoping that the emerging middle classes would soon buy NTV receivers and programming. Gusinsky was preparing to float the company on the New York stock market, to raise capital to repay the debts. But after the August 1998 crisis, those plans evaporated, as did the TV advertising market in Russia, and Media-Most found itself saddled with loans it could not repay. Its main creditor was the state-owned gas monopoly, Gazprom – and this gave the Kremlin great leverage when it decided to throttle Gusinsky. According to Kiselyov, Gusinsky had been in talks with Gazprom about restructuring the debt, but when Putin became president he ordered the gas company to demand immediate repayment of the entire debt – and, if Media-Most refused, to seize NTV's assets. On 11 May, four days after Putin's inauguration, dozens of armed and masked tax police and FSB troops stormed Media-Most's headquarters. By the end of the day they had carted out hundreds of boxes of documents, cassettes and equipment. Malashenko described the raid as 'purely political in character, an act of revenge and intimidation'.

There was, perhaps, still a slim chance to survive. At around the same time, Malashenko received an offer directly from the Kremlin: fulfil certain conditions and the reprisals would stop. The conditions, according to Shenderovich, were: to stop investigating corruption in the Kremlin, to change their coverage of Chechnya and, above all, to 'remove the "First Person" from *Kukly*' – in other words, Putin's latex physiognomy had to disappear from the show.

To Shenderovich, this was a red rag to a bull. He responded by writing a hilarious episode of *Kukly* that lampooned the edict itself. Since they could not show Putin, they showed a burning bush instead. Moses – in the form of Putin's chief of staff, Alexander Voloshin – receives tablets from his invisible leader with the Kremlin's 'ten commandments'. At the end the leader is referred to as '*Gospod Bog* (The Lord God), GB for short' (which for every Russian means KGB). In English it sounds convoluted. In Russian, it could not have been more direct, or more provocative.

Two weeks later, on 13 June, Gusinsky was arrested. Putin feigned complete innocence when asked about it by a television reporter. 'It was unexpected for me,' he said, barely able to stop a little smile playing on his lips. 'I hope the authorities who made this decision – I suppose it was the prosecutor's office, yes? – have good reasons to justify their action.'

Gusinsky was given a choice: sell his media empire to Gazprom or face prosecution for large-scale fraud. It was blackmail. He agreed and fled the country. Russia's freest media group was now under Kremlin control.

The other big media tycoon, Boris Berezovsky, fared no better. He had been accused of fraud under the premiership of Primakov, but the charges were dropped when Putin became prime minister, and he was seen as by far the most powerful oligarch – with a media empire as well as massive industrial and commercial assets, including the oil company Sibneft and the airline Aeroflot. As he was gradually squeezed out of Putin's inner circle, so his media became ever more critical. In

June he criticised plans announced by Putin for a recentralisation of power, and the day after Gusinsky's arrest the public prosecutor announced he was extending an investigation into Aeroflot's finances. Berezovsky was suspected of fraud and money-laundering on a massive scale.

Just before his election in March, Putin had pledged to outlaw the oligarchs: 'Those people who fuse power and capital – there will be no oligarchs of this kind as a class.' The phrase sent a chill down many spines, as it recalled Stalin's policy of liquidating the kulaks, or rich peasants, 'as a class'. What he objected to was the idea that wealth (especially fabulous, ill-gotten wealth) should render political influence. Even though Berezovsky had helped him come to power, Putin resented the influence he wielded through his media empire (which included not just ORT but another channel, TV-6, and several newspapers).

As in Gusinsky's case, Berezovsky's downfall may have been triggered, or hastened, by a television programme. When the *Kursk* nuclear submarine sank in the Barents Sea on 12 August 2000, leading to the deaths of 188 crew members, ORT excoriated Putin for his tardy response. The station's top presenter, Sergei Dorenko – the attack-dog taken on to help Putin's party win the election at the end of 1999 – now poured his bile on the president. Putin had remained on holiday in Sochi for a full five days following the accident, and it was another four before he visited the northern garrison town and met the dead servicemen's families. He had also turned down offers of help from Britain and Norway. Dorenko dissected an interview given by Putin to justify his response, and sneered at every phrase, as though he had nothing but contempt for the country's president. For example, Putin was shown saying that foreign help was offered only on the 16th. Dorenko heaved a big sigh and retorted: 'I'm sorry, but in fact they offered to help on the 15th, and they would have offered earlier if we hadn't been lying to the world that everything was OK and we didn't need help.' Dorenko also broadcast a secret recording of a meeting Putin held behind closed doors with relatives of the dead, in which he was heard blaming the *media* for the disaster: 'They're liars. They're liars,' he said. 'For the last ten years television has been destroying our army and navy, that people are dying in today ...'

Dorenko's show was axed. And soon it was Berezovsky's turn to follow Gusinsky into exile. At the end of August Berezovsky went to the Kremlin to see Putin's chief of staff, Alexander Voloshin, who gave him an ultimatum: to transfer his ORT shares to the state or 'follow Gusinsky' – that is, face prosecution. The next day Berezovsky was received by Putin himself, who accused the businessman of deliberately trying to destroy him. They had a furious row. According to Berezovsky, Putin said to him: 'You should return your shares under my personal control ... I will manage ORT on my own.' Berezovsky vowed never to do that, and stormed out.

In fact Berezovsky did surrender his control of the station, selling his stake to fellow oligarch Roman Abramovich, who meekly transferred his voting rights to the state, thus completing the government's takeover of the channel. But this did not stop the attacks against Berezovsky. On 1 November the state prosecutor accused him of defrauding Aeroflot of hundreds of millions of dollars. Berezovsky was abroad at the time and decided to stay there. From the safety of exile he claimed that the money he was alleged to have embezzled was partly used to finance Putin's election campaigns.

Berezovsky has lived in London ever since, despite repeated Russian attempts to have him extradited, and was granted political asylum in September 2003. Putin personally intervened to try to persuade Britain to send him back, and in so doing betrayed his lack of understanding of Western systems. He asked Prime Minister Tony Blair to put pressure on the courts to extradite Berezovsky. According to a well-informed source, Blair explained that this was impossible in the UK: it was a magistrate's decision, not the government's. Putin, unable to fathom the independence of the courts, took offence.* This was the KGB man speaking, the product of a Soviet upbringing unwittingly applying his own undemocratic standards to a Western country.

There is no reason to think that Putin was dissembling; rather, it seems clear that he actually believes that it is normal for Western politicians to influence the courts in the same way as Russian leaders can. His belief that governments control the media is similar: in 2005 he accused President Bush to his face of personally ordering the sacking of the veteran CBS news anchor Dan Rather. And on another occasion he told a journalist who questioned why Russian police routinely beat up peaceful protestors that in the West it was 'normal' for demonstrators who found themselves in the wrong place to be 'beaten around the head with a baton'.

The vertical of power

The crackdown on the free media was not the only reason why the West's admiration for President Putin's first steps in foreign policy and economic reform, described in the first two chapters of this book, was tempered from the start by wariness about his understanding of democracy.

One of Putin's earliest decisions as president was to start creating what he called the 'vertical of power' – the gathering-in of all political power to the centre, and effectively into

---

*   The magistrate who rejected the extradition request for Berezovsky (and also for an exiled Chechen leader, Akhmed Zakayev, who was also wanted by Moscow) was Judge Timothy Workman. A few months later, in January 2004, an 83-year-old man with the same surname, Robert Workman, was shot dead when he opened his front door to a stranger in a quiet village north of London. No motive for the murder has been established and the killer has not been found. There was speculation that the murder could have been a case of mistaken identity.

his own hands. He believed that lack of central control lay at the heart of Russia's woes, that Yeltsin's weak leadership had allowed crime and corruption to flourish, oligarchs to amass power and the country's regions to spin off into separate orbits. Yeltsin had encouraged the regions to 'take as much sovereignty as you can swallow', which had had the unwanted effect of allowing governors quietly to ignore or even sabotage edicts from the centre, threatening the disintegration of the federation. Many regions passed laws that contradicted the Russian constitution, withheld taxes from the centre and struck bilateral agreements with foreign countries. Some of them could have survived well as independent countries: the republic of Yakutia, for example, produces one-quarter of the world's diamonds (and has a population of less than half a million); Khanty-Mansiisk (population 1.5 million) is the world's second largest oil producer.

On 13 May – just six days after his inauguration – Putin announced that the country's 89 regions would be placed under the control of seven 'super-governors' personally appointed by the president. Five of Putin's seven enforcers turned out to be *siloviki* * – men with careers in the security services and armed forces. They included Viktor Cherkesov, first deputy director of the FSB, whose work in the past had included the persecution of Soviet dissidents.

Six days later Putin initiated a reform of the upper chamber of parliament (the Federation Council or 'senate'). Previously, elected regional governors and heads of regional legislative councils were *ex officio* senators; now the regional bosses were replaced by *nominated* representatives, allowing the Kremlin to

---

* The word *silovik* is often translated as 'strongman', but it really means 'a member of the security forces'. It derives from the term *silovye struktury*, or 'power structures', in other words the FSB, ministry of defence, police, and so on. In effect the *siloviki* are men (I can't think of any female *siloviki*) who derive their power from having worked in one of these structures.

fill the Federation Council with 'friendly' senators.

Putin then moved to centralise the collection and distribution of taxes, which had been about 50–50 between the centre and the regions, to 70–30 in favour of the central government.

The apex of the new vertical of power was not the federal government, however, but rather Putin himself – something he achieved by appointing trusted colleagues from the security services or from his home town, St Petersburg, to key positions. Many of them, moreover, were also given directorships in state companies, thereby enmeshing the country's political and business structures in a vast spider web, at the centre of which sat Putin.

Igor Sechin had the perfect pedigree: he had worked with Putin in St Petersburg, and by some accounts may also earlier have been a spy, working undercover as a translator in Portuguese-speaking African countries. He became Putin's most trusted adviser, and followed his master from St Petersburg to Moscow in 1996. When Putin became acting president he retained Yeltsin's chief of staff, Alexander Voloshin, but immediately appointed Sechin as deputy chief of staff, controlling the flow of papers that crossed his desk, and in effect running the energy industry. In 2004 he also became chairman of the board of Rosneft, the state oil company.

Viktor Ivanov, from the Leningrad KGB, became Putin's deputy chief of staff in charge of personnel matters – and also chairman of both the Almaz air defence corporation and Aeroflot. Sechin and Ivanov were considered the most powerful *siloviki* in Putin's circle.

Dmitry Medvedev, another former colleague of Putin's from St Petersburg, came to Moscow in 1999 to become a third deputy chief of staff, and also chairman of the state gas monopoly, Gazprom.

Putin brought his St Petersburg colleague Alexei Miller to Moscow to become deputy minister of energy and then CEO of Gazprom.

The two chief economic reformers, German Gref and Alexei Kudrin, also came from St Petersburg. Gref served on the board of Gazprom, and Kudrin became chairman of both VTB bank and the diamond producer Alrosa.

Sergei Naryshkin, another Leningrader and former colleague at KGB school, was promoted in Putin's second term to government chief of staff, as well as chairman of the board of Channel One television and deputy chairman of Rosneft.

Another old Leningrad KGB colleague, Nikolai Patrushev, became chairman of the FSB, following Putin himself.

Rashid Nurgaliyev worked under Putin in the FSB and then became interior minister. Cherkesov, mentioned above, was another subordinate of Putin's in the FSB.

Sergei Chemezov, a fellow spy with Putin in Dresden, was brought in to run Rosoboronexport, the country's chief arms exporter. And another 'Chekist', Vladimir Yakunin, was brought in to the transport ministry and eventually became head of Russian Railways.

Yakunin has another link to Putin: they are both founding members of a so-called 'dacha cooperative' known as *Ozero*, which manages their adjacent country houses on Komsomolskoye lake near St Petersburg. All of Putin's other friends from the *Ozero* group (as we shall see in Chapter 12) now hold top positions in government, banking and the media.

The Chechen war and the backlash

During Putin's first years as president events in Chechnya cast a long shadow over his claims to be bringing Russia into the 'European family'. I spent several months in Chechnya during the earlier war (1994–96) and saw for myself how the republic was ravaged by Russian forces. It seemed to me that there was more than sufficient evidence of serious war crimes and human rights violations, which I and scores of other journalists documented, but the international community – perhaps because it was preoccupied with the simultaneous wars in the Balkans – did nothing about them. The total devastation of the capital, Grozny, and the deaths of tens of thousands of civilians, whose apartment blocks were literally pulverised by Russian air power and artillery, could not be justified by the alleged purpose of destroying 'bandits', as the rebel forces were known. I interviewed survivors of Russian 'filtration camps' – notorious prisons where Chechens were tortured to extract confessions, or just for fun. I visited huge open graves, filled with hundreds of bodies, some with their hands tied behind their backs. I met dozens of grieving families, saw murdered women and children, hundreds of homes destroyed in villages all across Chechnya, streams of refugees fleeing from Russian troops, people cowering in basements from air attacks. I met defenceless, bedridden old people, all but freezing and starving to death in the rubble of their homes. But this was under Boris Yeltsin's presidency, and the West, besotted with his alleged devotion to democracy, offered only limp condemnation, considering the conflict to be an 'internal affair'.

The second war, unleashed by Putin in 1999, was by all accounts even more brutal. But fewer Western journalists covered it, because it was simply too dangerous. At least in the earlier war the Chechens had been generally well disposed to journalists; since then the republic had turned into a lawless quagmire, where the risk of kidnapping and murder were just too great. The rebel fighters themselves were now as barbarous as the Russians had been. It was left mainly to courageous journalists like Anna Politkovskaya of *Novaya gazeta* to bring the truth to the world this time. (And even so no Western leader has called for any Russian commander or politician to be tried for war crimes.)

In the first war it was relatively easy for journalists to move around in Chechnya. It was this that led to the highly critical coverage – not only in the West but in Russia too, especially on NTV. The authorities learned their lesson, and the second time around tried to restrict access to the war zone. One Russian journalist, Andrei Babitsky, who worked for Radio Liberty, was even kidnapped by federal forces in early 2000 because of his critical reporting. They then handed him over to Chechen fighters in exchange for Russian prisoners of war, as though he himself were a combatant – a fallacy apparently supported by Putin, who indicated that he saw nothing wrong with the swap because Babitsky – a *journalist*, let's not forget – was a traitor: 'This was his own decision,' Putin told the newspaper *Komsomolskaya Pravda*. 'He went to the people whose interests he effectively served.'[2]

If Putin believed that critical reporting was tantamount to serving the enemy, then there could be no doubt about what he must have thought of Politkovskaya. After the taming of NTV she became the most important chronicler of Russian barbarity in Chechnya, a patient listener to the cries of pain that the Kremlin wished to stifle.

The authorities maintained that the campaign in Chechnya was a 'security operation', aimed solely at eliminating terrorists. Politkovskaya spoke to eyewitnesses of Russian 'security sweeps', men like 45-year-old Sultan Shuaipov, a refugee from the Grozny suburb of Novaya Katayama. He told Politkovskaya how he had personally gathered up 51 bodies from his street and buried them. Here is just part of his story.

When 74-year-old Said Zubayev came out of No. 36 on Line [street] 5 he ran into the federals and the soldiers made him dance, firing their rifles at his feet to make him jump. When the old man got tired, they shot him. Thanks be to Allah! Said never knew what they did to his family.

At about nine at night, an infantry fighting vehicle broke into the Zubayevs' courtyard, taking the gates off their hinges. Very efficiently and without wasting words the soldiers brought out of the house and lined up by the steps 64-year-old Zainab, the old man's wife, their 45-year-old daughter, Malika (the wife of a colonel in the Russian militia); Malika's little daughter, Amina, aged eight; Mariet, another daughter of Said and Zainab, 40 years old; their 44-year-old nephew, Said Saidakhmed Zubayev; 35-year-old Ruslan, the son of Said and Zainab; his pregnant wife Luiza; and their eight-year-old daughter Eliza. There were several bursts of machine-gun fire and they were all left dead in front of the family home. None of the Zubayevs survived except for Inessa, Ruslan's 14-year-old daughter. She was very pretty, and before the massacre the soldiers carefully set her to one side, then dragged her off with them.

We looked desperately for Inessa but it was as if she had vanished into thin air [Sultan says]. We think they must have raped her and then buried her somewhere. Otherwise she would have come back to bury her dead. That same night Idris, the headmaster of School No. 55, was killed. First they battered him against a wall for a long time, and broke all his bones, then they shot him in the head. In another house we found, side by side, an 84-year-old Russian woman and her 35-year-old daughter, Larisa, a well-known lawyer in Grozny. They had both been raped and shot. The body of 42-year-old Adlan Akayev, a Professor of Physics at the Chechen State University, was sprawled in the courtyard of his house. He had been tortured. The beheaded body of 47-year-old Demilkhan Akhmadov had had its arms cut off too. It was one of the features of the operation in Novaya Katayama that they cut people's heads off. I saw several bloodstained chopping blocks. On Shevskaya Street there was a block with an axe stuck in it, and a woman's head in a red scarf on the block. Alongside, on the ground, also headless, was a man's body. I found the body of a woman who had been beheaded and had her stomach ripped open. They had stuffed a head into it. Was it hers? Someone else's?[3]

Despite all the documented cases of brutality, only one senior officer has ever been brought to justice. Colonel Yuri Budanov was accused of kidnapping, raping and murdering an 18-year-old Chechen woman, Kheda Kungayeva, in a drunken rampage. She was dragged from her home by soldiers and abducted in an armoured personnel carrier, allegedly because they thought she was a sniper. The rape charge was eventually dropped, and in court Budanov admitted strangling the woman, though he claimed to have been temporarily insane at the time, enraged while interrogating her. At first he was found not guilty, but then, after a retrial, was sentenced to ten years in prison. He was released in January 2009, 15 months early, and then murdered in a Moscow street in June 2011.

The payback for the Russian campaign was a decade of Chechen terrorist attacks across Russia – in aeroplanes, underground trains, schools and streets. On 18 April 2002, in his annual state-of-the-nation speech, President Putin declared the war over. But six months later terror struck right at the heart of the Russian capital. In October 2002, up to 50 armed Chechens, many of them women, strode into the Dubrovka Theatre during a performance of a musical called *Nord-Ost*, and took the players and the 850-strong audience hostage. They were armed with guns and explosives and the women put on suicide belts. They demanded the immediate and unconditional withdrawal of Russian troops from Chechnya – within one week, otherwise they would start shooting hostages.

For the next three days Putin was locked in almost constant crisis meetings with his security chiefs. At the first session the *siloviki* proposed storming the building, while the prime minister, Mikhail Kasyanov, sharply disagreed, calling for talks with the terrorists in order to avoid casualties. According to Kasyanov, the security chiefs argued there was no point in making concessions because casualties would be unavoidable in any case. Putin was scheduled to travel to Mexico for a summit of Asian and Pacific leaders, but sent Kasyanov in his place. Some have suggested the decision was taken in order to remove from the process the only man opposed to using force to free the hostages, but even Kasyanov concedes that there was no way Putin himself could have left the country at that point (especially in the light of the criticism he earned over his response to the *Kursk* disaster).[4] President Yeltsin had gone to a G7 meeting in Halifax, Canada, in the middle of the Budyonnovsk hostage crisis in 1995, leaving his prime minister, Viktor Chernomyrdin, to negotiate with the captors and allow them to escape. Putin certainly was not going to repeat that mistake.

A number of politicians and journalists (including Anna Politkovskaya) did try to reason with the hostage-takers, but to no avail. In the end the *siloviki* did it their way. Special forces pumped an anaesthetic gas into the theatre to sedate the terrorists (and the hostages), and then commandoes stormed in. There was a gun-fight, in which all of the terrorists were killed, including those who had already been knocked out by the gas. But 130 hostages also died – mostly from the effects of the toxic chemical and the failure to provide them with immediate medical care when they were brought out of the building. There was much criticism of the action, including the fact that the chemical composition of the gas used was so secret that even medics attending the scene were not told what it was or what antidote could be used, almost certainly worsening the death toll.

Putin later defended his actions, saying hundreds of lives had been saved. And in truth, no government in the world has ever worked out a perfect way to cope with such a situation. But had the strongmen really taken enough care to protect the hostages' lives? Or were they more intent on killing the terrorists? When the *Kursk* sank it is assumed that Putin turned down foreign offers of help primarily because he did not want NATO rescuers poking around a top-secret Russian nuclear submarine. The chemical agent used to end the theatre siege was also a military secret, the exact formula of which was never revealed.

The big issue that the Russian authorities refuse to face up to is what motivates the terrorists. Is it, as Putin always claims, part of an international Islamist movement, with its roots in Pakistan and Afghanistan, or is it a vengeful response to Russia's vicious attempts to subjugate Chechnya since 1994? The answer can be found in some of the gunmen's answers to Anna Politkovskaya during the theatre siege. She asked one of the captors to release the older children from the theatre (the younger ones had been released). 'Children?' came the response. 'There are no children in there. In security sweeps you take ours from 12 years old. We will hold on to yours.'

'In retaliation?' Politkovskaya asked.

'So that you know how it feels.'

Politkovskaya asked if she can at least bring food for the children.

'Do you let ours eat in the security sweeps? Yours can do without too.'

Taming the oligarchs

In his first address to the nation, 12 hours after becoming acting president, Putin had pledged to respect freedom of speech, freedom of the mass media and property rights. On 28 July 2000 he had a showdown with the country's top 20 businessmen and bankers to explain what he meant, and set out the new rules of the game.

These were men who had acquired vast fortunes during the Yeltsin years by exploiting every loophole, breaking and bending laws, bribery, thuggery, extortion, and, most simply of all, by helping themselves to companies and resources offered to them in exchange for ensuring Yeltsin's political survival. They owned the country's major oil and gas companies, pipelines, aluminium smelters, telecoms and advertising, automobile plants, iron and steel works, a brewery and the top banks. Mingling with them in a grand, columned Kremlin hall as they waited for the president to arrive were the government's young team of reformers – Kasyanov, Kudrin, Gref – who above all needed the tycoons to pay their taxes so they could get the country's finances in order. The oligarchs themselves had other concerns, having heard Putin threaten their exist-ence 'as a class'. They had just seen their colleague Gusinsky effectively stripped of his wealth and hounded out of the coun-try. His fellow media tycoon Boris Berezovsky was nowhere to be seen.

The oligarchs were seated democratically around a huge doughnut-shaped table. But when the president joined them in the circle there was no doubt about who was in charge. The meeting lasted two and a half hours, but Putin's offer was simple: there would be no reversal of the privatisation process, on two conditions – that the oligarchs started paying their taxes, and that they kept out of politics. Putin was careful not to put it in the form of an ultimatum, but that is what it was.

In an interview, German Gref summed up what happened: 'Putin sent a strong message that no nationalisation or expro-priation of property was planned. He put it to them like this: "We are making a gesture to you, we are sharply decreasing taxes, we are creating a favourable investment environment and defending property rights. But please, since we are lower-ing the taxes, you should pay them. And secondly, if it's busi-ness you've chosen, then do business."' [5]

The businessmen emerged from the meeting almost sing-ing with relief. Most of them had no desire to get into politics anyway, and paying taxes was a small price to pay for their fortunes. Vladimir Potanin, president of the mining and metals conglomerate Interros, sounded almost repentant: 'The oligarchs had set themselves up as an elite, but society doesn't accept this elite. We have to behave better.'

The initiative for this meeting had come from Boris Nemtsov, the former governor of Nizhny Novgorod who had helped to kick-start the privatisation process in the mid-1990s and now headed a political party, the Union of Right Forces, to defend the interests of the nascent middle class. He described the event as a watershed – the point where (he put it, with irony, in Marxist terms) 'the ten-year history of the primitive accumulation of capital' came to an end. In other words, this was the moment when Russia's 'robber barons' were given the chance to turn into respectable businessmen.

For the most part, the oligarchs went along with that. Gusinsky and Berezovsky went into exile – the former quietly, the latter continuing to wage battle against Putin from abroad. Roman Abramovich, the owner of the oil giant Sibneft, did become a member of the Duma, and also governor of the remote region of Chukotka. But he did not use his political influence to challenge Putin. He was far more interested in his British football club, Chelsea, which he bought in 2003.

Only one oligarch refused to toe the line – Mikhail Khodorkovsky. His intransigence would land him in a Siberian prison camp for many years and turn him into one of the greatest sources of tension between Russia and the West.

The Khordorkovsky affair

Khodorkovsky had taken his earliest steps in business almost as soon as it was possible, back in the days of Mikhail Gorbachev's tentative *perestroika* reforms. As a communist youth functionary, he used his connections to set up a café, an import business and, eventually, one of Russia's first commercial banks – Menatep. From then on his rise was vertiginous. In 1995, in the 'loans for shares' scheme designed to bail out the bankrupt Yeltsin government, he acquired a major stake in Russia's second-largest oil company, Yukos. The following year he bought the shares – effectively from himself – and ended up with a majority stake in Yukos for just $309 million, a fraction of its real value. Within months the company was worth $6 billion. None of this broke the law: the scheme was devised by the government itself.

There is no doubt that Khodorkovsky was a devious wheeler

and dealer as he built his empire. In his excellent study, *The Oligarchs*, the American journalist David Hoffman confesses that even after painstaking investigation he could not fathom some of Khodorkovsky's manoeuvres and schemes, involving offshore transactions, front companies and 'sleight of hand'.[6]

But once he had complete control of Yukos he underwent something of a conversion and decided (largely because he wanted to attract foreign investors) to adopt squeaky-clean Western standards of accountancy and transparency. Khodorkovsky became the darling of the West because he, more than any other oligarch, seemed to epitomise a new breed of Russian capitalist – not just a money-grabbing shark, but a philanthropist too. He adopted a corporate governance charter at Yukos, and was the first businessman to introduce US-standard accounting practices. He used some of his fortune to set up a lyceum on an eighteenth-century estate outside Moscow to provide education to 130 underprivileged children. His Open Russia Foundation distributed more than $15 million a year to civic projects and charities involved in education, public health, leadership programmes and cultural development.

And yet there is no name more certain to bring that look of icy contempt into Vladimir Putin's eyes. Khodorkovsky would end up in jail for economic crimes – tax evasion, fraud, embezzlement. But asked about him at press conferences, Putin would not shrink from throwing in a few other accusations – 'political' crimes, even murder.

To be sure, Khodorkovsky was no saint. John Browne, the chief executive of BP, was not won over when Khodorkovsky visited him in Britain in February 2002, to offer BP a 25 per cent share in Yukos. Browne later described how the soft-spoken Khodorkovsky made him nervous. 'He began to talk about getting people elected to the Duma, about how he could make sure oil companies did not pay much tax, and about how he had many influential people under his control. For me, he seemed too powerful. It is easy to say this with hindsight, but there was something untoward about his approach.'[7]

For the reforming Russian government 'untoward' was an understatement. According to German Gref, 'not a single draft went through without Yukos's say so'. In fact, the bribing of members of the State Duma was commonplace – deputies pocketed fortunes from all sorts of business interests – but the oil companies were most active, and Yukos most of all. When it came to a new oil export duty that would have reduced the oil company's profits, things got heavy. Gref recalls how he was visited on the eve of the Duma vote by Vasily Shakhnovsky, president of Yukos-Moskva. 'Mr Gref,' he said, 'we very much appreciate what you have done for the development of the market economy, but tomorrow you're going to introduce a law that contradicts our interests, so we would like you to know that, first of all, this law will not get through. Everybody will vote against it – we have agreed on that with everybody. And the second point: if you insist on it, we will write a collective letter from all oil producers asking for the resignation of you and Mr Kudrin for lack of professionalism. It's nothing personal, but maybe you could just postpone the discussion of this law, and we can come to some arrangement with you.'[8]

When Kudrin and Gref arrived in the Duma next morning they discovered a solid bloc, including the large communist faction, had been stitched together, which defeated the bill. Gref later mused on the irony of it all: 'The communists, supposedly the champions of social policy, voted against a tax on the super-incomes of the oil companies!'

It was a dramatic blow for the reformers. 'We didn't have enough resources in the budget to pay our debts,' Gref recalled. 'Oil prices were rising, but that was just making the oil companies richer. We got nothing from it.' It took another year before Gref managed to pass a diluted version of the law through parliament.

Even more seditious, from Putin's point of view, were Khodorkovsky's political ambitions. He funded several opposition parties, including the liberal Yabloko, the Union of Right Forces, and the Communist Party. In early 2003 he held secret meetings with party leaders and offered to donate tens or even hundreds of thousands of dollars to finance their campaigns in the coming December Duma elections.[9] According to the prime minister, Mikhail Kasyanov, it was the financing of the communists that particularly infuriated Putin. Kasyanov said later he was astonished to discover that while support-ing the two Western-oriented parties was 'approved', funding the communists – though perfectly legal – apparently required some special secret dispensation from the president.[10]

Khodorkovsky claimed that what he did was normal 'lobby-ing', as happens in any country, but the Kremlin saw it differ-ently: 'He was *buying up* the Duma!' Putin's spokesman, Dmitry Peskov, exclaimed to me, clearly as affronted by the idea as his boss was. The Kremlin apparently feared that Khodorkovsky was planning to use his influence in the Duma to change the constitution, to turn Russia into a parliamentary democracy – and perhaps even become prime minister himself, directly challenging Putin's power.

People who know Khodorkovsky often point to his reckless streak. It was on show at a dramatic and perhaps fateful meet-ing of leading businessmen with Putin in St Catherine's Hall in the Kremlin on 19 February 2003.[11] The main item on the agenda was corruption. Khodorkovsky was the main speaker, and he was planning to say some extraordinarily provocative things about corruption he suspected was going on in the top circles of government. He was nervous, and called his vice-president, Leonid Nevzlin, for advice. 'Do you think my pres-entation is dangerous?' he asked.

'Well,' Nevzlin conceded. 'What if Putin himself is actually mixed up in these deals?'

'Come on!' exclaimed Khodorkovsky. 'The president controls the state budget. Do you think he'd get involved for a few million dollars of kickback?'[12]

Khodorkovsky cleared his presentation with Putin's chief of staff, Voloshin, and prime minister, Kasyanov. He went into the meeting armed with graphs and bar charts to illustrate his points.

Much of his presentation was based on opinion-poll findings: 27 per cent of Russians believed corruption to be the most dangerous threat to the nation; 49 per cent believed most state officials were corrupt (15 per cent thought *all* officials were); a large majority felt the government either could not or would not do anything to combat corruption.

'If you look at the next slide,' Khodorkovsky went on, 'you can see that the level of corruption in Russia is in the region of 30 billion dollars – that's 10 to 12 per cent of GDP.'

Another slide showed that 72 per cent of Russians had no faith in the justice system because judges were institutionally corrupt. And Khodorkovsky raised a remarkable fact about applications for Russian university places. Young people were less interested in studying to become engineers or oilmen than ... tax inspectors! Their salaries would be low, but the opportunities to supplement them through bribery were enormous. 'If we are setting our young people on this course, it's something we should think about,' said Khodorkovsky.

'Well, there is food for thought there,' retorted Putin, 'but let's not apply the presumption of guilt to our students!'

But Khodorkovsky was only warming up. Now he moved on to a specific case of corruption that involved people in Putin's closest circle – specifically his deputy chief of staff and confidant Igor Sechin, who effectively controlled the state oil sector. (He would soon become chairman of the government-owned Rosneft.)

Khodorkovsky referred to Rosneft's purchase, the previous month, of a smaller oil company, Severnaya Neft, for $600 million – far in excess of its true value. 'Everyone believes that this deal had, so to speak, an ulterior motive.'

For everyone listening the implication was clear. As Andrei

Illarionov, Putin's adviser, recalled later: 'It was obvious that the difference between the sale price and the actual price was a pure and simple kickback – corruption.'[13] In other words, the huge excess payment to the small company was shared by its owners with the government officials who had authorised it.

'Yes, corruption is spreading in our country,' Khodorkovsky continued. 'And you might say that it started right here with us ... but it has to stop some time!'

Putin shot back, asserting that as a state company Rosneft was *obliged* to buy assets such as Severnaya Neft in order to increase its reserves. As for Khodorkovsky's own company, Putin hinted that he had acquired it illegally: 'Some companies like Yukos have huge surpluses of oil. How they acquired them is precisely what today's meeting is about! And let's not forget the question of the payment – or non-payment – of taxes. Your own company [Yukos] had problems with non-payment of taxes. I have to give you your due – you came to an agreement with the tax authorities and the case was closed, or is being closed. But how did these problems arise in the first place?'

And Putin ended with a clear threat. 'So I am passing the buck back to you,' he said. It meant: you talk to me about my people being corrupt, and my people will start looking at your corruption.

Kasyanov, who was sitting next to the president, says the oligarchs around the table 'nearly climbed under the table in fear'. Was Putin reopening the whole issue of how Russia's strategic industries were privatised in the 1990s?

Kasyanov says he went to see Putin in his office afterwards. 'Naively, I thought the president didn't know the details of the Rosneft deal. I said, "You shouldn't have reacted so sharply. Khodorkovsky's right." ' But Putin shot back, insisting that it was Rosneft's right as a state company to increase its assets and there was nothing wrong with the deal. Kasyanov was taken aback: 'He started citing various figures that even I, the prime minister, didn't know. He knew more about the affair than I did.'[14]

To try to pre-empt the reprisals at which Putin had hinted, Khodorkovsky came to Kasyanov two weeks later with a plan. Speaking, he said, on behalf of his fellow oligarchs, he proposed a new law, under which the tycoons who had bought up state enterprises on the cheap in the 1990s – businesses that were now worth billions of dollars – should pay compensation to the state, a sort of one-off tax to cover the massive increase in their worth. The windfall would go into a special fund to finance 'important reforms'. Kasyanov liked the idea, which could have given the government an extra $15–20 billion to spend on new highways, high-speed rail links, power lines, airports and the like. He asked Khodorkovsky to draw up a draft law, which he did within a week. Kasyanov presented it to President Putin. And that was the last that was heard of it.[15] Putin was already thinking of other ways to make Khodorkovsky pay.

Leonid Nevzlin remembers receiving disturbing news from a contact in Russia's intelligence service. 'I was given information that there was a special group answerable only to the FSB chief Patrushev and his deputy Zaostrovstsev, whose job was to build a criminal case against Yukos and watch its managers and shareholders.'

In the early summer a think-tank known as the National Strategy Council published an analytical report entitled 'The State and Oligarchy', written by an influential thinker, Stanislav Belkovsky, who was regarded as close to the *siloviki*. He argued that the oligarchs were preparing nothing less than a creeping putsch, which would bring the Duma under their control, leading to the rewriting of the constitution and the crowning of Khodorkovsky as all-powerful prime minister, with the presidency emasculated.

At Putin's annual press conference a few days later, a reporter was primed to ask a question about the Belkovsky report, and the president was ready with a chilling reminder of how he dealt with his political enemies: 'I am absolutely sure that the appropriate separation of business and power has been established ... Those who disagree with this policy, as the saying goes, either no longer exist, or have been sent far away.'

Putin had many reasons to fear or resent Khodorkovsky. For two and a half years he had defied the president's instruction to the oligarchs to keep out of politics. But even Khodorkovsky's purely business activities challenged the *siloviki*. They regarded the country's natural resources, particularly oil and gas, as vital strategic assets, not to be entrusted to private individuals – and certainly not to foreign states. Khodorkovsky had the opposite view: the private sector could run things more efficiently, and if foreign participation helped, so much the better.

In April 2003 Yukos (now Russia's largest oil producer) agreed to merge with Roman Abramovich's Sibneft to form what would be the world's fourth biggest oil company, worth $35 billion. (It was this deal that allowed Abramovich to buy Chelsea football club.) Khodorkovsky then took a further step towards disaster – by starting talks with both ChevronTexaco and ExxonMobil about selling one of them a major stake in the Russian company. The prime minister Kasyanov gave his approval for the deal. But the *siloviki* were incensed.

Through the summer of 2003 events moved fast. In June Yukos's security chief, Alexei Pichugin, was arrested and accused of murder. The following month Khodorkovsky's partner, Platon Lebedev, chairman of Group Menatep, the holding company that controlled Yukos, was also arrested. Prime Minister Kasyanov immediately condemned it and pointed out that arresting entrepreneurs on suspicion of economic crimes was bound to undermine the country's image and deter investors.

Leonid Nevzlin expected the worst. 'Life became intolerable. They didn't even bother to disguise the cars they watched us from. Every night I went to sleep with a bag packed so that if they came for me at five in the morning I'd have what I needed for prison.' He left Russia for Israel. But Khodorkovsky ignored the warnings to the last.

In October armed police raided Khodorkovsky's orphanage near Moscow and took away its computers. And a few days later the president of ExxonMobil, Lee Raymond, came to Moscow for an economic conference and talks with the president. He appears to have given Putin the – probably wrong – impression that Khodorkovsky planned to sell the American company not just 25 per cent but a controlling 51 per cent of Yukos-Sibneft. Khodorkovsky's deputy, Alexander Temerko, concedes, 'a company like Exxon cannot be a minority shareholder. Of course it says, we'll buy 25 per cent, but we need an option for a controlling stake.'

Putin was by now, it seems, incandescent with rage. BP's John Browne recalled later: 'Shortly before Khodorkovsky's arrest, in a private conversation, Putin made a passing but steely remark to me: "I have eaten more dirt than I need to from that man."'

Putin called in the prosecutor general, Vladimir Ustinov, to arrange Khodorkovsky's arrest. It came on 25 October. The oil tycoon had flown to Siberia, quixotically ignoring a fax that had arrived two days earlier, bearing Ustinov's signature, summoning him to report to the prosecutor's office in connection with 'irregularities in the tax regime of the Yukos oil company'. As his plane refuelled in Novosibirsk, armed FSB troops stormed it and led Khodorkovsky away in handcuffs. His defiance of the *siloviki* was about to cost him his freedom and his fortune.

The reaction

The headlines said it all: 'Capitalism with Stalin's face' (*Nezavisimaya gazeta*), 'A coup in Russia' (*Kommersant*). The *New York*

Times wrote: 'Russia lurched toward a political and economic crisis as the country's stocks, bonds and currency plummeted after the weekend arrest of Russia's richest man.'

Khodorkovsky's colleagues in the Union of Industrialists and Entrepreneurs issued a statement condemning the arrest: 'Today Russian business does not trust the law-enforcement system and its leaders. Thousands of small and medium enterprises suffer daily from their arbitrary rule. The authorities' crude mistakes have thrown the country backwards by several years and undermined confidence in their statements about the impermissibility of reversing the results of privatisation.'

Trading on the tumbling Moscow currency exchange was suspended. Putin's chief of staff, Alexander Voloshin, resigned. His successor, Dmitry Medvedev, publicly questioned the wisdom of the arrest, saying, 'This is a dangerous thing, as the consequences of measures not fully thought out will have an immediate effect on the economy ... and cause indignation in politics.' [16] Amid the turmoil, Putin rejected calls from other oligarchs for a meeting, and demanded an end to what he called the 'hysteria and speculation', adding (as if he were a mere bystander) that for the courts to arrest a man they must have had reasons to do so. 'There will be no meetings, no bargaining about the work of the law enforcement agencies.' Government ministers, he said, should not get dragged into discussing the matter.

The prime minister, Kasyanov, tells a curious story about a certain appointment that the Kremlin wanted him to make around this time. Viktor Ivanov, the former FSB general whom Putin had taken on as his chief head-hunter, called Kasyanov several times, urging him to appoint a certain young man as a deputy tax minister. Kasyanov demurred, not understanding the urgency of the appointment and unsure why the man, who had worked most of his career in St Petersburg furniture stores, was qualified for the job. He was not aware at the time that Anatoly Serdyukov was the son-in-law of Viktor Zubkov, the first deputy finance minister (and former St Petersburg colleague of Putin). When Kasyanov was sacked in February 2004, Serdyukov was immediately moved to the tax ministry – where he was put in charge of the case against Khodorkovsky, and within two weeks promoted to be head of the Federal Tax Service. Putin now had a man he could trust to assemble the most damaging evidence against his enemy.

The two faces of Putin

The events described in this chapter – the stifling of the media, the establishment of the 'vertical of power' and appointment of Putin's cronies to key jobs, the war in Chechnya, the callous response to the sinking of the *Kursk*, the taming of the oligarchs and the persecution of Khodorkovsky – all had a salutary effect on those in the West who had decided from the outset to do business with Putin. The man who was stretching his hand out to Western leaders, and implementing welcome economic reforms at home, was at the same time acting true to type, confirming his own phrase: there is no such thing as an ex-Chekist. His actions strengthened the hand of those in the West – particularly in the Bush administration – who from the start had advocated a tough stand against him.

In Britain, the *Observer* newspaper expressed a common view, saying it was now 'crunch-time' for Putin, and he must decide who he wanted to be. 'Is he the westward leaning ally of President Bush and Tony Blair, or someone whose real affection is for the bad old days of the Soviet Union? ... If Mr Putin opts for the authoritarian path, then it is time for London and Washington to reassess relations.' [17]

But just as the West was disillusioned with Putin, so Putin was also becoming disillusioned with the West he'd been so keen to court.

5

NEW EUROPE,
OLD EUROPE

A foot in NATO's door

It was Tony Blair, perhaps, who best understood the ache that gnawed at Vladimir Putin's KGB soul. The two men continued to meet regularly after the ground-breaking first visit to St Petersburg before Putin was elected. As well as formal talks they had jeans-and-shirt-sleeves get-togethers at Chequers, the prime minister's country residence, and tête-à-têtes over vodka and pickled gherkins at Pivnushka, a Moscow beer hall. Blair tried to soothe the Russian's anxieties about American plans for a missile defence shield. And behind Putin's bluster about how Moscow would have to take counter-measures he sensed a deeper problem.

One of Blair's aides, in an off-the-record interview, put it in terms that were so condescending they would have incensed Putin had he known this was what Blair thought: 'The main thing Tony took away from those meetings was the need to treat them seriously. Their problem was that they felt excluded from the top table and weren't being treated as a superpower. You had to show them respect. Even if they weren't really a superpower any more, *you had to pretend they were*. This was the point Tony made to the Americans.'

To put flesh on the idea, Blair came up with a proposal to create a new NATO–Russia Council (NRC), to bind the Russians more closely to the Western alliance – stopping well short of membership, but at least giving them a sense of belonging to the club. The NRC would represent a significant upgrading of relations from the consultative 'Permanent Joint Council' that had existed since 1997 and given Russia zero influence over the alliance's actions. Russia would now have a permanent ambassador at NATO headquarters, who would participate in sessions of the NRC on a par with each of the 19 other ambassadors – not 'Russia plus NATO', in other words, but 'Russia plus the US, France, Britain, Germany', and so on.

Blair's initiative went down well in Western capitals, where it was seen as a realistic alternative to the more fanciful vision of actual NATO membership, which some, including the German chancellor, had discussed. The idea soon got hijacked by the Italian prime minister, Silvio Berlusconi, who had also been striking up a bond with Putin. The two men were rather similar in temperament – equally 'blokeish', equally vain and with a similar taste in earthy or tasteless jokes. Putin also saw in Berlusconi's media empire some justification for his own control of Russian television.

One Friday evening early in 2002, NATO's secretary general, George Robertson, had just got off a plane at Edinburgh airport, heading for a weekend at home in Scotland, when his mobile phone rang. It was Berlusconi. He had decided that Italy would host a special NATO summit to launch the NRC.

'Hang on, Silvio,' said Robertson. 'We haven't quite got to that point yet.'

'No, no,' replied Berlusconi. 'I have spoken to Vladimir. It's all agreed. We will host the summit – and we will pay for it.'

Robertson was not going to be pushed around. 'You can't

just do a deal with Putin. There are 19 countries in NATO and I have to consult all of them. But we'll take your offer into account.'[1]

The proposal to pay for the summit, however, was a clincher. It didn't take long to persuade the others to let Berlusconi stage the show. And a show it was, with no expense spared. Berlusconi took a run-down air base at Pratica di Mare outside Rome and transformed it into the Roman equivalent of a Potemkin village – a palatial canvas conference centre modelled on the Colosseum, complete with ancient marble statues.

The historic agreement was duly signed on 28 May. It would allow Russian generals for the first time to have permanent offices in NATO's headquarters. And while Russia would not be able to veto alliance decisions, it would at least take part in joint discussions about issues such as peacekeeping, regional security, search-and-rescue operations and the fight against international terrorism and nuclear proliferation. In practice, according to Blair's chief of staff, Jonathan Powell, the original idea – to give Russia a 'real voice' – got watered down in the NATO bureaucracy.[2] Russia would later complain that NATO representatives would usually meet ahead of any Council session, coordinate their position and then effectively act as a bloc in their talks with Russia.

At the press conference after the signing ceremony, Putin said something that startled some of those present with its frankness. 'The problem for our country,' he said, 'was that for a very long period of time it was Russia on one side, and on the other practically the whole of the rest of the world. And we gained nothing good from this confrontation with the rest of the world. The overwhelming majority of our citizens understand this only too well. Russia is returning to the family of civilised nations. And she needs nothing more than for her voice to be heard, and for her national interests to be taken into account.'

His words were so powerful that Robertson remembered

them and could almost recite them from memory nine years later. 'That seemed to me to be quite a dramatic appraisal, a confession, by a Russian leader about the years of failure and what he aimed to do in the future.'

Putin's statement also confirmed exactly what Blair had understood about his craving for respect. But there were many in the West who looked at what was going on inside Russia and refused to believe that she really was a repentant daughter 'returning to the family of civilised nations'.

Just what do we think of Russia?

Within the Bush administration there were two diametrically opposed views of what to do about Russia – plus many shades of opinion in between. Those, like national security adviser Condoleezza Rice, who spoke Russian and had a background in Soviet studies, were not necessarily the best disposed towards the new Russia. Several of Putin's advisers have described her to me as 'a Soviet expert, not a Russia expert'. They felt that she still viewed Russia through red-tinted spectacles. She took a tough line on Russia's aggression in Chechnya, and an even tougher line on any Russian interference in neighbouring countries, which she took to be a sign of post-Soviet recidivism – but nonetheless she did try to understand the underlying causes of Russian policies.

Some of the Russia experts in the administration argued that there was not enough consideration of where Russia was coming from, that you couldn't expect it to become 'Western-ised' overnight (or perhaps at all), and that the way to win Putin round was to understand his fears (the Blair view) and accept that Russia had a legitimate right to expect its voice to be heard and its interests to be taken into account. This view was represented most strongly at the highest level by Secretary of State Colin Powell. According to one insider, speaking off the record, President Bush himself, having developed a real friendship with Putin, tilted in that direction, but policy tended to be shaped more by those who simply did not trust Russia, the so-called 'neo-cons' such as Vice-President Dick Cheney, Defence Secretary Donald Rumsfeld, Under-Secretary of State John Bolton, Dan Fried, who handled European and Eurasian affairs at the National Security Council, and Nick Burns, US ambassador to NATO (and later under-secretary of state). Somewhere between the two camps were national security adviser Condoleezza Rice and her deputy Stephen Hadley.

The insider went on: 'Some of the policy makers understood a lot, but they understood it from a particular perspective. The real drivers behind Russia policy were people who had been working on European security issues all the way through the 1990s, and the goal was to continue the unfinished business of the 1990s – a Europe free, undivided and peaceful and all the rest of it. And there was a view that if you took in the Russia perspective you were somehow affirming its right to assert certain interests or privileges.'

So Bush's Russia policy was largely forged by people who were above all concerned with the security of Central and Eastern Europe, who believed the West had 'won' the Cold War, and were determined to cement the former Soviet satellites into the free West, including NATO and the European Union – even at the risk of alienating Russia in the process. Poland, the Czech Republic and Hungary had already joined NATO in 1999, and now the alliance was about to embark on a second wave of enlargement, to include Slovakia, Slovenia, Bulgaria and Romania, plus – most controversially as far as Russia was concerned – the Baltic states of Estonia, Latvia and Lithuania, which had once been part of the USSR and stood right on Russia's present borders.

Dan Fried said in an interview: 'It was not sustainable to argue that the interests and freedoms of other countries, which suffered under Soviet occupation, should be held hostage to a Russian sense of deprivation of empire. I mean, to some degree the Soviets had achieved a sphere of influence in Europe thanks to Mr Molotov and Mr Ribbentrop, or if you prefer, Hitler and Stalin.'[3]

Over breakfast in a London hotel I put it to Nick Burns that Russia might have legitimate concerns in seeing NATO expand right up to its doorstep, and America installing new weaponry there. It was, after all, their 'backyard'. His answer was quite uncompromising: 'Tough! They lost that right. This was in the American national interest.'[4] It was an answer that seemed to me to preclude accommodating even a reformed, 'democratic' Russia: it had 'lost the right' to influence affairs in its backyard, apparently by having inherited the sins of the Soviet Union, whereas the USA did have the right to influence affairs there because it was 'in the American national interest'.

He went on: 'When it came to admitting the Baltic countries into NATO, there were really furious arguments about it – both with the Europeans and within Washington. Even George Tenet [the CIA director], for example, was against it. But many of us had essentially lost hope that we could trust the Russians or integrate them into the West. By 2002, there was a growing suspicion that Putin wasn't the person they thought he was, that he couldn't make Russia a reliable ally. We concluded that we wanted a good relationship with Russia, but the most important target in the region, post-Cold War, was the freedom and liberation of Eastern and Central Europe. There was lots of opposition in the US, and we had to fight hard, but we thought we had to be careful about the Russians. We thought it was more important to lock in the one real gain of the fall of the USSR. George W. Bush was a strong believer in that argument.'

The neo-cons believed the policy of putting faith in Russia in the 1990s had failed. 'I knew Russia would try to become dominant in Europe again, and we had to protect the Eastern and Central Europeans,' said Burns. 'Putin is all about bringing power back to Russia. This was becoming clear by late 2002.'[5]

That phrase was revealing: making Russia powerful again was precisely what Putin wanted – and precisely what many in Washington could not stomach.

The administration's 'Russophiles' found their views echoed in Western Europe, but not in Washington. One of them says: 'There seemed to be a viewpoint that by understanding and laying out the Russian point of view you were endorsing it and legitimising it. This was not the view you find in Europe. This is why we were at odds with the Germans and even the UK because most of the European interlocutors were trying to factor in what Russia felt about things, because they didn't want an open confrontation.'

There were many reasons why France and Germany felt closer to the Russians than the Americans. It was not that they underestimated the former Warsaw Pact countries' longing to join the West's structures and to protect themselves from the country that had oppressed them for 50 years. Germany, in particular, was still revelling in the joy of reunification after the collapse of the Berlin Wall. Nor was it just a matter of pragmatism and trade, although the latter was important for Germany. Rather, there was an ill-defined sense, especially in European intellectual circles, that Russia 'belonged' to Europe, that they shared a history and culture, and the time was right – whatever the shortcomings of Russian democracy – to welcome them 'home'. Indeed, the argument went, welcoming them home would be precisely the best way to improve democracy there.

President Jacques Chirac of France epitomised this view. He had a strong personal interest in Russia. His parents had had a Russian émigré in their home in the 1930s, and Chirac himself had learned Russian and even translated Pushkin's novel in verse, *Yevgeny Onegin*. According to his diplomatic adviser, Maurice Gourdault-Montagne, Chirac felt there was something 'eternal' about Russia, that it was neither fully European nor fully oriental. He had got on well with Yeltsin, who gave him the sauna and caviar treatment, and although he was cool towards Putin at first, he was willing to put his reservations aside, even regarding Chechnya.

'Chirac said everything possible to help Putin and not to criticise him, and to help him appear on the world stage as a responsible leader having to deal with enormous stakes – how to catch up from Soviet times and become a modern country,' says Gourdault-Montagne. 'Chirac thought there was no evidence for Russia going back to Soviet times. They had jumped into a new world, but it was a long task, and they had to be supported. And it was in the interest of the West to help the Russians as much as possible because we have common interests. Chirac thought the stability of the continent was on the axis of Paris, Berlin and Moscow – hence all these trilateral meetings we had until 2007. It was fascinating to see how the three got on together.'[6]

German chancellor Gerhard Schröder, the third in the trio, was like most of his compatriots eternally grateful to Russia for withdrawing its troops without fuss from Eastern Germany. As a gesture of goodwill he later wrote off €6 billion of debt that Moscow owed the former German Democratic Republic.

The relationship, it is true, did not get off to a very good start. During the German election of 1998 Schröder had promised to stop pouring vast amounts of cash into Russia, as his predecessor Helmut Kohl had done. He wanted a pragmatic relationship based on business interests and a certain diplomatic reserve – none of the bear-hugging that Kohl and Yeltsin had indulged in. His foreign minister, Joschka Fischer, almost caused a diplomatic incident during his first meeting with Putin in January 2000 by denouncing his Chechen campaign and demanding an immediate ceasefire. Schröder himself did not shy away from visiting the three Baltic republics (something Kohl had refused to do for fear of offending the Russians) just a week before President Putin's first visit to Berlin in June 2000.

But the visit itself changed things dramatically. The two men talked for five hours, without an interpreter, thanks to Putin's command of German. Despite Tony Blair's attempts to 'get in there first', it was clear that Putin regarded Germany as Russia's paramount European ally. Schröder himself understood that close collaboration with Russia was the best means to encourage democratisation: 'Russia has always been successful,' he wrote, 'when it has opened itself up to Europe, engaged in a lively exchange and linked itself with the economic and intellectual development in the rest of Europe.'[7] The two men initiated something unique among the European nations: the St Petersburg Dialogue, an annual Russian–German event which combined intellectual discussion with intergovernmental talks and intensive business-to-business deal-making. Soon Schröder would be drawn into Putin's sauna-and-vodka circuit. They became close friends, often visiting each other with their families. Putin would even fly out to the chancellor's home town of Hanover just to celebrate Schröder's 60th birthday with him. Putin enabled Schröder to adopt two children from St Petersburg. After leaving office Schröder became chairman of Nord Stream, a Gazprom affiliate that would bring natural gas straight from Russia to Germany (which he had supported as chancellor), and dropped all criticism of Putin's policies. (Chirac, by contrast, turned down Putin's offer of a highly paid job with Gazprom.)

In an interview, Schröder looked back at his relationship with Putin and described him as a 'man you can trust'. 'He was open, and in contrast to his image he has a lot of humour. He is very family-oriented, and he doesn't let down his friends. He's someone I would be glad to have a beer or glass of wine with even if I didn't have to deal with him politically.'[8] Those were clearly the words of a man who had no intention of disparaging a colleague who was still in office and with whom he maintained close business and personal ties. But that does not make them irrelevant. On the contrary, the close relationship between Putin and Schröder – and between Putin and Chirac – was a major factor in the early 2000s as Russia tried to position itself in the world.

With the UK balanced somewhere between the 'European' view and the American, compromises had to be thrashed out – among them NATO's two major decisions of 2002. In May the NATO–Russia Council was set up, bringing Russia *closer* to the club. But six months later, at a historic summit in Prague, NATO invited seven former Soviet satellites to become *members* of the club. It wasn't quite what Putin had in mind when demanding to be treated as an equal.

NATO's sun shines on eastern Europe

The lights go down in the seventeenth-century Spanish Hall of Prague castle. On a stage two dancers perform a hilarious piece by a Czech-born choreographer, Jiří Kylián, to music by Mozart. The dancers are dressed (somewhat scantily) in period costume and wigs. In one part of the performance they leap about like fleas, performing crazy mating rites on a huge four-poster bed. But the audience is not composed of President Václav Havel's bohemian buddies from a Prague theatre: they are the heads of state and 700 guests from NATO's present and future member states – not all of them expecting such a raunchy curtain-raiser to the alliance's enlargement process.

The Prague summit on 21 November 2002 was Havel's swansong as president of the Czech Republic. The playwright-turned-politician wanted it to be remembered both for its artistic panache and its historic significance. He had spent most of his life as a dissident, stubbornly resisting communist rule and protesting at the Soviet occupation of his country. His own country was already a member of NATO; now he wanted to celebrate the freedom of seven more nations.

It was hard for the Russians to understand that this really was about celebrating freedom (from communism), not threatening Russia. The foreign ministry spokesman, Alexander Yakovenko, spoke darkly about 'the appearance of NATO's military potential at Russia's borders, just a few dozen kilometres from St Petersburg'.

The foreign minister himself, Igor Ivanov, put a positive gloss on the event: 'Moscow no longer considers NATO's eastward expansion as a threat, since the alliance has undergone a radical transformation since the end of the Cold War and now concentrates on the fight against global terrorism.' But the Russians did not really understand why enlargement was necessary. It was not just that they believed that Gorbachev had been promised it would not happen. They also could not understand why, if Russia was accepted as a partner, anyone should feel they needed protection from them – and they understood perfectly well that despite all the protestations to the contrary, NATO *would* defend its new members against Russia if necessary. After the handshake of the NATO–Russia Council, Prague came as a slap in the face.

What the Russians failed to do was make any connection between their policies and behaviour *at home* and the way they were perceived *abroad*. This was a problem I had to grapple with a few years later when I worked as a media adviser for the Kremlin: my clients were unable to grasp that the key to improving their 'image' abroad was not better PR but better behaviour. (I will look at this in detail in Chapter 9.) My impression from working closely with them is that they genuinely do not comprehend why many East Europeans – and particularly the Balts – remain deeply uneasy about their big neighbour.

Naturally no one at the Prague summit spoke openly of their fear of Russia. But you did not have to dig very deep into history to understand its roots. Almost all of the East

European leaders attending Václav Havel's show had personally, like him, lived through the horrors of Soviet occupation and life in a totalitarian regime. There were many open sores. The Poles felt the Russian government had not done enough to acknowledge (far less apologise for) the murder by Stalin's secret police of thousands of Polish officers and intellectuals at Katyn in 1940. The Estonians, Latvians and Lithuanians had not just been occupied by the Soviet army but incorporated into the Soviet Union, where they had had to fight for their survival as nations. Thousands of their people had been sent to the Gulag. Their tiny republics had been swamped with Russian citizens, who brought with them their language and culture, and a Moscow-based Communist Party bureaucracy that turned them into second-class citizens. Native Latvians comprised less than half the population of their own capital city, Riga. There was widespread resentment of the Russian presence, and the three Baltic nations were the first to rise up against Soviet rule when Gorbachev's reforms opened the lid a little in the 1980s.

But their independence, restored in 1991, did not put an end to all the problems. Russia came to terms politically with the situation, but more than a million Russians lived in Estonia, Latvia and Lithuania, and the Kremlin felt it had a right and duty to protect them. The new independent governments did themselves no favours by not always treating their Russian minorities with much consideration. In their hearts, most Balts felt the Russians should never have been there in the first place: it was they who had colonised the Baltic and subjugated its people, so they had only themselves to blame. Language and citizenship laws which rendered most Russians stateless in Latvia and Estonia were criticised by the Organisation for Security and Cooperation in Europe, and the European Union demanded changes as a condition for the two countries' accession. Over the years since independence, Russia had kept up a litany of complaints about civil rights in Latvia and Estonia (Lithuania's Russian population was much smaller and had few complaints). At times the rhetoric was very hostile, so it should have come as no surprise to the Russians that Baltic nations were welcomed with open arms into NATO.

By common consent, it was Vaira Vīķe-Freiberga, the Latvian president, who stole the show at the Prague summit with a powerful, eloquent speech, delivered without notes. She herself had not personally endured the years of Soviet rule, as she had escaped with her parents at the age of seven, just as the Red Army 'liberated' her country and imposed communism there. But her words summed up what the event was all about:

> Latvia lost its independence for a very long time, and it knows the meaning both of liberty and the loss of it. Latvia knows the meaning of security and the loss of it. And this is why being invited in an alliance that will ensure our security is a momentous moment that will be writ large in the history of our nation.
>
> We in Latvia would like to build our future on the rock of political certainty, not on the shifting sands of indecision. We do not want to be in some sort of grey zone of political uncertainty, we would like to enjoy the full sunshine of the liberties and the rights that NATO has been defending so long. We do not want to be left out in the outer darkness, and we would not wish this to happen to any other nation who has expressed the desire to join those nations that hold the same values, that follow the same ideals, and that are ready for the same efforts and the same strivings. Our people have been tested in the fires of history, they have been tempered in the furnaces of suffering and injustice. They know the meaning and the value of liberty. They know that it is worth every effort to support it, to maintain it, to stand for it and to fight for it.

Her audience – all male heads of state – almost stopped

breathing as she spoke. Alexander Kwaśniewski, the president of Poland, recalled later in an interview: 'I had tears in my eyes, to tell you the truth. It was one of those touching moments that showed that the Second World War was really over. We were starting a new era. This feeling ... I sensed it through my skin, a shiver through my body. The Second World War was finally over in Prague, in the palace that was previously used for communist meetings, where Václav Havel, now president, was host.'[9]

Everyone present felt the same. Except, perhaps, the Russian delegation, which had turned up for a brief, *pro forma* session of the NATO–Russia Council the next morning. The foreign minister, Igor Ivanov, recalled how he tried to explain to his Western partners that by ensuring their own 'security' the new NATO members were making Russia feel less secure: 'What was the real interest of those states in joining NATO? Yes, there was a political interest, but where was the threat coming from? One should first formulate real threats and then think in what way one can minimise or confront those threats.' And he added: 'In reality this does not add to anyone's security, neither to NATO countries nor to Russia. It adds an element of distrust. You want to think about your own security, but you don't want to think about the security of Russia.'[10]

The Americans had an answer to such complaints. This is Nick Burns:

You know, by expanding NATO, we were also calling Russia's bluff. The Russians had been saying, since the fall of the Soviet Union in December 1991, that they were different, that they also believed that Europe should be a place where people should be free to decide their own futures without fear of external domination. By inviting those seven countries into NATO in November 2002, we were saying: if you choose freedom in a future democracy, we can help to guarantee that and to sustain it. The fact that many Russians subsequently said that this was a treacherous move by NATO, that this was an indication of bad faith by NATO, I think tells you everything you need to know about those Russian leaders – that they didn't believe in the promise of democracy.

The Russians don't, in the modern world, in the post-Soviet world, in the post-1991 world, the Russians don't have a right to decide other people's futures. They don't have a right to impose their empire on other peoples in what they call their near abroad. And if we had the strength, as we did, to see that other peoples could be free and democratic, it was certainly the right thing to do to help them achieve that freedom.[11]

The ability of the Russians and Americans to talk at cross purposes was astounding. The Russians could not understand why their own behaviour at home meant that their neighbours continued to fear them. The Americans and their allies could not see that the Russians were upset by being cast in the role of potential aggressor. NATO's two summits in 2002 were hailed as ending the Cold War. In fact they helped to blow on its embers and start a new one. Seen from Moscow, the old Iron Curtain, running through the centre of Europe, was being replaced with a new one, much closer to home.

Putin's tongue lets him down again

In his state-of-the-nation speech in the spring, President Putin spoke as if he was already where he wanted to be – accepted as a respected voice on the world stage, and virtually claiming joint leadership of the war on terror. 'Russia is today one of the most reliable guarantors of international stability,' he said. It was 'precisely Russia's principled position' that had allowed a durable anti-terrorist coalition to be created. By joint efforts, he said, 'we' liquidated the most dangerous centre of international terrorism in Afghanistan.

He then went on to talk of Russia's 'numerous concrete

steps towards integration with Europe' and his goal of forming a 'single economic space' with the European Union.

Fine words, but as so often with Vladimir Putin, he then blew it. On a trip to Brussels for a summit meeting with EU leaders in November 2002, he lapsed into the kind of language that labelled him not as a world statesman but as a bar-room thug. At a press conference a French journalist asked him a direct but not particularly offensive question about Chechnya: why was Russia using anti-personnel mines and shells that were killing hundreds of people? And did the president not think that by trying to wipe out terrorism in this way he was wiping out the population of Chechnya?

Perhaps the poor *Le Monde* correspondent did not know that this was Putin's rawest nerve. By merely asking such a question, he was in Putin's eyes a terrorist sympathiser. 'If you're so keen to be an Islamic radical,' he railed at the journalist, 'and are happy to be circumcised, then I invite you to Moscow. We are a multi-faith country and have specialists for this. And I'll recommend they do the operation so thoroughly that you have nothing left to grow back.'

This happened just one week before the Prague summit – a handy reminder to NATO's old and new members that Putin, perhaps, was not quite ready to join the civilised world.

Allies against the Iraq war

Had President Putin deployed such crude language with regard to the Iraqi dictator Saddam Hussein he might have earned a wry smile and some kudos in Washington. But the growing confrontation with Iraq was to drive another wedge between Russia and America, and demonstrate that, when it came to pursuing its foreign policy goals, Washington scarcely pretended that Russia was a superpower that mattered: certainly they would court Putin to try to get his backing, but if they failed it would not hold them back. The Bush administration was no more interested in taking Russia's advice on Iraq than Clinton had been on Yugoslavia.

The Iraq crisis had been deepening throughout 2002, as suspicions grew that Saddam Hussein was continuing to produce and store weapons of mass destruction, in defiance of United Nations Security Council resolutions. A new resolution, number 1441, passed on 8 November 2002 after two months of tough negotiations, gave Iraq a 'final opportunity' to disarm or face 'serious consequences'. Weapons inspectors returned to Iraq in late November. Over the coming months they discovered no banned weapons, but Iraq failed to prove they had destroyed stockpiles that had previously been documented. The diplomatic confrontation that now developed centred on two things: whether the weapons inspectors should be given longer to complete their task (as the chief inspector, Hans Blix, wished), and what to do next – given that Resolution 1441 did not authorise the use of force. It pitted the US and the UK, broadly speaking, against Russia, France and Germany. Since Russia and France were permanent members of the Security Council with the power of veto, it was clear that the US and Britain would not be able to push through a second resolution, authorising military action. The Americans disdainfully referred to the Putin–Schröder–Chirac alliance as the 'axis of weasels' – an ironic reference to Bush's 'axis of evil' (Iraq, Iran and North Korea). US defence secretary Donald Rumsfeld inadvertently alienated France and Germany still further when he referred to them disparagingly as 'Old Europe', as opposed to the more obliging ex-communist countries to the east – 'New Europe' – which by and large supported the American position.

Putin was implacably opposed to American plans to invade Iraq, for many reasons. Russia had major business interests there; it worried that oil prices could slump if Iraqi oil flooded the market after the war; it bristled at what it saw as US unilateralism, overriding international decisions; it opposed the hidden agenda of regime change; it felt UN weapons inspectors should be allowed to continue their work searching for weapons of mass destruction; and it wanted to exhaust all of its own diplomatic avenues to persuade Saddam Hussein to back down or resign from office. Putin was fully signed up to the war on terror, but unlike Bush he did not regard Iraq as a state that sponsored terrorism.

The Russians were dismissive of the unconvincing presentation given by Secretary of State Colin Powell to the Security Council on 5 February 2003, purporting to prove the existence of weapons of mass destruction in Iraq. 'We were shown photos taken from space,' Sergei Ivanov recalls, 'huge trucks, juggernauts, carrying chemical weapons. They said that it was reliable evidence. We said, "Well, maybe you have this intelligence, but we don't." ' [12]

Putin was not, however, initially inclined to spoil his budding relationship with George W. Bush by making a public stand. At first he stuck in his public pronouncements to a position of guarded support for American efforts to ensure Saddam's disarmament. He told French journalists: 'The only task facing the international community there is to satisfy itself that Iraq has no weapons of mass destruction or to find them and force Iraq to destroy those weapons. In this connection we share the position of our American partners which is that we must do everything in order that Iraq would engage in a full-fledged cooperation with the UN inspectors.'

When he travelled to Berlin on 9 February for a short meeting with Chancellor Schröder, Putin warned that the 'unilateral use of force against Iraq would only bring suffering to millions of people and further escalate tensions in the region'. But he also cautioned against stoking up anti-American sentiments.

His line became much tougher when he moved on the next day to Paris for a state visit, during which the three leaders issued a joint declaration condemning the use of force.

The tripartite declaration was a French–German initiative. Schröder and Chirac had forged a very close relationship, which had culminated just the previous month in celebrations at Versailles to mark the 40th anniversary of the historic Elysée treaty of friendship between the two countries. According to Chirac's adviser, Maurice Gourdault-Montagne (known in diplomatic circles as 'MGM'), 'we were close allies of the Germans and knew they shared the same assessment of the Iraq situation, but we didn't know about the other permanent members of the Security Council. The British were with the Americans, but what would the Russians and Chinese do? So it was utterly important for us to know what the Russians would do.' He says that until they met, neither Putin nor Chirac felt absolutely sure that the other would be prepared to veto a second resolution, and neither wanted to end up doing it alone. Germany, as a non-permanent member of the Security Council, had a vote but no power of veto, so Schröder was relying on Chirac to cast the veto on his behalf – and to get Putin on board too.[13]

MGM and his German counterpart drafted a joint statement and agreed that Chirac would try to get Putin to sign up when he arrived in Paris from Berlin. The French laid on a lavish reception for him at Charles de Gaulle airport – military band, red carpet, guard of honour provided by the three services and the National Guard. Chirac even went to the steps of the plane to greet Putin and presented him with an imposing bouquet of flowers. MGM says it was all designed to flatter the Russian: 'He wanted to show respect to Putin, to please him, and for the Russians to feel that they are a great country, and that they are a full partner in the international community.' Flying into the city on an air force helicopter, Chirac showed Putin the text of the declaration, and he said yes right away, asking only for a few small changes. MGM and Putin's diplomatic adviser, Sergei Prikhodko, went off to make the changes and agree them with Berlin. The declaration said:

'There is still an alternative to war. The use of force can only be considered as a last resort. Russia, Germany and France are determined to ensure that everything possible is done to disarm Iraq peacefully.'

But in essence, says Gourdault-Montagne, it was a 'pact': 'Putin, until that moment, had some doubts about France, because at that time there was a lot of talk to the effect that the French are showing their muscles, but at the last moment they will change their minds and go with the US. Now Putin knew that Chirac would impose a veto, and we knew the Russians would be with us. We knew that we were together.'

And Washington knew that if it went to war against Iraq it would have to be without the authorisation of the United Nations. Condoleezza Rice admits: 'We didn't much like this spectacle of America's closest allies standing with the Russians on a security interest of the United States.' [14]

In the month before the war started, Putin undertook two rounds of secret diplomacy to try to avert it. On 22 February he sent one of Russia's most experienced politicians, Yevgeny Primakov, to Baghdad. Primakov for some reason often attracts the epithet 'wily', and perhaps he is: he had opposed Putin's rise in 1999 but later supported him; before that he had served as head of the foreign intelligence service, foreign minister and prime minister; most importantly, a Middle East expert, he had known Saddam Hussein for years, so he was ideal for this mission. At the time, when news of his trip leaked out, there was speculation that he might have been trying to persuade Saddam to destroy his Al Samoud 2 missiles. The foreign ministry, forced to say something, said his purpose was to 'explain Russia's position on Iraq and receive an assurance it would fulfil UN resolutions and cooperate "completely and unconditionally" with weapons inspectors'.

In fact, his mission was much more dramatic than that. Putin had charged him with only one task: to persuade Saddam to stand down and thereby save his country from invasion.

Saddam listened to Primakov, took notes, asked him to repeat the message in front of his deputy prime minister, Tariq Aziz, then stood up, pressed his hand on Primakov's shoulder and left.

Primakov flew back to Moscow and reported the bad news – first to Putin, then to a full meeting of the Security Council in the Kremlin. They had one last trick up their sleeves. It was agreed that Putin's chief of staff, Alexander Voloshin, should fly immediately to Washington to try one last time to talk the Americans out of their plan for war.

He arrived late at night and went to a restaurant with the Russian ambassador, Yuri Ushakov. They drank into the small hours, and then Voloshin suddenly got a call to meet the CIA director, George Tenet, at 8.15. 'I'd only just got to bed,' he recalled later, with a smile. From the CIA he was taken to the White House to meet Condoleezza Rice, and during their conversation President Bush 'dropped by' (the only way diplomatic protocol allowed the president to meet someone of Voloshin's rank). 'He made a ten-minute speech about the threat of international terrorism,' says Voloshin. 'He was very passionate, standing up rather than sitting. Then pleasantries. Twenty minutes in all. I told him we didn't agree, but I felt he was not interested in my answers. He had made up his mind already so he wasn't much worried about the arguments – only in whether we would support him.' An American official confirms that 'the president wasn't there to listen to what Voloshin had to say and reply'.

Voloshin was granted access to every top official – Vice-President Cheney, Secretary of State Powell, the Senate leader. But it was his meeting with commerce secretary Donald Evans that astonished him most. Evans asked if they could speak privately, and they went to his office. Evans said: 'You are close to Putin, I am close to President Bush, and he has asked me to put it to you – what do you want in exchange for supporting us?'

Voloshin understood that they were offering a bribe: Russia stood to lose billions of dollars' worth of contracts in Iraq, and Washington was offering to compensate. 'We don't want to bargain,' Voloshin said. 'This is a bad war which will harm everyone. And Iraq has nothing to do with terrorism.'

In a final, rather pathetic, move the Americans tried to prove to Voloshin that there was a connection between Saddam and Chechnya. An American official recalled in an interview: 'We thought this would be an issue that would catch the Russians' attention, but Voloshin came out at the end saying, "That was totally uninteresting, there is nothing new in this presentation."'

Voloshin confirms: 'They told me a long, touching story about a terrorist who fought in Chechnya and later turned up in Iraq. It was pretty primitive, but they tried it on.'

Even scratching Putin's rawest itch achieved nothing. The two sides were poles apart. Operation *Shock and Awe* began on 19 March.

Putin snubbed

For Putin, Iraq was not the be all and end all. There were still important prizes to aim for: the cancellation of America's missile defence plans, WTO membership, increased trade, and so on. He decided not to let his failure stand in the way of his friendship with Bush.

Another opportunity was coming to impress the world with his openness and 'Europeanness'. At the end of May, his home town of St Petersburg - built by Peter the Great as Russia's 'Window on the West' - would celebrate its 300th anniversary. No wall was left unpainted, no stucco ornament ungilded, as the city was refurbished for a long weekend of partying, to which every major leader was invited. Putin planned to bask in the glory of St Petersburg's Italianate avenues and palaces.

On the Friday he opened a Baltic youth festival, hosted a

summit of Asian leaders on board a river ship, and took the leaders of Germany, Britain, France, Canada and Austria on personal guided tours of the city. In the evening the Mariinsky Theatre had never seen so many world leaders at one time. Next day he had talks with more presidents, and a summit with the entire European Union leadership. The world's elite toured the Hermitage art gallery, and attended a water festival on the Neva river.

And then, finally, on the second evening, George W. Bush turned up for the last supper. He had decided to visit Poland first – New Europe, a country that had contributed to the Iraq war. Putin was insulted.

Maurice Gourdault-Montagne caught the Russian mood. 'I think it was a tremendous disappointment for the Russians. It was surprising that Condi [Rice], with whom I have a good relationship and who is supposed to know what is in the Russian brain, gave Bush this terrible advice to go to Warsaw prior to St Petersburg. I just couldn't understand it.'

MGM then heard Putin and Chirac in conversation, and registered that the love affair with America was over. Putin was saying to Chirac: 'My priorities were the following: first a relationship with America, second with China, third with Europe. Now it is the other way around – first Europe, then China, then America.'

May 2002 had witnessed the triumphant signing of the Moscow treaty on nuclear arms reduction and the creation in Rome of the NATO–Russia Council. One year later, the mood had changed. And things were about to get even worse.

6

PUTIN MARK II

Georgia looks West

On the evening of Saturday 22 November 2003 Russia's leaders retired after their regular Security Council meeting to Genatsvale, one of the best Georgian restaurants in central Moscow. The solid oak table was laden with appetisers – hot khachapuri cheese bread, pots of red and green lobio beans, aubergine and walnut rolls, chicken tsatsivi ... Smoke from the logs burning in the hearth curled under the wooden rafters, and vines were growing on the timber walls. Waiters hovered with Russian vodka and Georgian wine, serving Russia's power elite: President Putin, Prime Minister Kasyanov, chief of staff Medvedev, security council secretary Rushailo, foreign minister Igor Ivanov, defence minister Sergei Ivanov, and FSB chief Patrushev.

The choice of venue had been influenced by the leadership's discussions earlier in the day about events unfolding in the Georgian capital, Tbilisi. For three weeks President Eduard Shevardnadze – the former Soviet foreign minister – had been facing down growing protests in the streets following parliamentary elections that everyone believed were fraudulent. Shevardnadze himself was due to rule as president for a further two years, but there was widespread dissatisfaction at the corruption and misrule of his government. Opposition leaders were demanding his resignation. Putin was no big fan of Shevardnadze, holding him partly responsible for the collapse of the USSR, but he did not like the idea of unruly crowds trying to seize power in a country on Russia's border. He was aware, too, that the student protests, under the slogan 'Kmara' (Enough) were modelled on the movement that had brought down Serbia's president, Slobodan Milosevic, in 2000, and were supported by American democracy groups, including the Open Society Institute of the billionaire philanthropist George Soros, and the National Democratic Institute, an organisation dedicated to the strengthening of democracy around the world (the kind of democracy Putin feared).

Suddenly an aide asked Putin to take a call on a secure telephone. It was Shevardnadze. Earlier that Saturday events had finally spun out of his control. He had gone to the parliament, determined to convene it and thereby legitimise the election results, but the main opposition leader, Mikheil Saakashvili, told a huge rally in the main square: 'We have only one aim – to rid the country of this man (Shevardnadze).' Mayhem broke out as the opposition leaders swept into the debating chamber, each carrying a rose, and Shevardnadze was hustled out to safety by his bodyguards. The speaker of parliament, Nino Burjanadze, declared that she was assuming presidential powers. It was the start of what became known as the Rose Revolution – the first of the so-called 'coloured revolutions' that brought democracy to countries on Russia's borders, revolutions that Putin came to regard as a threat to Russia itself. Shevardnadze retreated to his residence and declared a state of emergency. And then he called Putin.

Back in the 1970s, when he was Georgia's Communist Party leader, Shevardnadze had notoriously affirmed his republic's subservient position to Russia in the USSR by saying: 'For us in Georgia the sun rises in the north.' Now, as he desperately tried to cling to power in the independent state of Georgia, he effectively confirmed that little had changed, by turning to Putin for help. To the group seated around the table in Genatsvale it was obvious which of them should be dispatched to Tbilisi. Igor Ivanov, the foreign minister, had a Georgian mother and even knew a smattering of the language. He also knew Shevardnadze from the 1980s, when he had worked as his adviser in the foreign ministry. Putin sent him straight to the airport, with a posse of security guards and clear instructions to do whatever he could to avoid bloodshed in the streets of Tbilisi and ensure things were done in accordance with the Georgian constitution (which effectively meant: don't let a mob overthrow the president).

'You know,' Ivanov said in an interview, 'we didn't always have very easy relations with Shevardnadze, but Putin was nonetheless quite clear – he was the legal, legitimately elected president, and we must help him.'[1]

Ivanov flew into Tbilisi after midnight and had a meeting scheduled with Shevardnadze in the morning. But before then he wanted to test the mood, so he took two bodyguards and set off to where the protesters were camped out in the city centre. He picked his way among the tents and campfires trying to gauge how explosive the atmosphere was. 'I don't really understand Georgian,' he told us, 'but you could get a sense of the place.'

Suddenly somebody recognised him, and a buzz spread through the square: 'Ivanov is here, Ivanov is here!' The word quickly reached the ears of Zurab Zhvania, a popular politician and former speaker of parliament, who, together with Saakashvili and Burjanadze, was one of the leaders of the Rose Revolution. By now the crowd was becoming restless, and Zhvania urged Ivanov to get up on to the podium and address them. Ivanov recalled: 'I asked him how to say in Georgian, "Long live friendship between Russia and Georgia." I repeated that a few times into the microphone, and it seemed to go down well! I got the feeling that the people felt Russia could help somehow in resolving this conflict.'

Nino Burjanadze, the speaker of parliament and since the previous afternoon self-proclaimed acting president, was in her office. 'Zhvania and Saakashvili and I had been working till about four in the morning,' she recalled later, 'and now I was dozing in my armchair, when my secretary came in and said: "Ivanov is addressing the crowd." I thought I was dreaming! But I went downstairs, and sure enough there he was, even saying something to them in Georgian!'[2]

Ivanov now ended up in the role of mediator, shuttling between the opposition and President Shevardnadze. In the small hours of the morning he held talks with Saakashvili, Zhvania and Burjanadze to find out exactly what their demands were. Retelling these events, Ivanov insisted that at no stage did anyone insist on Shevardnadze's resignation; rather it was a question of re-running the parliamentary election that the opposition knew had been stolen from them. Ivanov spent the rest of the night consulting Georgian friends and diplomats, and came to the conclusion that 'the pendulum was swinging in the direction of the opposition'.

That was the message he took to President Shevardnadze in the morning. 'I had known him since 1985, and felt I could say to him quite openly that I had met all these people, in the opposition and in his own entourage, and sensed that he had lost almost all support.' Ivanov felt that he failed to convince Shevardnadze that he was so isolated, but he did persuade him to meet the opposition leaders.

Ivanov finally brought Zhvania and Saakashvili to Shevardnadze's residence for talks in the afternoon of the 23rd. At this point he felt he had done all that was required of him. 'I sat down at the table. Shevardnadze and his assistant were on one side; Zhvania and Saakashvili were on the other. I said: "I think I have done what I came to do. President Putin asked me to help you find a political solution. That's up to you now – to hold talks and avoid bloodshed. So I will leave you now." '

Thereupon Ivanov left the residence and flew to the city of Batumi in western Georgia, where he was due to meet the local leader, Aslan Abashidze. The outcome he expected from the talks he had arranged in Tbilisi was an agreement to re-run the elections, with Shevardnadze staying on as president, at least for the moment. But when he got off the plane in Batumi, Abashidze greeted him with the words: 'What on earth have you done? Shevardnadze has resigned!'

Looking back, Ivanov now laughs wryly at how he inadvertently brought about the end of Shevardnadze's rule, without ever understanding how it happened. Of the triumvirate who led the Rose Revolution, he speaks most warmly of Zurab Zhvania, describing him as 'wise, calm, balanced, and intent on having good relations with Russia' – more or less the opposite of what he says about Mikheil Saakashvili, the man whose charisma made him the pre-eminent leader of the opposition. 'Misha', as he was universally known, was a big, ebullient bear of a man – Westernised in mentality (he had studied in Strasbourg and New York, and had a Dutch wife), but at the same time oozing Georgian charm and spontaneity. Aged only 36, he swept to victory in the early presidential election held on 4 January 2004. Taking 96 per cent of the vote, Saakashvili embodied the hopes not only of the thousands of demonstrators who had backed the Rose Revolution but of the vast majority of Georgians, who saw the ballot as an opportunity finally to turf out the corrupt Soviet-era regime and orientate their country towards the West and democracy.

I interviewed Saakashvili a year or so later, when his pro-Western policies were already raising hackles in Moscow, and reminded him of his predecessor's famous phrase about the 'sun rising in the north'. Was he not afraid of provoking the Russian bear, I asked? 'Don't worry,' he told me. 'I also know where the sun rises. We want the best relations with the West *and* with our great neighbour to the north.'[3]

In fact, Saakashvili's first moves as president were uncannily like Putin's at the start of his rule. He immediately pushed through constitutional amendments that increased his presidential powers, while drastically reducing the role of parliament. He replaced regional governors and began to impose state control over television stations.[4] In a crackdown on corruption he had former ministers and businessmen arrested, and (unlike in Russia) carried out a radical overhaul of the police which dramatically reduced bribe-taking. He and his prime minister, Zurab Zhvania, transformed the economy by, among other things, slashing taxes and attracting major foreign investments.

Like Russia, Georgia also faced the threat of separatism. After the country gained independence from the USSR in 1991, the provinces of Abkhazia and South Ossetia both broke away and after brief civil wars enjoyed *de facto* independence – with Russian support. A third 'autonomous republic', Ajaria, did not declare independence but was ruled like a personal fiefdom by its autocratic president, Aslan Abashidze. Regaining control over Georgia's lost provinces was as much of an obsession for Saakashvili as retaking Chechnya was for Putin. On the eve of his inauguration as president on 24 January 2004 Saakashvili solemnly swore on the grave of Georgia's twelfth-century King David the Builder that, 'Georgia will be united and strong, will restore its wholeness and become a united, strong state.'

It was that resolve, that determination to reintegrate Georgia's minority nationalities, that four years later would bring his country to war with Russia.

Saakashvili also flaunted his love affair with the West like a reckless divorcee, thumbing her nose at the bullying ex-husband. The US secretary of state, Colin Powell, was guest of honour at Saakashvili's inauguration ceremony. He recalls: 'We all stood up when the national anthem was played. And when it was over I was about to sit down again when another anthem started up – it was "Ode to Joy" and the European Union flag was being raised. I thought: oh boy, I bet Igor [Ivanov, the Russian foreign minister] isn't enjoying this part of the performance.'[5]

Igor certainly would not have enjoyed what followed. Saakashvili invited Powell to come with him into the City Hall, which was decorated with dozens of Georgian and American flags, side by side. 'Then we went into the chamber where the city legislature meets,' Powell remembers, 'and we sat behind a table in front of all these people ... and we had a town hall meeting with the whole population, televised throughout Georgia. Just President Saakashvili and the American secretary of state, while all the other guests and senior people from around the world, including those from the Russian Federation, were outside wondering what's going on.'

Saakashvili did have the prudence to head north, not west, though, for his first presidential visit abroad. And remarkably, his trip to Moscow on 10–11 February 2004 was a great success. Igor Ivanov was present when the two presidents met in the Kremlin, and recalls that – considering the hatred the men would later develop for one another – the mood was very positive: 'Saakashvili greeted Putin very emotionally, very joyfully, and said that he greatly respected him as a politician and had always dreamed of being like him. He said he would do everything in his power to develop good relations between our countries, and that the previous leadership of Georgia had made many mistakes which he would try to put right.'

Saakashvili's own foreign minister, Tedo Japaridze, confirmed that the Georgian president emerged from the meeting almost bewitched by Putin: 'He came out of it very much excited and thrilled with that encounter and with the man himself: "He's a real leader, a resolute and strong man who controls everything – Duma, the mass media and so forth." These were his first words when we were driving back to the airport.'[6]

Saakashvili himself described in an interview what happened when the presidents left their foreign ministers and retreated to a separate room for private talks. Having proposed that they take off their jackets and ties, Putin apparently launched into a tirade about the subject that worried him most – Georgia falling into the all too warm embrace of the United States. It was not just American involvement in supporting – or, as the Russians firmly believed, planning – the Rose Revolution that concerned Putin. The US had also had a small military presence in Georgia for two years. Ironically the American troops had been invited in by the previous president, Shevardnadze, to help him deal with a problem that was spoiling his relations with *Russia*. After Putin had launched the second Chechen war at the end of 1999, thousands of Chechens, including armed militants (and foreign Islamist fighters), had moved over the mountains from Chechnya into Georgia and settled there in the Pankisi Gorge. Russia claimed the gorge was being used as a terrorist base and threatened to bomb it. Alarmed at the prospect of Russia attacking Georgia, Washington offered instead to help the Georgians themselves clear terrorists from the Pankisi Gorge by training their armed forces. Launched in May 2002, the Georgia Train and Equip Programme involved only a couple of hundred American soldiers at first, but it gave the US its first foothold in the Caucasus. Attending Saakashvili's inauguration two years later, Colin Powell remarked upon the marching styles on show in the military parade: 'I was just fascinated to sit there and watch some Georgian troops march by, marching like Soviet troops, the way they had been trained, and then the next contingent go by marching like American soldiers – 120 steps per minute just the way we teach our soldiers. And I said, times they are a changing.'

So it was not surprising that Putin's toughest message for the new Georgian president was to cool it on the American front.

According to Saakashvili, Putin stressed on the one hand that Russia was a friend of America and developing relations with it, but on the other hand claimed that Eastern European countries had become 'slaves to America', doing whatever 'some second secretary' at the US embassy told them to do. 'Basically, it was all about America, a 20–25 minute tirade, until I finally politely stopped him and said, "Look, it's very good you're telling me about your relations with America, but I'm not here to talk about America." I said, "Do you really believe that what happened in Georgia is an American plot? Do you really believe that our government is paid by Americans, or George Soros or, you know, that we are directed by them?" And he said, "No, no. Not you for sure. But some people in your government might be in that position, to be closely working with the Americans." '[7]

(In fact, Putin was almost certainly aware that Saakashvili's senior adviser was an American, Daniel Kunin, who previously worked for the National Democratic Institute and was paid not by the Georgian government but by the American, through the US Agency for International Development. Kunin was the first port of call for Washington officials trying to contact – and influence – the Georgian leader.[8])

Saakashvili says he proposed they should start from a clean sheet – that as a small country Georgia would do whatever it could to accommodate Russia's interests, in exchange for some understanding of its own, much smaller interests. He says Putin seemed very receptive. 'Actually I liked him. I cannot blame George Bush for looking into his soul because my first impression was that I liked him. I thought, well, yeah, he comes from this KGB kind of background, he is very different from what I come from and what I believe in, but this seems to be a pragmatic guy. He likes his own country, and maybe he would act on behalf of his county in a very pragmatic way and we can find some understanding. And you know, he was basically also trying to show, by the end of our conversation, that he could go a long way to solving some issues.'

The good rapport led to regular telephone calls and genuine efforts on both sides to mend fences. But it was never going to be easy for Saakashvili to balance his desire for good relations with Moscow with his two major obsessions – restoring the territorial integrity of Georgia (ending the *de facto* independence of three provinces with close ties to Russia) and tethering his country to the West's great alliances, NATO and the European Union.

On 25 February 2004 Saakashvili made his first trip as president to the United States, and immediately raised the issue of Georgian membership of NATO. He announced a new five-year deal under which US army instructors would train thousands more Georgian troops.

The honeymoon with Moscow lasted until May 2004, when Putin did what he called his 'last favour' for Saakashvili. The new Georgian government was close to civil war with the province of Ajaria – under its maverick Soviet-era leader, Aslan Abashidze. Saakashvili did what his predecessor Shevardnadze had done: he called Putin for help. And once again, Putin dispatched Igor Ivanov – now no longer foreign minister but secretary of the National Security Council – to the scene. Ivanov flew first to the Ajarian capital, Batumi, planning to negotiate with Abashidze and then fly on to Tbilisi. But as they had dinner that evening of 5 May, Ivanov recalls, news came of a Georgian armoured column heading for Batumi. Despite his call to the Georgian prime minister, requesting him to stop the advance, a fierce fire-fight soon broke out, right on the outskirts of the city. 'It was so intensive we felt the smell of powder in the palace.' According to Ivanov, Abashidze told him he had sufficient military power of his own to confront the Georgian troops and force them out of the region, but Ivanov replied: 'I have a plane at the airport. If you are prepared to leave with me to Moscow, you are welcome to take this opportunity.' Abashidze seized the chance of political asylum in Russia, and fled, taking his son, who was the mayor of Batumi, with him.

Within hours Saakashvili's troops entered the city, and Ajaria was reclaimed as part of Georgia. The next day, Saakashvili himself made a triumphant appearance in Batumi and addressed a jubilant crowd in the city square: 'You are heroic people,' he told them. 'You have achieved your Georgia. We have shown the world we are a great people. Only we could have staged two bloodless revolutions in six months.' Surrounded by jubilant supporters chanting 'Misha! Misha!', he walked to the Black Sea beach – out of bounds to Georgia's leaders for many years – and splashed seawater on his face. And he uttered the promise, or threat, that the restoration of central control over Ajaria was only the start of his mission: 'We must start negotiations, serious and peaceful negotiations with Abkhazia and South Ossetia, about reuniting the country and settling problems which are not settled. We have proved in Ajaria that it is possible to act peacefully but resolutely. This means that Georgia will be strong and we will definitely get to Sukhumi [the capital of Abkhazia]. Exactly when? We shall see.'

Aware of Moscow's crucial role in defusing the crisis and getting rid of Abashidze, Saakashvili telephoned Putin to thank him. According to the Georgian, Putin gave a tart reply: 'OK, Mikheil Mikheilovich, we helped you on this one, but remember very well, there will be no more free gifts offered to you, on South Ossetia and Abkhazia.' Russia had much deeper interests in Georgia's two breakaway territories than in Ajaria. Abkhazia is a republic of some 200,000 people (the figure is disputed) – less than half its pre-1992 population, since almost all the Georgians fled in the civil war. Its Black Sea coastal towns – Sukhumi, Gagra, Pitsunda – used to be principal holiday resorts for Russians during the Soviet period. South Ossetia is much smaller – less than 100,000 in Soviet days (roughly two-thirds Ossetian, and one-third Georgian), and only some

70,000 following the civil war of the early 1990s. The majority Ossetians had close links to their kinsfolk living in North Ossetia (a republic inside the Russian Federation). Both the Abkhaz and the South Ossetians looked to Russia for protection against the Georgians, and received large subsidies and other support. Since most of them did not have, and did not want to have, Georgian citizenship, Putin introduced a policy of 'passportisation' – issuing residents of the two provinces with Russian passports, which then allowed the Kremlin to claim the right to protect its citizens. In both republics ethnic Russians held important jobs, and in South Ossetia former KGB officers were brought in to staff key government posts.

If Putin's words about 'no more favours' were meant as a warning – and they certainly were – Saakashvili paid little heed. Perhaps he even misunderstood a hint that Putin is said to have given during their first meeting in the Kremlin, to the effect that he was prepared to do a deal over South Ossetia that would see it restored to Georgian sovereignty. In May, Giorgi Khaindrava, a film director whom Saakashvili appointed as his conflict resolution minister, saw maps hanging in the deputy security minister's office showing plans for a military attack on South Ossetia. As he told the Caucasus expert Thomas de Waal, 'All the days were mapped out – they wanted to do an exact copy of what they had done in Ajaria.'[9] On 26 May 2004, Georgia's Independence Day, Saakashvili held a huge military parade in Tbilisi at which he addressed the Abkhaz and South Ossetians in their own languages, urging reintegration with Georgia. The South Ossetian president, Eduard Kokoity, a onetime wrestler and businessman with strong links to Russia, recalled in an interview that Saakashvili's call for reintegration sent an unambiguous message: 'I want to emphasise that he did it in front of a column of tanks moving down Rustaveli Avenue. It was not a call but a threat for Ossetians. And everyone in Ossetia regarded this call as a threat.'[10]

Five days later Saakashvili moved troops to the South

Ossetian border to launch a massive 'anti-smuggling' operation. Ostensibly, the aim was to close down a huge market at the village of Ergneti, through which vast quantities of goods passed illegally between Russia, South Ossetia and Georgia. The Georgian attack caused the worst fighting in the region since 1992. Perhaps the real aim was to trigger the collapse of the South Ossetian government, but it had the opposite effect. Kokoity's position was strengthened, and anti-Georgian attitudes hardened among ordinary South Ossetians, for whom the Ergneti market had provided their only source of income.

With the Russian ministry of foreign affairs issuing a warning that 'provocative steps' might lead to 'extremely negative consequences', Saakashvili headed to Washington for help. But there too, his actions were seen as impulsive and dangerous. The secretary of state, Colin Powell, recalled: 'I think the president over-reached too early. I had to make clear to him that, "You might think this is in your vital national interest – we're not so sure it is. But it isn't in our vital national interest. So don't get yourself into a situation that may overwhelm you and think we are going to race in to rescue you from any difficulties you get into. So be careful." '

Saakashvili took note, and in August Georgian troops were withdrawn.

Election night

Throughout history, Moscow has been afflicted by fires. The original wooden structures of the Kremlin – the fortress at the heart of the capital – burned down time after time. In the sixteenth century Tatar invaders torched the city. In 1812, as Napoleon's Grande Armée entered Moscow, a great conflagration destroyed almost everything, leading to the city being rebuilt virtually from scratch.

On the evening of Sunday 14 March 2004, the Manezh exhibition hall, the former tsarist riding school which stands right next to the Kremlin, caught fire in unexplained circumstances and blazed for hours into the dark night sky.[11] Vladimir Putin climbed to a vantage point inside the Kremlin's dark red walls and observed the scene. Television pictures showed him staring out at the inferno, then turning and walking away, with a look of apprehension in his eyes. Perhaps he saw it as some of kind of omen. It was election day. Polling stations had closed just a few hours earlier, and he had been chosen as Russia's president for a second four-year term, with 71 per cent of the vote. Napoleon had seen his prize burn down before his eyes. Would Putin's vision also be destroyed by foreigners, encroaching on Russia with their alien concepts of democracy?

I have no idea whether such thoughts really ran through the president's mind at that moment. But events a few months later in the south of Russia would show that Vladimir Putin, the strongman, was haunted by almost paranoid illusions of weakness and external danger. Another bloody terrorist attack, which ended with the deaths of hundreds of children in a school, apparently served as proof for Putin that his grip on the country was too feeble, and that Russia was an emasculated rump state surrounded by enemies. Cornered, he would lash out to prove his strength. Putin Mark II would be an angry phoenix, born in fire.

Beslan and the 'constitutional coup'

The tragedy began on 1 September, the day Russian children traditionally return to school after the summer holidays. In Beslan, a small town of 36,000 people, just north of the Caucasus mountains and less than an hour's drive west of Chechnya, children turned up at school No. 1 in cheerful mood and fresh uniforms. Just after 9 o'clock, as they held a ceremony with their parents in the schoolyard, a group of armed fighters screeched up to the school in an army truck, firing their guns into the air, and herded more than 1,100 people – children, parents and teachers – into the school building. It was a repeat of the Moscow theatre tragedy – except that the terrorists had learned lessons that made it even harder for the authorities to deal with the crisis. The hostage-takers had planned the attack meticulously and knew every inch of the school. A dozen hostages were shot within the first hours, and over the next three days the country watched horrific events unfold, as the gunmen laid trip-wires and explosives around the school and refused to allow food, water or medicine to be brought into the building. Once again, President Putin faced the most awful dilemma – how to free hostages and save lives without giving in to the terrorists' demands, which as usual included outright independence for Chechnya. Negotiations with a doctor who had helped during the theatre siege and with a local government leader got nowhere. Packed into the school gymnasium, in sweltering heat, the children were traumatised and parched. On the third day, special forces stormed the school following two unexplained explosions. The rebels fought back. Twenty-eight terrorists were killed, but so were 334 hostages, mostly children.

It was the bleakest day yet in Russia's failing battle against terrorism on its own soil. The ability of gunmen and suicide bombers to wreak havoc almost at will demonstrated the impotence of the authorities and the nonsense of Putin's claim to have 'won' the fight. The Beslan tragedy was the sixth major terrorist incident in 2004 alone.

In February 41 people were killed in a bomb attack on the Moscow underground.

In May the pro-Moscow president of Chechnya, Akhmat Kadyrov, was assassinated at a Victory Day parade in the capital, Grozny.

In June a group of terrorists from Chechnya attacked the capital of the neighbouring republic of Ingushetia. They killed 95 people and captured a large cache of weapons which were later used at Beslan.

In August 90 people died when two aircraft were simultaneously blown up in mid-air by suicide bombers.

And at the end of the same month, just the day before Beslan, a woman blew herself up in a Moscow metro station, killing herself and ten passers-by.

Vladimir Putin finally addressed the nation on television on the evening of Saturday, 4 September, a day after the violent end to the school siege and a few hours after travelling to the scene to meet some of the survivors. He looked deeply shaken, and spoke slowly and emotionally about the 'terrible tragedy on our soil'. Like a priest addressing a funeral service, he asked people 'to remember those who perished at the hands of terrorists in recent days', and dropped his head in sorrow. But then he quickly moved on from the immediate crisis to draw far-reaching and startling conclusions that in many ways defined the rest of his presidency.

'Russia has lived through many tragic events and terrible ordeals over the course of its history,' he said. 'Today, we live in a time that follows the collapse of a vast and great state, a state that, unfortunately, proved unable to survive in a rapidly changing world. But despite all the difficulties, we were able to preserve the core of what was once the vast Soviet Union, and we named this new country the Russian Federation.'

The style was odd – a history lesson delivered at the nation's moment of grief, evoking the greatness of the USSR. In his next words Putin betrayed his nostalgia for the iron fist of the communist police state, which had been replaced by laxity:

We are living through a time when internal conflicts and interethnic divisions that were once firmly suppressed by the ruling ideology have now flared up. We stopped paying the required attention to defence and security issues and we allowed corruption to undermine our judicial and law enforcement system. Furthermore, our country, formerly protected by the most powerful defence system along the length of its external frontiers overnight found itself defenceless both from the east and the west. It will take many years and billions of roubles to create new, modern and genuinely protected borders. But even so, we could have been more effective if we had acted professionally and at the right moment.

In an intimation of the crackdown that would soon follow, Putin went on: 'We showed ourselves to be weak. And the weak get beaten.'

Putin was putting a whole new spin on the terrorist attack. There was no mention of his own forces' brutality in Chechnya – the main factor that lay behind all the home-grown terrorism. In fact, he did not mention the word 'Chechnya' at all. Instead he was blaming the West! He couched his accusation in strange, ambiguous terms:

> Some would like to tear from us a 'juicy piece of pie'. Others help them. They help, reasoning that Russia still remains one of the world's major nuclear powers, and as such still represents a threat to them. And so they reason that this threat should be removed. Terrorism, of course, is just an instrument to achieve these aims.

The attack on Beslan, Putin seemed to be saying, was part of a Western conspiracy to dismember the Russian Federation. Foreign governments were using terrorists as an 'instrument' to achieve that end. He addressed his people now in apocalyptic terms, like a leader on the brink of war:

> As I have said many times already, we have found ourselves confronting crises, revolts and terrorist acts on more than one occasion. But what has happened now, this crime committed by terrorists, is unprecedented in its inhumanness and cruelty. This is not a challenge to the president, parliament or government. It is a challenge to all of Russia, to our entire people. Our country is under attack.

Putin swore that as president he would not be blackmailed or succumb to panic. 'What we are facing is direct intervention of international terror directed against Russia. This is a total, cruel and full-scale war.' He warned Russians they could no longer live in such a 'carefree' manner, and demanded tough action from the security services. He promised 'a series of measures aimed at strengthening our country's unity'.

Those measures were announced over the coming days, and they shocked those who believed Russia was already far too authoritarian. Putin's former prime minister Mikhail Kasyanov (who had been sacked half a year earlier) called it an 'anti-constitutional coup'.

First, in the name of fighting international terrorism, Putin abolished the direct election of regional governors. From now on, he himself would nominate them, and their appointment would be rubber-stamped by regional assemblies. (The implication, never properly explained, seemed to be that Beslan would not have happened if regional governors were not 'out of control'.) Second, it was made almost impossible for independent politicians or radical opposition parties to get into the State Duma. Until now, half of the 450-seat parliament had been elected from party lists, while the other half were individual politicians directly elected by voters in 225 constituencies. From now on, all would be chosen from party lists; the single-member constituencies were abolished. The threshold required for a party to enter parliament at all was raised from 5 to 7 per cent. The rules for setting up new political parties were also tightened.

Putin was ratcheting up his own control, and strangling the opposition. The 'vertical of power' created in 2000 was now made rigid. Putin's 'ideologist', Vladislav Surkov, was wheeled out to dignify the crackdown with a pseudo-academic term. He called it 'sovereign democracy', or sometimes 'managed democracy'. In fact, it was the end of democracy. In an interview with the newspaper *Komsomolskaya Pravda*, he gave an Alice in Wonderland version of the latest reform package. Everything was the opposite of how it seemed: the new election system would not weaken the opposition but 'bring it back from political oblivion'; the reforms would strengthen not Putin but the state; the appointed governors would have greater, not fewer rights. A further initiative announced by Putin – the creation of a new 'Public Chamber', an assembly of 126 appointed worthies who would discuss civic initiatives and draft laws – had caused some bewilderment, since it was assumed that this was what the elected State Duma was supposed to do. Surkov explained that the trouble with parliaments is that deputies are always thinking about re-election; in the West this is known as 'being held to account by the electorate', in Russia according to Surkov, it leads to populism. The experts in the Public Chamber would be less dependent on the political climate and thus be more objective.[12] (A measure of Surkov's grasp on reality was given a few years later, when he said on television that 'Putin is a person who was sent to Russia by fate and by the Lord at a difficult time for Russia. He was preordained by fate to preserve our peoples.' [13] Clearly such a God-given leader could interpret democracy any way he liked.)

And what were people to make of the president's talk of foreign powers trying to seize a 'juicy piece of pie'? According to the experienced analyst Dmitry Trenin, Putin's foreign policy was entering a new stage. Until 2003, he wrote, 'Russia had been mostly moving toward rapprochement with the West under the slogan of its "European choice" and with a quest to become allied with the US.' Henceforth, 'Moscow pursued a policy of nonalignment, with an accentuated independence from the West, but combined with reluctance to confront it.' [14]

It was the beginning of a new isolationist stance. In Putin's second term there would be no more sucking up. He believed Russia had dropped its guard and needed to defend itself against twin evils – terrorism (now defined as part of a foreign conspiracy) and Western-style democracy, which was infiltrating the former Soviet space, first through Georgia, and soon ... through Ukraine.

7

ENEMIES EVERYWHERE

The Orange Revolution

The scenes in Kiev in late 2004 caused apoplexy in the Kremlin: a sea of orange clothes and banners, a million protesters braving sub-zero temperatures, day and night, to bring the Ukrainian capital to a standstill. Bad enough that this was a repeat of the Tbilisi events a year earlier – protests against a rigged election, mass support for a pro-American, nationalist candidate who offered an alternative to corrupt, authoritarian, pro-Russian rule. But this was happening in Ukraine, the most important for Russia of all the former Soviet republics. With 47 million inhabitants, Ukraine was ten times the size of Georgia. One in six of the population was an ethnic Russian, and there were millions of mixed Russian-Ukrainian families. Putin (like many Russians) saw it as a mere extension of Russia itself. He reportedly told President George W. Bush in 2008: 'You don't understand, George, that Ukraine is not even a state. What is Ukraine? Part of its territory is Eastern Europe, but the greater part is a gift from us.' One part – the Crimean peninsula – really was a gift, transferred by decree from Russia to Ukraine by the former Soviet leader Nikita Khrushchev.

Crimea was strategically vital to Russia, as the Black Sea Fleet was based there – and indeed the whole country stood like a great boulder across many of the strategic links between Russia and Europe – the oil and gas pipelines, the electricity grid, the military highways – the last buffer between Russia and the ever-expanding NATO. And yet the man who would be president there, Viktor Yushchenko, with his American wife, was talking of *joining* NATO!

Putin would not make the mistake of sending his foreign minister to Ukraine to 'sort things out' and risk letting it slip away like Georgia. In Ukraine, Putin would do whatever it took to stop the rot. He put his new chief of staff, the future president, Dmitry Medvedev, in charge of working out a strategy.

The danger had been clear to Putin since the Ukrainian election campaign started back in July. The Western-oriented opposition was led by a charismatic duo: Yushchenko, who had already served as the country's central bank chairman and prime minister, and Yulia Tymoshenko, a fiery politician renowned for the trademark blond plait wound like a pie-crust around her head and for her controversial career in the gas business which had made her one of Ukraine's richest people. The two formed an electoral coalition, Force of the People, and struck a deal under which, if Yushchenko was elected president, he would nominate Tymoshenko to be his prime minister. Both wanted to assert Ukraine's independence from Russia and, in particular, its right to join the European Union and NATO if it wished.

The establishment candidate was the prime minister, Viktor Yanukovych, a man with an unprepossessing past – he had two criminal convictions as a youth for robbery and assault – that made even Vladimir Putin wary of him, though he was clearly preferable to Yushchenko. Several well-placed Russians have indicated to me that Putin did not think Yanukovych was the best candidate, but acquiesced because he had the full support of the incumbent president, Leonid Kuchma, who threw all the government's resources behind his campaign. State television gave Yanukovych wide and positive coverage, while disparaging Yushchenko as an extreme nationalist, damningly married to an American of Ukrainian extraction who may even have been a CIA agent, plotting her husband's seizure of power.

In an interview, Kuchma confirmed that he and Putin had discussed who the preferred candidate should be. 'It was not a secret. Didn't the West discuss who should be president of Ukraine? The whole Western community did that, but on the other side just Russia, just Putin. Putin knew Mr Yushchenko's statements and opinions. And he did not have a great desire that he come to power.'[1] Once Kuchma had chosen Yanukovych as his 'successor', Putin threw the Kremlin's support behind him. Ukraine now became a battleground for influence, with the United States and Russia both openly supporting opposing candidates.

Just as in Georgia the previous year, Western NGOs were heavily involved in the campaign, advising Yushchenko and the home-grown groups that supported him. The biggest youth group was called Pora ('It's Time'), which borrowed the electioneering and civil disobedience techniques of the Serbian group Otpor and the Georgian Kmara. The Russians for their part sent so-called 'political technologists', including the well-known Gleb Pavlovsky (a one-time Soviet dissident and now an adviser to Putin) and the political consultant Sergei Markov, to work as spin doctors with the Yanukovych team and act as a channel between them and the Kremlin.

The American ambassador to Kiev, John E. Herbst, recalled in an interview that Western embassies 'developed tools' to make sure the elections would be free and fair. 'I remember the Canadian ambassador took the lead on this to develop a working group of interested embassies keeping an eye on things relating to the election. I also then organised a regular meeting, first on a monthly basis but then it happened maybe every couple of weeks, with all interested international and Ukrainian NGOs, to find out what they were doing to encourage free and fair elections, and to brainstorm on how we might better coordinate to get the outcome we want. And the outcome was a free and fair election, not any particular winner.' As in Georgia, the USAID contributed millions of dollars to promote civil society, free media and democracy awareness. Herbst says all parties, including even the Communist Party, were free to avail themselves of these funds and programmes.[2]

At one point during the campaign Herbst reached out to the Russian spin doctors to try to gauge what they were up to. 'I invited Pavlovsky and Marat Gelman, who was his partner in this enterprise, to lunch. We had a pleasant lunch ... but a very restrained conversation. They really did not want to talk too much about what they were doing.' Herbst says he made no bones about what the Americans were doing in Ukraine: 'In a sense I had an advantage because everything we were doing was pretty much right out in the open. We wanted to encourage a free and fair election, and we said what we were doing publicly. I had no problem telling them that NGOs in Ukraine, and for that matter internationally, were trying to encourage this result too. They were more reticent to describe to me what they were up to, and I can understand why.'

What Herbst described as merely supporting free and fair elections, Pavlovsky saw differently: 'I could see consultants and a large number of NGO activists who were completely pro-American or pro-Atlantic.' Pavlovsky was also reticent when asked what he had been trying to achieve. He acted as a 'channel of communication', he said, but found it hard to influence Kuchma, who insisted on running his candidate's campaign on his own. 'We never understood why Kuchma selected him. There were other governors much more acceptable to the electorate. As I understood it, Kuchma was expecting a conflict, and Yanukovych seemed like a tough man who could handle it. It was his mistake. Yanukovych's rudeness, his coarseness, irritated voters. And of course Putin noticed that, and was unhappy about it.' By the end of the campaign, Pavlovsky says he was reduced to writing sad reports back to Moscow about how the campaign headquarters had 'lost command'.[3]

In an interview, Sergei Markov was more forthcoming about the advice Russian consultants gave to the Kuchma/ Yanukovych team – and made some startling claims about the role the Russians believed Western NGOs were playing. Markov openly acknowledged – indeed stressed – that he and his colleagues were commissioned to do this work (to influence the election of a sovereign state) *by the Russian presidential administration*. Part of their work, according to Markov, consisted in providing Kuchma and Yanukovych with daily expert analyses of the developing situation, to enable them to respond better. Secondly, he said, 'We saw that experts who were appearing in the mass media were by and large firmly under the influence of Western foundations. And basically these Western foundations forbade them to say anything good about Russia. If they did they were thrown out of the projects they were working on, lost their grants and ended up penniless. So we came and started organising seminars, conferences, joint media projects with them, to try to get around this "ban".'[4]

It should be said that this assessment is precisely the opposite of what the opposition themselves (and most Western observers) believed: that the media were totally controlled by the government, and served a consistent diet of pro-Russian views.

Markov gave this outlandish assessment of the opposition candidate. 'We were firmly of the opinion that Yushchenko was completely controlled by his wife, and she belonged to a circle of radical Ukrainian nationalists connected with the Nazi movement and with, not so much the American special services, rather with circles of various East European diasporas, especially the Poles, who hate Russia as only Polish nationalists can. I was certain that Yushchenko, as a weak person, would totally carry out the programmes of these radical nationalists, whose aim was to create the maximum conflict between Ukraine and Russia – even a small war. In order to cause a quarrel between these fraternal nations, the Russians and Ukrainians, blood had to be spilt. I am convinced that these people were determined that Ukrainians and Russians should start killing each other – and I mean *killing each other.*'

These are quite astonishing claims, but they are important, for it is highly likely that Markov's apocalyptic view was shared by his masters in the Kremlin.

At the same time, the Russians were fully aware that Yushchenko had a big chance of winning, and made strange undercover overtures to his team. Oleh Rybachuk was Yushchenko's campaign chief, and future chief of staff. He says he received a call out of the blue from an old student friend whom he had not seen for 24 years. 'When he called me I knew he was in the KGB. He suggested that I come to Moscow to meet people who were close to Vladimir Putin.'[5]

Over the next month and a half Yushchenko's adviser made weekly visits to Moscow, meeting 'in dimly lit restaurants and speaking in whispers'. The Russians wanted to know what Yushchenko would do if elected. Rybachuk told them: 'Our policies are simple. We want to be a democratic country, a European country. We want to be a NATO member for European security. When we come to power we won't be a problem because you'll know what to expect from us.' It was hardly the reassurance the Kremlin was hoping for.

On 5 September, just two months before election day, Yushchenko fell seriously ill after a dinner with the head of the Ukrainian security service. He took painkillers when he got home, but in the morning was feeling worse. Rybachuk recalls: 'It was around ten in the morning and he said, "Let's have this meeting fast because I feel really bad. Something's not right." ' The cause of the pain could not be found and after three days Yushchenko was flown to a private clinic in Vienna where he was diagnosed with dioxin poisoning. The poison caused stomach ulcers, problems with his spleen and considerable disfigurement to his face.

'I remember waking up in the clinic at 5.30 in the morning,' Yushchenko recalled, 'and half of my face was paralysed, and within three hours I could barely make a sound. I was losing my speech. Every morning I looked in the mirror and my face was getting bigger and bigger.' [6]

For two weeks, Yulia Tymoshenko stepped into the breach, addressing rallies and blaming Yushchenko's enemies for 'cynically poisoning him'. When he finally returned to the campaign trail he was more popular than ever, the scars on his once handsome face visible proof of his enemies' desperation. Thanks to Channel 5 – a television station owned by a wealthy businessman in Yushchenko's Our Ukraine party – his words were broadcast live to public squares across the country: 'The last two weeks, dear friends, have been the most tragic in my life.'

Moscow had to step up a gear now to promote its candidate, who was trailing in the opinion polls. On 9 October Putin invited Kuchma and Yanukovych to Moscow at short notice – to celebrate his recent birthday. The television coverage was designed to demonstrate how chummy they all were, in the hope that some of Putin's stardust would land on Yanukovych's dowdy shoulders.

'Thank you for responding to my invitation to come at such short notice,' Putin gushed. 'It's a good pretext.'

'It's a wonderful pretext,' the Ukrainians gushed back. With the cameras still on him, Kuchma took the chance to sound presidentially 'neutral' while warning his countrymen back home that, as Eduard Shevardnadze might have said, the sun rises in the north: 'When I am asked about our two main presidential candidates, I reply that for me it's not so much a question of who but of what will be after the election.

Which path will Ukraine take? The tried and tested one we have today, which has given results – even if our countrymen perhaps do not fully feel those results – or the path that will scupper everything that's been done these past ten years, and put everything in doubt? I think our meeting [with Putin] will help to push things in the right direction.'

Lest anyone was in any doubt, Putin then travelled to Ukraine for a three-day visit at the end of October – an unprecedented intervention right on the eve of the first round of the election. He did not need to do anything so crude as to publicly praise Yanukovych or disparage Yushchenko. His very presence was a reminder of what was most at stake in this election, and everyone knew who the pro-Russia candidate was. Putin began with a live interview simultaneously broadcast on three Ukrainian state television channels, to which viewers could phone in or email their questions. Over the next two days he held talks with the leadership and stood beside Yanukovych at ceremonies to mark the 60th anniversary of Ukraine's liberation (by the Russians) from Nazi occupation. The spin doctors were doing a pretty good job. And at this stage the Russians were firmly convinced that Yushchenko stood no chance of being elected.

But polling on 31 October proved them wrong. Yushchenko emerged fractionally ahead of Yanukovych, with both taking just under 40 per cent. A run-off between the two leading candidates was required, and this was set for Sunday 21 November.

In that second round, an exit poll paid for by Western embassies put Yushchenko 11 percentage points ahead of his rival. But official results put the prime minister three points ahead. The result was denounced by Western election observers who said they had witnessed abuse of state resources in favour of Yanukovych. Yushchenko's campaign chief, Oleh Rybachuk, recalls: 'I was voting in a small polling station in the centre of Kiev. There were always very few people voting there, but on the day of that election there was a sudden queue of people with additional voting slips, who had arrived from the Donetsk region [Yanukovych's heartland]. There were more of them than there were Kiev people who came to vote at their own polling station!'

The fraud was so evident that Yushchenko supporters began to pour into Independence Square (known as Maidan) in central Kiev, setting up a tent city where they planned to sit it out until the result was changed. Orange became the colour of the revolution – chosen rather than the blue and yellow of the Ukrainian flag in order to avoid nationalist overtones. Over the next week or so, a million people joined in, besieging government buildings.

Vladimir Putin, however, immediately rang Yanukovych to offer his congratulations. 'It was a sharp fight,' he said, 'but an open and honest one, and your victory was convincing.' Apart from 'sharp', every adjective could scarcely have been further off the mark. Being charitable, one might point out that he was in Brazil at the time, and maybe out of the loop. But what were his intelligence services telling him? His adviser Gleb Pavlovsky says it was no mistake, but a deliberate attempt by Putin to challenge the West in what he describes as an 'international fight' over the election result. 'The congratulations served as a political signal. The fight for recognition of the results had started, and Putin took part in that fight. In the end, Russia lost, but if it had not, the result would have been different.'

President Kuchma was paralysed. His capital city was witnessing the biggest display of people power Europe had seen since the fall of communism. He toyed with the idea of using force to remove the protestors, hoping all the while that the sub-zero temperatures would drive them away. They did not, and the demonstrators themselves remained entirely peaceful to avoid provoking violence. In the early hours of 23 November Kuchma called President Kwaśniewski of Poland for advice. 'He was incredibly nervous,' Kwaśniewski recalls, 'and kept repeating, "I will not allow blood to be spilt here" – two or three times. He asked me to go to Kiev. I said, "It's the middle of the night, I'll see what I can do by morning." '[7]

In the morning Kwaśniewski called Tony Blair. Blair's chief of staff, Jonathan Powell, recalls: 'He was urging Tony to go with him to Kiev. But Tony was reluctant to do that because the Russians had this obsession that we were trying to surround them, that the West was moving into their sphere of influence. Tony decided not to do it.'

The Polish president pulled together a European Union mission to mediate between the two candidates and President Kuchma. They would travel to Kiev by the end of the week. But events were moving fast.

On Tuesday 23 November Yushchenko declared himself the winner and symbolically took the presidential oath. His running-mate Yulia Tymoshenko impetuously announced she would lead a march on the presidential administration, declaring, 'Either they will give up power or we will take it.' Her call provoked a row within the team. Rybachuk told her: 'You shouldn't be provoking the crowds like that. What if somebody gets killed?'

'Then they'll die as heroes,' she replied, according to Rybachuk.

The next day the Central Election Commission officially declared that Yanukovych had won. The United States, which had invested so much in trying to ensure a fair election, had to decide what to do in the face of such apparently blatant manipulation. The secretary of state, Colin Powell, recalled in an interview: 'I came into the office while all this was unfolding and called in my team, and I said, "Look, this is too big. We cannot simply stand by and say nothing and put out mealy-mouthed statements." ' He went down to the press room and made a statement that set Washington at odds with Moscow: 'We cannot accept this result as legitimate because it does not meet international standards and because there has not been an investigation of the numerous and credible reports of fraud and abuse.'

On his way back from his Latin American trip, President Putin stopped in at The Hague for a summit with EU leaders, where he picked up the gauntlet. 'We have no moral right to push a big European state into any kind of mass disorder,' he said. 'We should not allow the resolution of such conflicts through mob rule to become part of international practice.'

Behind the scenes, it seems that Putin was advising Kuchma to get a grip and clear the crowds from the streets. Asked about it in an interview, Kuchma admitted: 'Putin is a hard man. It wasn't like he was saying directly, "Put tanks on the street." He was tactful in his comments. But there were some hints made, that's no secret.' The hints were evidently rather heavy, and Kuchma had to insist: 'I will not use force to clear demonstrators from the Maidan. Because I know there are children there, and it's obvious how it would end.'[8]

On the Friday, five days after the election, the EU mission arrived in Kiev, led by Kwaśniewski and the EU's foreign policy chief, Javier Solana. But as a million Yushchenko supporters waited patiently in the streets, some 40,000 miners from Yanukovych's heartland, Donetsk, were marching on Kiev. Kwaśniewski told Kuchma: 'What are you saying? This means a massacre! I am telling you that if this happens I go straight to the airport with Solana, and we will hold a huge press conference in Brussels where we will accuse you of starting a civil war in Ukraine.'

Kuchma took the necessary measures to prevent disaster. 'I have leverage with influential people,' he recalled later. 'We just managed to stop them.'

Before the mediation talks began Kuchma put through a call to President Putin in Moscow to stress that the Round Table must have a Russian representative present. Putin proposed sending Boris Yeltsin, which sounded like a joke to

Kwaśniewski. He told Kuchma: 'Listen, I'm sorry, but I can't treat this seriously, because much as I appreciate Yeltsin and I enjoyed working with him, we want to have serious talks, not a show.'[9]

Putin sent a trusted functionary instead – Boris Gryzlov, a former interior minister and chairman of the State Duma, whom Putin had just made head of his party, United Russia. Gryzlov's contribution to the talks was scarcely more productive than Yeltsin's might have been. Yushchenko says the tension was overpowering. 'I knew I was the last person Russia wanted as president. These falsifications, the way the Russians were taking an interest, their slanted position during the election, this interference in Ukrainian internal affairs ... it was obvious to all.'

Gryzlov's starting point, according to Kwaśniewski, was that Yanukovych was president, and that all the stories about irregularities were a waste of time, stirred up by foreign forces. There was nothing to talk about and the Round Table made no sense.

Yushchenko and Yanukovych each accused the other of rigging the vote in different constituencies. Someone suggested that overall the vote wasn't forged by more than 10 per cent. Kwaśniewski says he looked at him and said: 'Okay, put that in your constitution, then – that if an election is not forged by more than 10 per cent, it's valid!' Gryzlov then referred to the US presidential election of 2000, when the final outcome depended on hanging chads and a recount in Florida, and suggested that, like the Americans, they should just accept an apparently flawed result and agree to it. 'Let's stick with the constitution.'

There was stalemate in the talks. Kwaśniewski knew that only one man could break the deadlock. He asked the German chancellor, Gerhard Schröder, to talk to Putin. 'I said: "You know Putin. Tell him – if you persist in claiming that this is some artificial movement, financed by Western forces, which has no legitimacy, and that the elections were not rigged, then you're getting it wrong; it means you don't understand the seriousness of this situation." '

Schröder called Putin – but got an earful. Putin believed he understood the situation perfectly well, much better than Kwaśniewski and his EU mission. Schröder reported back to Kwaśniewski that it was one of the hardest calls he had ever had with Putin.

It is not clear what effect Schröder's call had, or what Putin may have subsequently said to Kuchma. But on Sunday evening, one week after the election, the US embassy received news that the worst was about to happen: heavily armed police units were being sent in to disperse the demonstrators. Ambassador Herbst called Washington and told them, 'I think Secretary Powell needs to call President Kuchma.'

Powell was told that interior ministry troops were massing on the outskirts of the city. 'I tried to call the president, but he suddenly wasn't available.' Kuchma explained in an interview that the reason he refused the call was because it was 3am and he had no interpreter available for the conversation. In the meantime the ambassador got through to Kuchma's son-in-law, Viktor Pinchuk, and told him: if any repression happens tonight, we will consider Kuchma personally responsible.

The troops were called off. When Powell finally got through to the president in the morning Kuchma told him nothing would happen: it was a 'false panic'. But he added, 'Mr Secretary of State, if the White House was surrounded as our presidency and government offices are at this moment, what would you do?' Powell, according to Kuchma, had no answer.

Kuchma was becoming ever more desperate and was now prepared to ditch his own man as well as Yushchenko and hold a fresh election with new candidates. He says: 'If Yanukovych had become president then, Ukraine would have become a pariah state. There was all that pressure from the street. Plus the diplomatic blockade from the West, especially the USA.'

But nothing could be done without Moscow's blessing. On Thursday 2 December Kuchma flew to Moscow for consultations with Putin at Vnukovo airport. Putin seemed to give his backing to the idea. 'Re-running the second round [with Yanukovych and Yushchenko] might also achieve nothing,' he told Kuchma. 'You'll end up doing it a third, a fourth, and a twenty-fifth time, until one side gets the result it needs.'

Putin spoke of his fears that Ukraine could split into two parts – the western, more nationalistic part that overwhelmingly supported Yushchenko, and the eastern, heavily industrialised part bordering Russia, where Yanukovych drew much of his support. 'I have to tell you straight,' he told Kuchma. 'We are very worried about the trend towards a split. We are not indifferent to what is happening. According to the census, 17 per cent of Ukraine's population are Russians – ethnic Russians. In fact I think there are far more of them. It's a Russian-speaking country, in both the east and the west. It's no exaggeration to say that every second family in Ukraine, if not more, has relatives and personal ties to Russia. That's why we are so worried by what is happening.'

It was clear from this that Putin regarded Ukraine (as he later revealed to George W. Bush) as almost a province of Russia – certainly what would later be termed a 'sphere of privileged interest'. His adviser, Sergei Markov, says he had prepared briefing papers for Putin earlier in his presidency that suggested 'public opinion in Ukraine wanted there to be no borders between Ukraine and Russia, that all the citizens should have the same rights, the same currency, the same education and information policy. But at the same time Ukraine would keep its sovereignty – separate flag, anthem, president, citizenship and so on.'

This was what the Kremlin leadership believed. Just as strongly, the American administration believed Ukraine was ripe to align itself with the West, and that the majority of its citizens aspired to membership of NATO and the EU.

In fact, both the Russians and the Americans underplayed the most important thing – that Ukraine is a finely balanced entity, divided and pulled in many directions. There is a linguistic split between Russian and Ukrainian speakers, a religious divide between Orthodox and Catholic Christians; there are those who pine for the old days (more security, less tension, less corruption, little ethnic strife) and those who want to move on (openness, democracy, free enterprise); there are Ukrainian nationalists and ethnic Russians – distributed across an imprecise geographical 'east–west' divide. Opinion polls did not show an overwhelming desire across the country for NATO membership, although joining the EU was more popular. The family ties of which Putin spoke were real. But at the same time this was not the same Ukraine that was once part of the Soviet 'family'; it had developed for 13 years already as a separate entity, and a new identity was growing. The use of the Ukrainian language was far more widespread than it was in Soviet days when I once embarrassed the head of the Ukrainian Communist Party, Vladimir Shcherbitsky, by asking him what language was used at Ukrainian central committee meetings. There was a new pride in the nation, and an awareness that economically, at least, they would be far better to tie their future to the West than to the semi-reformed and corrupt economy of Russia.

It was these sentiments that prevailed when the 2004 election was finally re-run, following a Supreme Court decision, on 26 December, under new rules to tighten up procedures and reduce fraud. Viktor Yushchenko was declared the winner with 52 per cent of the vote, to Yanukovych's 44 per cent. International observers declared the ballot had been run fairly.

The result was a humiliation for Putin, who had staked everything on preventing what he saw as the 'loss' of Ukraine to a Western conspiracy.

The Orange Revolution was like a door slamming on

Russia's and the West's efforts to understand one another. It is hard to think of any event that could be interpreted in such diametrically opposed ways. The West saw it as a triumph of democracy. Here is what the *Washington Post* wrote, looking back a few years later: 'Ukraine's Orange Revolution erupted in 2004 because of an attempt by Russian leader Vladimir Putin and his proxies to impose on Ukraine a version of Russia's corrupt authoritarianism – beginning with a fraudulent presidential election.' [10]

In Russia, it was seen as essentially the work of US special operations. Gleb Pavlovsky described the Orange protestors as 'Red Guards', trained and funded by American consultants. 'But this isn't rocket science. There are plenty of local specialists who've been working on the "Destroy Russia" project since 1990–91, ever since the Chechen project.' [11]

Sergei Markov said it was a coup aimed at breaking Ukraine away from Russia, and that Yushchenko triumphed only through falsification. 'The Orange never came to power as the result of free elections. They came to power as the result of an anti-constitutional coup, being supported, of course, by the American administration and the Western observers. No matter how many American senators say that it was legal, it was anti-constitutional.'

Pavlovsky, the Kremlin's main operator during the revolution, had to sneak away in disguise. 'My departure from Kiev was quite funny. I was living in a hotel right in the centre of the city, in the middle of the orange crowd which was blocking the presidential administration. I was forced to change clothes – like Kerensky [Russian prime minister overthrown in the 1917 revolution], who our Soviet textbooks say escaped dressed as a female nurse. I went out through the crowd wearing an orange scarf and hat.'

The backlash

Few people can say they know very much about Vladislav Surkov, even though for more than a decade he has been one of the most influential people in the Kremlin. Hiding behind the innocuous title of deputy chief of staff to the president, he is in fact the architect of Russia's political system – changing chameleon-like at his master's command, thinking up ever new structures and ideologies to justify whatever twist or turn Vladimir Putin required. His most notorious coinage – the notion of 'sovereign democracy' – essentially meant that Russia would decide for itself, as a sovereign state, what kind of democracy it needed. If today it meant that parties needed 7 per cent of the vote, not 5, to get into parliament, Surkov was on hand to explain why. If a few years later, it was decided that 5 per cent was, after all, better, Surkov would justify that too. If governors should no longer be elected, Surkov would explain why appointing them was also democratic.

He was born in 1964, and for a long time concealed the fact that his father was Chechen (his name was originally Dudayev). He studied at a metals institute, did his compulsory military service in military intelligence, and then turned to the arts, training to become a theatre director before studying economics and going into business. He composed lyrics for rock bands, and still writes novels. This post-Soviet renaissance man worked with Mikhail Khodorkovsky as head of PR, before moving briefly to central television and then into Putin's office as what the Soviets would have called 'ideology secretary'.

Following the 'catastrophe' of the Orange Revolution, it fell to Surkov to devise strategies to prevent the contagion spreading to Russia (as the entire ruling elite believed it would). In doing so he was guided by the assessments of those who had been on the ground in Ukraine during those tumultuous events.

Gleb Pavlovsky, having safely escaped in his orange

disguise, wrote in the press: 'Kiev is a serious wake-up call for Russia. I believe that our political system is not ready for the new revolutionary technologies of the age of globalisation. The combination of the internal weakening of the political system and external pressures and provocations could lead to a new revolution, and a global revolution in Russia would not be a small thing. We avoided bloodshed in 1991, almost by a miracle. We avoided bloodshed in Russia in 1996 and 1999 everywhere except in Chechnya. But that doesn't mean that another miracle is coming.'[12]

He told the BBC, looking back in February 2008: 'This catastrophe was very useful for us. We learned a lot of valuable lessons. Putin started to take much more seriously the threats he faced. It very quickly became clear that they would try to export this to us. We needed quickly to prepare, to strengthen our political system and make it ready for a blow from the outside – a blow in a "velvet glove", but a blow that would topple us nonetheless. Putin in 2005 very quickly prepared, consolidated the elite, the political system, the cooperation, so there could be no orange revolution in Russia. Within a year we had turned back the wave of coloured revolutions.'

Surkov and his comrades targeted two lurking dangers – the 'unguided' energies of young people, and foreign-funded NGOs. To tackle the first problem, it was decided to set up a mass youth organisation that would be totally loyal to Putin and the current regime. It was called Nashi – meaning 'Our Own People'. The word has a strongly nationalistic or chauvinistic connotation, implying that all those who are not 'nashi' are 'against us', even traitors.

Sergei Markov describes himself as one of the ideological team, under Surkov, that begat this monster, which smacked so strongly of the Soviet communist youth movement, the Komsomol. In an interview, Markov stated without embarrassment: 'The main aim of Nashi was to prevent an orange revolution in Russia. So the first guys who joined were super patriotic. And the first rule was geography. They had to live within ten hours' drive of Moscow so that they could take the night bus and be in Moscow in the morning and occupy Red Square to protect the sovereignty of the state.'

Nashi quickly had its own website (www.nashi.su, using the still valid domain of the Soviet Union rather than Russia). Over the coming years they would hold patriotic summer camps at Lake Seliger, north of Moscow, dedicated to a healthy lifestyle, political education and paramilitary exercises; they would turn out regularly in their red T-shirts not just for their own demonstrations but to swamp opposition protests; and they mounted campaigns against any institution or individual they didn't like – including Western ambassadors, critical newspapers and even a kebab shop unluckily named 'Anti-Soviet'. Nashi describes itself as a 'democratic anti-fascist youth movement'. Its membership soon grew to well over 100,000.

The Surkov team felt their mission was already accomplished on 15 May 2005 when Nashi mobilised its first large rally. Some 60,000 activists, mostly transported into Moscow overnight on thousands of buses, brought Leninsky Prospekt to a standstill. According to Markov, 'after that the talk about orange revolution stopped'.

Mission accomplished, but role far from over. Nashi became the self-appointed voice of public outrage, a potent political force that purported to be independent but in fact enjoyed the absolute protection of the state, however lawless or thuggish their behaviour became. Their activities had little to do with preventing a coloured revolution in Russia. The British ambassador, Tony Brenton, would find himself in their sights after he attended a conference held by The Other Russia, a coalition of opposition groups, in July 2006. Brenton recalls the incident in the self-deprecating manner of a British diplomat: 'I went along to this Other Russia conference to express our support for Russian civil society, which I did in a deeply dull speech. I wasn't the only ambassador there, but for some reason the Russians picked me out. And this youth group, Nashi, which is a ruling-party youth group, so in effect works for the Kremlin, demanded an apology for Tony Brenton's interference in Russian politics. Now there was no way I was going to apologise, so then they said, well we are going to hassle Tony Brenton until he does apologise. It was my job to put up with it, which I did.' [13]

What he and his family had to endure, however, bordered on the criminal. Hooligans from Nashi camped outside his house, waving banners, followed him around town and shouted abuse at the back of public meetings he addressed. When his wife drove out to go shopping, they hammered with their fists on the roof of her car. Brenton complained about this intimidation, which clearly violated the Vienna Convention on the status of diplomats (not to mention laws against harassment), but it took half a year before the foreign ministry took action to force Nashi to back off.

Nashi undertook similar actions against the Estonian ambassador to express the 'outrage of the Russian people' against her country's decision to remove a memorial to Soviet 'liberators' of Estonia (considered occupiers by most Estonians) from the centre of the capital, Tallinn.

Whenever complaints were made, Kremlin spokesmen would shrug their shoulders, claiming it was nothing to do with them, almost laughing it off as a bit of harmless fun. But the link with the Kremlin is explicit. The Nashi website is full of articles by Surkov, Putin and Medvedev, all of whom also attend their conferences and summer camps. Putin's party, United Russia, also has its own official youth wing, Molodaya Gvardiya (Young Guard – another Soviet-era term), which is rather more disciplined than Nashi.

Surkov's second line of attack, to ward off the orange 'contagion', was aimed against non-governmental organisations, particularly those which received funding or support from abroad. These had been identified by the paranoiacs in the

Kremlin not just as factors in the revolutions in Georgia and Ukraine (and a third grass-roots revolt in the former Soviet republic of Kyrgyzstan in February 2005) but as the means by which the United States was allegedly plotting the downfall of the Putin regime.

Civil society had burgeoned in Russia ever since Gorbachev's *glasnost* policies had allowed the first 'informal organisations' to be registered. Now there were hundreds of thousands of them, and about 2,000 dealt with human rights and democracy issues. Organisations such as the Carnegie Centre provided independent expert analysis of Russian politics; Memorial chronicled the crimes of the past and kept alive the memory of the victims of communism; the Helsinki Group monitored human rights abuses. And some of them received grants or subsidies from Western governments or from parent NGOs abroad.

Less than a year after the Ukraine revolution the State Duma introduced legislation to rein them in. The law, which would severely hamper the activities of foreign-supported NGOs operating in Russia, caused an outcry in the West, and President Bush, among others, successfully lobbied for some of its terms to be softened. Nonetheless, the version signed into law by President Putin on 10 January 2006 required all Russian NGOs to disclose their finances and sources of funding, and ensure that their activities complied with Russian 'national interests' or risk closure. It became considerably more difficult for foreign groups to fund and support their partners in Russia. (By October, Human Rights Watch, Amnesty International, the Danish Refugee Council and two branches of Doctors Without Borders had been forced to halt their work temporarily for allegedly failing to comply with registration requirements.)[14]

Aware of the bad publicity surrounding the new law, the Kremlin resorted to Soviet-style propaganda to make the public aware of how heinous NGOs could be.

A fortnight after the law was signed, Lyudmila Alexeyeva, a 78-year-old human rights activist and chairperson of the Moscow Helsinki Group, was at home in Moscow when a friend called and told her to switch her television on, quickly. 'I switched on the TV,' she told me, 'and saw some strange silhouettes. The presenter, in a dramatic voice, was saying that some English diplomats had made some kind of transmitter, inside a rock, in some square, stuffed with top-notch technology.' [15] State television had been given an extraordinary scoop: clandestine footage of British spies in action. The pictures showed named British diplomats, including one Marc Doe, a 'second secretary' (often a euphemism for an MI6 agent), retrieving data from a fake rock, in reality a transmitter, planted in a park. The report showed the rock being opened up, to reveal a James Bond-style gadget inside.

The story was bizarre, but it was not untrue. Tony Blair's chief of staff, Jonathan Powell, admits: 'The spy rock was embarrassing. I mean, they had us bang to rights. The rock was there for all to see, on television. Clearly they had known about it for some time and had been saving it up for a political purpose.' [16]

The political purpose became clearer as Lyudmila Alexeyeva continued to watch. 'Suddenly they are talking about this diplomat at the British embassy, Doe, or something like that, who "managed" our human rights organisations. And then they show some piece of paper with the words "Moscow Helsinki Group".' In fact, the document, signed by Doe, appeared to be authorisation for the transfer of £23,000 to the Moscow Helsinki Group.

The Russians did not expel any of the British spies they had caught red-handed. The story had a different purpose: to demonstrate that NGOs like the Helsinki Group were in the pay not just of the West but of the British secret service. Alexeyeva says she had never met Marc Doe, and the Helsinki Group had only received one grant from the Foreign Office's

Global Opportunities Fund, which was merely processed by the embassy. The Foreign Office says that all its payments to Russian NGOs are openly published on its website. But by using a spy to handle some of those payments, it had played straight into the Russians' hands.

Two days after the 'spy rock' exposé, President Putin justified the controversial NGO law by making an explicit link between espionage and NGO activities: 'We have seen that attempts are made to use secret services to work with NGOs and that they are financed through the channels of the secret services. No one can say that this money doesn't stink. I assume that many people will now understand why Russia has passed a law regulating the activities of non-governmental organisations in this country. The law is intended to block the interference by other states in the internal affairs of the Russian Federation.'

Triumph of the strongmen

In his annual presidential address in April 2005, Putin uttered a sentence that has often been quoted as proof of his nostalgia for communism. 'The collapse of the Soviet Union,' he said, 'was the greatest geopolitical catastrophe of the century.' In fact, he was not talking about the communist system as such. What he regretted was the passing of a mighty, unified, multi-ethnic state, whose collapse – as he went on to say in that speech – left 'tens of millions of our fellow citizens and compatriots outside Russian territory'. This was, as he put it, 'a genuine drama' for the Russian nation – and it is hard to dispute that.

It was an unfortunate choice of words, however, since so many of his actions at the beginning of his second term really did look as if he was trying to restore the Soviet Union, communism and all. In response to the Beslan siege he had removed many of the most democratic elements of the electoral system, tightening his personal grip on power. In response to the popular revolutions in Georgia and Ukraine he had squashed human rights groups and set up an ugly chauvinistic youth organisation. All the while, his stranglehold on the media was tightening.

There was little reason now for genuine liberals to remain in Putin's team. As early as February 2004 Putin had lost his prime minister, Mikhail Kasyanov, who was sacked after a series of disagreements – the final straw being Putin's decision to appoint his friend Igor Sechin to the chairmanship of the state oil giant Rosneft. Sechin was just one of Putin's cronies (others included ex-KGB man Viktor Ivanov, ideology chief Vladislav Surkov and deputy chief of staff Dmitry Medvedev) who ended up running massive state companies, in addition to their administration jobs. Kasyanov saw this as proof that 'Putin was drifting away from liberal approaches, towards a command economy'.[17] Out of government, Kasyanov went on to become a leading opposition figure, and one with much credibility, having worked side-by-side with Putin for three years – and having considered him initially a reformer.

Next to go was Putin's economics adviser, Andrei Illarionov – the man he had taken on despite his views on the futility and brutality of the Chechen campaign. Illarionov walked out in December 2005 after five years with Putin, delivering a devastating verdict on the country Russia had become. The country was no longer free and democratic, he said, but run by state corporations acting in their own interests. Until recently, he said, he could express his views freely, but now the political and economic system in Russia had changed, and he could no longer stay in post.

In the year following the arrest of Mikhail Khodorkovsky, the *siloviki* moved to grab his assets for themselves, even before he was found guilty of anything. The sell-off of his oil company Yukos to the state was accomplished in a stunningly cynical way. Claiming that it was owed more than $27 billion by Yukos, the government arranged an auction on 19 December 2004 to sell off the company's main production unit, Yuganskneftegaz, to cover the tax claim. The state gas monopoly Gazprom registered to participate in the auction through a new oil subsidiary, Gazprom Neft. So did a company called Baikal Finance Group, which had only been created on 6 December. Its registered office was at an address used by a vodka shop, a mobile phone operator and a travel agency in the city of Tver, north of Moscow. Who its owners were, no one knew. Nonetheless it secured a massive loan from the state-owned Sberbank in order to participate in the auction. On the day, Gazprom Neft declined to place a bid, leaving the obscure Baikal Finance Group to buy Russia's largest oil company for $9.3 billion.

Two days later, on a visit to Germany, Putin declared with a breathtaking pretence of innocence that the shareholders of Baikal Finance Group were 'people who have been in the energy business for many years', and that 'as I have been informed, they intend to develop some sort of relationship with other energy companies in Russia, which are interested in this stock'. He didn't know which companies they might be, of course, but 'state companies have the same right as other players in the market'.

At his annual press conference on 23 December, Putin couldn't quite remember the name 'Baikal Finance Group' any more. That day it had been bought in its entirety by none other than Igor Sechin's Rosneft. Sechin, it is thought, was the founder of the mysterious and short-lived Baikal Finance Group. 'Today, the state, using absolutely legal, market mechanisms, is ensuring its interests,' said Putin. 'I consider this perfectly normal.'

Meanwhile the trial continued of the man who had built Yukos into an oil giant in the first place. In May 2005 Mikhail Khodorkovsky was found guilty of fraud and sentenced to nine years in jail.

The energy weapon

Western governments – and Western investors – watched these events unfold with some trepidation. But there was worse to come. The repercussions of the Orange Revolution were far from over.

The new Ukrainian president, Viktor Yushchenko, headed straight for Moscow on 24 January 2005, the day after his inauguration, and President Putin seemed to appreciate it. When the Ukrainian referred to Russia as a 'permanent strategic partner', Putin noted, with a hint of surprise, 'What you just said about strategic partnership is a very good and very pleasant sign.'

Nonetheless it was a meeting without smiles. Yushchenko felt misunderstood. He said in an interview: 'My major concern was that all the steps we were taking, especially when it came to our democratic reforms, or the revival of our history, or the integration of Ukraine into the rest of the civilised world – Russia took all of these as anti-Russian steps.' [18]

It was a perfunctory visit, lasting only half a day. Then Yushchenko headed straight for Strasbourg to the Council of Europe, and to Brussels for a speech to the European Parliament. When he went to Washington in April he was received as a hero. He earned rapturous applause when he told Congress: 'Today Ukraine is looking into the future with great hope and expectation. Free and fair elections have brought to state office a new generation of politicians not encumbered with the mentality of the Soviet past.'

Then he was taken to the Oval Office to meet George W. Bush. The president's chief Ukraine adviser, Damon Wilson, recalled in an interview that Yushchenko seemed to lack focus. 'He began the conversation by discussing the challenges he was facing as president of Ukraine, in particular the relationship with Russia. He began to set out, I think it may have been 12 points or so, a whole series of particular issues that he saw he needed to work through with Russia. And as he began to enumerate these challenges in a rather longwinded way, President Bush stopped him. He said, you don't need to worry about these 12 challenges, you have one challenge you need to be concerned about with Russia – is Moscow prepared to see an independent sovereign democratic Ukraine make decisions about its own future? That's the strategic challenge you face.' [19]

Wilson says the Americans were rather worried after that first visit. 'We were quite concerned whether he understood the scale of the task before him – whether he understood how to go about addressing these issues. And, you know, while there was still a lot of enthusiasm and a lot of support, and a commitment in policy terms to figure out how to help him succeed in his task, his visit to Washington really did raise the first alarm bells – that we might have more difficulty than we thought, and how he could follow through on the promise of the Orange Revolution.'

The alarm bells rang louder at the end of the year when Yushchenko surprisingly struck a shady deal that the Americans thought stank of corruption, in order to dig himself out of a major crisis over Russian gas imports.

The first of Putin's 'gas wars' began in March 2005, when the Russians apparently decided to punish the Ukrainians for their Orange Revolution by announcing that, from the following January, Gazprom would more than quadruple the price of its exports to Ukraine from $50 per 1,000 cubic metres to around $225. The situation was complicated by the fact that Gazprom also supplied 25 per cent of the European Union's gas, mainly through pipelines crossing Ukraine, for which Kiev charged Gazprom transit fees. (Some countries relied 100 per cent on Russian supplies through Ukraine.) Russia supplied gas to all its former Soviet republics at prices far below world levels. But now that Ukraine was snubbing it and declaring itself to be allied with the West, Moscow saw no reason to continue to subsidise it.

In October Yushchenko's chief of staff, Oleh Rybachuk,

was summoned to Moscow and given a stern warning: agree to the price hike, or your gas will be turned off. 'Putin was warning us that this isn't a threat, we're not bluffing,' Rybachuk recalls. 'If we don't do a deal by 1 January, our supplies will be cut.'[20]

Two days before the deadline, Putin offered a solution: a Russian commercial loan worth $3.6 billion to enable Ukraine to adjust to the new price. Yushchenko turned it down. On New Year's Eve, Putin made another last-minute offer: a three-month price freeze if Kiev would agree to the higher price after that. Yushchenko said he would pay no more than $80. Early on New Year's Day, Gazprom engineers turned the taps on the pipelines entering Ukraine, and the gas stopped flowing.

It stopped flowing to Europe too. Hungary and Poland quickly saw their supplies disrupted. The export pipelines should not have been affected, but Gazprom claimed the Ukrainians were stealing supplies from the transit routes to make up for the shortfall in its own deliveries. European governments were livid. Moscow claimed it had no choice, that it was a commercial dispute. But the West saw it as a strong-arm tactic, retribution for Kiev's display of independence.

The European Commission summoned ministers back from their Christmas holiday to an emergency meeting on 4 January. But before they met it was suddenly announced that the Russian and Ukrainian presidents had reached a deal. On the face of it, the agreement was a decent compromise: Ukraine agreed to pay the market rate for Russian gas, but Gazprom would also sell it much cheaper gas from Turkmenistan, bringing the overall price down to $95 per 1,000 cubic metres; to sugar the pill Gazprom would also pay 47 per cent more to Ukraine for transporting gas to Europe.

The West's new worries arose because all the gas would now be sold not directly by Gazprom but by a murky Swiss-registered trading company called Rosukrenergo, which was half-owned by Gazprom, partly owned by two shady Ukrainian businessmen. Rosukrenergo's creation in July 2004 was overseen by Putin and ex-President Kuchma of Ukraine. Western observers could not understand why Yushchenko had now got involved with it.

The American ambassador John Herbst recalls: 'The Ukrainians came in and described the deal. And I was dumbfounded. My German colleague and my other European colleagues were all dumbfounded. Because again we thought that the Ukrainians had a reasonable negotiating position and a reasonably strong one. And the result was less than optimal, to be diplomatic.' [21]

Damon Wilson described the consternation back in Washington: 'Here we are with a president who presides over a deal with Russia that introduces Rosukrenergo, an intermediary with all sorts of shady transactions and dealings, in a process that, it became increasingly clear to us, was a vehicle for facilitating side payments, facilitating the worst of business practices in Ukraine. This was corruption at the heart of the Orange Government.'

Yushchenko's chief of staff, Rybachuk, conceded it was a controversial deal, but they had no choice: 'Yushchenko's position was: Putin is president; yes I understand that gas is a dirty business but we can't do business with Russia in any other way.'

So now Washington and Europe found their dreams fading. The Ukrainian democrat they had championed was proving to be decidedly flaky. Wilson described it as a moment of disillusionment, of realisation that old habits were still strong in the "new Ukraine'. And in Moscow, Putin had demonstrated his willingness to use a weapon never tried before – energy supplies. Those few days of gas cuts in early January caused immense nervousness throughout Europe and triggered a radical rethink of the EU's energy policies. From now on, Vladimir Putin was not a man the West enjoyed doing business with.

8

A NEW COLD WAR

Tempers get frayed

Now a spiral of disenchantment began to wreck relations between Washington and Moscow – and even between the 'friends', Bush and Putin, each of whom began to accuse the other of bad faith. At a bad-tempered summit in the capital of Slovakia, Bratislava, in February 2005 (just after the Orange Revolution), Putin pulled a pack of 3-by-5 cards from his inside jacket pocket – the Americans called them his 'grievance cards' – and began lecturing Bush about ... well, about how fed up he was being lectured to by the Americans. The rant went something like this: We've done everything we can to accommodate you, we supported you in the war on terror, we closed down bases, we let you destroy the ABM treaty without making a big fuss, we didn't even let Iraq get between us, and what did we get in return? Nothing. You haven't abolished Jackson-Vanik, you keep moving the goalposts on our WTO entry, you don't even ratify the Conventional Forces in Europe arms control treaty, you want to build a missile shield that makes us vulnerable, and you're trying to bring all our neighbours into NATO. Instead of praise for our policies aimed at reforming our economy and tying it into the world system, all we hear are complaints about our internal affairs – about human rights, about our supposed 'backsliding' on democracy, about Chechnya, about our media, about Khodorkovsky. When will it end?

Bush's new national security adviser, Stephen Hadley, recalled that this was 'probably the testiest meeting the two leaders had had'.[1] It was here that Putin tried to turn the tables on Bush by claiming that America did not have a free press – as witnessed by the fact that Bush had allegedly had CBS's senior news anchor Dan Rather fired for criticising him.[2] Bush tried to explain that this was not the case, but Putin was in no mood to listen. Instead, he hit back on American democracy, too. The American people did not elect their president, Putin asserted, but an electoral college did. Bush replied: 'Vladimir, don't say that publicly whatever you do. You will just show everyone you don't understand our system at all.'

Three months later there was a chance for reconciliation. Putin invited a host of world leaders to Moscow on 9 May to celebrate the 60th anniversary of the Allies' victory over Nazi Germany. The guests included Chirac and Schröder, but it was Bush who stood beside Putin on the reviewing stand on Red Square to observe a Soviet-style display of military might, complete with goose-stepping soldiers and communist banners. Putin appreciated the gesture. But he did not like what went before or after it.

On his way to Moscow Bush had stopped in Riga, the capital of Latvia, where he sided fully with the Baltic nation's interpretation of post-war history – namely, that the liberating Soviet army had overstayed its welcome and become an occupation force, replacing Nazi rule with another totalitarian regime. Soviet oppression in Europe, said Bush, was 'one of the greatest wrongs of history'. The fact that the Baltic nations perceived Soviet 'liberation' as occupation is a truth the Russian government finds very hard to stomach, because, it claims, it insults the memory of Soviet servicemen who fought to free the country from the Nazis.

Even worse than his interpretation of the past was Bush's gloss on the present. From Moscow he flew straight to Tbilisi, where the Georgians laid on a hero's welcome and Bush reciprocated by calling the country a 'beacon of liberty for this region and the world' and apparently urging other former Soviet states to follow suit. He praised Georgia for providing troops in Afghanistan and Iraq, and proclaimed: 'Your courage is inspiring democratic reformers and sending a message that echoes across the world – freedom will be the future of every nation and every people on earth.' The words caused fury in the Kremlin, which was at that very moment tightening the screws on Georgia – banning imports of its world-famous wines and mineral waters on 'health grounds'.

As 2005 progressed, and the West watched powerless as Putin curtailed democracy, created Nashi, cracked down on NGOs and turned off gas supplies to Ukraine, the rhetoric on both sides peaked. In early May 2006 Vice-President Dick Cheney travelled to another former Soviet Baltic republic, Lithuania, with the express purpose of delivering another broadside at Russia – one that was intended to be seen not as a wayward attack by a sometimes off-message vice-president, but as the considered view of the administration. Damon Wilson, at the National Security Council in the White House, explained: 'We knew that this would be an important opportunity to continue to echo the president's messages about the freedom agenda. There was a tendency often in Moscow to discount what Vice-President Cheney said, to say, this is Vice-President Cheney, we all know he's radical, he's the neocon in the administration, but at the end of the day, we're doing business with President Bush. And so we worked very closely with the vice-president's office and his speech writers to make sure that this wasn't Vice-President Cheney out on a limb. We prepared a speech that was actually well vetted, very much circulated in the Interagency, delivering key messages on the democracy front, pretty tough-hitting words on what was happening in Russia.'[3]

Cheney delivered a paean to freedom and the spread of democracy, and let loose at the Putin regime:

> In many areas of civil society – from religion and the news media, to advocacy groups and political parties – the government has unfairly and improperly restricted the rights of her people. Other actions by the Russian government have been counterproductive, and could begin to affect relations with other countries. No legitimate interest is served when oil and gas become tools of intimidation or blackmail, either by supply manipulation or attempts to monopolise transportation. And no one can justify actions that undermine the territorial integrity of a neighbour, or interfere with democratic movements.

He called on Russia to return to democratic reform, and become a 'trusted friend' by sharing the Western values: 'We will make the case, clearly and confidently, that Russia has nothing to fear and everything to gain from having strong, stable democracies on its borders, and that by aligning with the West, Russia joins all of us on a course to prosperity and greatness.' In a flagrant display of double standards, Cheney then flew to Kazakhstan where he praised the Putinesque dictatorship of President Nursultan Nazarbayev, expressing his 'admiration for what has transpired here in Kazakhstan over the past 15 years, both in terms of economic development as well as political development.'

It was not the sort of thing that Vladimir Putin could let pass without comment. Six days later, in an address to parliament, he made a cryptic remark that left the Americans scratching their heads, although its target was clear. During a long passage devoted to the importance of the military, he snarled: 'We can see what's going on in the world. We can see it! As they say, "Comrade Wolf knows who to eat." He keeps on eating, and listens to nobody. And apparently doesn't intend to listen.'

The Russian foreign minister, Sergei Lavrov, traditionally suave and restrained, lost his cool at talks in the Waldorf Astoria Hotel in New York. The meeting was about Iran, which the US suspected was trying to build a nuclear weapons capability by developing civilian technology provided by the Russians. The previous year Russia agreed to join a troika of EU nations (the UK, France and Germany) plus the United States and China in elaborating a joint approach. At one point Moscow had helpfully suggested that it could enrich fuel for Iran's as yet uncompleted Bushehr power station and have it shipped back to Russia. But in April 2006 the Russians announced the sale of an advanced air-defence system to Iran, infuriating the Americans.

Now, at the Waldorf, the six foreign ministers of the Iran group were exploring the possibility of sanctions against Iran. But after Cheney's Vilnius speech the gloves were off. Condoleezza Rice and her political director Nicholas Burns faced an increasingly agitated Lavrov across the dinner table. Burns recalls: 'Ordinarily in diplomacy people are polite to each other. And they don't personalise things. But at some point, midway through the dinner, Lavrov became very red in the face and very angry, and kind of pounded on the table and attacked me over public statements I had made, objecting to Russia's arms sales to Iran.' Lavrov invoked Cheney's speech and demanded that the Americans keep their criticisms to themselves. Burns was about to respond in kind, and Rice had to grip his arm to calm him.[4]

Such was the fraught atmosphere when the simmering conflict between Georgia and Russia erupted into violence. In September 2006 South Ossetian forces fired on a military helicopter carrying Georgia's defence minister, Irakli Okruashvili, causing him to make an emergency landing. Okruashvili had earlier promised to celebrate the following New Year in the

South Ossetian capital Tskhinvali – in other words, to accomplish the reincorporation of the region into Georgia by the end of 2006. Skirmishes broke out between Russian-armed South Ossetian soldiers and American-trained Georgians. Then, at the end of the month, Georgia arrested four Russian officers and accused them of espionage. International mediators were brought in, and after a few days the Russians were released – but not before they were paraded in front of television cameras, handcuffed and escorted by female Georgian police.

'The message of Georgia to our great neighbour Russia,' Saakashvili proclaimed, 'is: enough is enough.'

The Russians took it as a deliberate humiliation and retaliated with the harshest of sanctions: they recalled their ambassador, and cut all rail, sea, road, air and postal links. Georgians living in Moscow began to feel the heat: hundreds who could not produce legitimate papers were rounded up and put on planes bound for Tbilisi; schools were asked to provide lists of children with Georgian-sounding names so that the authorities could investigate whether they were illegal immigrants.

Murder of Anna Politkovskaya

Western governments were only getting into their stride with criticism of Russia's démarche against Georgia when something much more shocking happened. On 7 October 2006, Putin's 54th birthday, the journalist Anna Politkovskaya – known around the world for her bold reporting from Chechnya and criticism of the Kremlin – was shot dead in the lift of her apartment block in Moscow. The murder stunned people around the world – but not, apparently, Vladimir Putin. At first he gave no reaction at all. Then, four days later during a trip to Germany, he finally responded to a reporter's question by dismissing her as essentially unimportant.

It was, he said, 'a disgustingly cruel crime' and her killers should not go unpunished. But he added: 'Her impact on Russian political life was only very slight. She was well known in the media community, in human rights circles and in the West, but her influence on political life within Russia was very minimal. The murder of someone like her, the brutal murder of a woman and mother, was in itself an act directed against our country and against the Russian authorities. This murder deals a far greater blow to the authorities in Russia, and in Chechnya, to which she devoted much of her recent professional work, than did any of her publications.' It was one of Putin's more grotesque utterances: Politkovskaya's death, he was saying, was actually aimed against *him*, and would have a greater effect than her insignificant writings had. He lamented the murder of 'a woman and mother', not of the journalist.

I once asked his spokesman, Dmitry Peskov, whether Putin had read much of Politkovskaya's work. 'No,' he replied, shaking his head as if to underline that she wasn't worth reading. But it is hard to believe that Putin did not know of her work. She worked for the most prominent opposition newspaper, *Novaya gazeta*, co-owned by ex-President Mikhail Gorbachev. Her articles contained stinging criticism of human rights abuses in Russia and particularly of Putin's war in Chechnya. She had negotiated with the hostage-takers in the Dubrovka theatre crisis, and might have done the same during the Beslan school siege had she not been poisoned on the plane as she flew down from Moscow (another unexplained crime). Leaders of other countries condemned her murder and demanded a thorough investigation. The State Department described her as 'personally courageous and committed to seeking justice even in the face of previous death threats'.

Yet the Kremlin was unmoved.

Suspicions automatically fell on the leadership of Chechnya, and specifically its prime minister, Ramzan Kadyrov, whom Politkovskaya had fiercely criticised for human rights abuses. Some speculated that people loyal to him might have killed her for revenge, others that his enemies killed her to cast suspicion on him.

Kadyrov became prime minister of Chechnya, and later president, following the assassination of his father, Akhmat Kadyrov, whom Putin had installed as a pro-Russian president by means of a rigged election in 2003. Both had previously been on the rebel side – the elder Kadyrov was the mufti, or religious leader, of Chechnya under its separatist leader, Dzhokhar Dudayev, and had even called for a jihad against Russia. I once had tea with him in a house in rebel-held Chechnya in 1995. I recall that he asked rather disarmingly whether the British people were generally converting to Islam. The Kadyrovs later reversed their anti-Russian stance, however, and supported the war launched by Putin against the insurgents in 1999. Ramzan's militia, known as *kadyrovtsi* or Kadyrovites, acquired an unsavoury reputation – accused of torture, abductions and murders. Moscow installed first Akhmat, then Ramzan, as 'quisling' leaders – Chechens loyal to Moscow – under a new strategy to pacify the republic.

In the wake of the Chechen terrorist attack on the school in Beslan, the Kremlin deputy chief of staff, Vladislav Surkov, gave this explanation of Russia's strategy towards Chechnya: 'The solution is complex and hard. And we have begun to put it into practice. It entails the active socialisation of the northern Caucasus, the gradual creation of democratic institutions and the foundations of civil society, of an effective system of law and order, and of industrial capacity and social infrastructure, the overcoming of mass unemployment, corruption and the collapse of culture and education.' In reality, Kremlin policy amounted to the surrender of the republic to the loyal Ramzan Kadyrov, allowing him to enrich himself and run the place as he pleased so long as it was kept inside the Russian Federation. Kadyrov professes 'love' for Putin and calls him his 'idol'. He renamed the main street in Grozny, the capital, Putin Avenue.

The strategy has been partially successful. Despite the continuation of terrorist atrocities, mainly outside of Chechnya, by the remaining Islamic rebels, Kadyrov has restored a semblance of order within the republic. Grozny, totally destroyed in the two wars, has been largely rebuilt, using petro-dollars thrown at it from Moscow. It boasts Europe's largest mosque. It has normal shops and cafés again – something I thought I would never see when I reported from the bombed-out city in the late 1990s. But the strategy is a double-edged sword for Putin. The muscular, bearded Kadyrov is a wayward and ruthless individual. I visited his palace outside the village of Tsentoroy in 2008 and got a taste of his fabulous wealth – the grounds include an artificial lake and a zoo with panthers and leopards – and his primitive way of thinking. Asked what he thought about the death of the rebel leader Shamil Basayev, the mastermind behind most of the recent terrorist attacks in Russia, Kadyrov replied: 'I was delighted when I heard he was killed ... and then sad, because I wanted to kill him with my own hands.' He has introduced elements of Sharia law in his fiefdom, and congratulated men who sprayed paintballs at women who appeared in public with their heads uncovered.

American diplomats attending a riotous wedding reception in Dagestan in August 2006 witnessed Kadyrov, the guest of honour, dancing with a gold-plated pistol stuck down the back of his jeans and showering dancing children with hundred-dollar bills.[5]

True to Chechen tradition, Kadyrov is quick to promise retribution and blood vengeance on his enemies. On his watch many opponents have disappeared. His former bodyguard, Umar Israilov, who went public about torture and killings by the Kadyrovites that he had witnessed, was shot dead in Vienna in January 2009. Six months later Natalya Estemirova, who worked for the Memorial human rights centre in Grozny, was abducted and murdered. Kadyrov described her as a woman 'without honour, dignity or conscience'. As for Anna

Politkovskaya, in 2004 she published an account of a terrifying meeting with Ramzan Kadyrov, during which he boasted that his hobbies were fighting and women. The interview included the following comical exchange:

'What kind of education do you have?'

'Higher. Law. I'm graduating soon, sitting my exams.'

'What kind of exams?'

'What do you mean, what kind? Exams, that's all.'

'What's the name of the college you are graduating from?'

'A branch of the Moscow Business Institute, in Gudermes. The law faculty.'

'What are you specialising in?

'I'm a lawyer.'

'But is your diploma in criminal law, civil law ...?'

'I can't remember. I wrote something, but I've forgotten. There's a lot of events going on.'

Kadyrov was later made an honorary member of the Russian Academy of Natural Sciences.

Politkovskaya was taken back to see him again the next morning, and found him with a Kadyrovite in a black T-shirt who snarled at her: 'You should have been shot back in Moscow, in the street, the way they do it in Moscow.' And Kadyrov chimed in: 'You're an enemy. You should be shot.'

Politkovskaya described him as a 'baby dragon, raised by the Kremlin. Now they need to feed him. Otherwise he will set everything on fire.' She was about to publish another article about human rights abuses and torture in Chechnya when she was killed.

Her murder took place not only on Putin's birthday but two days after Kadyrov's. (I know this because I happened to be sitting next to Putin's spokesman, Dmitry Peskov, in a Moscow restaurant that evening, when he took out his mobile phone and called 'Ramzan' to congratulate him fulsomely on turning 30.) Could the murder have been someone's slightly belated 'birthday present' to the Chechen strongman? Or could it

have been Kadyrov's gift to his 'idol', Putin? In Russia's criminal underworld, such an idea is not implausible. Or was the
murder designed to discredit one or other of them? Or was
there some other motive? One thing was clear: the Kremlin
was intensely annoyed by Politkovskaya's work – particularly
some of her more extravagant claims, such as her assertion
that the 2002 Moscow theatre siege, which ended with 130
deaths, was stage-managed by one of Russia's secret services.

Prosecutors brought three Chechens to trial, but they were
acquitted in 2009 for lack of evidence. A retrial was later
ordered, and a fourth man, accused of being the actual assas-
sin, was arrested. In August 2011 a former police officer, Lt.
Col. Dmitry Pavlyuchenkov, who had appeared as a witness
in the earlier trial, was charged with plotting the murder. As
for who might have commissioned the crime – the courts have
not even come close to establishing that.

It's our oil

Russia faced more criticism during 2006 as Putin and the *siloviki* moved to assert greater control over the country's energy
resources, some of which belonged to foreign companies. We
saw earlier that the prospect of Yukos selling out to an American oil major was one of the factors that prompted the arrest
of Khodorkovsky and the nationalisation of his assets. Now
Putin turned his attention to so-called Production Sharing
Agreements which Boris Yeltsin had signed with Western oil
companies. Under a PSA, the foreign company finances all the
development and exploration, and when the oil or gas comes
on stream it is allowed to keep the first revenues to recoup its
costs; after that the profits are shared (in agreed proportions)
by the government and the company.

Putin believed these were humiliating agreements, the kind
of deal a Third World country enters into because it doesn't
have the skills or knowhow to extract the oil itself. The first

PSA, signed in 1994, was known as Sakhalin-2: a consortium called Sakhalin Energy, comprising Royal Dutch Shell (55 per cent) and two Japanese companies, Mitsui and Mitsubishi, was developing huge oil and gas fields near the island of Sakhalin in Russia's far east. The development costs foreseen in the agreement came to $10 billion, so this was the sum that Shell and its partners would be able to recover from the first sales before any revenues would begin to flow to the Russian state.

In 2005, however, Shell revealed that the development costs had doubled, to $20 billion. On a visit to the Netherlands in November, Putin 'gave a roasting' to Shell's CEO, Jeroen van der Veer. It meant Russia was going to lose $10 billion. It gave Putin the excuse he needed to overturn the 12-year-old deal, which he did by means of plotting and pressuring over the course of 2006. Instrumental to the government's strategy was Oleg Mitvol, a fierce environmental activist who was deputy head of the government's Service for Supervision of Natural Resources, Rosprirodnadzor. In May 2006 the service's representatives from the far east region came to see Mitvol in Moscow and showed him some photographs. 'It was unbelievable,' he recalls. 'There were photos of forests that had been turfed upside down, landslips, total chaos, on a huge scale. I said to them, "What is this?" and they said, it's Sakhalin Energy building pipelines.'[6] The construction work included almost a thousand pipes laid across spawning rivers, preventing fish from swimming upstream.

Mitvol made it a personal crusade. He took journalists to Sakhalin to show them the damage. Rosprirodnadzor estimated it would cost $50 billion just to clean up Aniva Bay, where large-scale dredging had ruined fishing grounds (something denied by Shell).

It was assumed by most observers at the time that Mitvol was simply doing the government's bidding, digging up dirt to bolster its case against Shell. The press called him the Kremlin's 'attack dog'. But he insists that he was motivated entirely by environmental concerns and worked more closely with Greenpeace and other environmental groups than with the Kremlin. He even says he had a call at one point from a 'very high official' who was concerned he was being too strident in his criticisms, and 'spoiling the investment climate'. Other environmentalists I have spoken to say they believe this: they too were appalled by the damage done to the forests and marine life, and they knew Mitvol to be a real eco-warrior, who, among other achievements, also helped to persuade Putin to ban seal-hunting.

That said, Mitvol could never have waged such a campaign against a major foreign investor without top-level backing, and Shell's position became impossible. In December Sakhalin Energy buckled to the pressure and sold 51 per cent of the project to Gazprom. Putin had succeeded in renationalising the world's biggest combined oil and natural gas project. At the signing ceremony, the president declared that the environmental problems could now be considered 'resolved'. The Sakhalin crisis was over, but the Kremlin's strong-arm tactics caused long-term damage to Russia's efforts to woo foreign investors.

For Putin, this was just part of a strategy, aimed at ensuring that Russia's strategic energy resources remained, or were retaken, under state control. Foreign companies were welcome to participate in joint projects, but Russia would never again give away its resources as Yeltsin had so recklessly done. New legislation was drafted to limit non-Russian involvement in 42 industries, including arms and aircraft, fisheries, precious metals and hydrocarbons.

Putin was less squeamish about other countries' strategic assets. As oil prices rose and the Kremlin's coffers filled up with petro-dollars, Russia started looking to invest abroad. Gazprom showed an interest in buying Centrica, Britain's major gas supplier. Then it began talks on acquiring a 50 per cent stake in the Central European Gas Hub at Baumgarten in Austria – the main distribution centre for EU gas supplies. The European Commission blocked the move.

In September 2006 it become known that the state-controlled bank VTB had quietly bought a 5 per cent stake in EADS, the world's biggest aerospace company, producer of Airbus and a great deal of defence equipment. Putin's diplomatic adviser Sergei Prikhodko then suggested they would like more – perhaps 25 per cent, enough to block major decisions. When Angela Merkel heard about it she told President Chirac of France in no uncertain terms that this could not be allowed to happen. Chirac and Merkel met Putin at Compiègne, outside Paris, towards the end of September and told him this was one investment that was not welcome.

On a visit to Bavaria the following month, Putin mocked the West for its nervousness: 'Why the hysteria? It's not the Red Army coming, but Russian businesses with money to invest.'

A Cold War encounter

It was Saturday 21 October 2006. The last, yellowing leaves were falling from the birch trees outside Putin's window at his country residence, Novo-Ogaryovo. It was cold and raining. He was already in a foul mood. The previous day he had attended a summit with 25 European Union leaders in Lahti, Finland. It was supposed to be an 'informal' meeting, a cosy gathering with no set agenda or agreements to be signed, but nonetheless he had had to listen to a litany of complaints – about the murder of Anna Politkovskaya, about his government's attempts to squeeze Shell out of the multi-billion-dollar Sakhalin-2 project, about Russia's unreliability as an energy provider, and about Georgia.

The Europeans explained that they were keen to build a close partnership with Russia's southern neighbour and deplored the sanctions recently introduced by the Kremlin.

But Putin expounded at some length his view that President Saakashvili was hell-bent on regaining the breakaway regions of Abkhazia and South Ossetia, and warned them that this would lead to bloodshed. Only his friend Jacques Chirac supported him, telling the others that relations with Russia were more important than Georgia.

It was the middle of the night before Putin got home. On Saturday afternoon he called his 11 most powerful colleagues – his Security Council – to his residence. He told them about his uncomfortable meeting with the EU leaders, and they considered their options in Georgia. Putin also had an appointment with the US secretary of state, Condoleezza Rice, who was waiting at her hotel in Moscow, but he was not looking forward to it. 'He didn't feel like meeting her,' one of his close aides recalls, 'but he knew he had to.'

Rice was wondering why their meeting was so delayed. 'Usually he saw me right away, unless he wanted to make a point,' she said later.[7]

After their working session the members of the Security Council drove to a nearby government lodge – a baronial-style chateau at Barvikha – for a special dinner. Three members, including the security council secretary, Igor Ivanov, and the future president, Dmitry Medvedev, had recent birthdays to celebrate.

Here, Putin decided to play a 'joke' on Rice. According to one of those present, he looked at his watch, and a mischievous smile appeared on his face. 'Why do we have to wind things up in a rush? Let's put on a little show for her. If she wants, tell her I will meet her here, but don't tell her I've got the entire Security Council with me.'

'It was five o'clock, five-thirty, six o'clock, six-thirty,' Rice recalls. 'Finally about seven-thirty they said, he's ready to see you now.'

She and the American ambassador, Bill Burns, were whisked out into the dark, wet countryside, along the elite

Rublyovo-Uspenskoye highway, dotted with ostentatious red-brick mansions, through the 'Luxury Village of Barvikha' with its Lamborghini showroom and designer boutiques, and then through the tall iron gates of the government estate.

Rice and Burns had never seen such a building in Russia before – all turrets and dark stairways, like Dracula's castle. Suddenly the doors of the dining room were flung open and the Americans were confronted with an unexpected sight – the full Russian Security Council, the very heart of Russian power, around a banquet table. Burns 'could hardly take breath', according to one witness, while Condi was full of composure. 'Oh,' she said, 'it's the Security Council.'

The Russians appreciated her sang-froid. 'She wasn't even an iron woman – much higher,' said a Putin aide.

Her old friend Sergei Ivanov joked to her: 'We are discussing top-secret matters. Here's some top-secret military intelligence documents. Would you like to see them, Condoleezza?' There was much laughter – and some raised eyebrows on the American side when the Russians brought out bottles of Georgian wine. This was just after the arrest of the Russian officers and the embargo on Georgian products. The Russians started telling crude jokes about Georgians – which Rice could understand, despite the interpreter's attempts to clean them up.

After a while, Rice said to Putin: 'You know, we have some work to do.'

Putin took his guests off to a side room, with defence minister Sergei Ivanov and the foreign minister Sergei Lavrov, who acted as interpreter. Here, the talk got serious.

Putin started lecturing Rice about Ukraine, its history and demographics, and why America was wrong to even contemplate bringing it into NATO. Ivanov recalled in an interview: 'Putin explained what Ukraine was – at least a third of the population are ethnic Russians – and the negative consequences that could arise, not only for us but for all of Europe if Ukraine and Georgia were dragged into NATO.'

According to Bill Burns, Rice retorted that sovereign states had the right to make their sovereign choices about which institutions or alliances they wished to belong to, and that this should not be seen as threatening.

But Putin was not at all persuaded by that. 'You do not understand what you are doing,' he said. 'You are playing with fire.'

Then the 'lecture' turned to the recent events in Georgia, and Rice decided to give as good as she got. 'President Bush has told me to come and say that if Russia does anything in Georgia, there will be a rupture in US–Russia relations.'

Ambassador Burns recalls that Putin's answer was unmistakable: if Georgian provocations caused a security problem, Russia would respond. Rice could feel Putin's tone turning hard-edged.

All of a sudden Putin stood up, looking angry and intimidating. Reflexively, Rice also stood up, and in her high heels she was now taller than the Russian, looking down at him. She remembers it as 'not a nice moment – probably the toughest moment between the two of us'.

Putin decided to tell it straight. 'If they [the Georgians] provoke any violence,' he said, 'there will be consequences! And you tell that to your president.'

Lavrov, interpreting, did not translate the last phrase, but Rice had understood. This was a forceful warning from an angry Putin – one that she would remember clearly two years later when Russia brought down the might of its armed forces on Georgia after Saakashvili launched an ill-conceived attack on South Ossetia.

A Cold War murder

There is, perhaps, no enemy more hateful to the KGB than one of their own who turns against them. Forgiveness for disloyalty is not something they teach their agents.

Alexander Litvinenko was an officer in the Soviet KGB and its successor, the FSB. In the 1990s he specialised in counter-terrorism and fighting organised crime. After service in Chechnya he was assigned to a new FSB unit called URPO, the Directorate for the Analysis and Suppression of Criminal Organisations, which in effect consisted of hit squads designed to take out the country's top mafia crime bosses. But Litvinenko became aware of corruption and links to organised crime in the organisation itself and began to rebel. In March 1998 he confided to the oligarch Boris Berezovsky that he and four other agents from his unit had been ordered to kill him. (Berezovsky at the time was the ultimate wheeler-dealer in the Kremlin, who had engineered Boris Yeltsin's re-election in 1996 and would soon help to organise his succession.) When Vladimir Putin was appointed director of the FSB in July that year, Berezovsky immediately took Litvinenko to see him and report on corruption in the organisation. According to the oligarch, Putin did not respond, so on 13 November Berezovsky went public, with an open letter to Putin in the newspaper *Kommersant*. Four days later Litvinenko and his four colleagues from the URPO unit held a press conference at which they made public their claim that they had been ordered to kill Berezovsky.[8] Litvinenko was immediately dismissed from the FSB, apparently on the personal orders of Putin, who told the journalist Yelena Tregubova later: 'Soon after becoming director of the FSB I fired Litvinenko and liquidated the unit in which he worked.' His objection was not that FSB agents were carrying out extra-judicial killings but that Litvinenko and his colleagues dared to go public about it. 'FSB officers should not stage press conferences. This is not their job. And they should not make internal scandals public.'[9]

During 1999 Litvinenko was twice arrested and imprisoned for months, but eventually acquitted. In November 2000 he fled to London and applied for political asylum, which he was granted. In London he worked for the now exiled Boris Berezovsky, campaigning against the Putin regime, and in October 2006 became a British citizen. His activities in London would have infuriated the Russian government in many ways. First, he was on the payroll of Berezovsky, one of Russia's most wanted men, whom the British government refused to extradite. (He was also alleged to receive a retainer from the British secret intelligence service, MI6.) Second, he was totally convinced of the complicity of the FSB in the 1999 apartment bombings which had triggered the second Chechen war, and published preliminary findings in a Russian newspaper and in a film. As noted earlier, several journalists and politicians who investigated these allegations died in mysterious circumstances.

In exile in London, Litvinenko did everything he could to provoke the Kremlin. His allegations seemed to grow ever more fantastic and obsessive, perhaps delusional: he accused the FSB not only of being behind Chechen terrorist attacks such as the Moscow theatre siege and the Beslan school crisis, but even of responsibility for terrorist attacks worldwide, including the 2005 London bombings. Even close friends regarded him as a fantasist, consumed by his hatred for Putin and the FSB. He claimed, with no proof, that the KGB had trained al-Qaeda's number two, Ayman al-Zawahiri, and that Putin was a paedophile. He developed close links to the Chechen separatist government in exile and lived next door to its foreign minister, Akhmed Zakayev. At a discussion of Anna Politkovskaya's death at London's Frontline Club, he stood up and accused Putin of personally ordering her murder.

A couple of weeks later, on 1 November 2006, Litvinenko met two visitors from Russia – both former intelligence officers, Andrei Lugovoi and Dmitry Kovtun – and had tea with them. He fell ill and died after an excruciating illness on 23 November. Investigators established that he had been poisoned with a rare radioactive substance, Polonium-210. A police investigation eventually concluded that the poison had been brought to Britain, possibly by Kovtun via Germany, where traces of the element were detected, and administered by Lugovoi, who had put it in Litvinenko's tea during their meeting. The agonising slow death of Litvinenko topped the news throughout November. Few had heard of the Russian, but as journalists and investigators pieced together the story of his poisoning, the British public was both scandalised by what seemed to be the enactment of a John le Carré-style plot, and terrified by the discovery of Polonium-210 traces around their capital city and on aeroplanes that had flown from Moscow. The events brought to mind the KGB's 'umbrella-tip' poisoning of a Bulgarian exile in London in 1978, at the height of the Cold War. The *Daily Mail* wrote that the 'tentacles of the KGB reach as far and formidably as ever'. It was suddenly remembered that in July 2006 the Duma had passed legislation allowing the security forces to hunt down and eliminate extremists worldwide. The definition of 'extremism' was explicitly widened to include anyone who libelled the Russian authorities – which Litvinenko certainly did, in spades.

Gruesome though the situation was, it was also expertly exploited by Berezovsky and his spin doctors, a PR company run by Margaret Thatcher's former image-maker, Lord Bell. They released a shocking photograph of Litvinenko on his deathbed, hairless and emaciated. Just before he died Litvinenko signed a statement composed for him by his friend Alex Goldfarb, who also worked for Berezovsky, in which he accused Vladimir Putin of personally ordering his murder. 'As I lie here I can distinctly hear the beating of wings of the angel of death,' he wrote, in somewhat over-elegant English, and continued: 'You may succeed in silencing one man, but a howl of protest from around the world will reverberate, Mr Putin, in your ears for the rest of your life.' Berezovsky could scarcely have found a more powerful weapon in his battle against the Kremlin than the death of his protégé.

Putin was in Helsinki, at an EU–Russia summit, the day

after Litvinenko's death, when his posthumous accusation was read out. Putin, of course, had no option but to answer questions about it at a news conference. Just as he had done with Politkovskaya, he seemed to play down Litvinenko's importance, saying merely, 'the death of a human being is always a tragedy'. Regarding the personal accusation against him, he dismissed it as a political provocation, probably written by other people. But privately – I was told by his press secretary Dmitry Peskov, who had to tell him about the deathbed note – Putin was livid. 'He can't believe that people are accusing him personally of ordering this murder,' he said. 'As a person, he is very upset by that.' When I asked why Putin didn't show that anger in public, since it might convince people of his innocence better than his normal stonewalling, Peskov replied: 'He doesn't like showing his feelings in public.'

Putin showed his feelings somewhat a few years later, though, when he spoke about the agent who betrayed 11 Russian spies, including the celebrated Anna Chapman, in the USA in 2010: 'They live by their own laws, and these laws are well known to all the special services. Things always end badly for traitors. They usually end up in the gutter, from alcohol or drugs.' Or poisoning, he might have added.

With the polonium trail leading inexorably to Moscow, Litvinenko's death – less than two months since Politkovskaya's – had a dramatic effect on Western perceptions of Russia, and in particular on its relations with the UK. The prime minister Tony Blair, anxious to preserve his good relationship with Putin, urged a cautious approach, but some members of his cabinet strongly objected to the idea of 'going soft' on a regime that was flouting human rights. Blair convened an emergency session of COBRA, the government's crisis response committee. Ironically, Vladimir Putin himself had once been invited to witness a security briefing in the COBRA room at 10 Downing Street. That was in October 2005, not long after the bombings in London. Putin had shocked his hosts by declaring, according to an eyewitness, 'We know well how you pursue terrorists, and we are impressed with your professionalism. But when we identify a terrorist, he's dead.'

In January 2007 British investigators concluded that Litvinenko's murder was a 'state-sponsored assassination orchestrated by Russian security services', and in May the Foreign Office officially asked the Russians to extradite the chief suspect, Andrei Lugovoi. The Russians retorted that their constitution does not allow for the extradition of Russian citizens. The Russians offered to put Lugovoi on trial in Russia, but claimed that the evidence provided by the British in their extradition request was insufficient for them to base a case on. This was almost certainly true: the UK authorities were hardly going to hand over all their evidence to the Russians, since much of it was based on their own top-secret intelligence gathering. But without it, the Russians would neither extradite Lugovoi nor put him on trial. There was deadlock. Lugovoi used the time to have himself elected to the Duma, where he would enjoy immunity from prosecution. He freely gave interviews, in which he blamed Boris Berezovsky for the murder.

On 28 June 2007 a cabinet reshuffle gave Britain a new foreign secretary, David Miliband. He spent his first weekend with briefing papers that shocked him. 'What I hadn't quite recognised,' he recalled in an interview, 'was the rotten state of Anglo-Russian relations, dating back to Iraq and then to the whole Berezovsky business, which the Russians saw as a political move by us. So there was a deep political problem, even without the terrible events of the murder of Litvinenko.' [10]

A week later the Kremlin turned down Britain's request for the extradition of Lugovoi. 'We had to decide how to respond, and we didn't want the Russians to go wildly over the top – we didn't want to break off diplomatic relations.' Britain expelled four Russian diplomats and froze relations with the FSB, even though that meant cutting off the main channel for collaboration in the fight against international terrorism. It is not clear whether the British side actually understood this. Russia's foreign minister, Sergei Lavrov, recalls: 'We had to explain that the FSB, in the Russian Federation, is the lead agency that coordinates anti-terrorist activities and heads the national anti-terrorism committee. So if cooperation with the FSB was no longer in the plans of our British counterparts, we would have to freeze our cooperation in that area, and this was regrettable.' [11]

Russia expelled four British diplomats in retaliation, and sneered at London's persistent request for extradition. President Putin reminded Britain that '30 people are hiding out in London who are wanted by Russian law enforcement agencies for serious crimes – and London does not even think of extraditing them'. He was sitting, in classic Putin fashion, in a forest clearing, discussing current affairs with youth activists. He went on: 'They don't extradite people hiding on their own territory, and give insulting advice to our country to change our constitution. They need to change their brains, not our constitution.'

Clearly relations had hit rock bottom. It was time for Miliband to try to calm things. 'We had to cooperate together on Iran, on terrorism, even on climate change. So I suggested that we meet with foreign minister Lavrov, and we proposed that we meet him in the UN building in September. It was important to show that we were open for business on the diplomatic front, even though we were pursuing justice in the Litvinenko case.'

The rookie British foreign minister was in for a shock. Lavrov had practically lived in the UN headquarters for about 17 years, including ten as Russia's envoy. He is one of the shrewdest operators I have met, with an encyclopaedic knowledge of two decades of diplomacy. He likes to chain-smoke, sip whisky and deploy his arguments like rapiers. 'I went in with a football analogy,' Miliband recalls. 'I was talking to him about which football team he supported, but I got very short shrift on that, and then the rest of the 30 to 40-minute meeting was a very, very tough lesson in diplomacy from someone who felt that they'd been around the block, they knew what the score was and they weren't going to take any lessons from me. So it was a pretty robust encounter and a pretty tough way to start a relationship.'

In fact, Lavrov has a different memory of Miliband's small talk, equally inappropriate. He recalls with a laugh: 'David started our conversation by asking why our party, United Russia, was a partner of the Tories, and not the Labour Party. For me, it was unexpected. Inter-party cooperation has nothing to do with me, but he was extremely interested in this.' As for fresh ideas on how to get over the Litvinenko crisis, says Lavrov, 'I heard nothing. I repeated the Russian position, including the prosecutor general's offer to open a joint investigation with the British, if they were provided with all the materials at the disposal of British investigators.'

Putin had referred to Britain's 'insulting' demand as a 'remnant of colonial thinking', and Lavrov took up the theme. Miliband recalls: 'He said we needed to stop looking at ourselves as an imperial power, who could tell other countries to change their constitutions. He was absolutely clear about that.'

Far from healing the rift, it widened even further after Miliband's meeting with Lavrov. In December the Kremlin announced it was closing two British Council offices in Russia, on the pretext of unpaid taxes and irregularities in its official status. Many saw it as an own goal, since the British Council's main tasks include teaching English and organising cultural exchanges. But Lavrov decided the offices were 'in violation of an international convention on consular relations' – while at the same time explicitly saying the action was further retaliation for Britain's 'unilateral actions' against Russia – specifically the freezing of negotiations on visa facilitation.

David Miliband looks back at his time jousting with Lavrov

and sees it is a clash of post-imperial nations. 'I've come to believe that Russia believes that Britain is a declining power and Britain believes that Russia is a declining power. That is a recipe, not for misapprehension, but it's a recipe for the sort of toughness and difficulty and, in some ways, unwillingness to compromise, that seems to go with the territory of British–Russian relations.'

For five years political contacts between the two countries remained virtually frozen. And even after a new prime minister, David Cameron, visited Moscow in September 2011, relations remained in the doldrums, beached on the sandbar of that atrocious Cold War murder in London in 2006.

Showing initiative

The spate of murders, which would continue over the coming years, destroyed Putin's attempts to portray his country as a free and modern democracy. Dozens of journalists were murdered in Vladimir Putin's two terms as president. Not all the cases were politically motivated, and few of the victims had the stature of Anna Politkovskaya. But hardly any of the murders have been solved, giving the impression that journalists can be killed with impunity in Russia, especially if they have angered the authorities. The journalist Politkovskaya and the political exile Litvinenko had both earned themselves enemies in high places. They were extremely hostile to the Putin regime – indeed both wrote in rather similar terms, accusing the FSB of terrible subversive acts that allegedly sacrificed hundreds of innocent lives in order to shore up the regime.

In his investigation of the Litvinenko affair, Martin Sixsmith concludes that Putin himself did not order the killing, but that he can be implicated in the affair 'because he created the atmosphere and conditions in which the killing could take place, in which an enterprising group of current or former FSB men read the signals from the Kremlin and embarked on their own initiative.' [12] I think the same can be said about the Politkovskaya murder. In both cases, it is likely that the assassins did not receive, or even require, a direct order, nor did they need permission to kill, because they knew that 'taking out' an 'enemy of the state' had the tacit approval of the authorities. They may have been acting on their own initiative, for revenge or to 'please' their masters. Either way, they knew they would not be punished.

The very fact that the FSB had a unit known as URPO, whose operatives specialised in unlawful killings, speaks volumes about Russia today. The unit may have been disbanded by Putin, but it would be naïve to think that the FSB has suddenly become a club of amiable Clouseaus. Or that the fair trial and the jury have replaced the revolver and the phial of polonium.

MEDIA, MISSILES, MEDVEDEV

A Western PR machine

Two thousand and six should have been a landmark year in Russia's post-communist history, and in President Putin's campaign to bring his country back to prominence as a respected and valued player on the world stage. Russia had become a member of the G8 group of leading industrialised nations in 1997, and this year, for the first time, it was its turn to chair it – a chance to shape the global agenda and to impress with a flawless summit in July, to be hosted by Putin in his home town, St Petersburg.

As we have seen, however, the year began with Russia cutting off gas supplies to Ukraine – hardly the image it was looking for. In the preceding months Putin had already unnerved the West with a series of moves aimed at tightening his own grip on power and stifling the opposition, including his curbs on NGOs and the unleashing of the youth group Nashi to cow both political opponents and uppity foreign ambassadors.

Already there were calls from conservative quarters to expel Russia from the G8, or at the very least for President

Bush to boycott the St Petersburg summit.

In the gloomy corridors of the presidential administration, hidden behind the dark-red walls of the Kremlin, they came up with a novel idea: Russia needed to project its image better. They needed a Western public-relations company to help them. There was no tender.[1] Personal contacts led them to a leading New York PR firm, Ketchum, and a European partner, GPlus, based in Brussels. The most senior executives from the two companies flew into Moscow and made a joint pitch to Putin's press secretary Alexei Gromov, and his deputy Dmitry Peskov. (The two men divided the role of spokesman between them: Gromov was in overall charge, but the fluent English-speaker Peskov dealt almost exclusively with the foreign press.)

It was at this point that the directors of GPlus – former journalist colleagues of mine – asked me to join their team as chief Russia consultant. Much of this chapter is based on my experiences there.

We saw our main task as Kremlin advisers as a rather simple one: to teach the Russians about how the Western media operate and try to persuade them to adopt the best practices of government press relations. We were advisers, not spokespeople. But whereas the Westerners who advised Boris Yeltsin's government on economics in the 1990s were beating on an open door, advising Putin's team on such an 'ideological' subject as media relations was never going to be so easy. Peskov did, in fact, show great interest in studying Western practices, but after some initial success we watched our 'client' drifting back into their old ways. As the Politkovskaya murder was followed by the Litvinenko murder, and then by the Russian invasion of Georgia, I began to wonder whether the very reason the Kremlin had decided to take on a Western PR agency was because they knew in advance that their image was about to nosedive.

They were prepared to pay big money to try to burnish that image. Ketchum declarations filed with the US Department of

Justice show that the Russians paid, in the early years, almost $1 million a month.[2] (A separate Ketchum contract with Gazprom – in deep trouble over its 'gas wars' with Ukraine – cost about the same). The financial arrangements were not directly with the Kremlin, but with a Russian bank, thus avoiding the need to be approved in the state budget.[3] The whole idea was criticised by some Russian media, which wondered why the Kremlin needed a Western (as opposed to a Russian) PR agency, and why it was not put out to tender as a state contract.[4]

The biggest problem Ketchum faced was that the Russians had little clue about how the Western media function. Based on their experience of the domestic media, they were genuinely convinced that we could *pay for* better coverage – that a positive op-ed in the *Wall Street Journal*, for example, had a certain price. They believed that journalists write what their newspaper proprietors (or governments) order them to write, and wanted to 'punish' correspondents who wrote critically about them by refusing to invite them to press events (thereby, in fact, forfeiting the chance to influence them). They subjected the *Guardian*'s Moscow correspondent Luke Harding (and his family) to constant harassment, apparently because of an interview his paper published with Boris Berezovsky in which he called for Putin to be overthrown – even though Harding had nothing to do with the conduct or content of the interview.[5] At the height of the Litvinenko affair, three members of the BBC's Russian team in Moscow were attacked in the street. All this was hardly likely to incline the journalistic community towards the kind of positive coverage the Kremlin craved. They would constantly demand that Ketchum 'use our technologies' to improve coverage. I had no idea what they meant. The technology we wanted them to use was a West Wing-style press room, every morning at ten o'clock. But it never happened.

In briefing-paper after briefing-paper we hammered away at our basic theme – open up to the press. Mix with journalists, take them for lunches, schmooze, give them titbits off the record, and gradually win them over. Speak to them, explain yourselves, and they will begin to trust you. Give interviews and get on air, because if you don't your opponents will, and they will set the agenda. It worked for a while. Peskov held a few dinners for Moscow correspondents in fancy restaurants (rather more formal than the kind of thing we really had in mind), and that went down well. They instituted 'Tuesday briefings' with selected ministers. The Moscow press corps was delighted. But after the murder of Anna Politkovskaya, Peskov became too worried: he knew that whatever the formal topic of a briefing, journalists would end up asking about human rights and democracy. Safer not to meet them.

Much of Ketchum's work involved the kind of things that most governments get done internally, by their embassies and foreign ministry – in whom the Kremlin evidently had little faith. We organised press conferences for government ministers when they travelled abroad, and provided briefing papers for them with the questions they were likely to be asked (and sometimes with the answers we thought they ought to give – though they rarely used them). We drafted articles for ministers (and even the president) which were generally redrafted out of all recognition in Moscow and became so unreadable that they were difficult to place in any newspaper. Part of the mystery of this aspect of the work was that Peskov would ask us to draft an article for, say, the energy minister, or the foreign minister, but give us no guidance whatsoever as to what they wished to say. He would usually reply, if asked: 'Just put in what you think he should say.' So we would draft articles –and speeches – blind. And then they would be completely rewritten. Foreign minister Lavrov, in particular, (rightly) had no interest in having his articles drafted by ignorant foreigners.

Every day Ketchum provided the Kremlin with three press reviews, compiled in Japan, Europe and the United States, which gave a comprehensive – perhaps rather too detailed –

picture of coverage of Russia around the globe. The reviews often came to well over a hundred pages, with summaries and full texts of any article that mentioned the word Russia, but with little analysis. During the period of the first contract, for the G8 year, Ketchum employed an outside agency to colour-code every article in the press, with red, yellow or green, to indicate negative, neutral or positive stories, so that by the end of the G8 year this could be plotted on a graph to demonstrate that there were more greens and fewer reds. This is a common PR technique which unfortunately did not transport well to the nuanced world of Kremlin politics. Often the colours seemed to be picked at random, and bore little relation to the content – even sports news or a weather report could turn up with a red or green button. (This 'service' was eventually dropped, after it was realised it was useless.)

The Kremlin received regular 'road-maps' – 'big picture' PR strategies for the coming three months / six months / year, wrapped in management-speak about 'leveraging opportunities going forward', 'deliverables' and 'reaching out to stakeholders'. In practice much of the work boiled down to the more mundane business of helping with ministerial visits, organising press conferences and briefing on key developments in the West.

As a newcomer to the PR world I was amused by the nebulous concepts of 'influencer' relations and 'third-party outreach' – cultivating contacts with experts and 'thought leaders' who had an interest in Russia. Ketchum was meticulous in reporting any contact, such as having lunch with someone from a think-tank or attending a lecture, which would all end up in the record of completed tasks sent each month to Moscow. And if one of those influencers produced a positive line in some article, this could then be quoted in a report-back as a 'success'. I remember one report of Ketchum's achievements included a quotation from the Canadian prime minister, saying, 'I think Russia's made an enormous amount of progress in recent years.' It was not clear whether the Kremlin really believed that we contributed to that.

One undoubted success was the introduction of 'tele-briefings', where journalists could call in to participate in a news conference with Peskov or a government minister. The Russians found these more agreeable than face-to-face meetings, and finally acquired a way to interpret their actions to the press.

Over the three years working with him I got to know Dmitry Peskov fairly well. Tall, smartly dressed and in his early 40s, he has a charming, easy-going style, and speaks excellent English (and also Turkish, having worked for many years in the embassy in Ankara). He was spotted by President Yeltsin during a trip to Turkey in 1999 and brought back to work in the presidential administration. When Putin came to power he became head of the Kremlin's press relations office and deputy spokesman to the president. Ever since then he has been a priceless asset, almost the only person in Russia with the ability, the authority and the willingness to give on-the-record interviews to the foreign press. As a result he was in huge demand. My colleagues in the BBC Moscow bureau, who had an insatiable demand for talking heads, used to plead with me: 'Please get them to provide other spokespeople. Dmitry's great, but he just doesn't have the time ...' But other than a few ministers, no one else in Russia was willing to give interviews to the Western press. No wonder they found it so hard to get their message across.

I gave Dmitry media training to help him feel more comfortable in front of the television camera. It was an opportunity not just to draw his attention to his voice or mannerisms, but also to subject him to the toughest possible questions, and train him in the art of expressing a few essential ideas succinctly and coherently. Many interviewees who have not studied how a Western news bulletin works tend to ramble on interminably, never getting to the point.

During a G8 summit in Germany in 2007, Peskov approached me with a special task – to rewrite and spice up a speech President Putin was to make in Guatemala City in support of Russia's bid to host the 2014 Winter Olympics in Sochi. The bid was successful – for which I naturally take the entire credit! (In truth, most of my suggestions were not accepted!) When Dmitry Medvedev became president in 2008 I gave advice about videos and podcasts, and saw at least some of my ideas incarnated in his innovative video-blogs.

Dmitry's boss, Alexei Gromov, was one of the most important men in the Kremlin during Putin's presidency. He was described to me as 'the only person who could walk into Putin's office without an appointment'. He saw him every day and was a constant sounding board for policy ideas. He also exercised tight control over the Russian media. I was once drinking tea in his office when the head of Russian state television walked in. Gromov introduced me briefly to him, then waved him through to his back office, asking him to pour himself a drink and wait. This was the regular weekly pep-talk, where Gromov talked through the agenda for the coming period and made sure coverage would be 'correct'.

Like Peskov, Gromov started out in the diplomatic service, posted to Prague and Bratislava, and was brought back to head Yeltsin's press service in 1996. He has a penchant for patterned cardigans and smokes Marlboros through long cigarette-holders. As Putin's press secretary he dealt exclusively with the Russian media, leaving the foreign press to Dmitry Peskov. During one meeting with Gromov I raised one of my perennial themes: the West regarded Russia as reverting more and more to Soviet ways of thinking and behaviour, and in order to combat this it was necessary not only to stop *acting* like the Soviets (by banning opposition demonstrations, for example) but also to forcefully repudiate the Soviet past in speeches and in documentaries that could be shown on state television. Gromov's reply was revealing. He conceded that this would have a positive effect on the West's attitudes, but, he said, 'we have to think about domestic public opinion, which generally is positive about the Soviet Union. We have to think about political stability inside the country first and foremost.' I found it depressing that he simply accepted that many Russians, especially older ones, were nostalgic about the past, and that challenging this view could lead to 'instability'. With his influence over the state media, he could have launched a campaign to *change* perceptions of the past. After all, this had been done under Gorbachev and Yeltsin, and attitudes had changed. Now the government, by its inaction, was allowing Stalinism and communism to enjoy a revival. Worse than that – as we shall see in a later chapter – school textbooks were being rewritten to play down Stalin's crimes.

Over the years I tried to be as candid as possible in my advice, even if it went beyond the normal bounds of 'public-relations advice'. This was a period when the authorities began to break up demonstrations staged by a new opposition coalition known as The Other Russia, led by the chess champion Garry Kasparov. I explained to my Kremlin colleagues that no amount of PR would lessen the damage done by a photograph of riot police beating up old ladies. But of course my comments were misdirected. I have little doubt that Dmitry Peskov agreed with me wholeheartedly: but it was not his job to change the police tactics.

I was once asked to comment on an article drafted in Russian for President Medvedev, with a view to having it published in the prestigious *Foreign Affairs* magazine. This was in 2008, following the war against Georgia. The article was so badly written (as though at least three people with divergent views had contributed to it) that I sent back an excoriating review, suggesting that unless they wanted their president to be seen as a crazy schizophrenic they should tear the article up. The eyebrows of my professional PR colleagues shot up, concerned about upsetting their employers. But Peskov

President Yeltsin hands Vladimir Putin the seals of office,
31 December 1999. (www.kremlin.ru)

President Putin's
inauguration speech,
7 May 2000. (www.
kremlin.ru)

Putin's St Petersburg friend Alexei Kudrin became Russia's
most successful finance minister. (www.kremlin.ru)

Putin with his early team of reformers, German Gref,
Alexei Kudrin and Andrei Illarionov.
(Courtesy of RIA Novosti)

President George
W. Bush with Putin
in 2001, when Bush
looked into Putin's
eyes and saw his soul.
(www.kremlin.ru)

Bush and Putin
became good friends
despite serious policy
clashes.
(www.kremlin.ru)

US Secretary of State Condoleezza Rice and Russian defence minister Sergei Ivanov came to trust one another after 9/11. (www.kremlin.ru)

Tony and Cherie Blair with the Putins at the Mariinsky Theatre, St Petersburg, March 2000. (www.kremlin.ru)

Putin with one of his closest Western allies, Italian leader Silvio Berlusconi. (www.kremlin.ru)

Putin got on less well with German chancellor Angela Merkel, whom he tried to scare with his dog. (www.kremlin.ru)

Victims of the Putin regime? Top left: oil tycoon Mikhail Khodorkovsky. (Photo by Oleg Nikishin/Getty Images). Top right: journalist Anna Politkovskaya. (Photo by Schreibstube). Bottom left: ex-KGB agent Alexander Litvinenko. (Photo by Natasja Weitsz/Getty Images). Bottom right: Putin's placeman in Chechnya, Ramzan Kadyrov. (Photo by Ruslan Alkhanov/AFP/Getty Images)

All smiles at Putin's first meeting in 2004 with the Western-oriented Georgian leader Mikheil Saakashvili. Saakashvili later mocked the Russian as 'Liliputin'. (www.kremlin.ru)

Viktor Yushchenko and Yulia Tymoshenko, leaders of Ukraine's Orange Revolution.
(Courtesy of European Peoples Party)

Putin's patriots. The Russian leader holds regular meetings with his young supporters in Nashi. (www.kremlin.ru)

ТОВАРЫ ДЛЯ ОФИСА

Putin's portraits for sale in a stationery store.
(Vladimir Menkov)

Putin as a child dreamt of joining the KGB. (www. kremlin.ru)

After university he fulfilled his dream. (www.kremlin.ru)

Putin with his wife Lyudmila on a rare public appearance together.
(www.kremlin.ru)

Putin's appearances with his dog Koni are more frequent.
(www.kremlin.ru)

Putin the judoist.
(www.kremlin.ru)

Putin discovers
two Grecian
urns in the
Black Sea in the
summer of 2011.
His spokesman
later admit-
ted they were
planted for him.
(Courtesy of
RIA Novosti)

Doing the butterfly stroke in an icy Siberian river.
(Courtesy of RIA Novosti)

Putin at the controls of a jetplane. (www.kremlin.ru)

Putin and Dmitry Medvedev celebrate the latter's election as president in May 2008. The crowd on Red Square chanted only Putin's name. (www.kremlin.ru)

During the 2009 financial crisis, Putin forces billionaire Oleg Deripaska to sign a paper promising to get the one-factory town of Pikalyovo working again. (Courtesy of RIA Novosti)

July 2009: President Barack Obama explains his plans for a US–
Russian 'reset' at Putin's dacha. (www.kremlin.ru)

June 2010: President Medvedev heads off with Barack Obama
for a hamburger lunch. (www.kremlin.ru)

Foreign minister Sergei Lavrov and Secretary of State
Hillary Clinton press a toy 'reset button'. (www.kremlin.ru)

The modernis-
ing Medvedev
is rarely seen
without his
iPad. (Cour-
tesy of RIA
Novosti)

Dmitry Medvedev became president in 2008 knowing he would probably hand back to Putin four years later. (www.kremlin.ru)

In September they told a congress of the United Russia party that they had agreed to swap roles, allowing Putin to regain the presidency for as much as 12 more years. (www.kremlin.ru)

thanked me for my advice.

However much Peskov came to trust my judgement, I came to realise that it made little difference. The Kremlin wanted us to help distribute the message, not change it. They did not entrust us with anything at all in advance. We would ask for advance copies (or at least extracts) of important speeches, for example, so that we could prime the early morning news bulletins, whet the appetite for more, and ensure maximum effect by the end of the day. This is standard practice in Western government press offices. But the Kremlin did not trust its media advisers. We received the texts of Putin's speeches at the same time as the journalists. As for the public-relations efforts that received attention in the West – Putin's macho photo-shoots, for example – they had nothing to do with us. We always learned about them after the event.

Ketchum won a prestigious public relations award for its efforts in 2007, but I know the Kremlin wanted its PR consultants to be 'pushier' – not just arranging press conferences and interviews, or providing them with briefing materials and analytical papers, but actually trying to manipulate journalists into painting a more positive picture of Russia. I remember a conversation with Peskov's deputy in which he criticised us for failing to follow up an interview given by a government minister to ensure that the journalist wrote it up in 'the right way'. Newspapers would describe us as spin-doctors, endeavouring to play down Putin's human rights record – and, indeed, perhaps that is what the Kremlin wished for. But in fact, Ketchum's principal role was to inform the Kremlin about how they were being perceived, and to encourage them to take the initiative to change things. What really needed changing, of course, was the message, not the way it was conveyed – but that was a political challenge far beyond Ketchum's remit.

Other Western approaches

The Ketchum project was not the only 'propaganda tool' employed by the Kremlin at this time. Russia Today (later rebranded RT) was set up at the end of 2005 as a 24-hour satellite television station, aiming to give a 'Russian take' on world events and to inform worldwide audiences about Russian politics and life. With a budget of $60 million in its first year, it employed Russians with first-class English and also foreign nationals as presenters, and looked as professional as many of its competitors in the global television market. Unlike rivals such as BBC World News, CNN or newcomers like France-24, however, it did not set out to be a dispassionate news source, covering stories on their merits. RT's mission is to explain Russia to the world, so there is an emphasis on domestic political stories and little attempt to provide comprehensive coverage from other countries. The method used is much less crude than its Soviet precursors, which painted a black-and-white picture of a West riven by class struggle and poverty, contrasted with a Soviet Union free of problems. RT – understanding that viewers also have other sources of information – does not shrink from covering opposition activities and even criticism of Russian policies. It thereby manages to create an illusion of plurality in the Russian media which in fact belies the truth: RT is the exception in Russia's television system, because it is aimed at a foreign audience. It showed its true colours and purpose during the 2008 war with Georgia, when all pretence at balance was dropped and Russia Today became a full-blooded propagandist for the Kremlin.

The station was founded by a state-owned news agency, RIA Novosti, which grew out of the Soviet-era Novosti Press Agency (APN) and like it combines two separate roles: firstly, it is a news-gathering organisation which provides news reports primarily to foreign audiences (APN's network of foreign correspondents also included a large number of undercover

KGB spies); secondly, its foreign bureaus serve as hubs for the propagation of Russian government information. The latter function overlapped greatly with the role Ketchum and GPlus were expected to play, and this led to a certain amount of friction. I got the impression that RIA Novosti was none too happy about its role as official Kremlin propagandist being usurped by foreigners. Occasionally GPlus, for example, would be asked to set up a press briefing with the Russian envoy to Brussels, Yevgeny Chizhov, only to find that the ambassador was already working with RIA Novosti on the same project – except that RIA, with its enormous resources, was doing it in style, with a video link to Moscow.

RIA Novosti was the prime mover behind another image-making innovation – the Valdai International Discussion Club which began its work in Putin's second term. The Valdai Club brings together about 50 foreign 'Russia watchers' (mainly journalists and academics) each September for ten days of debates with Russian specialists, combined with sightseeing (every year a more exotic location) and meetings with top Kremlin officials (every year a better, more senior crop). The first session, in 2004, was at Lake Valdai, north of Moscow, from which the Club derived its name, and the surprise guest of honour was President Putin himself – fuming in the aftermath of the Beslan tragedy – who was willing to spend several hours with the group, letting off steam and answering their questions. Since then the itinerary has included trips to Kazan, Chechnya, Siberia and St Petersburg, and featured lavish lunches with Putin and Medvedev (separately) at their dachas outside Moscow or in Sochi. In 2009 Medvedev apparently decided that Valdai was too closely associated with Putin; he held his own event for foreign experts, the 'Yaroslavl Global Policy Forum', instead.

Valdai was a brand-new way of influencing outsiders – much more subtle than giving an interview on CNN or the BBC, or trying to steer Moscow correspondents towards giving more favourable coverage. This was soft propaganda – quite a risk, since hosting 50 foreigners in five-star hotels for ten days is not cheap and certainly not guaranteed to change perceptions overnight. The idea was that the guests – experienced Kremlin-watchers who write in academic journals, advise governments, and appear as pundits in the media – would become better disposed towards Putin if they were given the opportunity to meet him over a long lunch and spend a week or so debating issues with friendly Russian experts and officials.

Critics in the Moscow intelligentsia are utterly dismissive of the project, claiming that the majority of participants are 'useful idiots' who have the wool pulled over their eyes and go home parroting the propaganda that's served up to them with the lobster terrine and fine wines.

Lilia Shevtsova of the Carnegie Endowment, for example, says the Kremlin uses Valdai to 'co-opt' and manipulate Western commentators: 'Foreign guests come to the Valdai meetings to absorb the opinions of Russia's leaders and then transmit them to the rest of the world.'[6] I would agree entirely that this is what the Kremlin wants to happen. Otherwise they would not spend so much time and money on it. But having attended three Valdai conferences, I think she overestimates the effect. Maybe some participants become less critical – and it is certainly true that almost everyone, Valdai member or not, tends to be mesmerised by personal contact with Vladimir Putin (Margaret Thatcher used to have a similar effect, even on her critics). But the coverage that spills out from these weeks is not all sycophantic. Ariel Cohen of the conservative Heritage Foundation and the experienced Marshal Goldman are hardly Kremlin stooges.

Meeting officials is always better than not meeting them, and most of the Valdai participants are experienced enough to be able to separate the propaganda from the truth. By and large those who arrive well disposed leave well disposed, and those who arrive believing Putin is crooked and undemocratic rarely change their minds. Most journalists and scholars would welcome the opportunity to meet so many government officials in any country; it does not mean you automatically accept their views, far less 'transmit' them. Spending several hours listening to Putin, for example, does not necessarily make one fall in love with him, because one has a chance to scrutinise his mannerisms and obsessions, even at times his anger, and for a democrat the experience is far from comforting. My criticism of the participants is not that they fall for the propaganda, but that few of them – perhaps being too much in awe of him – take this unique opportunity to *argue* with Putin: it's a case of asking a (usually soft) question, and patiently listening to the interminable answer – and never daring to follow up or interrupt, or tell him why he is wrong. Too many of the questions – even from the 'nasty' crowd – come larded with flattery and compliments. I know privately from Dmitry Peskov that Putin himself (who quite clearly enjoys an argument) despairs at the lack of combative questioning.

Putin also appears to doubt the efficacy of the Valdai effort. At his fourth meeting with the group, in 2007, he kicked off with a rather caustic comment that underlined his apparent belief that the Western media follow some kind of 'instructions': 'In recent years I've become convinced that the media in Europe and North America are very disciplined. I don't see any obvious results from our meetings in your publications, though I'm sure that you personally are getting to understand our country better. We'd be glad if you would transmit something of what you learn to your readers and viewers, to combat the strong stereotypes that exist in the West.'

Much more pernicious than the Valdai Club (at least in intent, if not in reality) is the Institute for Democracy and Cooperation – yet another innovation of the second Putin term. With offices in New York and Paris, it is the ultimate Soviet-style revival in today's Russia: a think-tank that aims to prove that human rights and democracy are trampled on in the West rather than in Russia. According to its mission statement, the Institute hopes to 'improve the reputation of Russia in the US' and to provide 'analysis' of US democracy. Its New York office is run by Andranik Migranian, an Armenian by birth but a fierce supporter of Russia's alleged right to interfere in neighbouring states; its Paris office is run by Natalia Narochnitskaya, a Russian nationalist and apologist for Slobodan Milosevic. Having given them both media training before they were deployed to the front, I could say with some confidence that the West had little to fear from their mission to undermine faith in Western democracy, but I was sure they would both enjoy their sinecures in America and France.

Munich

In February 2007 I was asked by the Kremlin to travel to Germany, where President Putin was due to make a speech at the prestigious Munich Security Conference, held each year in the Bavarian capital. His press team was anticipating a strong reaction and wanted some help in arranging interviews for Dmitry Peskov afterwards. As usual, we were not given any details about the content of the speech, but Peskov and his deputy, Alex Smirnov, were excited: 'This will be very tough!' they said. 'We'll want to speak to journalists to make sure they've understood.' They needn't have worried: it was the bluntest, most powerful speech of Putin's career.

The Bayerischer Hof hotel was ringed with security officers and teeming with senior world figures – not only dozens of defence ministers and generals but parliamentarians, politicians and eminent journalists. None of them was expecting the tongue-lashing Putin was about to deliver. Early in 2007, according to those in the know, the Russian president had finally lost patience with the Americans. '*Dostali!*' he told his aides: 'I've had enough!' The immediate cause of frustration was Washington's decision to push ahead with its plans for a national anti-missile defence system based in Europe. It had just begun talks with Poland about the possibility of basing ten interceptor missiles on its territory, and with the Czech Republic about building a state-of-the-art missile-tracking radar station there. Early in his presidency Putin had reluctantly acquiesced in Bush's decision to abandon the Anti-Ballistic Missile treaty, but he had no intention of being so lame when it came to the new defensive system that the Americans wanted to deploy. Russia was convinced that this could neutralise its own nuclear deterrent.

Putin strode into the conference hall armed with more than just the usual grievance cards. He began with a jocular warning to his audience:

> This conference's structure allows me to avoid excessive politeness and the need to speak in roundabout, pleasant but empty diplomatic terms. The format will allow me to say what I really think about international security problems. And if my comments seem unduly polemical, pointed or inexact to our colleagues, then I would ask you not to get angry with me. After all, this is only a conference. And I hope that after the first two or three minutes of my speech Mr Teltschik [the chairman] will not turn on the red light over there.

The audience was already bristling, as Putin launched a blistering attack on what he described as the USA's attempt to rule the world as its 'sole master':

> Today we are witnessing an almost uncontained hyper-use of force – military force – in international relations, force that is plunging the world into an abyss of permanent conflicts. As a result we do not have sufficient strength to find a comprehensive solution to any one of these conflicts. Finding a political settlement also becomes impossible. We are seeing a greater and greater disdain for the basic principles

of international law. And independent legal norms are, as a matter of fact, coming increasingly closer to one state's legal system. One state – of course, first and foremost the United States – has overstepped its national borders in every way. This is visible in the economic, political, cultural and educational policies it imposes on other nations. Well, who likes this? Who can be happy about this?

The United States was guilty of 'ideological stereotypes' and 'double standards.' He accused the Americans of lecturing Russia about democracy, while invading other countries, flouting international law and causing an arms race. He suggested that the US, instead of destroying missiles intended for elimination under a recent arms treaty, might 'hide them in a warehouse for a rainy day'. Referring to President Bush's missile defence plans, Putin condemned the 'militarisation of outer space', and proposed a treaty to outlaw such weapons. The expansion of NATO, he said, was a 'provocation':

> We have the right to ask: against whom is this expansion intended? And what happened to the assurances our western partners made after the dissolution of the Warsaw Pact? Where are those declarations today? No one even remembers them. But I will allow myself to remind this audience what was said. I would like to quote the speech of NATO General Secretary Mr Woerner in Brussels on 17 May 1990. He said at the time that: 'The fact that we are ready not to place a NATO army outside of German territory gives the Soviet Union a firm security guarantee.' Where are these guarantees?

Putin warned that a new iron curtain was descending across Europe – and his words seemed to ring with hurt, as he pointed out that Russia too – just like the East Europeans – had abandoned communism but was not getting any credit for it:

> The stones and concrete blocks of the Berlin Wall have long

been distributed as souvenirs. But we should not forget that the fall of the Berlin Wall was possible thanks to a historic choice – one that was also made by our people, the people of Russia – a choice in favour of democracy, freedom, openness and a sincere partnership with all the members of the big European family. And now they are trying to impose new dividing lines and walls on us – these walls may be virtual but they are nevertheless dividing, ones that cut through our continent.

Robert Gates, the American defence secretary, was sitting in the front row, scribbling on a piece of paper throughout the speech. Afterwards, his aides, Dan Fata and Eric Edelman, rushed to ask him whether they could help him rewrite the speech he was due to give the next morning, in view of what they had just heard. Gates pulled out the paper he had been writing on and said: 'Well, tell me what you think about this?'

Fata and Edelman listened, looked at each other, and said, 'Sir, that's fantastic!'

'Well, it's not my first rodeo,' responded their boss.[7] Indeed, Robert Gates had many years of experience, not unlike Putin's, having joined the Central Intelligence Agency in 1966, rising to become its director under President George H.W. Bush. He referred to this when he rose to make a conciliatory response to Putin at the Munich Security Conference the next morning.

'Many of you have backgrounds in diplomacy or politics,' he said. 'I have, like your second speaker yesterday, a starkly different background – a career in the spy business. And, I guess, old spies have a habit of blunt speaking. However, I have been to re-education camp, spending four and half years as a university president and dealing with faculty. And, as more than a few university presidents have learned in recent years, when it comes to faculty it is either "be nice" or "be gone." The real world we inhabit is different and a much more complex world than that of 20 or 30 years ago. We all face many common problems and challenges that must be addressed in partnership with other countries, including Russia. One Cold War was quite enough.'

The analyst Dmitry Trenin described Putin's Munich speech as the start of a new phase in his thinking. If phase one was 'rapprochement with Europe and the US', and phase two (following the Iraq war) was 'non-alignment, but reluctance to confront the West', then phase three, after Munich, was one of 'coerced partnership'. Trenin wrote: 'Putin laid out conditions under which he expected to coerce America and Europe into partnership with Russia: accept us as we are, treat us as equals, and establish cooperation based on mutual interests.'[8] In the end, Trenin wrote, the 'coerced partnership' never took place, because in 2008 and early 2009 Russia began moving towards increased isolation from its would-be partners.

But during 2007, in the months following the Munich speech, President Putin did make one last attempt to reach an accommodation with the Americans over missile defence. Perhaps he hoped that the speech would shock them into cooperation. The two sides would come tantalisingly close to an agreement, and when the attempt failed, this time it would be as much the Americans' fault as Putin's.

The threat from Iran ... or Russia

From the start of his presidency, George W. Bush had insisted that the planned national missile defence (NMD) system was intended to protect the United States from attack by 'rogue states' such as Iran and North Korea. Even if they did not have the capability yet, they appeared to be building medium and long-range systems that might one day reach America. The trajectory of Iranian missiles, it was argued, would pass over Eastern Europe, and so the European element of the NMD system would require a radar facility in the Czech Republic (to track missiles in the early stage of their flight) and interceptor missiles in Poland (to shoot them down).

'From the very outset,' Putin's foreign policy adviser Sergei Prikhodko recalls, 'these plans were unacceptable to us.'[9] The Russians rejected the idea on several grounds: Iran did not yet have the long-range missiles against which the NMD system was aimed and would not have them for many years; even if they did, Poland and the Czech Republic were not the best places to intercept them; and, crucially, the Czech radar would be able to spy on Russian facilities, while the Polish missiles would undermine Russia's own nuclear deterrent.

Until now, Russia had criticised the plans but offered no constructive alternative. But in June 2007 Putin came to a G8 summit in the German seaside resort of Heiligendamm with plans of his own. Apart from the main summit business Putin had a bilateral meeting with President Bush, for which he had prepared so thoroughly that it took the American by surprise. In the week before, he consulted military experts, and the night before, in his room, Putin sketched out maps of missile trajectories and other data. Now he placed them in front of Bush and expounded in great detail why the American plans were all wrong. According to an aide who was present, Putin 'delivered a real thesis', explaining where the radars needed to be, why Bush was being misled by his advisers about Iran and North Korea, and why Russia felt threatened.[10]

Bush is said to have looked at him and said, 'OK, I see this is really serious for you. Nobody advised me you treat this so seriously.'

'We can't sleep for thinking about this!' said Putin.

'Well, as your friend,' said Bush, 'I can promise that we'll look into what you've said.'

But Putin had a new and concrete proposal, designed to trump the American move – while simultaneously calling their bluff on whether the system was really aimed against Iran and not Russia, as Bush claimed. 'Look,' he said. 'I spoke to the president of Azerbaijan yesterday. We have a radar station there, in a place called Gabala. I'm willing to offer this to you. It's closer to Iran. We can have a joint system. You use our radar in Azerbaijan, and there'll be no need for one in the Czech Republic.'

Putin had a stick as well as a carrot. Just days before the summit he had hinted darkly that if the Americans deployed their missile interceptors in Eastern Europe then Russia would have to retaliate by re-training Russian missiles on European targets. Now he offered to remove that threat if the Americans rethought their plans: 'It would allow us to refrain from changing our position and retargeting our missiles. There would be no need to deploy our missile strike system in the immediate vicinity of our European borders, and no need to deploy the US missile strike system in outer space.'

It was an opportunity the Americans could not ignore: for the first time, Putin was offering to drop his opposition to missile defence, under the condition that Russia would also be involved in it. Bush promised to talk to his military advisers about it.

But within a month, sensing he had Bush's ear, Putin was offering more. On 1 July he flew to Kennebunkport in the state of Maine for informal talks at the Bush family home at Walker's Point, a little peninsula jutting out into the Atlantic Ocean. He took a speedboat ride with George W. Bush and his father and ate a supper of lobster and swordfish with the family, together with the foreign ministers and national security advisers from each side – Condoleezza Rice and Stephen Hadley, and Sergei Lavrov and Sergei Prikhodko. 'It was a very relaxed setting,' says Rice. 'We sat, I'll never forget, in this lovely chintz-covered living room, with the ocean in the background.' [11]

Next day they did a spot of fishing, and Putin pulled out more initiatives. Not only would he offer the Gabala radar in Azerbaijan but he would get it modernised. And then there was a brand-new radar the Russians were about to commission at Armavir in southern Russia. That could also be used. Together they would form a joint early-warning system for common missile defence involving not just the US and Russia but the whole of NATO. The NATO-Russia Council could finally have something concrete to work on. Putin offered to host an 'information exchange centre' in Moscow and proposed there could be a similar one in Brussels too. 'This would be a self-contained system that would work in real time,' Putin went on. 'We believe that there would then be no need to install any more facilities in Europe – I mean those facilities proposed for the Czech Republic and the missile base in Poland.'

Bush wasn't too sure about the latter point, but the rest of Putin's proposal made a lot of sense to him – especially as Putin seemed to place these specific missile defence proposals in the context of a whole new strategic alliance. As Sergei Lavrov recalled later: 'Putin stressed that if we could work together on this, it would, to all intents and purposes, make us allies. The proposal was prompted by a wish to create an absolutely new relationship between us.'

The talks ended, and the two leaders were about to go outside to brief the press. Stephen Hadley took President Bush aside for a moment: 'That was a terrific statement, exactly what we've been looking for from Putin. Do you think he'd be willing to say that publicly?'

'I don't know. Let's ask him,' said Bush. He approached the Russian leader and told him he thought it would help accelerate progress between the two countries if he would repeat on camera what he had said privately.[12]

Putin was only too happy to oblige. 'Such cooperation,' he told the press, 'would bring about a major change in Russian-American relations regarding security. In fact, this would lead to the gradual development of a strategic partnership in the area of security.'

So far, so good, but the Americans had yet to see what kind

of facility Putin was offering. The neo-cons in the defence establishment were highly sceptical, and saw the move as a ploy to drive a wedge between the US and the Poles and Czechs. Under-secretary of defence Eric Edelman recalls: 'I was doubtful that this actually indicated a Russian desire to cooperate on missile defence. My view was that a lot of what they were doing was tactically aimed at preventing us moving forward on missile defence by drawing us into unproductive discussions or into other issues.'[13]

In September a team of experts led by the director of the Missile Defence Agency, General Patrick O'Reilly, flew out to Azerbaijan to inspect the Gabala radar station. They were not impressed by what turned out to be an ageing Soviet installation. The neo-cons were not unhappy to have their suspicions confirmed. According to Edelman, 'What [O'Reilly] said was that this was a radar that had some capability. That it could be useful. But that it was also quite old. That it needed major upgrade. And that in order in the future to really play a role it was going to need some considerable expenditure and work.'

The team concluded that Putin's offer could help only to monitor the threat of a missile attack. But the American vision was of a system that could defend against it – and for that they would still need other sites in Poland and the Czech Republic.

The more Russia-friendly axis in the administration accepted this, but did not want to throw away an olive branch they had not even expected to see, after Putin's Munich speech. Condoleezza Rice and Robert Gates met alone in the defence secretary's office at the Pentagon. Rice recalls: 'We're both Russianists, and we said: what we have to do is, we have to break the code somehow, we have to find a way to scratch the itch that the Russians have about being left out of this, about it being in the Czech Republic and Poland, which was obviously a lot of the problem. And are there some things we can do as confidence-building measures?'

Gates and Rice batted ideas back and forth and eventually

came up with an idea that might do the trick. In October they headed out to Moscow for what were dubbed 'two plus two' talks – between the foreign and defence ministers on each side: Rice and Gates, plus Lavrov and Serdyukov.

On the morning of Friday 12 October they drove out to the president's Novo-Ogaryovo residence, travelling the same road Rice had taken a year earlier for the surprise birthday party that had ended so testily. Putin wanted to see them before the 2+2 talks got going – and he was in much the same mood as a year before. Again he kept the Americans waiting for half an hour, though he had no other meetings. Then, when he assembled the two delegations around the table, with the television cameras running, he launched into a fresh tirade against the American plans: 'The one point I would like to make is that we hope that you will not push ahead with your prior agreements with Eastern European countries while this complex negotiating process continues. You know, we could decide together to put a missile defence system on the moon some day, but in the meantime, because of your plans, we could lose the chance to achieve something together.'

According to Gates, Putin questioned whether the Americans really needed a system to defend them from an Iranian attack. 'He passed me this piece of paper that showed the range arcs of Iranian missiles, and he was basically saying that their Russian intelligence was that the Iranians couldn't have a missile that could hit Europe for years and years and years. That's when I said, "You need to get a new intelligence service."' [14]

News reports at the time quoted Putin's sarcastic comment about missiles on the moon, and concluded that the talks had failed. But behind the scenes, Gates and Rice made an offer that the Russians liked. It was intended to bridge the divide over whether or not the Iranians posed a threat. Lavrov remembers: 'They suggested that the US would not activate their missile defence system until we, together with them, established that there was a real threat.'[15]

According to Rice, 'Bob [Gates] said: suppose we dig the holes, but we'll do a joint threat assessment on Iran, and won't actually start deploying interceptors until there is some shared understanding of where the Iranians are going.'

'It was going to take some period of years anyway to get these sites operational,' said Gates, 'so we could wait for the installation of the interceptors until the Iranians had flight-tested a missile that could hit Europe.'

The suggestion went down well because it at least delayed things, but it did little to disabuse the Russians of their conviction that they, not Iran, were the Americans' real target. At this point Gates came up with a proposal which he now admits, with a wry smile, was certainly not agreed with the hawks back home. 'I thought that there were a lot of things we could offer in the way of transparency, in terms of giving them access. We could even have a more or less permanent Russian presence there, like arms inspectors.'

Within minutes the idea evolved into an offer to the Russians to have a permanent military presence, 24/7, at the US installations in Poland and the Czech Republic. The Russians were astonished. Their chief negotiator, Anatoly Antonov, recalls: 'We didn't actually discuss the technicalities of where they would live and who would pay for them ... but it was an interesting idea.'[16]

Gates recalls rather ruefully: 'All these measures that I talked about, I was just making up on the spot. If Condi and I agreed then why not see if we could make some headway with Putin?'

Lavrov asked the Americans to put it on paper. But when Gates and Rice returned to Washington with their ad hoc proposals, there was, in Gates' words, 'consternation'. The ideas had to be assessed by all the relevant administration departments – defence, state, national security – in the so-called 'interagency process'. It soon became clear that the neo-cons had not the slightest intention of giving the Russians 24/7 access to their most state-of-the-art facilities. They also belatedly consulted the Czechs and Poles, and were given short shrift. As Gates recalls, with smiling understatement: 'There were several areas in which the interagency process here sanded off some of the sharp edges of the offers and made them less attractive.'

The offer was put in writing, as requested, but in place of 'permanent Russian presence', it suggested that embassy attachés could occasionally visit the Czech and Polish sites. The Russians shook their heads with derision. Lavrov recalled in an interview: 'We got the paper in November and not one of the proposals was in it.'

A second 2+2 session was held in March 2008, but it was bad-tempered and unproductive. By now it was clear to the Russians that the Bush administration would not be deflected from their plans. Within a few months Washington signed the agreements it needed with Prague and Warsaw (despite the opposition of public opinion in both countries). Once again, Putin had attempted to force Washington to take Russia's views into consideration, and failed.

Paralysis in the Kremlin

Putin's increasingly tough line abroad coincided with a time of growing uncertainty at home. Working with the Kremlin, I became aware of something close to paralysis in the president's team as he plotted his own future during 2007, the last year of his second term. Under the constitution, he could not run for a third consecutive term, and Putin repeatedly stated that he would not change the constitution to serve his own personal ends. There were many in his entourage who urged him to do so – and public-opinion polls suggested it would have been the most popular option – but Putin wanted to find another way to preserve his role.

It was the dilemma of an autocrat who was determined, at least formally, to abide by the rules. He had no intention of leaving the scene: his statements indicated that he was afraid the course he had set Russia on could still be reversed, that he did not fully trust anyone else to defend that course as he himself would, and that he certainly did not trust ordinary people, through a democratic election, to choose the 'correct' path – not even by offering them two 'approved' candidates to choose from. Somehow, he needed to manoeuvre a trusted substitute into the driving seat – someone who would both continue his policies and not challenge his position as the ultimate 'national leader', running things behind the scenes. The trouble was, Putin himself did not know how to achieve this. Nor did he know for many months who the right substitute might be.

Not the current prime minister, certainly. Whereas Boris Yeltsin had appointed Putin to that job in 1999 in order to position him to become president, Putin had appointed his most recent prime minister, Mikhail Fradkov, for precisely the opposite reason – to have a grey yes-man with no ambitions at the head of the government.

There were two front-runners: Dmitry Medvedev had been first deputy prime minister since November 2005 and was seen as a 'liberal', with no obvious connections to the *siloviki*, while Sergei Ivanov, the former spy and defence minister, was promoted to the same rank – first deputy prime minister – on 15 February 2007, prompting speculation that he was a serious rival for the future presidency. I could tell from my dealings with senior officials that no one knew which of them to side with. Both men began forming their own loyal teams, including press secretaries, but the wisest functionaries kept aloof.

As a result, people at all the top levels of government became immobilised, afraid of taking long-term decisions and unsure which of the possible candidates to support. The hesitation was palpable from the middle of 2007 through to the parliamentary election in December, and even beyond the presidential election on 2 March 2008. For a good year, the strongman's dilemma left the country weak and irresolute.

One thing was clear: no ordinary Russian – indeed no one below the top circle of power – would have the slightest say in who Russia's next president would be. But it would take Putin months to work out how to do it. I am pretty sure he did not have a plan in place at the beginning of the year. It emerged – and evolved – over the months. I often asked my contacts in the Kremlin what was going on, and I am sure they were not dissembling when they told me they had no idea. Even Putin didn't know.

The situation gave rise to the rebirth of Kremlinology, long dead since the days when people like me used to pore over photographs of Politburo line-ups on Red Square, or count how many words *Pravda* dedicated to various up and coming Soviet leaders. It did not escape attention that in January 2007 Medvedev received a warm welcome for a relatively liberal-sounding speech at the World Economic Forum in Davos, nor that it was just five days after accompanying Putin to Munich in February that Sergei Ivanov was promoted to the same rank as Medvedev.

The new Kremlinologists, including those working in the Kremlin itself, fearful for their own futures, avidly debated the merits of the two contenders. Medvedev was seen as perhaps too liberal or weak (though, on the other hand, that might be exactly what Putin was looking for, to project a softer image abroad). Ivanov was a *silovik*, surely closer to Putin, who had promoted so many spies and military men in the past years ... but then again, perhaps he was *too* strong, too much of his own man, too much of a threat. Might Putin even allow them to stand against each other, representing different facets of the establishment? Or would Putin finally change the rules and run for a third term?

It was Ivanov who seemed to be being groomed for the top job, shown more often on television, travelling more often with Putin, haranguing the West in Putin-like tones. Opinion polls, to the extent that they could be believed, put Medvedev marginally ahead of him until June, when the ex-spy pulled ahead by about four points.

Suddenly, on 12 September, Putin pulled off an excruciatingly bad piece of political theatre, in which the prime minister Mikhail Fradkov was shown on television walking into the president's office and falling – metaphorically and rather clumsily – on his sword. 'In view of the political processes going on at the moment,' Fradkov mumbled, 'I want you to have complete freedom in your decisions and appointments. So I want to take the initiative and free up the position of prime minister so that you have a free hand in configuring your cabinet as you see fit.' That was code for: obviously I am not going to be the next president, so I will resign and let you appoint the person you want. (This was based on the assumption that Putin, like Yeltsin, would appoint his chosen heir as prime minister.)

'I completely agree with you,' said President Putin, pretending to have had no say in the cabal, and immediately appointed a new prime minister. But it was neither Medvedev nor Ivanov. Instead Putin nominated an old colleague from St Petersburg, Viktor Zubkov. He was as grey and uninspiring as Fradkov, but for most of the Putin presidency he had headed a powerful anti-money-laundering unit, the Financial Monitoring Committee, which made him privy to the financial secrets of the elite. Few people had heard of him, yet within days the 66-year-old declared that he might indeed run for president.

It wasn't just outside observers that were shocked. I happened to be with the Valdai group in Moscow that day, and we had an appointment with Ivanov just two hours after he received the news that he was not, after all, heir presumptive. He laughed it off as best he could, but it was clear from his demeanour that the news was as big a shock to him as to everyone else. His soaring career had suddenly belly-flopped. He said Putin had not even discussed the move with him.

So was Zubkov the next president? Only if Yeltsin's manoeuvring was seen as a precedent. But Putin was inventing new ways of doing things, and unlike Yeltsin he had no intention of anointing a successor and then obligingly stepping out of politics. Two days later Putin opined that there were 'at least five' viable candidates. Kremlinologists assumed he meant Zubkov, Ivanov, Medvedev, and ... two others. I understood from a Kremlin source that this was not merely flak thrown up to disorientate the pundits: Putin himself had not yet decided.

It was only after the elections to the State Duma on 2 December that Putin finally revealed his choice – not that the result, which unsurprisingly gave his party, United Russia, 64 per cent of the votes, affected his decision. It was neither Zubkov nor the former KGB man Sergei Ivanov, on whom the dice fell, but the man who it seemed had been pipped at the post, Dmitry Medvedev.

Again, it was a staged event, a pretence at democracy. The leaders of four parties, just elected to the Duma, came to Putin and put forward Medvedev's name. Putin feigned surprise, and turned to Medvedev, who happened to be present: 'Dmitry Anatolievich, have they discussed this with you?'

'Yes, we had some preliminary discussions,' replied the candidate.

'Well,' Putin had to agree, 'if four parties representing different strata of Russian society have made this proposal ... I have known Dmitry Anatolievich Medvedev for more than 17 years, and we have worked closely together all these years, and I fully and completely support this choice.'

The following day, Medvedev declared that if he were elected he would nominate Putin for the post of prime minister. After months of confusion and manoeuvring, the way forward was suddenly clear. Putin would ensure his political longevity by transforming the post of prime minister (without so much as touching the constitution) from the quiet back-office occupied by Fradkov and Zubkov into the country's real power-base.

Though born in the same city as Putin, and a graduate from the same law faculty, Medvedev was 13 years younger and had a very different background. Born in 1965, into an intellectual family, he graduated in 1987, at the height of Gorbachev's efforts to democratise the communist system. The zeitgeist of the time was all about debunking the KGB that Putin had chosen for his career. Medvedev helped run the campaign of the liberal reformer Anatoly Sobchak (one of his law professors) in the first genuine elections of the late 1980s. Sobchak later became mayor of St Petersburg and hired both Medvedev and Putin to work in his external relations office – this was when the two men met. Medvedev later followed Putin to Moscow, becoming his deputy chief of staff in 1999 and running his election campaign in 2000. As president, Putin appointed Medvedev as chairman of Gazprom, and later as his chief of staff.

There were several reasons why Putin may have decided Medvedev was preferable to his main rival, Ivanov: he was less charismatic, had no power-base of his own, was less of a threat than a fellow *silovik* (who might be tempted to ease Putin out of the way) and – not unimportant for a small man – was even shorter than Putin. All in all, he was much less imposing and threatening than Ivanov, the tall cavalier who had once swept Condoleezza Rice off her feet. And there was the added benefit that with his liberal reputation, Medvedev would go down well in the West, perhaps acting as a lightning rod and removing the strain from Putin for a while. The task for the next four years would be to keep Medvedev on a tight leash, and at least leave the door open for Putin's own return to the presidency.

We in the Kremlin's hapless PR team saw another opportunity to impress the West evaporate. An election between two establishment candidates with different views on how to run the economy would have been the same as in most Western democracies. But the Russian people were not to be asked for their opinion. Putin's choice was the only one that mattered, and as the head of the Central Election Commission, Vladimir Churov – a friend of Putin's appointed less than a year earlier – stated, 'Churov's First Law is that Putin is always right.'

State television gave Putin's choice blanket coverage, and Medvedev was duly elected on 2 March 2008 with 70 per cent of the vote. The Communist Party leader, Gennady Zyuganov, won almost 18 per cent, and the nationalist Vladimir Zhirinovsky 9.5 per cent. The former prime minister Mikhail Kasyanov, the candidate for the 'democratic' opposition, was registered as a candidate but later disqualified on the grounds that too many of the signatures gathered in his support had allegedly been forged.

When the result was announced Putin and Medvedev walked out together on to Red Square in leather jackets and jeans, Medvedev trying to ape Putin's macho gait. Interrupting a rock concert in front of St Basil's Cathedral, Medvedev made a short speech affirming that the course of the last eight years would be continued. When Putin took the microphone to praise his protégé, the crowd of supporters drowned him out, chanting, 'Putin, Putin, Putin ...' Nobody chanted 'Medvedev!'

Even after the election, and for a month or so after Medvedev's inauguration in May, the turmoil continued, as bureaucrats scrambled for what they thought would be the best seats. What I observed in the Kremlin press department was probably mirrored throughout the administration: officials were trying to work out where the real power would lie, in President Medvedev's Kremlin or in Prime Minister Putin's government, ten minutes away in the 'White House' on the Moskva river. In retrospect, the clever ones were those who moved to the White House, hoping to have a supervisory role over their counterparts in the Kremlin. Dmitry Peskov took us on a valedictory tour of the Kremlin in April, as Putin appointed him as his spokesman.

'How will it feel to move away from here?'

Peskov twisted his moustache: 'Who knows? Who knows ...?'

Peskov's move was part of a clever matrix of appointments designed to maintain Putin's control over the new president. Peskov took with him to the White House his long-time deputy Alex Smirnov, who became head of the prime minister's press service, an entity that had scarcely functioned under its predecessors. It was Peskov (rather than the president's press secretary) who appointed a new, young team to the president's press service, making it clear that they answered to him. Putin's old spokesman and ally, Alexei Gromov, remained in the Kremlin, promoted to become President Medvedev's deputy chief of staff, in a blatant attempt to maintain 'ideological control' over the president's media operation. But there was a fly in the ointment. Medvedev retained Natalia Timakova, who had been his press adviser during the election campaign, as his spokeswoman. She was a rival rather than a protégé of Peskov's, and soon began to co-opt the team Peskov had put in place in the presidential press service. She was fiercely devoted to the president, not the prime minister. Within a year, a clear split was developing: not surprisingly, Medvedev's team soon felt they owed their allegiance to the president, not to the people who had appointed them. Over the next years I gained a strong impression that the two press offices grew rather far apart, to the extent that each no longer knew what the other was planning.

I understand from well-connected sources that this situation was echoed in other departments too, so that by 2010–11 two competing bureaucracies existed, each knowing that their futures depended on their respective bosses, and each therefore dedicated to their own boss's survival. This was not what

Putin had intended.

Putin took with him from the Kremlin to the White House his presidential chief of staff, Sergei Sobyanin, and also the influential economist Igor Shuvalov. But he left behind some of his trusted senior staff, to ensure 'continuity' under Medvedev. They included not only Alexei Gromov, in charge of the mass media, but also Vladislav Surkov, who became Medvedev's first deputy chief of staff, Sergei Prikhodko, his foreign affairs adviser, and Arkady Dvorkovich, his economics adviser. The goal was to intertwine the two branches of the administration while ensuring that Putin's appointees in the Kremlin held sway. Instead they became drawn into their separate teams, serving their new masters. Even the 'ideologue' Surkov changed his colours to support Medvedev's new initiatives, some of which contradicted what he had earlier preached for Putin.

Putin's presidential legacy

On 8 February 2008, in the middle of the election campaign, Putin gave his last major speech as president – effectively his own assessment of his achievements. In foreign policy, he insisted that 'we have returned to the world arena as a state which is taken account of'. Yet the detail sounded more like a bitter admission of failure: 'We drew down our bases in Cuba and in Vietnam. What did we get? New American bases in Romania, Bulgaria. A new third missile defence region in Poland.' Russia had failed to prevent the United States from 'unleashing a new arms race with its missile defence system', obliging Russia to respond by producing 'new types of arms, with the same or even superior specifications compared to those available to other nations'. And he protested, like a stuck gramophone needle, that 'irresponsible demagogy, attempts to split society and to use foreign assistance and interference in the course of political struggle in Russia are not only immoral, but also illegal.'

But he delivered a glowing account of his own achievements at home. Russia, he said, was now one of the seven biggest economies in the world. 'The main thing we have achieved is stability. We have established that life will continue to improve. [Under Yeltsin] wealthy Russia had turned into a country of impoverished people. In these conditions we started to implement our programme to take the country out of crisis. We consistently worked to create a robust political system. We were able to rid ourselves of the practice of taking state decisions under pressure from financial groups and media magnates.'

Economic growth was at its highest in seven years. Russia's foreign debt had been reduced to just 3 per cent of GDP. The last two years had seen a 'real investment boom' in Russia. The birth rate was rising.

And there was a reason, he implied, for certain political restrictions. 'Political parties,' he said, 'must realise their huge responsibility for the future of Russia, for the stability of society. It is never worth taking the country to the edge of chaos.' This was a subtle reminder of the specious, unspoken deal Putin had offered, or rather imposed on, the country: that in exchange for growing prosperity and stability, political freedoms had to be curbed.

Putin's opponents decried both elements of his claim: there was no correlation between authoritarianism and economic growth, they said, and there was no real economic success anyway because the early liberal reforms had run their course.

In a damning report published in February 2008, two of Putin's major political opponents, Boris Nemtsov and Vladimir Milov, conceded that some of the official statistics looked good: under Putin the country's gross domestic product had grown by 70 per cent; incomes had more than doubled; poverty had been reduced, so that only 16 per cent lived below the poverty line (as opposed to 29 per cent in 2000); the budget was balanced, gold reserves stood at $480 billion, and the Stabilisation Fund had reached $157 billion.

But ... most of this had been achieved thanks to the soaring price of oil, which had gone from an average of $16.70 a barrel under Yeltsin to an average of $40 under Putin (and was now heading for $100). Instead of using the oil windfall to modernise the economy and carry out economic reforms, the authors argued, 'our army, pension system, health care and primary education have all degraded under Putin'.[17] Meanwhile corruption had attained 'gigantic proportions, without analogy in Russian history', and those oligarchs whom Putin had not driven into exile or put in prison were making themselves fabulously rich at the state's expense. The recovery from the post-communist collapse had begun, they argued, not under Putin but earlier, in the final years of the Yeltsin presidency. Under Putin, instead of 'authoritarian modernisation' – which, had it worked, theoretically might have allowed one to forgive some of the anti-democratic tendencies of his rule – there was 'authoritarianism without modernisation'. The brief period of progressive reforms had been replaced by 'the greedy redistribution of property and the transformation of Russia into a police state'.

Writing in *Foreign Affairs* magazine at exactly the same time, the American scholars Michael McFaul (later nominated by President Obama to become ambassador to Moscow) and Kathryn Stoner-Weiss came to similar conclusions. They wrote that although state resources had increased under Putin, allowing pensions and government salaries to be paid on time, and greater spending on roads and education, overall the state still performed poorly: 'In terms of public safety, health, corruption, and the security of property rights, Russians are actually worse off today than they were a decade ago.'[18] Security, 'the most basic good a state can provide for its population', had worsened: the frequency of terrorist attacks had increased under Putin; the number of military and civilian deaths in Chechnya was much higher than during the first war, and conflict in the North Caucasus region was spreading; the murder rate was rising; the death rate from fires was around 40 a day in Russia – roughly ten times the average rate in Western Europe. Health spending had gone down under Putin, the population was shrinking, alcohol consumption had soared and life expectancy had declined during the Putin years. 'At the same time that Russian society has become less secure and less healthy under Putin,' McFaul and Stoner-Weiss wrote, 'Russia's international rankings for economic competitiveness, business friendliness, and transparency and corruption all have fallen.' Corruption, in particular, had skyrocketed. Property rights had been undermined: not only had the state engineered the sell-off of Yukos assets to Rosneft, but the oil company Shell had been compelled to sell a majority share in Sakhalin-2 to Gazprom.

Such was the state of the Russia that Dmitry Medvedev took over after his inauguration on 7 May 2008. There were signs that he shared, or at least understood, the kind of criticisms levelled at his predecessor's record. The main sound-bite to emerge from his only election campaign speech was 'Freedom is better than non-freedom', and in his inauguration address he promised that 'we must achieve a true respect for the law and overcome legal nihilism'.

In foreign affairs, Medvedev wanted to make a quick impression. He rushed to Berlin (just as Putin had done) shortly after becoming president to make what he hoped would be a ground-breaking speech, in which he grandly called for a new European Security treaty. This, apparently (though it was not made clear), would replace all existing treaties and alliances, making NATO and the OSCE redundant and, of course, giving Russia its rightful place at the top table of a new organisation. The initiative was largely ignored, and not just because it was half-baked and raised more questions than it answered. It was ignored mainly because it was divorced from reality: Russia was still acting in ways that reminded most people of the USSR, it played gas wars with its neighbours, appeared to condone the murders of Politkovskaya and Litvinenko, it bullied Georgia and Ukraine ... nobody wanted lectures about European security from a country like that. We in Ketchum sent memos explaining that foreign policy initiatives like this had to be part of a 'package', together with internal liberalisation, if they were be taken seriously. We pointed out why Mikhail Gorbachev had been so successful: he was a communist leader, but his arms-control gestures were taken seriously because he had also initiated *glasnost* and freed political prisoners. No one, we told the Kremlin, would take their security proposals seriously so long as they were rolling back democracy at home.

Maybe – one liked to think – President Medvedev actually wanted to implement changes at home. But any hope of liberalisation was about to be dashed, as Russia for the first time since its invasion of Afghanistan in 1979 went to war with one of its neighbours. The invasion of Georgia in August 2008 destroyed at a stroke all the efforts made by Putin, and then Medvedev, to present their country as a truly post-Soviet, European, democratised and trustworthy power. The events leading up to the 'five day war', and the question of who bore ultimate responsibility for it, were surrounded with controversy – and obfuscated by a fierce PR war in which the Georgians proved considerably more adept than the Russians. In the following chapter I will attempt to shed some light on what happened – without claiming to provide definitive answers.

10

THE DESCENT
INTO WAR

From Kosovo to Bucharest

On Sunday 17 February 2008 Serbia's breakaway Albanian-majority province of Kosovo declared itself independent. The next day the United States recognised it, and on Tuesday a reporter asked President Bush, 'Isn't this a poke in the eye to Vladimir Putin and others who say you're approving of secession movements everywhere implicitly?'

Bush replied: 'Actually we've been working very closely with the Russians ... You know, there's a disagreement, but we believe, as do many other nations, that history will prove this to be a correct move to bring peace to the Balkans.'

It was not the Balkans that Putin was worried about. Russia had good reasons to oppose the recognition of Kosovo – and its 'brotherly ties' with Serbia were the very least of them. Pandora's box was open. However forcefully the Americans and their allies insisted that the Kosovo case for independence was *sui generis* – a unique set of circumstances, setting no precedent – there were a number of other secessionist nations around the world who were delighted. If the Kosovars could vote for independence and secede from Serbia, against the 'parent state's' wishes, citing military attacks, ethnic cleansing and acts of brutality committed against them, then could not the Chechens say the same about their position within Russia, or the Abkhaz and South Ossetians about theirs within Georgia?

Above all, Russia did not want to encourage Chechen separatism, but it was also wary of encouraging the South Ossetians and Abkhaz to secede – precisely because of the precedent it could set for other tiny nations within the former Soviet Union, not least the chain of restive Muslim republics in Russia's northern Caucasus region. At a summit meeting of leaders from the Commonwealth of Independent States – the loose grouping of former Soviet republics – President Putin delivered an unambiguous warning of the consequences: 'The Kosovo precedent is a terrifying one,' he said, shifting nervously in his seat and almost spitting out the words. 'It in essence is breaking open the entire system of international relations that have prevailed not just for decades but for centuries. And it will without a doubt bring on itself an entire chain of unforeseen consequences.'

Mikheil Saakashvili, re-elected as president of Georgia the previous month, was sitting in the audience, and gulped hard as he heard the Russian accuse Western governments of a grave miscalculation: 'This is a stick with two ends, and that other end will come back and knock them on the head one day.' In a separate meeting on the margins of the summit, Putin tried to reassure Saakashvili: 'We're not going to ape the Americans, and recognise the independence of South Ossetia and Abkhazia just because Kosovo was recognised.' But Saakashvili did not believe him, and in any case he was as aware as Putin was of the precedent set by Kosovo, and knew his own breakaway provinces might follow suit if he did not act quickly. His attempt to move against South Ossetia in 2004 had failed. Since then, with American help, he had transformed his military into a much more capable force. But if he was going to use it to retake Abkhazia and South Ossetia – risking confrontation with Russia – he would need much more than just logistical support from the Americans.

Speaking nine days after Kosovo's declaration of independence, Saakashvili explained why Georgia was now keener than ever to join NATO. 'Why do we need NATO membership?' he asked. 'We need it because Georgia should be strategically protected in this very difficult and risky region, and receive its share of security guarantees.' A crucial NATO summit was approaching – in Bucharest in April – at which the alliance would consider whether to allow Georgia and Ukraine to embark on a Membership Action Plan or 'MAP', considered the first concrete step on the road to membership. To garner support, Saakashvili flew to Washington in March to flash his democratic credentials around the corridors and committee rooms of Congress and the White House.

He was not short on flattery, telling George Bush in front of the television cameras: 'What we are up to now is to implement this freedom agenda to the end, for the sake of our people, for the sake of our values, for the sake of what the United States means to all of us, because the US is exporting idealism to the rest of the world.'

Bush could not suppress a smirk of delight; no one in the world supported him like this guy did. Damon Wilson, the president's adviser on European affairs, recalls: 'He was terrific, he was on message. He came into the president with a message about the importance of recognising that his legacy was building a democratic Georgia. This was music to our ears, this was the right message.'[1]

And Saakashvili got exactly the answer he was hoping for. 'I believe Georgia benefits from being a part of NATO,' Bush told reporters. 'And I told the president it's a message I'll be taking to Bucharest.'

Not all the allies were so convinced, however, especially

the French and the Germans. When Saakashvili arrived in Washington – before he even reached the Oval Office – he received a call from the German chancellor, Angela Merkel. Saakashvili says the first thing he told Bush was, 'I just had a call from our common friend, Angela Merkel, and she said, "I know you are going to meet with Bush to discuss the pending NATO summit, and I wanted you to know from me that our German position is that you are not ready for membership, and we will not support it." ' [2]

According to eyewitnesses, Bush smiled and told Saakashvili there were big players and small players in the alliance: 'You take care of Luxembourg and leave Angela to me. I'll take care of her.'

That was easier said than done, however. Both the French and the Germans had two reasons to doubt Georgia's fitness for NATO membership, and neither had to do with 'appeasing Russia'. Firstly, they felt it was dangerous to admit a country with 'frozen' internal conflicts, such as South Ossetia and Abkhazia. Secondly, they were worried by Saakashvili's personality and recent signs that he was far from the democrat George Bush saw in him.

In November 2007 police had violently broken up huge anti-government demonstrations in Tbilisi. Saakashvili closed down an opposition television station, Imedi, which had extensively covered the violence, and declared a nationwide state of emergency, accusing Russia of plotting a coup d'état against him. Even the White House had been appalled, and Condoleezza Rice dispatched her assistant, Matthew Bryza, to Tbilisi to read Saakashvili the riot act.

But Washington and Berlin had a tacit agreement not to air their doubts in public, and the Americans were furious when Merkel went to Moscow, just days before Saakashvili's meeting with Bush in March, and stood side by side with Vladimir Putin to denounce Georgia's (and Ukraine's) NATO aspirations.

Merkel was hardly a member of the Putin fan-club. A year earlier, during talks in Sochi, she had been horrified when Putin brought out his dog, Koni, and allowed her to sniff around the chancellor's legs, knowing she was terrified of dogs. (One of Merkel's senior aides told me they regarded this as 'typical KGB intimidation'.) Having grown up in communist East Germany, she knew at first hand what totalitarianism meant and what Putin's background, working hand in hand with the Stasi secret police, said about him.

But Merkel did agree with Putin that if Georgia and Ukraine began the process of joining NATO, it would steeply raise tensions with Russia. At a joint press conference in Moscow, Putin pointed out that a majority of Ukrainian citizens did not want to join NATO, and added: 'Ultimately, each country decides for itself how best to ensure its security, and we will most certainly accept whatever the Ukrainian and Georgian peoples decide, but this has to be the decision of the people and not the political elite.' Merkel concurred that 'it is important that the public in all future NATO members support their country's membership', and added: 'One of the obligations of NATO member states is that they be free from conflicts. This is something we must reflect upon in our discussions, and it is also something we will be discussing at the upcoming summit in Bucharest.'

Two days later, in Berlin, addressing a meeting of Germany's military top brass, Merkel again went public with her doubts: 'I mean this seriously – countries ensnared in regional or internal conflicts cannot in my view be part of NATO. We are an alliance for collective security and not an alliance where individual members are still looking after their own security.'

According to Bush's Georgia adviser, Damon Wilson, the president realised he would have to work 'personally and privately' on Merkel to bring her round. 'He decided the pivot point was the chancellor herself and that if he could help get her on board that he could help close the deal across the alliance.' Bush and Merkel held a series of video conferences in the run-up to the Bucharest summit. 'And the remarkable thing is,' says Wilson, 'that when you listened to her articulate her concerns, they actually weren't very different from President Bush's concerns. In Ukraine, we were concerned about the lack of coherence in governance, the lack of popular support for NATO among the population. In Georgia we both shared concerns about the durability, the depth of democratic institutions.' The big difference lay in how to move forward. Bush argued that giving Georgia a MAP for NATO membership would encourage them to 'do their homework', but Merkel was sceptical about even beginning the process. 'She wasn't convinced that Saakashvili was a democrat,' says Wilson.

In their final video conference there was deadlock. For Bush it was a matter of principle to be supporting fragile democracies, and he told Merkel he would go to Bucharest to achieve that. 'OK,' Bush told his aides afterwards, 'we're headed for the OK Corral – guns drawn.'

Bush also put in calls to other allies. The British prime minister, Gordon Brown, indicated support for the American position. But the French president, Nicolas Sarkozy, was another matter. The feedback the Americans were getting from Sarkozy's advisers had put them on guard. A member of Bush's National Security Council recalls: 'Many of them had argued to us that they were sceptical that Georgia was even a European country, much less that we should be willing to begin this conversation about them moving towards alliance membership eventually.'

When Bush got through to Sarkozy personally, he felt the Frenchman was 'gettable': he talked of Ukraine and Georgia having a 'European and Atlantic vocation'. But Sarkozy also wanted Bush to think about Russia. According to the French president's diplomatic adviser, Jean-David Levitte, Sarkozy 'tried to get him to understand that in this situation, we were side by side with the Germans, in an approach which aimed to give Russia time to understand that its future was actually bound with that of Europe and its security should not be something that separates us, but rather something that brings us together, and that this vision meant that we shouldn't try and push too quickly to obtain a MAP, though we should give a positive signal in Bucharest to our partners in Ukraine and Georgia.'[3]

And Sarkozy made a forceful new point to the American president about what exactly NATO membership would mean for Ukraine and Georgia. MAP was a 'foot in the door', an irreversible step that would lead to full membership of NATO – and then you had to think about Article Five, the alliance's mutual defence clause. 'How many troops,' Sarkozy asked, 'would we be willing to send to assist our new members in the case of an attack?' That was why France preferred to make a partnership with Russia the real priority, 'so that everybody within the continent had the same vision of security'.

Even within the US administration, there were doubts. Defence Secretary Robert Gates and Secretary of State Condoleezza Rice shared some of the Europeans' concerns about democracy in Georgia and Ukraine. Gates recalls: 'It seemed to me that in terms of the progress of the reform effort, there was still a distance to be covered by both countries.'[4] But it was the 'freedom agenda' advocates that won the day. 'If the United States were to back down in the face of Russian pressure and not give them MAP,' national security adviser Stephen Hadley remembers, 'then actually that in itself could be provocative, by suggesting to the Russians that they could permanently keep Georgia and Ukraine out of NATO. And that was not a prescription for stability in Europe, that was a prescription for continued tension.'[5]

The Bucharest summit, held on 2–4 April in the bombastic palace built by the former Romanian dictator Nicolae Ceausescu, turned out to be as dramatic as any in the alliance's history, with a good deal of undiplomatic mud-slinging passing between the Americans and East Europeans who broadly supported Ukraine and Georgia, and the French and Germans who found themselves cast as 'appeasers' of the Russians. On the first evening, foreign ministers had discussions over dinner and failed even to come close to a wording that the summit would be able to approve. The Polish foreign minister, Radoslaw Sikorski, said he had the impression that 'some allies' (meaning the Germans) had made commitments to the Russians that MAP would not be granted to Georgia and Ukraine.[6]

Condoleezza Rice says she had the feeling that some of the East Europeans were coming rather close to saying to the Germans that 'you of all people should not be standing in the way of countries that suffered under tyranny thanks to what the Germans did in the 1930s and 1940s'.[7]

The German foreign minister, Frank-Walter Steinmeier, was simply insulted. He had tried to argue that there was a conflict situation in the Caucasus region and NATO risked getting drawn into it. But, he says, 'things were said that I never want to hear again, where people who were against NATO enlargement were compared to [the appeasers of] Munich in 1938. Absolutely inappropriate.'[8]

The plenary session of NATO leaders was due at nine the following morning, but the Americans decided to try to sort it out over an early breakfast beforehand – with officials from the US, the UK, Germany and France, plus Poland and Romania. Damon Wilson admits it was a case of gathering reinforcements: 'We decided we needed to invite the Romanians as host of the summit and the Poles as big players within the alliance. Obviously, these are two countries that were quite supportive of our position.'

Jean-David Levitte, the French national security adviser, recalls: 'At one o'clock in the morning and again at three o'clock I was telephoned to make sure I fully understood at what time and where the breakfast meeting was being held.'

But it turned out not to be an intimate, friendly breakfast, says Levitte, 'but more like a tribunal'. A text was cobbled together which foresaw a period of 'intensive engagement' by NATO towards Georgia and Ukraine, with another assessment of progress in December.

When the text was distributed just before the full session at nine o'clock, some East European leaders were furious. The presidents of Lithuania, Poland and Romania all made it clear they found the wording 'not even close to what we expected'. 'They went ballistic,' says Stephen Hadley. 'They thought the document was a capitulation to Russian pressure and Russian veto, and they wanted changes made.' NATO adopts its decisions by consensus, but as the leaders settled around the huge round conference table, there was no sign of one. Frantic efforts continued to broker a compromise, but not at the main table. Behind the heavy curtains draped around the hall, small constellations of advisers and foreign ministers gathered for ad hoc negotiations.

In an interview, Stephen Hadley recalled the remarkable scene that followed. 'All the foreign ministers get up and go to the back of the room, all men in grey hair and suits. And then Angela Merkel gets up, in a nice lime-green jacket, and goes back and sits down with these grey-haired men from Central and Eastern Europe. And soon Condi goes back too, dressed to the nines, and joins them too. And what language are they using? Of course it's Russian! The language Angela learned in her youth in East Germany and Condi knows from her time as a Russian scholar.'

It was Merkel who then grabbed the pen and wrote the deal-breaker sentence on a piece of paper: 'We agree today that Georgia and Ukraine shall one day become members of NATO.' No mention of MAP – just affirmation that the two countries *will* join NATO. The East Europeans then protested that the words 'one day' were as good as saying 'never', so the phrase was deleted. Condoleezza Rice, who had stepped away for a few minutes, came back and was pleasantly surprised: 'It said Georgia and Ukraine will become members of NATO, and I thought, this is a pretty good deal, and I went to the president and said, "Take it!"'

When the whirlwind passed, and the document was adopted, Gordon Brown leaned over to George Bush and joked: 'I'm not sure what we've just done. I know we didn't give them MAP, but I'm not sure we didn't just make them members!'

It was a compromise whose consequences would only sink in later. Bush and the East Europeans were happy because it promised Ukraine and Georgia membership of NATO; Merkel was happy because it left it entirely open-ended as to when that might happen; Georgia and Ukraine were generally pleased, but unhappy to have their membership plans kicked into the long grass; and Russia was furious.

Watching these events unfold, I found myself wondering: would it not have been better if NATO had taken Putin's early innocent-sounding inquiries about joining NATO more seriously? Would it not make more sense for the allies to be taking decisions together with Russia – and Georgia and Ukraine – rather than cobbling together compromises explicitly designed to take Russia's views into account while pretending they did not?

The roots of the problem

In the summer of 1991 I had spent several weeks in Georgia, and witnessed the first ethnic convulsions in Abkhazia and South Ossetia. Georgia had just declared itself independent of the Soviet Union, under an earlier nationalist leader, Zviad Gamsakhurdia. Like Mikheil Saakashvili some 13 years later, Gamsakhurdia moved to restrict the autonomy of the two territories, both of which wanted to remain within the Soviet Union. It provoked a savage backlash.

Abkhazia's Black Sea beaches were once renowned as the Soviet 'Riviera', but now they were almost deserted, as Russians stayed away. The capital Sukhumi seemed to be braced for violence, and it soon came. The civil war of 1992–93 led to a mass exodus of a quarter of a million Georgians (almost half of Abkhazia's population), leaving the 93,000 Abkhaz, who had accounted for just 18 per cent of the population, as the main group in their nominal national territory. The region now had *de facto* independence, supervised by Russian peace-keepers and United Nations monitors.

In tiny South Ossetia, where Ossetians accounted for two-thirds of the almost 100,000 population, civil war had already begun. The Ossetians had tried to declare independence, and Gamsakhurdia sent in Georgia's National Guard to restore order. It was my first experience of war. I remember the road leading into the capital, Tskhinvali, empty and blocked at either end by armoured vehicles and soldiers behind sand-bagged barricades, as one of the bleakest places I had ever seen. Knots of Georgian refugees stood around, staring down the road to where their houses had burned down. Some were waiting for a military escort to accompany them through Osse-tian territory to Georgian villages. In Tskhinvali, still full of the communist slogans already abandoned in the rest of Georgia, an Ossetian woman told me the kind of horror story that I would hear so often in other tortured parts of the former Soviet Union in later years: 'Georgia doesn't feed us. They just kill us. They pull out people's fingernails, gouge their eyes out, burn their houses.' I heard Georgians tell the same kind of hysterical stories about Ossetians. In one village I was shown a smoked-out bus in which, it was said, four Georgians had been doused with petrol and burned to death.

In a Tskhinvali school, I saw a fresh graveyard for 'the victims of Georgian fascist terror'. Ossetians now received all their supplies from North Ossetia, through the Roki tunnel. I wrote at the time that it was 'hard to imagine how the two communities could ever again live at peace'.[9]

For the next 17 years, Abkhazia and South Ossetia lived as separate entities, with tense and tenuous ties to Georgia, and a growing reliance on Russia. Under Putin their stateless citizens received Russian passports. Like Abkhazia, South Ossetia was patrolled by a Russian-led peacekeeping force. OSCE monitors tried to keep the lid on trouble.

Logically, Putin and Saakashvili should have been on the same side over these 'frozen conflicts'. Russia supported the regional governments, but had resisted their calls for recognition for many years, and Putin was not at all keen to add to the Kosovo precedent by recognising them. He would then have had no argument whatsoever against the demands of Chechen separatists. Putin's preference was to negotiate the two regions back into Georgia, with appropriate guarantees for their autonomy. But on the other hand he would not, and could not, allow them to be taken by force.

Galloping to war

Campaigning for re-election in January 2008 Mikheil Saakashvili vowed to recover both regions. He described the South Ossetian capital Tskhinvali as a 'loose tooth ready for removal' and promised to recapture it 'within months at the most'.[10]

The Kosovo precedent and the Bucharest fudge seemed to spur him on. Perhaps he felt he must resolve the 'frozen conflicts' quickly, since these had been cited as the main impediment to NATO membership. The day after the Bucharest summit, the Swedish foreign minister Carl Bildt had dinner with Saakashvili in Tbilisi, and was so alarmed by the latter's talk of possible military action to retake Abkhazia and South Ossetia that he called his American colleagues to warn them. Bush responded to Bildt's news by calling Saakashvili: 'Dear friend, let me be clear: there is no way we will support you. Yes, you are a sovereign leader and we respect you. But you will not get US support if you choose to initiate the use of force.'

It has been suggested that Saakashvili had returned from his trip to Washington in March with the false impression that he had been given some sort of green light by President Bush to reincorporate the rebel republics. Damon Wilson strongly denies that Bush gave any sort of encouragement for military action. 'The president couldn't have been clearer in underscoring that the military course was not a viable path at all. He was encouraging the diplomatic track, cautioning against taking matters into their own hand.'[11]

But Saakashvili was losing faith in the diplomatic route. A few weeks before Bucharest, the State Duma had declared that 'the path taken by the Georgian authorities towards full integration in NATO deprives Georgia of the right to consolidate its territory and the peoples living on it'. Then, on 16 April, Russia suddenly 'upgraded' its diplomatic relations with the two territories. The two moves had all the appearance of a concerted strategy to prevent the reintegration of Georgia's regions – or even to annexe them. According to a Russian military analyst, Pavel Felgenhauer, it was around this time that Moscow took a decision to go to war: 'The goal was to destroy Georgia's central government, defeat the Georgian army, and prevent Georgia from joining NATO.'[12]

That was certainly the feeling in Tbilisi, where some in the leadership were itching to go. A senior US official had a conversation with Georgian security ministers in April where they said: 'The Russians have already positioned themselves to take over. We think they are preparing to move forces into our country, assembling them in Russia. We Georgians have our sources. So we think it is better to move first rather than just wait and let them march in and take over.'

The US official responded: 'You know that is suicide.'

And the Georgians replied: 'Well, if they cross that red line, maybe we would rather die as true patriots and real Georgian men!'

Throughout the spring of 2008 Russia and Georgia each claimed the other was about to attack – and Abkhazia seemed the likelier flashpoint rather than South Ossetia. Russia sent troop reinforcements to the region; the Georgians increased their forces in the Upper Kodori Valley district which they controlled. Georgia flew unmanned reconnaissance drones over the region to monitor Russian troop movements. The Abkhaz called this a violation of their sovereignty, and Russian fighters shot some of the aircraft down. In late April the Russian foreign ministry claimed that Georgia was planning a military intervention in Abkhazia, and Russia vowed to use 'all' its resources to protect Russian citizens in the two disputed territories. In early May Condoleezza Rice expressed concern over the rising Russian troop levels in Abkhazia, and a week later the Georgians released footage shot by a reconnaissance drone which apparently confirmed the movement and deployment of Russian troops and military hardware in Abkhazia.

At the end of May Russia announced it was sending 400 'unarmed' troops to Abkhazia to repair a railway line. The Georgians took this as proof that they were preparing for an invasion, and the leadership began frantic discussions about whether to launch a pre-emptive strike. In interviews, three members of the Georgian leadership recalled the kind of arguments they were making at the time. Giorgi Bokeria, deputy foreign minister, said, 'The major question was at what point does it become impossible for a sovereign state not to react, even when we don't know for sure if the aggression will be massive or not?'[13] Batu Kutelia, deputy defence minister, said, 'Our citizens need to know that Georgia can protect them and that Georgia can react to these actions that cause concern for the Georgian people, that their country will use all its resources to destroy that threat.'[14] Nino Burjanadze, chair of the Georgian parliament, cautioned some restraint: 'Some people tried to persuade the president and myself that the Russians had rusty tanks, that we had modern equipment and that Georgia would defeat the Russians in one night. Almost all the Security Council wanted to start a military intervention in Abkhazia.' [15]

President Saakashvili, for all his eagerness to reclaim the 'lost' territories, decided to give diplomacy another chance. Russia, after all, had a new president, Dmitry Medvedev. And even Prime Minister Putin was sending mixed signals. Just as the Russians were sending railway troops into Abkhazia, Putin was asked by the French newspaper Le Monde what he thought about Saakashvili's 'peace plan for Abkhazia granting an unprecedented degree of autonomy' and 'giving the post of vice-president of the Georgian state to an Abkhaz national'. 'I very much hope that the plan proposed by Mikheil Saakashvili will gradually be introduced,' Putin replied, 'because it is on the whole a sound plan.'

A few days later, on the margins of a summit of post-Soviet states in St Petersburg on 6 June, Saakashvili held his first talks with Medvedev. Both men appeared to approach them in a positive mood, as if they were really starting from a fresh piece of paper. 'I think we will be able to resolve all the difficulties we face today and find long-term solutions. What do you think?' said Medvedev.

'I agree,' replied Saakashvili. 'There are no unsolvable problems. There are plenty of unsolved ones, but no unsolvable ones.'

Recalling the meeting later, Saakashvili said: 'He seemed to have a very different style from Putin. He was open, he was engaging.' (Saakashvili has a similar recollection of his first meeting with Putin.) The Georgian was encouraged to hear Medvedev suggest that he had 'inherited these situations and didn't initiate them', and wanted to resolve the Ossetian and Abkhazian conflicts 'within the framework of the territorial integrity of Georgia'.[16] That amounted to a pledge that Russia was not interested in annexing the two regions and regarded them as part of Georgia.

Saakashvili said he left the meeting 'full of hope' and that Medvedev had suggested getting together in Sochi to 'sit down and look at the different options'. But he did not mention that – as Sergei Lavrov points out – the prerequisite for any progress, as far as Russia was concerned, was that Georgia, given its stated intention to regain the two territories, should sign a non-use-of-force pledge. In an interview, Medvedev's diplomatic adviser Sergei Prikhodko confirmed: 'The key thing was a proposal to put together a document on non-use of force. They even named the venue where it could happen, in Sochi. Saakashvili reacted, as far as I recall, quite positively.' [17]

But the question of a non-use-of-force agreement would bedevil relations over the next months. Saaskashvili says the Russians wanted Georgia to sign such an agreement with the Abkhaz and South Ossetians – with the Russians as guarantors. But for Saakashvili that was 'like giving a fox a mandate to guard a chicken house'. He would only agree to sign a non-use-of-force agreement with the Russians. But the Russians responded: why should we do that? We are not combatants in the area, we only have peacekeepers there.

Both men agreed that there was no point in meeting until they had narrowed their differences sufficiently for there to be a practical outcome. In the middle of June they exchanged confidential letters, which I have seen. Saakashvili sent Medvedev what he believed were a few helpful proposals to reduce tension in Abkhazia, but his letter – and Medvedev's reply – revealed fundamental disagreements. Saakashvili proposed the removal of Russian peacekeepers from the areas of Abkhazia closest to Georgia, and the return of Georgian refugees to these areas (Gali and Ochamchira) which would be jointly administered by Georgia and Abkhazia. Only after this (in December, Saakashvili conjectured) could there be an agreement on the non-use of force, and on the return of Georgian refugees to the rest of Abkhazia. As a sweetener, Saakashvili offered Georgia's help in preparing the 2014 Winter Olympics in Sochi, which is just north of Abkhazia – but in the meantime he called for the 'rapid withdrawal' of Russian military reinforcements and the annulment of Putin's directive of 16 April upgrading relations with the breakaway regions. In his reply Medvedev welcomed the offer to help with the Sochi Games, but politely rejected everything else as pie in the sky. It was hard to imagine, he said, joint Georgian–Abkhaz administration of any part of Abkhazia, and it was premature to speak of the return of refugees. The priority was for Georgia to take real measures to reduce tension, and, above all, to sign a non-use-of-force agreement with the Abkhaz side and to withdraw Georgian troops from the Kodori Valley. If Saakashvili would agree to that, Medvedev offered a summit meeting to sign the relevant documents in July or August.

The Russians tried to work through the Americans to put pressure on their ally. Sergei Lavrov called Condoleezza Rice and said: 'Saakashvili is playing with fire. Keep him away from adventuring. Convince him to sign an agreement for non-use of force.'

Rice replied, according to Lavrov: 'Sergei, don't worry. He wants to be a member of NATO. He knows very well that if he uses force, he can forget about NATO.' Rice remembers the conversation. She says she even added: 'It will be another generation before they are in NATO if they use force.' But she also told the Russians that their own menacing actions were making it 'difficult for Saakashvili in terms of domestic audiences to sign a no-use-of-force pledge'.

Medvedev and Saakashvili had one more encounter before war became inevitable. It was a steamy Saturday night in Astana, the capital of Kazakhstan. The next day, 6 July, was President Nursultan Nazarbayev's birthday, and he had brought exalted guests from many countries to an exclusive nightclub to celebrate. Medvedev had declined to meet Saakashvili for formal talks, but the Georgian approached him several times. Medvedev recalled later: 'He's a difficult man to avoid, because if he wants to get hold of you he sticks to you! We talked while sitting on a bus, and we talked while taking a walk in the park. In the evening we went out for a cup of tea and a glass of wine ... we sat on a sofa and kept discussing the prospect of a meeting.'

The two men have different, and contradictory, memories of these conversations. Since it appears to have been a crucial moment in the breakdown of communication, leading a month later to war, the two versions deserve to be told.

Saakashvili says that he pressed for a follow-up summit in Sochi, as discussed at St Petersburg, but that Medvedev was evasive and hinted he was not in control: 'He said, "You know, I'm so pleased to be with you here, and we are listening to the same music, we like the same social environment, we are at ease with each other. In many ways we might have the same background, but back in Moscow there are different rules of the game, and I would not be easily understood if I rushed to a meeting with you now."

'And I said, "Look, a meeting is better than no meetings and we should get somewhere." But he said, "A meeting now will be a disappointment because we will not get anywhere, and we might come off even worse than before." And I tell him, "Dmitry, come on, what could be worse than we have now? We have daily provocations, things are really spiralling out of control, we have these incidents on the ground, it cannot get any worse." And here he stopped me and said, "Well, I think you are deeply mistaken here. You will see, very soon, it might get much, much worse." And then he basically turned around and left.'

It must be stressed that Saakashvili was speaking with the benefit of hindsight – after the war that broke out one month later. One must also remember that he has a mission to shape the history of those events to his own advantage. But he implied two interesting things: first, that Medvedev had indicated he was not fully in charge of policy (this is credible, given that Medvedev had been in office for only two months), and, second, that he had hinted darkly that Russia was planning military action (though Medvedev's words can also be read as simply meaning that events were spinning out of control). The important thing, when piecing together the events that led to war, is that Saakashvili *interpreted* Medvedev's words as a threat – which he might have been tempted to forestall.

Saakashvili concludes his story of the nightclub encounter somewhat melodramatically. 'Apparently I was looking nervous. Nazarbayev came to me and said, "Misha, what's wrong with you? I've never seen you so pale – what did he tell you?" I said, "Nothing." And then he said, "Don't worry, things will be sorted out, you know, give him some time, I'm sure you can find a way." ' [18]

In an interview with Ekho Moskvy three years after the war, Saakashvili said that after Astana he tried repeatedly to call Medvedev but was always told: 'Wait. We'll call you when it's time.' Saakashvili interprets Medvedev's evasiveness as proof that 'he was no longer inclined to have a serious conversation' because 'he knew what could [be about to] happen'.[19]

Medvedev's account is entirely different. He says the two did agree to meet again for 'a serious discussion' in Sochi, but Saakashvili then went ominously quiet. 'I can tell you earnestly: I spent the next month checking regularly for any feedback from our Georgian counterpart. There was nothing.' Both Medvedev and three other senior Russians all made the same point in interviews (clearly it is the conclusion they reached in their internal discussions later): that Saakashvili, for whatever reason, fell silent after he was visited by Condoleezza Rice in Tbilisi four days later. Medvedev said: 'Following that visit, my Georgian colleague simply dropped all communications with us. He simply stopped talking to us, he stopped writing letters and making phone calls. It was apparent that he had some new plans now.' [20]

It is undeniable that Rice sent mixed signals during her visit – indeed she says so herself. She flew to Georgia on 9 July. The day before, the Russians had engaged in a little more sabre-rattling – flying warplanes over South Ossetia 'to cool hot heads in Tbilisi', as the foreign ministry put it. Dining in the Kopala restaurant, on a veranda overlooking the Mtkvari river, Rice again insisted to the Georgian leader that he had to reject the use of force.

'Why should I do that?' he replied. 'I will get nothing for it.'

Rice replied: 'You're going to have to do it, you have no option … If you engage Russian forces, nobody will come to your aid and you will lose.' [21] Her tough words in private, though, gave way in her public statements to what Saakashvili may have seen as encouragement for his plans. At a press conference before leaving Tbilisi, Rice strongly endorsed Georgia's territorial integrity and criticised Russia, adding, 'We take very, very strongly our obligation to help our allies defend themselves, and no one should be confused about that.' In an interview Rice said this was no idle promise: 'It was very important for the Georgians to know that if they did the difficult things, the United States would stand by them, if the Russians didn't stand by *their* obligations. And I absolutely, deliberately – in front of the press – said that the United States would stand by Georgia.'

The Russians, it seems, believe that Saakashvili heard in this the encouragement he needed. Medvedev says: 'I don't believe the Americans *urged* Georgia's president to invade. But I do believe that there were certain subtleties and certain hints made … which could effectively feed Saakashvili's apparent hopes that the Americans would back him in any conflict. In politics, connotations and nuances are very important.'

In short, Medvedev believes Saakashvili took encouragement from Rice's words and decided to invade South Ossetia, and therefore stopped communicating with Moscow.

Saakashvili believes Medvedev stopped communicating because he had been told to shut up by Putin, who had already taken a decision to invade Georgia. Whatever the truth, there was now silence, and therefore little hope of avoiding war through diplomacy.

A few days later, the Russian 58th Army began massive military exercises across the whole of the North Caucasus, involving 8,000 troops, 700 combat vehicles and 30 aircraft. At the same time 1,630 US and Georgian forces conducted military exercises in Georgia called 'Immediate Response 2008'. Remarkably, despite the tension and continuing skirmishes in South Ossetia, the leaderships in both Georgia and Russia appeared to think the situation was calm enough to go on holiday. One senior American who visited Tbilisi in July recalls having dinner with members of the Georgian leadership before they went away, Saakashvili to a health farm in Italy, deputy foreign minister Bokeria to Spain: 'They were pretty happy, and totally relaxed, hugging each other with "see you in a month or three weeks, make sure you don't think about work!"'

In the first week of August almost the entire Russian leadership also went on holiday, just as the worst Georgian–Ossetian skirmishes in four years erupted in South Ossetia. In the next days thousands of Ossetians evacuated their families to the safety of North Ossetia. On Wednesday 5 August an official in the Russian government gloomily told me it was not a question of 'whether' there would be war: 'There *will* be war.' It erupted finally on the night of 7–8 August, with a massive Georgian assault on the South Ossetian capital, Tskhinvali, followed by a Russian invasion that swarmed deep into Georgia, far beyond the confines of the disputed region itself. The war was almost universally blamed – at least at first – on Russia, and comparisons were drawn with the Soviet invasions of Hungary and Czechoslovakia. Russia's reputation suffered its greatest blow since the end of communism, though a European Union commission which was set up to investigate the war apportioned blame more evenly, concluding that Georgia aggressed first, with force that was not 'justifiable under international law'. The report also said that both sides had contributed to the build-up of tensions beforehand, and that Russia's reaction was disproportionate, going 'beyond the reasonable limits of self-defence'.

The war and its consequences

President Saakashvili, who had announced a ceasefire at 19:00 on 7 August, ordered his forces to attack Tskhinvali at 23:35. A huge artillery bombardment, using tanks, howitzers and Grad multiple-rocket launchers, destroyed swathes of the city and caused many civilian casualties. Georgian ground troops moved in. Russian peacekeepers were killed, as well as many Ossetians, who by virtue of Putin's 'passportisation' policy were now Russian citizens. The Russians evoked 'genocide', claiming 2,000 civilians had been killed in the Georgian attack, a figure that proved to be grossly exaggerated. The next day hundreds of Russian tanks poured through the Roki tunnel, with massive air support. Over the next five days 40,000 Russian troops entered Georgia, half of them through South Ossetia, the others through Abkhazia. They quickly drove Georgian forces out of Tskhinvali and proceeded into Georgia proper, bombarding the city of Gori, attacking airfields and army bases across the country, and even destroying the port of Poti, many miles from the disputed areas. Hundreds of thousands of Georgians fled their homes as Russian forces headed south towards the capital, Tbilisi. In Gori, South Ossetian militias rampaged through the empty city, while Russian troops turned a blind eye. Eventually, international diplomacy brought hostilities to a halt, and the Russian advance stopped. The five-day war left 850 dead and 35,000 people displaced from their homes.

Such are the basic facts, but how and why it all started was, and remains, a subject of bitter dispute. Shortly after the initial assault on Tskhinvali, Georgia's military commander, Mamuka Kurashvili, appeared to confirm that President Saakashvili had decided to press ahead with his long-held desire to re-conquer South Ossetia, when he told reporters that Georgia had 'decided to restore constitutional order in the entire region'. It was later said that this statement had not been authorised, though Saakashvili himself announced that 'a large part of Tskhinvali is now *liberated*'. The Georgians later tried to justify their actions by claiming that they had resorted to force only to counter a huge Russian invasion that was already under way, but most observers (including the EU mission) say there is no evidence of a large-scale Russian invasion in the hours before the Georgian attack. Indeed Saakashvili himself did not make such a claim at the time, and the Georgian government told a UN Security Council session on 8 August that 'at 05:30 [that day] the *first* Russian troops entered South Ossetia through the Roki tunnel'. In interviews conducted two years later with several members of the Georgian government, they seemed hopelessly confused about the timeline.

That the Georgians attacked first, and that it was an attempt not to repulse a Russian attack but to retake South Ossetia, is also confirmed by a conversation the Polish foreign minister Radoslaw Sikorski had with his Georgian counterpart Eka Tkeshelashvili the day before the attack on Tskhinvali. 'Eka called me and said they were going to establish constitutional authority over South Ossetia. What I understood was that they were moving in. I warned her not to overplay their hand and to be very careful, because allowing yourself to be provoked would have dire consequences.' [22]

The fact that President Medvedev was on holiday on a Volga riverboat, Prime Minister Putin was in Beijing for the opening of the Olympic Games and foreign minister Lavrov was in the middle of Russia (four-and-a-half-hours' flight from

Moscow), and all had to rush back to Moscow to deal with the crisis, also suggests that Russia was taken by surprise and did not instigate the attack – even though its army was clearly well prepared to respond.

So why did this war erupt when it did? Only a week or so earlier, Georgia's leaders had been on holiday. Their best troops were serving in Iraq. Although Saakashvili wished to regain the lost territories, he appeared to be giving diplomacy a last chance. As late as 7 August, Georgia's negotiator, Temuri Yakobashvili, even went to Tskhinvali for planned talks that failed to materialise (because the South Ossetian side refused to take part and the Russian special envoy failed to arrive, saying he had a flat tyre). Russia, it is true, had been sabre-rattling – but mainly to dissuade Georgia from attacking rather than because it was contemplating an attack itself; Moscow in fact had little to gain from attacking Georgia and had never (despite claims to the contrary) shown any desire to annexe or even recognise the two regions. Its clobbering of Georgia and subsequent recognition of South Ossetia and Abkhazia as independent 'states' should not be seen as retrospective proof that this was what it intended to do all along.

It seems to me that right up until the eve of battle neither side was seriously planning to go to war (though both were preparing for it). That would mean that the fatal decision was taken at the last minute by Saakashvili and his closest advisers. Perhaps they felt that the world's eyes were on the Olympics in Beijing; perhaps they weighed up everything they had heard from the Americans recently and decided that, on balance, they would have their support; perhaps they really were given intelligence (even if it was false) that the Russians were already streaming through the Roki tunnel; perhaps they saw the fail-ure of the Russians and South Ossetians to turn up for talks with their negotiator as an ominous sign, and Medvedev's evasiveness and hint that 'things could get worse' as a threat; perhaps they jumped at what they thought was an unexpected opportunity to retake South Ossetia. Whatever the reasons, the decision confirmed the worst fears of Saakashvili's American and other Western colleagues – who liked him, respected him, loved his democratic credentials, but were very alive to his unpredictability, his impulsiveness, even his instability. One of the enduring images of the war is of Saakashvili, recorded by a BBC camera as he waited to go on air for a live broadcast, nervously stuffing the end of his tie into his mouth. The Russians leapt on this as proof of his 'insanity'. But many of his Western colleagues also had their doubts. When Angela Merkel had talks with him as a peace settlement was being thrashed out, he was extremely agitated, drank from an empty glass and knocked a bottle of water across the table.

One senior American official (extremely close to Saakashvili) witnessed a top-level get-together in Tbilisi, after midnight, a few weeks before the war: 'My impression was just – what a rip-roaring and disorganised way to make really important decisions. But it is the Georgian way – it is at least how that group does things. I mean, they weren't drunk, they weren't juvenile or stupid, they were just kind of shooting the breeze. I came in and they said, "You say we don't have an interagency coordination process, well this is how we do it. Would you like some wine?" '

Though it was Georgia, in the end, that lit the touch-paper, it was Russia that found itself in the dock for the conflagration. Partly, this was because views were coloured by the initial international television coverage of the war, which showed little, if any, of the Georgian bombing and destruction of Tskhinvali and a great deal of the subsequent Russian bombing of Gori. That in turn happened because the Russians kept journalists out of South Ossetia, whereas the Georgians positively encouraged the press to go to Gori. The BBC's foreign editor, Jon Williams, noted in a blog: 'It's not been safe enough to travel from Tbilisi to the town of Tskhinvali in South Ossetia, the scene, say the Russians, of destruction at the hands of the Georgians. Not until Wednesday – six days after the first shots were fired – was a BBC team able to get in to see what had happened for themselves, and then only in the company of Russian officials.'

The role of PR advisers in the war has been much written about, and much exaggerated. Georgia's principal asset was President Saakashvili himself, who gave a constant stream of interviews, in fluent English and French – without, I fancy, much encouragement from his Western PR team. Moscow, on the other hand, steadfastly resisted the urgings of its PR advisers to allow journalists to travel to South Ossetia, and only belatedly began to offer English-speaking interviewees to stations such as the BBC and CNN.

But the main reason for the opprobrium heaped upon Russia rather than Georgia was because – whatever the circumstances – it invaded a neighbouring, independent country. It did this in order to prevent that country from doing something absolutely legitimate under international law – restoring (albeit in brutal fashion) its territorial integrity in precisely the same way as Russia had restored its rights over Chechnya. The Russian leadership was incapable of seeing this parallel. It accused the West of tolerating Georgia's aggression, forgetting that the West had by and large also tolerated Russia's much more brutal assault on Chechnya. Both cases were seen by the West as internal affairs. Attacking a foreign country is different. As the Russian journalist Andrei Kolesnikov of *Novaya gazeta* put it, 'Russia behaved as if it were the mother country and Georgia was its remote, rebellious province.'

The result was the dismemberment of Georgia, a sovereign state, and the permanent displacement of hundreds of thousands of people, mainly Georgians, from their homes on land that they and their ancestors had inhabited for centuries. In the case of Abkhazia, the Russians effectively handed the territory, now 'ethnically cleansed' of Georgians, to a tiny nation who prior to 1991 had comprised just one-fifth of the population.[23] One-sixth of Georgia's territory is now occupied by Russian troops.

In Beijing, only hours after the Georgian assault began, Vladimir Putin met both President Bush and President Sarkozy. Both tried to caution restraint in Russia's response, and both were rebuffed. Putin was no longer commander-in-chief, but he acted as if he was. Sarkozy introduced Putin to his son, Louis, who received a warm hug – but that was the last of Putin's friendly gestures. Sarkozy's aide, Jean-David Levitte, recalls his boss's attempt at peacemaking. 'He said to President Putin, "Listen, I currently hold the presidency of the EU and I can make the EU do everything possible to stop this war, a war that would be a catastrophe for Russia, for Europe, and for Russian and European cooperation. But for that, Vladimir, I need 48 hours." The answer? "Nyet." So President Sarkozy said, "Hang on, Vladimir, do you realise what's at stake here? At least give me 24 hours." "Nyet, impossible." The president said, "Well, give me until 8pm." "Nyet." ' [24]

It was President Medvedev, though, who took the decision to send in Russian forces. He claims, somewhat improbably, that he did not even discuss the matter with Putin for 24 hours, due to the absence of a secure line to Beijing. Medvedev says that he was woken by the defence minister to be told of the attack on Tskhinvali, but hoped it was just a provocation. It was only when he was told that a tent full of Russian peacekeepers had been hit, killing them all, that he gave the order to counterattack. Anyone who believed that Medvedev was a 'softie' compared to the strongman Putin would be mistaken. It was the president (he says) who ordered the invasion – without even consulting his Security Council. The Council did eventually meet, and supported the decision, but this was still before Putin arrived back from China. Eventually Putin returned, flew to Vladikavkaz in North Ossetia, to see the situation on the ground for himself, and then to Sochi, where he finally met Medvedev to discuss the situation.[25]

On the second day of the war, Russian bombers flew 120 sorties, aiming to destroy Georgia's defence infrastructure – including all the shiny new hardware acquired from the USA, Israel and Ukraine.

The next day Condoleezza Rice, who had just started a vacation with her aunt and sister at the luxury Greenbrier resort in West Virginia, called Sergei Lavrov and demanded an end to the invasion. The conversation became a major bone of contention between the two. Lavrov said the Russians had three conditions: 'First, the Georgians have to go back to their barracks.'

Rice said, 'OK.'

'Second, they have to sign a non-use-of-force pledge.'

'OK.'

'And three, just between us, Saakashvili has to go.'

Rice could not believe her ears: 'Sergei, the American secretary of state and the Russian foreign minister do not have a private conversation about overthrowing a democratically elected president.'[26]

She decided to go public with what she regarded as a Russian threat of regime change in Georgia. On 10 August the US envoy to the UN, Zalmay Khalilzad, announced: 'Foreign Minister Lavrov told Secretary Rice that the democratically elected president of Georgia – and I quote – "Saakashvili must go" – end of quote. This is completely unacceptable and crosses a line.'

Lavrov was incensed. He said in an interview: 'To announce to the entire world what you have discussed with your partner is not part of our diplomatic practice.' He did not entirely deny that he had said it, though, but insisted he merely indicated 'that we would never deal with him again'.[27]

By 11 August the Georgians, having seen Gori bombarded and emptied of its citizens, believed the Russian army was planning to move on the capital, Tbilisi. There was panic in the president's chancellery: pictures were taken off the walls, documents stuffed into boxes in readiness for a quick evacuation. Carl Bildt and the American envoy, Matt Bryza, were there, calculating they had little more than half an hour before the Russians would enter the city.

Saakashvili appealed to President Bush for the help he thought had been promised. 'I told him, "Look, right now, on your watch, you might see the reversal of the demise of the Soviet Union. It might be restored right now in my country, and it would be a very sad turn of history – for us certainly, for us it would be the end – but certainly for the US and for the world."' [28]

His allegation that Russia was about to enter his capital and reincorporate Georgia into some new version of the Soviet Union could have been seen as either paranoid, manipulative or simply as a disingenuous attempt to cover up his own calamitous decision to go to war. But Medvedev later indirectly confirmed that, while 'our mission at the time was to destroy Georgia's war machine', more radical options were considered: 'Saakashvili should be grateful to me for halting our troops at some point. If they had marched into Tbilisi, Georgia would most likely have a different president by now.'

The threat was taken seriously in Washington, especially in view of Lavrov's comment to Rice. Bush convened his national security team. Defence Secretary Robert Gates recalls: 'There was a clear feeling on the part of virtually everybody in the situation room that the Russians had flat out committed an aggression against an independent state, and were proceeding to dismember it.' [29]

The Americans even contemplated intervening militarily themselves. According to Secretary of State Rice: 'There was a little bit of chest beating around the table about what we would do and about how we could signal the Russians militarily, that this would be a foolhardy thing to do.'

National security adviser Stephen Hadley says: 'The issue was, do we put in combat power or not? What you needed was ground troops if you were going to save Tbilisi.' [30]

But that would have risked conflict between the world's greatest nuclear powers, and voices such as that of Robert Gates urged caution: 'I was pretty adamant that we not give weapons assistance to Saakashvili. My feeling at the time was that the Russians had baited a trap and Saakashvili had walked right into it, and so they were both culpable.'

In the end, the Russians stopped and turned around, and the Americans no longer needed to consider a military response. They did send navy transport planes to Tbilisi airport, and warships through the Black Sea to the port of Batumi, to deliver humanitarian aid (and even that infuriated the Russians), but the decision was to let diplomacy work. Despite considerable misgivings about the competence of President Sarkozy, they decided to allow France, which at that point held the rotating presidency of the European Union, to take the lead.

Although the Russians maintained at the time that only Medvedev was involved in the talks with Sarkozy, Putin was there too, predictably playing the hard man. It was during those talks that he declared, 'I am going to hang Saakashvili by the balls.' (The Russians denied the report, but Putin has since himself indirectly confirmed that he did use the expression.[31])

Sarkozy took with him to the talks a draft agreement which Lavrov says, 'we corrected a little bit'. In fact the six-point document was almost obliterated with amendments, so that, for example, the first sentence read 'The Georgian ~~and Russian~~ forces will withdraw fully.'

Sarkozy's adviser, Jean-David Levitte, recalls: 'They'd completely changed the logic, it was no longer a ceasefire, it was no longer a retreat of troops, it was essentially a way of imposing a kind of diktat on Georgia.'

Sarkozy proved to be, in the words of President Medvedev's adviser, Sergei Prikhodko, 'tough, very tough'. Eventually he tired of the Russians' negotiating tactics. 'Listen,' he said, 'we've been going round in circles with this draft. I'm picking up my pen and writing a new draft. Right, first of all the conflicting parties agree to the non-use of force. Agreed – yes or no? Yes.'

There then followed five more points: cessation of hostilities, free access for humanitarian aid, Georgian forces to withdraw to their normal bases, Russian forces to withdraw to their position before the outbreak of hostilities, and international talks to be held on the future status of Abkhazia and South Ossetia.

Point 5 contained an extra clause which would soon cause trouble. 'Pending an international mechanism', Russian 'peace-keepers' were to put in place 'additional security measures'. That was a fluid prescription, which Moscow would use to justify maintaining its troops in a wide security zone, and even in parts of Georgia proper, long after the peace deal went into force.

Sarkozy flew to Tbilisi with the paper. But it was to point 6 that Saakashvili refused to sign up, because 'talks on future status' seemed to leave the question of Georgia's territorial integrity open. Lavrov said in an interview that the whole point of having the clause about international talks on the regions' status was to demonstrate that Russia did not intend to recognise them unilaterally: it would be up to an international conference to decide. But Saakashvili was adamant, and the point was changed, after a quick midnight phone-call from Sarkozy to Medvedev in Moscow, to read: 'talks on security and stability' in the two regions. Those talks have continued off and on, achieving little, in Geneva ever since.

But Saakashvili had already lost the big point. On 26 August, President Medvedev suddenly announced that Russia was recognising the independence of both South Ossetia and Abkhazia. Two new states were born, which would be recognised by only Venezuela, Nicaragua and the Pacific island of

Nauru. Even Russia's former Soviet allies would not go down that road. Russia had finally accepted the Kosovo precedent (though not, of course, in relation to Kosovo itself). For all the world it gave the impression that annexation would be the next move, and that this had been Russia's intent from the outset.

I have yet to meet a Russian who looked very happy about the situation. It can be pointed out that Georgia's NATO aspirations have been knocked for six, or that Russia has allegedly 'increased its security', and is now building a new naval base in Abkhazia. But without doubt Russia's security interests would have been better served by having a peaceful relationship with Georgia.

In the end, the tragedy of Georgia and its war with Russia may come down to the personal tragedy of one mercurial and deluded man. Nino Burjanadze, formerly a close ally of Saakashvili, says he 'rushed into war totally convinced he would defeat the Russian army. The last time I spoke to him was five days before the war began, and I said to him: "If you start this war it will mean the end for my country, and I will never forgive you."' But another question is why Saakashvili's supporters in the West, especially in the United States, while cautioning him against starting a war, at the same time encouraged his belief that he could get away with it. Angela Merkel and others knew about his impetuousness, yet NATO recklessly insisted on promising his country (and Ukraine) membership – even though that made Russia feel insecure. To this day, no serious attempt has been made to visualise a future in which all the countries of Europe and North America might act together to ensure their security, rather than imagining that the security of some can be built at the expense of the security of others.

The events described in this chapter illustrate better than any in the past 12 years the failure of Russia and the West to understand one another and to take one another's concerns and fears into account. Bush preached and lectured. Putin raged and menaced. America said that Russia must give up its 'sphere of influence' in its 'near abroad'. Russia said that America should stop acting as if it ruled the world. Bush accused Putin of communist-style authoritarianism. Putin accused Bush of Cold War thinking. Both were right. The result was inevitable.

11

RESETTING RELATIONS
WITH THE WEST

Repercussions of the Caucasus war

The Russians were livid with the West for siding with Georgia over a war that it had started. They lashed out at everyone in sight, demonstrating a fragile grip on reality. The Georgian attack on Tskhinvali was compared to the 9/11 attack on the United States. In the true tradition of Russian conspiracy theory, Vladimir Putin declared that the Americans had instigated the whole conflict in order to shore up the position of Senator John McCain, Barack Obama's Republican rival in the American presidential election.

The foreign minister Sergei Lavrov claimed that certain foreign powers decided to use Saakashvili 'to test the strength of Russian authority' and 'to force us to embark on the path of militarisation and abandon modernisation'. The minister insisted the Russians had done nothing more than take out positions from which the Georgians could attack them. Speaking to the British foreign secretary David Miliband on his cellphone, Lavrov referred to Mikheil Saakashvili as a 'fucking lunatic'.

The Russians appeared to be oblivious to the fact that they were in the international doghouse having invaded and occupied a large part of a neighbouring country. At the end of August, President Medvedev made his first – of several – attempts to draw weighty conclusions from the war. He enunciated five new 'principles' of Russian foreign policy, some of which had alarming implications. Principle number four declared that defending the lives and dignity of Russians, *wherever they might be*, was the priority. This included 'protecting the interests of our business community abroad'. Anyone who committed an aggressive act against them would be rebuffed, Medvedev promised. Point five declared that there were regions where Russia had 'privileged interests'. This appeared to include all the neighbouring post-Soviet countries, where ethnic Russians lived. Medvedev pointedly did not use the expression 'sphere of influence' – but that is essentially what he meant. It implied that former Soviet republics such as Estonia and Latvia, now members of the EU and NATO but with large Russian minorities, were officially considered part of Moscow's domain. The new policy was, perhaps, the precise opposite of what one might have expected a chastened Russia to adopt following the Georgia crisis.

Showing no sign of humility, the Russians saw the war as a pretext to plough on with their old, already rejected initiatives. In October President Medvedev rushed to a conference in Evian, France, and reiterated his call for a new European security treaty, saying events in the Caucasus had 'demonstrated how absolutely right' his idea was, and were 'proof that the international security system based on unipolarity no longer works'. What was he saying? Had he forgotten that it was his country that had just violated the security and territorial integrity of a neighbour? His long-winded appeal for a new treaty fell mostly on deaf ears. This really was, as Saakashvili might have put it, the fox demanding co-ownership of the chicken-house.

As for Vladimir Putin, his new post as prime minister meant that the economy, rather than foreign policy, was now his major responsibility. That, too, gave him the levers to meddle in a region of 'privileged interest'. The main lever was Gazprom, the huge state monopoly he had refused to allow his ministers to split up in 2002, which was now a handy instrument of foreign policy. Energy had become a convenient whip with which to punish neighbours. In 2006, a few months after the gas dispute with Ukraine, Russia cut oil supplies to Lithuania after it sold its Mazeikiai refinery to a Polish company rather than to Rosneft. The same year, power lines to Georgia were mysteriously bombed, and Russia refused to allow Georgian investigators to see the evidence or help with repairs. In 2007 Russia cut oil shipments to Estonia following a row over the removal of a Soviet war memorial.

Towards the end of 2008 another gas conflict with Ukraine was brewing, as Russia again insisted on raising its prices to world levels, and Ukraine refused to pay. This time, with a Western public relations firm on board, the Kremlin tried to pre-empt the bad publicity. They warned Ukraine (and customers farther west) of the impending conflict, and Gazprom sent its top executives on a tour of European capitals to ensure that, if supplies were interrupted, like three years before, people would know it was Ukraine's fault, not Russia's. But no one predicted that Putin would go so far as to deliberately cut supplies intended not for Ukraine but for Western Europe.

Gazprom was owed $2.4 billion by Ukraine for gas already delivered, and wanted to raise the price for 2009 to $250 (and after a few days to $450) per 1,000 cubic metres – a price Ukraine could not pay. On 1 January 2009 Gazprom cut gas supplies, just as it had done in 2006. To make up for the shortfall – again, just as in 2006 – Ukraine began siphoning gas from the export pipelines, and soon customers in Hungary, Austria, Bulgaria, Romania and other countries noticed a considerable drop in pressure. But this time there was no quick resolution, and European countries began to panic. Slovakia even considered restarting a mothballed nuclear power station.

On 5 January Putin took an astonishing decision. He called in the head of Gazprom, Alexei Miller, plus television cameras, and used the following stilted conversation to announce that for the first time ever Russia would cut gas supplies to customers in Western Europe – mere bystanders to the dispute with Ukraine – in the middle of a freezing winter.

Alexei Miller: Ukraine has failed to pay its debt for gas supplied in 2008, and that debt amounts to more than $600 million. If things continue like this and Ukraine continues to steal Russian gas, the debt will soon amount to billions of dollars.

Vladimir Putin: What do you suggest?

Alexei Miller: It has been suggested to cut the amount of supplies to the border between Russia and Ukraine by exactly the amount Ukraine has stolen, 65.3 million cubic metres, and to subtract the amount of gas stolen in the future.

Vladimir Putin: Day by day?

Alexei Miller: Yes, day by day.

Vladimir Putin: But in that case, our Western European customers will not get the full amount they have contracted for.

Alexei Miller: Yes, in that case our Western European partners will not be receiving the amounts of gas stolen by Ukraine, but Gazprom will do all it can to compensate for that volume in other ways. We may increase supplies of Russian gas via Belarus and Poland and increase supplies of Russian gas via the Blue Stream to Turkey.

Vladimir Putin: What about consumers inside Ukraine? They will also be undersupplied. We are talking about large amounts: as far as I remember, Ukraine consumes 110–125 million cubic metres a day. Ukrainian consumers will suffer. I feel sorry for the common people.

Alexei Miller: According to our reliable information,

Ukrainian president Viktor Yushchenko personally ordered a unilateral suspension of talks with Gazprom on gas supply to Ukraine this year. Apparently, he does not feel sorry for the common people.

Vladimir Putin: He is not sorry, but we are; everyone should feel sorry for them, because we are related to the people who live there.

Alexei Miller: We also know that Ukraine produces about 20 billion cubic metres of gas a year, and the amount of stored gas in Ukraine at present exceeds its annual output. Given the good will of the Ukrainian leadership, the people of Ukraine should not suffer.

Vladimir Putin: I agree. Start reductions as of today.

Thus it was that Putin, feigning pity for the poor people of Ukraine, 'agreed to a suggestion' to cut supplies of gas intended for transit through Ukraine to Central and Western Europe. It was the first time Russia – or the Soviet Union – had ever cut supplies to its customers in the West. The action destroyed Russia's fundamental argument, that it had always been, and would always be, a reliable energy supplier.

The decision was the last straw for the European Union. The Americans had long been urging its partners to diversify supplies in order to break Moscow's stranglehold. Now it became urgent. The EU began exploring every possible alternative energy supplier – from Algeria to Iran to Turkmenistan. Putin's decision gave fresh impetus to the so-called Nabucco project, a planned pipeline that would bring gas to central Europe from Turkmenistan or Azerbaijan via Turkey, Bulgaria and Romania – avoiding Russia.

Nabucco was seen as a rival to Russia's own 'alternative' route – the South Stream pipeline, which would supply Russian gas via the Black Sea, Bulgaria and Serbia. Plans were already well advanced, too, for the Nord Stream pipeline under the Baltic Sea – yet another alternative to supplying Europe via Ukraine. Russia didn't quite get (or pretended not to get) the Western argument, which was that Russia itself could no longer be trusted as a reliable supplier. Russia put the blame entirely on Ukraine as a transit country, and proffered Nord Stream and South Stream as routes for Russian gas that would avoid potential disruption in the future by Ukraine. The EU feared that this could leave not only Ukraine but also Poland (another transit country) open to blackmail in the future: Russia, faced with a dispute with Poland or Ukraine, would be able to cut gas to those countries while continuing to supply countries further west via the new pipelines. For the Europeans, Nabucco seemed a safer bet, cutting Russia out of the equation altogether. But the fact remained that potential supplies for Nabucco were scarce (Russia had already bought up Turkmen gas for years in advance), and in any case Russia, with its enormous energy resources, was fated to remain a major supplier for the foreseeable future. But after Putin's intervention on 5 January 2009 it would never be fully trusted.

It took until 20 January for Europe's gas to start flowing again, following a deal struck in the middle of the night between Putin and the Ukrainian prime minister Yulia Tymoshenko. Ukraine would pay European prices, but with a discount for 2009, and in return Ukraine left the fee it charged for transit unchanged. Both sides agreed no longer to use the shady intermediary, Rosukrenergo, linked to Tymoshenko's erstwhile colleague and now rival, President Yushchenko.

The postscript to this story comes a year later. In February 2010 Viktor Yanukovych, the man supported in 2004 by Putin but overthrown by the Orange Revolution, was finally elected as Ukraine's president. The Yushchenko presidency had proved disastrous, riven by internal rivalries, corruption and inept economic policies. Some saw it as the defeat of the Orange Revolution – but that was short-sighted. Yanukovych beat his main rival, Tymoshenko, in a fair election, so democracy itself was not an issue. Moreover, Yanukovych in power proved to be not entirely a Russian poodle. He did, it is true, quickly sign an agreement with President Medvedev to extend Russia's lease on its Black Sea Fleet base in the Crimea for up to 30 years. In exchange he extracted a multi-year discount on Ukraine's contracts for Russian gas deliveries. But the price Russia would have to pay for its Crimean base was extortionate. Putin commented: 'The price we are now asked to pay is out of this world. I would be willing to eat Yanukovych and the prime minister for that sort of money. No military base in the world costs that much. Prices like that simply do not exist. If we look at what the contract would cost us over ten years, it amounts to $40–45 billion.'

Later, Yanukovych also began to question again how much Ukraine was paying for its Russian gas. (The deal signed by Tymoshenko with Putin in 2009 was deemed so unfavourable that she was jailed for abuse of office.) In summer 2011 Yanukovych demanded that Russia halve its prices, to less than $200. As for Ukraine's westward orientation, although plans to join NATO were dropped, Yanukovych continued to move towards closer integration with the EU – spurning Putin's attempts to woo him into a free-trade agreement with Russia.

The Obama effect

In the summer and autumn of 2008, while Russia was gazing at its Georgian navel, its leadership failed to notice that on the other side of the world something important was happening. George W. Bush, Putin's nemesis for the past eight years, would soon stand down, and there was every chance that the November presidential election would be won by a young, liberal black man who was enthralling the entire world. Firstly, the Russians did not believe that a black candidate could possibly beat Senator John McCain. But they also refused to believe that if Barack Obama did win anything would change. I remember sitting in a Kremlin office trying to explain to officials that an Obama victory looked very likely and that it could present a real opportunity to improve relations. They should start thinking now about how to reach out to him. The reaction was a smirk and a shrug of the shoulders: 'Nothing will change. It's all the same people.'

Russia really was stuck in a time-warp. It was not just the West that still treated Russia as essentially a communist country minus a few of the trimmings. Russia also suffered from a world view shaped by Cold War-era *Pravda* cartoons of Uncle Sam feeding the 'military-industrial complex' with one hand and launching missiles at the Soviet Union with the other. For them, Barack Obama was just a product of the system, and nothing would change.

On 4 November Obama was elected, to a parade of delirious headlines almost everywhere. Whatever else was true, Obama was not George W. Bush, and for many people it seemed like the dawn of a new era. President Medvedev had been preparing for his first state-of-the-nation speech for some weeks – it was first announced for late October, then rescheduled for 5 November. As news of Obama's victory came in, the Kremlin's PR firm, Ketchum, quickly sent a recommendation that this was the ideal chance to make an overture to the new president, with some warm words about future cooperation. But it was not just Ketchum's advice that failed to get through; it was as if nobody had bothered to pass on the news that Obama had won.

Medvedev spoke for an hour and half in the dazzling white hall of the Great Kremlin Palace, but he did not even mention Obama's name, far less congratulate him. He did, however, blame US foreign policy for the war in Georgia, and he announced that Russia might deploy Iskander missiles in Kaliningrad, bordering Poland, to neutralise Bush's missile defence system.

The next day's headlines recorded a missed chance. 'Russian President Dmitry Medvedev orders missiles deployed in Europe as world hails Obama,' said the London *Times*.

'Russia gives Obama brisk warning,' said the *Washington Post*.

It has often been pointed out that Russia's foreign policy is essentially reactive, and this was certainly largely the case throughout the Putin years. He made few, if any, initiatives off his own bat: as we have seen, he expected NATO to 'invite' Russia to join, he responded to the 9/11 attacks with positive gestures, and to NATO expansion and missile defence plans with negative ones – but he rarely came out with initiatives of his own for others to react to. The same was clearly going to be the case now: Russia's foreign policy might change, but only if the Americans made the first move.

Obama chose Stanford University professor Michael McFaul as his chief Russia adviser, and the new team immediately came up with a new, pragmatic philosophy which they called 'dual-track engagement'. It meant that the administration would not link country-to-country relations with Russian behaviour on human rights or democracy. It would continue to challenge the Kremlin robustly on its human rights record and over its occupation of Georgia, but it would not make diplomatic or military cooperation in other areas (on Iran, for example, or missile defence) hostage to that. The two would operate on separate tracks. 'The idea's very simple,' McFaul says. 'We're going to engage with the Russian government on issues that are of mutual interest and we're going to engage directly with Russian civil society, including Russian political opposition figures, on things that we consider are important as well.' [1]

The first public hint of a new approach came in a speech by Vice-President Joe Biden at the Munich Security Conference in February 2009. This was the same venue where two years earlier Putin had virtually turned his back on the United States. 'The last few years have seen a dangerous drift in relations between Russia and members of our alliance,' Biden said. Now, the US wanted to 'press the reset button'. The phrase quickly became shorthand for Obama's new approach to Russia. His secretary of state, Hillary Clinton, tried to turn it into a television image a month later by presenting her opposite number, Sergei Lavrov, with a large red button marked 'reset'. The word was unfortunately rendered into Russian as 'overload' or 'overcharged' – which at least ensured some smiles as the policy was formally inaugurated.

Behind the scenes, more important resetting was getting under way. A week after Biden's speech, Michael McFaul went to Moscow to hand-deliver a personal letter from Obama to Medvedev. The letter was intended to be a kind of bait, laid outside the cave to tempt the growling bear to come out. 'We are taking a careful look at the missile defence programme,' it said, hinting that it should become an issue for cooperation, not confrontation. The letter laid out in big, broad terms a vision of US–Russian relations which recognised that, in fact, America's interests were by and large also Russia's interests, and they should be looking for 'win-win' situations rather than the 'zero-sum' attitude that had dogged the past.

The bear sniffed the package and seemed to like it. Medvedev had his first face-to-face meeting with Obama in London on 1 April, on the margins of a G20 summit convened to tackle the global financial crisis. They got through the preliminaries – how nice that we're both young, both lawyers, both new to the job – and then Obama decided to try out his new 'win-win' approach on a troublesome example that had recently arisen. A few months earlier, President Bakiyev of Kyrgyzstan had suddenly announced he wanted the Americans to leave the Manas air base, a vital transit centre for the Afghan war, having been leant on – and bribed – by the Russians. Bakiyev's decision came on the same day as Russia offered Kyrgyzstan a $2 billion loan. Sitting together in the US ambassador's Regent's Park residence, Obama explained to Medvedev, a trifle condescendingly, why it was in Russia's interest to let the Americans stay at Manas: 'I need you to understand why we have this base here. It supports our activities in Afghanistan.

It's where our troops fly in and out of Afghanistan. They take showers. They have hot meals and they get ready to go in to fight in Afghanistan, to deal with enemies of ours that are also enemies of yours. And if we weren't fighting these people, you would have to be fighting these people. So tell me, President Medvedev, why is that not in your national interest, that we would have this base of operations that helps what we're doing in Afghanistan?' Medvedev did not respond immediately. But three months later the Americans signed a deal that allowed them to stay at Manas.

Michael McFaul recalls that Medvedev also made a surprising gesture at the London meeting, offering to expand the so-called 'Northern Distribution Network' for Afghanistan, to allow the US to transport lethal cargoes through Russian air space for the first time.

This became a key accord to be announced during Obama's first official visit to Moscow in July 2009, together with a framework agreement for talks to begin on a new disarmament treaty to replace the old START nuclear arms reduction treaty, which was due to expire in December. The treaty, which would become known as New Start, was to be the centrepiece of the reset. But even agreeing wording for the framework agreement required some diplomatic acrobatics, to accommodate the two sides' diametrically opposed views on whether the treaty should also impose limits on missile defences.

President Obama had promised to 'review' George W. Bush's missile defence plans, and in September he would delight the Russians by cancelling the plans for a radar in the Czech Republic and interceptors in Poland. But he still intended to build something in their place, and the Americans were determined not to include in the New Start treaty anything that would impede their development of a missile shield. The Russians were equally determined to link the two. They insisted that building defences against offensive nuclear missiles destabilised the general strategic balance by making the side without the shield vulnerable to a first strike.

'We were categorical that we were not going to have this conversation together,' says McFaul. 'We could have a separate conversation about missile defence, but here we were going to talk about reducing offensive strategic weapons. That's what the negotiations had to be about. The Russians wanted to do it all together. We said no.'

Russia's deputy foreign minister, Sergei Ryabkov, recalls: 'It was clear from the beginning – for us at least and I think for our American friends too – that the subject of missile defence would become a stumbling block.'[2]

They agreed a compromise, but it was a messy fudge. Their memorandum of understanding included a 'provision on the interrelationship of strategic offensive and strategic defensive arms'. The two presidents interpreted this in quite different ways. At their joint press conference, Medvedev said: 'We have agreed that offensive and defensive systems of both countries should be considered *as a complex*.' Obama said: 'It is entirely legitimate for our discussions to talk not only about offensive weapons systems but also defensive weapon systems.' He did *not* say they should be 'considered as a complex', indeed he explicitly pointed out that America's planned missile shield was aimed exclusively at dealing with a strike from Iran or North Korea and had nothing to do with Russia's strategic forces, and added: 'And so, in that sense, we have not thought that it is appropriate to link discussions of a missile defence system designed to deal with an entirely different threat unrelated to the kinds of robust capabilities that Russia possesses.' So was there linkage or not? The fudge allowed negotiations to start ... but on a fatally flawed basis.

The July summit in Moscow was designed to demonstrate the new 'dual track' approach, taking in not just summit talks with the Russian leadership but also 'civil society' – a speech at an independent college, the New Economic School, and a meeting with opposition figures, 'the biggest critics we could find of the Russian government', according to McFaul.

The first day was devoted to talks with President Medvedev, but Obama was also keen to meet the man who had shaped Russia for the past ten years. The second morning began with breakfast on the veranda at Putin's dacha – a sumptuous meal that included three types of caviar ('at least one of which must have been illegal', according to one of the Americans). The meeting was scheduled to last one hour, but went on for two and a half. Obama started by asking Putin, 'How did we get into this mess – this low point that US–Russian relations have been in for the past years?' Luckily Obama is a good listener. Putin's answer took up the whole of the first hour.

He delivered a history of the two countries' relations, going back to his hobby horse, the West's bombing of Serbia, and enumerating every slight he had felt in the years that followed: ABM, Iraq, WTO, NATO expansion, missile defence, Kosovo … Putin's tale of unrequited love. McFaul felt that while one could argue over the substance 'the prime minister was actually saying things that I think President Obama also agreed with – that if we just focus on our interests and talk very pragmatically about where we agree and disagree, we can cooperate'. For Obama, the history lesson was even rather helpful because it enabled him to emphasise to Putin: well, I'm different, I'm new, and I don't want the past to haunt the future. I actually want to reset the relationship with Russia.

The summit achieved its goals – but in a surprisingly unspectacular way. There was none of the euphoria (or tension) that used to accompany East–West summitry during the Cold War. Obamamania just did not infiltrate Russia. The student audience for his major public speech looked rather bored.

Gradually, though, the reset began to bear fruit – including a marked shift in Russia's stance towards Iran. Since joining the six-nation Iran group in 2005, Russia had consistently argued that while it, too, opposed the proliferation of nuclear weapons, it did not believe that Iran was trying to build them or could build them in the near future. It defended its right to help Iran develop a civil nuclear programme, and was reluctant to support sanctions. But at their first meeting in London in April 2009, Obama was astonished when Medvedev admitted that the Americans had 'probably been more right' than the Russians when it came to assessing Iran's ballistic missile threat.

In September the Americans had a unique chance to prove they were right about Iran's nuclear ambitions too. The presidents were due to meet at the United Nations in New York. Just before the meeting, Obama's national security adviser, General James Jones, called his Russian opposite number, Sergei Prikhodko, and told him they needed to meet urgently. In a room at the Waldorf Astoria hotel, Jones showed Prikhodko spy photographs of a secret uranium enrichment plant that the Iranians were building near the holy city of Qom. Prikhodko admitted in an interview: 'This was not the nicest surprise we could have got.'[3] Jones says the Russian was shocked and kept shaking his head, saying, 'This is bad, really bad ...'[4]

Foreign minister Lavrov couldn't believe what he was seeing. He took Michael McFaul aside and said: 'Why didn't you tell us before, Mike?'

McFaul replied: 'Well ... we thought you knew. I mean, these are *your* guys, not ours!'

Obama and Medvedev then met to discuss the news, and Medvedev's reaction at a press conference generated positive headlines in Western countries, as for the first time he stated that 'sanctions rarely lead to productive results, but in some cases the use of sanctions is inevitable'. It was only two days later, when news of the Qom facility was revealed to the world at a G20 summit in Pittsburgh, that the reason for Medvedev's change of attitude could be guessed at. For the first time, Russia and the West now started to work more closely on Iran. The following June, Moscow would back new UN sanctions, and in September even cancel the sale of an S-300 air defence system to Iran, losing a billion-dollar contract.

Negotiations on New Start, meanwhile, began on a permanent basis in Geneva. Two sticking points quickly became evident. One was the exchange of what was known as 'telemetric information' – sharing data about missile tests and launches. The second was 'unique identifiers' – essentially, bar-coding every missile so they could all be accounted for and tracked.

Both Obama and Medvedev became deeply involved in the process, hammering out all the most important details in telephone calls and face-to-face meetings. Medvedev joked later that 'telemetry' had become his favourite English word.

One of their meetings took place in December in Copenhagen, where both leaders were attending climate-change talks. With every venue in the city apparently taken up with global warming discussions, Obama and Medvedev found themselves in a makeshift meeting-room in a curtained-off area of a women's dress shop, surrounded by naked mannequins. It proved to be a conducive atmosphere. Obama explained the concept of unique identifiers: 'Look, we just put these barcodes on the missiles, so we can count them. That's what the treaty's all about, after all.'

Russia's negotiators had been resisting this, insisting that 'if we sign a treaty, we fulfil it' and that it should not be assumed they would cheat. But Medvedev saw the sense of it. 'OK,' he said, 'so long as it's done in a fair way. That you do it and we do it, and we do it in a symmetrical way.'

The breakthrough was followed by one on telemetry, and it seemed agreement was close. In January General Jones called Obama from Moscow airport after talks that seemed to clinch the deal.

But there was a hitch. The Americans had been assuming that the Russians agreed that the strategic arms treaty would stand alone, with no reference to missile defence. But now

Obama's replacement for the Bush missile shield was beginning to take shape, and the Russians did not like it. Instead of a radar in the Czech Republic and interceptors in Poland, Obama was developing what he called a 'Phased Adaptive Approach', which in many ways might pose even more of a potential threat to Russia. It would involve highly mobile sea-based missiles and radars, and short-range missiles based in Eastern Europe. On 4 February 2010 it was announced that those missiles would be located in Romania. It seemed to cause a hardening of attitudes in Moscow, where they realised they were about to agree a treaty that would considerably reduce Russia's strategic arsenal, while the Americans were building a fence right on their border.

On 24 February the hot line between the Kremlin and the White House glowed red for almost an hour and a half. Medvedev was again trying to couple the arms cuts with legally binding missile defence restrictions – within the new treaty. Obama was angry. 'We'd agreed, Dmitry! If the conditions for the treaty are this, then we're not going to have a treaty.' Obama was also angry with his staff, who had led him to believe the deal was all but done. In fact, his negotiators had done him a bad service by letting the Russians think they could insert a condition in the treaty that would freeze missile defence systems as they currently stood.

It took three more weeks of intense negotiation in Geneva and Moscow, and another Medvedev–Obama phone call on 13 March, to settle the deal. The New Start treaty was finally signed in Prague on 8 April. It dealt only with arms reductions, as the Americans wished, while both sides appended unilateral statements regarding missile defence. The Americans stated that US missile defence systems were not intended to affect the strategic balance with Russia. But the Russian statement invoked the right to withdraw from the treaty should it deem a future American build-up of missile defence capabilities to be a threat to its own strategic nuclear potential. The Russians thereby achieved some kind of linkage, as they had wanted: if at any point they decide that the US missile shield has become too strong, they can leave the treaty and build up their own nuclear forces.

iMedvedev

So far, internationally, President Medvedev had acted in much the same way as one would have expected Vladimir Putin to have acted. It did not go unnoticed that as prime minister, Putin continued to express his opinions on foreign affairs and even to make trips to other countries. It was he, for example, who publicly stated that missile defence was in fact an obstacle to the search for a strategic arms agreement – just weeks before Medvedev infuriated Obama by repeating the same thought.

Medvedev's views on defending Russia's interests, and being treated as an equal partner, were identical to his mentor's. Even the rapprochement with the West over Iran did not signify a strategic shift: for a variety of reasons – commercial, political and strategic – Moscow was never going to risk making an enemy of Tehran.

Medvedev, as we shall see in the next chapter, was slowly changing the agenda at home but struggling to make an impact. The same was true of his early foreign overtures. His keynote speeches in Berlin and Evian had flopped. But now that the ice was broken with President Obama, he spotted a way, perhaps, to boost his image at home and abroad. Since 'modernisation' was his watchword in domestic politics, it made sense for him to be seen hobnobbing with a modern American president. It wasn't enough just to own an iPad and record video-blogs for his website. He needed to get out West and visit Silicon Valley. He was never going to compete with Putin's Action Man holiday stunts, but he could try to look cool in the company of Barack Obama and Arnold Schwarzenegger. Or would he just look puny? That was the problem.

A couple of months after the Prague treaty was signed, Medvedev set off on his first state visit to the United States. He did everything a modernising president should do. He opened a Twitter account, visited Cisco and Apple and Stanford University, met Russian émigrés working in Silicon Valley, then flew to Washington for talks with congressmen and an impromptu shirt-sleeves lunch with Obama at Ray's Hell Burger joint. They discussed whether jalapenos were better than pickles, but what Barack did not tell Dmitry over lunch was that the FBI had just uncovered a nest of Russian spies. That only emerged after Medvedev was back in Moscow, and a grand spy swap was executed at Vienna airport, in true Cold War style, on 9 July. Ten Russian 'sleeper' agents, including the glamorous and instantly celebrated Anna Chapman, were exchanged for four Americans who had been jailed in Russia, accused of espionage.

The incident did more than remind everyone that espionage is still a thriving business. It also involuntarily brought to mind the spymaster who was President Medvedev's patron and now his prime minister. Putin welcomed the spies home as heroes – notwithstanding the fact that they had, in fact, proved to be almost useless during their many years as 'sleepers', with fake identities and jobs in the United States. They had failed to penetrate any worthwhile institution and allowed themselves to be caught doing the most basic of espionage tricks. But Putin's loyalty to his profession is unequivocal, and he fell comfortably into his role as godfather of Russia's spies. A week or so after the agents' return, Putin organised a morale-boosting meeting with them, where they sang patriotic Soviet songs and he promised them 'an interesting, bright future' working in 'worthy places'. He also promised retribution for the traitor who exposed them to the Americans: 'This was the result of treason, and traitors always end badly. They finish up as drunks, addicts, on the street.'

One of the songs they sang together was 'Where Does

the Motherland Begin?', from a 1968 film, *The Sword and the Shield*, about a Soviet spy working in Nazi Germany. Putin also played it on the piano, with two fingers, at a charity event in December. It's clearly a favourite – sentimental and patriotic ...

Where does the motherland begin?
With the song your mother used to sing,
With your comrades good and true,
The neighbours always there for you.
With the birch-tree in the windy field,
The steady sound of wagon-wheels,
The never-ending country track,
The windows lit in a distant shack ...
Where does the motherland start?
With the pledge you made in your heart.

THE STRONGMAN AND HIS FRIENDS

Weathering the global financial crisis

Vladimir Putin once remarked that he was 'tired of foreign policy' and glad to be prime minister rather than president. But in September 2008, just four months into the new job, he had to deal with an economic and financial crisis for which he was ill prepared. Eight years earlier he had received intensive tuition in economics from his team of bright young reformers. But little in Putin's experience prepared him for the tornado that was about to hit his country.

Immediately prior to the global financial crash, things were looking good. Buoyed by record-high oil prices, the Russian economy had grown by an average of 7 per cent a year between 1999 and 2008. The Stabilisation Fund, set up to provide a cushion if oil prices should drop, was huge, and had been split into a Reserve Fund, with $140 billion, and a National Welfare Fund, with $30 billion, the latter mainly earmarked to solve the looming pension crisis. Only in February 2008 Putin had been boasting that 'the main thing we have achieved is stability'. But Russian business had borrowed heavily from Western banks, and those were about to start crashing.

Luckily Putin still had his team of experts, who had watched America's subprime crisis gathering, and were only too aware that the tsunami would soon engulf Russia. The day after Lehman Brothers went bankrupt on 15 September, Putin's economics team gathered at the office of his deputy prime minister, Igor Shuvalov. They included President Medvedev's economic adviser, Arkady Dvorkovich, and the finance minister, Alexei Kudrin, who would later be named 'Finance Minister of the Year' by *Euromoney* magazine. 'When we realised that everyone in the market could go bankrupt overnight, we knew we had to do something,' he recalls. 'We came up with a plan to provide a line of credit for 295 businesses. They'd get special rights to credit from banks.'[1] Those 295 companies represented 80 per cent of the country's income.

The plan was to offer loans through two state-owned banks, Vneshekonombank and Sberbank. The latter was headed by the architect of Putin's early reforms, German Gref. He was hesitant: 'I said that I was willing to do this but only with state guarantees, because I had the money of our shareholders. I had to answer to them if the risks were too high.'[2]

The team came up with a scheme whereby the Central Bank would guarantee the loans. 'We spent two days and nights here in Sberbank,' Gref recalls. 'We sifted through all the papers working out who owed what to whom. My staff didn't sleep for two days.'

In the end the Central Bank spent about $200 billion, about a third of its cash reserves, keeping the economy afloat. Most of this was used to recapitalise banks, buy up plunging shares and support the declining rouble. $50 billion was disbursed to the 295 key businesses, so that they could repay hard currency loans from foreign lenders. The beneficiaries included private oligarchs such as Oleg Deripaska ($4.5 billion) and Roman Abramovich ($1.8 billion), but also state companies such as Rosneft ($4.6 billion) and Russian Technologies ($7 billion).

At 13 per cent of GDP, it was the biggest bail-out package in the G8, dwarfing even the huge US stimulus package of $787 billion or 5.5 per cent of US GDP.

The strategy worked. Within a couple of years almost all of the loans were repaid, as Russia swung out of the recession in rather better shape than some Western countries. GDP fell during the crisis by 8 per cent, more than any other economy in the G20, but within a year growth had recovered to plus 5 per cent.

Sergei Guriev, a respected economist with whom President Obama had a meeting on his first visit to Moscow, says the government's response to the crisis was 'resolute and effective'. 'The Russian financial system came out of the acute financial crisis virtually unscathed, and unemployment remained under control. The government prevented the collapse of the banking system. Moreover, the crisis did not result in major nationalisations of private companies. The government could have nationalised all banks and companies in financial distress under the banner of fighting the crisis, but it did not.'[3]

Nonetheless, in the year of recession, thousands of Russian banks and businesses collapsed. Foreign investors began to flee, wiping a trillion dollars off the value of the Russian stock exchange.

Putin himself refused to accept that the crisis revealed any structural shortcomings in Russia's economy. He blamed it all on American recklessness and saw it as yet more proof of the iniquity of American hegemony. 'Everything that is happening in the economic and financial sphere has started in the United States. This is a real crisis that all of us are facing. And what is really sad is that we see an inability to take appropriate decisions. This is no longer irresponsibility on the part of some individuals, but irresponsibility of the whole system, which as you know had pretensions to (global) leadership.'

He went to the Davos World Economic Forum in January to deliver this message, but like Medvedev's homily on world security after the invasion of Georgia, no one was much interested in Putin's recipes for the world economy. It was, after all, only days since Russia had frozen Europeans in their homes by cutting their gas supplies.

The crisis hit Russia differently from the more established Western economies. It exposed the dependency of the country on its oil exports, as the price plummeted from $145 to $35 a barrel. Russia produces almost no manufactured goods for export – neither electronics nor clothes nor machinery – to provide more stable revenues. The crisis also laid bare the calamitous state of much of Russia's industrial base, inherited from the Soviet planned economy. The Soviets had created industrial zones on a scale unknown in the West – so-called 'mono-cities', where literally everything revolved around and depended upon a single enormous engineering plant. If you didn't actually work at the factory, or one of its subsidiaries or supply units, you were employed by the local government or the schools or health system, or in the shops that fed the workers. If the central plant – be it a car factory or aluminium plant or steel works – stopped producing, then the entire network built around it would also collapse. Soviet planners did not envisage economic downturns. Now the mono-cities they built, even if they had passed into private hands, were hopelessly vulnerable to the vicissitudes of Wall Street.

One such mono-city was at Pikalyovo, near St Petersburg. It grew up around a cement works, now a complex of three intertwined factories, one of which was owned by one of Russia's richest men, Oleg Deripaska. The economic crisis caused thousands to be laid off with no pay at the beginning of 2009. When the factory could not pay its bills to the local heating and power station, supplies of hot water and heating to the entire town were cut. The population, facing a huge social crisis, took matters into their own hands. Protestors blocked the main highway leading to St Petersburg, causing a 400-kilometre tailback of vehicles, just as Vladimir Putin was visiting his home town – inaugurating, of all things, a shiny new Nissan car assembly plant. Now there was a full-blown crisis. At a meeting with the factory owners and government ministers in Pikalyovo on 4 June, Putin read the riot act. He ordered unpaid wages – more than 41 million roubles – to be paid that day, and lectured the owners: 'You made thousands of people hostages to your ambition, incompetence and greed. It's absolutely unacceptable!' Suddenly the hallowed precepts of the market economy were forgotten as Putin seemed to threaten a state takeover: 'If the owners can't come to an agreement by themselves then no matter what, this complex will be restarted one way or another. But if you can't come to an agreement, then we'll do it without you.'

In a scene that left television viewers astonished, he then demanded that the owners, whom he likened to cockroaches, sign a pledge to get the factories working again. 'Did everybody sign this agreement? Yes? Deripaska, have you signed? I can't see your signature ... Come here!' The billionaire shuffled up and meekly signed the paper, only to hear Putin snarl at him: 'Give me back my pen!'

It was as if Leonid Brezhnev had come back to haunt Russia – the Communist Party general secretary stepping in to whip the local bosses into order. But this was 2009, almost two decades after Russia was supposed to have espoused capitalism. Putin's solution could only be a quick fix. In the longer term Russia had to find a way to make even the mono-cities respond to the market.

The city of Tolyatti on the Volga, 800 kilometres southeast of Moscow, is the country's biggest mono-city – a conurbation of 700,000 people where every fourth adult works in the AvtoVAZ factory producing Lada cars. Shortly before the recession, in February 2008, the French manufacturer Renault bought a 25 per cent stake in AvtoVAZ for $1 billion. But like automobile makers around the world, the company suffered badly during the crisis. Renault failed to streamline production or reduce the bloated workforce. As many as 100,000 cars were unsold. Again, the prime minister's instinct was to put workers' welfare ahead of all else. The factory simply could not be allowed to fail: in a city like Tolyatti, the collapse of the dominant industry would have catastrophic consequences for hundreds of thousands of people – and threaten the very stability of the state. On 30 March 2009 Putin visited the factory and praised its managers for not causing massive lay-offs (in contrast to Pikalyovo) and promised 25 billion roubles ($830 million) of government aid in the form of loans, cash and guarantees. Sergei Guriev describes the bail-out of 'this behemoth of inefficiency' as one of the few mistakes of the crisis.

But Putin also engaged in some tough diplomacy to ensure the company's longer-term survival. In October he issued a public ultimatum to Renault to help bail out the plant or see its 25 per cent stake in the company reduced. 'Either they participate in the further financing of the company or we will have to negotiate with them about our relative stakes.' Then, on 27 November, he made a dash to Paris and got what he wanted. Renault promised to provide new technology for the factory, in return for which the government put in an extra 50 billion roubles.

It was a good couple of days in Paris for Putin. As well as the Renault success, he also supervised the signing of a deal between Gazprom and the French energy giant EDF on the latter's participation in the controversial South Stream project – the pipeline designed to bring Russian natural gas to Europe while bypassing 'unreliable' transit countries such as Ukraine and Belarus – while the other French energy major, GDF-Suez, held talks with Putin about taking a 9 per cent share in the other bypass pipeline, Nord Stream. Both pipelines were now making good progress: the German government and energy companies supported Nord Stream, while the Italian ENI was a partner in South Stream. The EU's alternative, Nabucco, by contrast, was making slow progress.

Meanwhile, at a private dinner with the French prime minister, Putin discussed something even more sensational – the purchase of a French-built Mistral amphibious assault ship, the second-largest vessel in the French fleet, with room for helicopters, tanks, landing craft and 750 commandoes. The sale of two Mistrals was confirmed a year later, representing an unprecedented transfer of NATO naval technology – and causing considerable unease among Russia's East European neighbours.

The prime minister seemed to relish his job as international salesman for Russia. But he suffered one notable failure – again involving the automobile industry. In the spring of 2009 he and the German chancellor, Angela Merkel, together supported a bid to rescue Opel, the German division of the bankrupt American manufacturer General Motors. The deal would see one of Russia's state-controlled banks, Sberbank, club together with a Canadian firm, Magna, to buy a 55 per cent stake in Opel and save tens of thousands of jobs, mainly in Germany. Merkel and Putin met regularly to discuss and promote the deal. For Merkel, facing elections in September, it was politically vital, and for Putin it was another chance for Russia to get its hands on Western technology: Sberbank's partner in the deal was the GAZ car factory, owned by Oleg Deripaska, which stood to gain access to Opel's latest technologies and build cars that might finally shed the impression that Russians could only produce shoddy Ladas.

On 10 September GM agreed to the deal. Putin was jubilant. 'I hope that this is one of the steps that will lead us to true integration into the European economy,' he told members of the Valdai Club at his country residence. Over the next couple of months the chairman of Sberbank, German Gref, oversaw the final negotiations, flying back and forth to GM headquarters in Detroit. They produced a 5,000-page contract. 'Then, one evening in early November,' Gref recalls, 'I happened to be in a meeting with Putin, and I was supposed to fly to Russelsheim that evening to sign the contract the next morning. I came out of the meeting and was given a message that GM had decided not to sell Opel!' At first, Gref thought it must be a joke. 'The whole deal was worked out. We'd done colossal work, getting agreement with all European governments!'

Eventually the president of GM, Frederick Henderson, called Gref to apologise and explain that it had been a decision of the board. Gref told him it might be better for them not to have a conversation right then, because he might use language he would regret: 'It was a short call. I was so shocked, it took me ages to recover. We had worked day and night for half a year on this deal – with a huge team of people.'

Putin himself hit the roof. It was not just a huge blow to his hopes of reviving the Russian car industry, but also confirmation of American perfidiousness: 'We will have to take into account this style of dealing with partners in the future, though this scornful approach toward partners mainly affects the Europeans, not us. GM did not warn anyone, did not speak to anyone ... despite all the agreements reached and documents signed. Well, I think it is a good lesson.'

The need to reform

The financial crisis exposed the weakness of Russia's semi-reformed economy. You could not rely solely on a hyperactive prime minister to rush around chivvying owners to sign pledges or foreigners to invest. The economy itself had to become more responsive, and more attractive to investors. Putin's team of reformers understood this, and so did his president. Medvedev's adviser, Arkady Dvorkovich, says: 'We had to ask ourselves, why was the Russian economy hit harder than any other? And the main conclusion we came to was that the structure of the Russian economy just didn't match up to modern demands and was open to far too big risks. Of course, that was obvious back in 2000 when we worked out the reforms under Putin. We achieved some things in those eight years, but the structure of the economy didn't change.' [4]

Constantly rising oil prices had helped to raise living standards, but also induced complacency with regard to economic reform. 'When oil prices fell again in 2008,' says Dvorkovich, 'we realised this was not enough – we had to change direction. Medvedev decided we just couldn't stay on the old path.'

The change in direction was signalled in an article entitled 'Go, Russia!', published by Medvedev in an online (of course) journal on 10 September 2009. It took him just four lines to get to the point, condemning Russia as 'a primitive economy based on raw materials and endemic corruption'. The more cynical Russian commentators refuse to see even a glimmer of difference between Medvedev and Putin, but the fact is that Putin never uttered such words about the economy. The article reminded me a little of some of Mikhail Gorbachev's reformist tracts in the late 1980s: he too would be accused of being better on analysis than solutions, and he too found that many of his reforms were either smothered by the Old Guard or withered in the unyielding ground of the Soviet system.

Medvedev declared that '20 years of tumultuous change has not spared our country from its humiliating dependence on raw materials. Our current economy still reflects the major flaw of the Soviet system: it largely ignores individual needs. With a few exceptions domestic business does not invent or create the necessary things and technology that people need.' Referring, it seems to his predecessor's reforms, Medvedev said: 'All this proves that we did not do all we should have done in previous years. And far from all the things were done correctly.' He promised 'modernisation' in almost everything: the country would hire the best specialists from around the world; there would be inward investment, modern information technologies and even political reform – whereby parliamentary parties would periodically replace each other in power, 'as in most democratic states'.

It read like an election manifesto – the one he might have published *before* the election rather than a year after, had there been a free election. This was the first of many such liberal-sounding prospectuses Medvedev would deliver during his presidency, but very few of the ideas found their way into real life. Analysts argue over why. Is it because Medvedev is simply a Putin puppet, dancing his liberal dance to entertain the West, while the puppeteer keeps a tight control of everything behind the scenes? Or is it because a real would-be reformer is thwarted at every turn by his master? Or is the task of reforming Russia simply too great, and the system – the corruption, the sheer enormity of the task – fights back and kills every initiative?

Like Gorbachev, Medvedev's first visible measures were top–down initiatives designed to bring about what the market achieved, with very little help from governments, in the West. In March 2010 he chose the town of Skolkovo, in Moscow region, as the site for what he hoped would become Russia's 'Silicon Valley'. But was it not a contradiction in terms for a government to be establishing by decree an 'innovation centre'? Not if the Kremlin ideologue Vladislav Surkov was to be believed. He advocated what he called 'authoritarian modernisation' (sic) and said political liberalisation was not needed for economic reform. According to Surkov 'spontaneous modernisation' only worked in Anglo-Saxon countries, whereas France, Japan and South Korea (and by implication, Russia) relied on 'dirigiste methods'.

The following month Medvedev announced another 'reform from above': Moscow was to be turned into a leading global financial centre. But how? It smacked of Medvedev's earlier attempt to 'establish' the rouble as an international reserve currency (this was announced in the same ill-conceived speech at Evian in which he called for a new security treaty in the wake of the Georgia war). There seemed little understanding of the psychology of markets, with their unfathomable mixture of gambling, guesswork, experience and foresight. Alexander Voloshin, former chief of staff to both Yeltsin and Putin, was put in charge of the project. He is a renowned wheeler-dealer, but this seemed a task too great even for him. A year later Medvedev announced that the project was 'half-complete'. So apparently if such progress keeps up, Moscow will be an international financial capital by mid-2012.

Medvedev became obsessed with Russia's inability to become integrated into the world economy. In 2009 foreign capital investment fell by 41 per cent. In February 2010 the president put deputy prime minister Igor Shuvalov personally in charge of improving Russia's investment image, with a 'special structure in the ministry to analyse obstacles that hinder it'. Shuvalov is a clean-cut, crew-cut, smart young politician much admired by Western businessmen. He personally contributes to Russia's international links by renting a 400-square-metre apartment in London and a 1,500-square-metre villa in Austria. Shuvalov has led Russia's efforts (crucial for integration into the world economy) to join the World Trade Organisation – an on-off process hampered both by American obstacles and by Putin's apparently lukewarm approach. In June 2009, for example, two days after the US and EU trade representatives successfully completed a round of talks with Shuvalov that would lead to WTO membership 'by the end of the year', Putin announced out of the blue that Russia would only join together with Belarus and Kazakhstan, as a 'single customs union', even though both countries were miles behind Russia in their negotiations with the WTO. The announcement appeared to take Medvedev and Shuvalov by surprise and put off Russian membership indefinitely.

When he returned from his eye-opening trip to California in July 2010, President Medvedev called in Russia's foreign ambassadors for a private talk in which he hauled them over the coals for their antediluvian approach to their work. (It reminded me of the foreign ministry official who told us, when asked to explain why it took so long to organise interviews with deputy ministers, that 'we still work in the nineteenth century here'.) Medvedev sternly told his diplomats to stop sending him pointless dispatches about world events. 'I can read about them perfectly well on the internet,' he said, 'and a lot sooner than you tell me about them.' In future, the foreign service was to devote itself to Medvedev's Big Idea – modernisation – by advancing Russia's cause and attracting investment, especially from key countries, which he named as Germany, France, Italy, the EU in general and the USA. A Kremlin official who was present summed up the president's lecture as 'either change your views and your brains, or get out of the diplomatic profession'.[5]

But a question remained unanswered – one that has bothered me over many years since the fall of communism in Russia. Why is it that Russia did not – could not – turn itself into a thriving manufacturing country like China or many other developing economies? It has the brains and skills, an educated but relatively cheap workforce, limitless natural resources, all the space you could want for the construction of new facilities, a market desperate for Western goods ... and yet when do you ever look at the label on an article of clothing and read 'Made in Russia', or buy a computer or camera or piece of furniture imported from Russia?

There are many explanations. But by far the biggest obstacle to foreign investment (or the creation of an international financial centre in Russia) can be summed up in one word – corruption – a word so complex that one leading Russian businessman told me I would never, as a Westerner, ever, understand it. 'Theft,' he said, 'is not theft as you know it. It is the entire system – the political system, the business establishment, the police, the judiciary, the government, from top to bottom, all intertwined and inseparable.'

Crooks and thieves

In Chapter 3 I described how IKEA became one of the first stores to open up outlets in Putin's Russia. There are now 12 stores around the country, where millions of Russians love to spend their weekends buying affordable and fashionable furniture. IKEA has done more than any other institution to enhance the look and comfort of Soviet-built apartments. Yet the Russian machine – local mayors, bureaucrats, judges, police – did everything in their power to stop it from happening. Not because they objected to the Swedish business moving in, but because, being part of the Russian machine, they could not even imagine letting that happen without reaping fabulous profits for themselves – and IKEA righteously refused to pay the bribes that would have smoothed the way. The company even sacked two senior executives who were discovered, not even to have paid bribes themselves, but to have turned a blind eye to a corrupt transaction between one of IKEA's subcontractors and a power-supply company. But its ethical stance caused unimaginable problems that might easily have prevented one of the world's most ubiquitous and successful stores from penetrating the Russian market.

The tactic most often used by crooked authorities (and they are almost all crooked) to extort money from businesses is to invent a problem (lack of some permit, for example), then demand cash for that 'problem' to be ignored. Unless the bribe is paid, the problem remains, and permission for development is withdrawn – or worse, the police are called in and the entrepreneur ends up in prison for 'violating' some regulation or other. The size of the bribe depends on the size of the company – so Russian authorities naturally saw IKEA as a big, friendly, blue-and-yellow cash cow.

IKEA's Russia manager, Lennart Dahlgren, came to Moscow in 1998 and stayed for eight years, battling with the authorities to open the first IKEA stores and 'Mega malls'.

He has since written his memoirs, *Despite Absurdity: How I Conquered Russia While It Conquered Me*,[6] detailing with remarkable good humour his near impossible mission to do business in Russia without paying bribes. When the company built its first distribution centre in Solnechnogorsk, outside Moscow, at a cost of $40 million, the police suddenly turned up and closed the entire site down because they didn't have all the correct permits. 'To build a big shopping centre like IKEA or Mega it is necessary to get more than 300 separate permits,' he says. The district mayor demanded 10 million, then 30 million roubles (more than $1 million) to relaunch construction. Dahlgren agreed to pay the money – not to the mayor but to a charity fund, openly and publicly. It worked.

A year later IKEA tried to open a huge store in the Moscow suburb of Khimki, but was obstructed because the shopping centre operated on reserve generators and a traffic interchange had not been built. To overcome this problem IKEA had to build two bridges for $4 million and pledge $1 million for the development of children's sports. IKEA's founder, Ingvar Kamprad, says Russian power companies cheated the company out of $190 million by overcharging it for electricity and gas. He said it only happened because they refused to pay bribes.

The World Bank publishes an annual survey in which it ranks 183 countries of the world according to 'ease of doing business'. In 2011 Russia came in at 123 – far behind other post-Soviet states such as Georgia (at 19) and Kyrgyzstan (at 44). In terms of 'dealing with construction permits' Russia sits in 182nd place, ahead only of Eritrea.[7]

Dahlgren wanted to arrange a meeting for IKEA's owner – one of the wealthiest people in the world, and a man with great enthusiasm for doing business in Russia – with Putin. At first they palmed him off with meetings with a deputy prime minister. Then Dahlgren had an opportunity to discuss the proposal with someone from Putin's entourage, who told him they didn't think IKEA would really want to have a meeting with Putin. Dahlgren writes: 'I don't know whether they meant it seriously or as a joke, but they said: "IKEA is penny-pinching, and the going rate for a meeting with Putin is 5 to 10 million dollars, which you will never pay." '

The *New Times* magazine has cited government sources as saying that an appointment with deputy prime minister Igor Shuvalov, by contrast, costs a mere $150,000. A member of the public wrote to President Medvedev on Twitter that he requested a meeting with first deputy chief of staff, Vladislav Surkov, in February 2011 and was asked for $300,000. Medvedev even replied to him: 'I showed your tweet to Surkov. Call his office. Tell him who is trying to extort money.'

Needless to say, all such suggestions that top officials grant audiences only in exchange for bribes are officially denied. But there is absolutely no attempt to hide the scale of the problem generally in Russia – nor that it is escalating at a phenomenal rate under the current Russian leadership. At a Kremlin meeting devoted to corruption on 29 October 2010 Medvedev himself stated that Russia loses up to $33 billion a year due to corruption. Officials in charge of state purchases rake in so much in kickbacks from suppliers that it officially accounts for one-tenth of all state expenditure. According to the chief military prosecutor, 20 per cent of the military procurement budget is stolen by corrupt officials.[8] Overall, according to Medvedev, 'the level of theft could be reduced by a trillion roubles, by the most conservative estimates. That is, we already understand that in [the sphere of state procurements] gigantic sums are being taken by bureaucrats, and by unscrupulous businessmen working in this area.'[9] An independent report puts the level of corruption even higher – at $300 billion a year, equal to one quarter of GDP.[10]

The financial crisis made no difference in the world of Russian corruption: between 2008 and 2009 the average size of a bribe in Russia nearly tripled – according to an official interior ministry report – to more than 23,000 roubles ($776).

By July 2010, according to the same official body, the average bribe had reached 44,000 roubles ($1,500), and by July 2011 the incredible sum of 300,000 roubles, or $10,000. The chief of the interior ministry's Main Economic Security Department, Denis Sugrobov, told reporters: 'Officials in charge of purchase and the placement of orders for state and municipal needs are particularly infected by bribe-taking.' The head of Transparency International's Moscow office added that $10,000 was the *average* business bribe, not connected with 'mega projects': 'It is a bribe that medium-level businesses give to officials.'

The strange thing is that while these investigators know the size of the average bribe they do not apparently know who the bribes are paid to – or at least rarely take action. In terms of how much of a deterrent this rampant corruption is to foreign investors, it is enough to consider Transparency International's corruption index, which ranks the countries of the world according to the level of perceived corruption among public officials and politicians: since 1996 Russia has slumped from number 46 in the world, to 82 in 2000 when Putin came to power, to 154 in 2010. There are, in other words, only a dozen countries in the world considered more corrupt than Russia.

There have been a few small successes in combating corruption. At a Kremlin meeting on 10 August 2010, the head of the Presidential Control Directorate, Konstantin Chuichenko, reported to President Medvedev on an audit of medical equipment purchased by state hospitals. He had discovered that, among other things, 7.5 billion roubles ($250 million) had been spent on 170 CT scanners – many of them costing 'two or three times' more than the manufacturer's prices. Chuichenko opined that public funds were being used 'inefficiently'. But Medvedev's reply was more blunt: 'You know, I think this is not just corruption but an absolutely cynical and brazen theft of public funds. The people who perpetrate this fraud have absolutely no shame and no conscience.'[11] This led to a number of prosecutions of officials responsible for medical procurement, not just at lower levels but even in the presidential administration itself. Two of them, Vadim Mozhayev and Andrei Voronin, operated an extortion racket: they informed manufacturers of medical equipment (for example, Toshiba) that they had been placed on a fictitious blacklist, barring them from participating in public procurement tenders for their products, and offered to remove the companies from the blacklist if they paid $1 million. Toshiba reported the extortion attempt to the police, who investigated, and the officials were arrested. Voronin was sentenced to three years in prison.[12] In another high-profile case, the head of the defence ministry's medical administration, Alexander Belevitin, was arrested on 2 June 2011 for taking a $160,000 bribe from a foreign supplier of a CT scanner.[13]

Sometimes, though, it seems that US legislation – the Foreign Corrupt Practices Act – is more effective in uncovering bribery in Russia than anything the Russians do. In 2010 Diebold, the American ATM manufacturer, complied with the FCPA by dismissing five top managers of its Russian subsidiary after it discovered they had given kick-backs to officials to get business. The German car-maker Daimler was charged under the FCPA with giving bribes worth more than €3 million to secure contracts with Russian government customers for the purchase of vehicles. The cars were bought mainly by the interior ministry, the defence ministry and the 'special purposes garage' which serves the political elite. Daimler paid the money into offshore accounts. After a long delay, in November 2010, President Medvedev ordered an investigation into the case.[14]

Corruption goes hand in hand with the lack of an independent judiciary. Little has changed despite Medvedev's calls for an end to what he termed 'legal nihilism'. The most notorious case concerned the young lawyer Sergei Magnitsky, who died in prison in November 2009 after being arrested by the very officials he had accused of fraud. Magnitsky was a lawyer representing a UK-based firm, Hermitage Capital, the largest foreign portfolio investor in Russia. Its founder, Bill Browder, had done much to attract investors to Russia and was a self-professed supporter of Vladimir Putin. He had even applauded the arrest of Mikhail Khodorkovsky as an attempt to clean up Russian business. Part of his strategy was to promote good corporate governance and fight corruption in the Russian companies in which he invested, in order to increase their share price and increase profits. In November 2005, after he had tried to force a secretive oil company, Surgutneftegaz (which is rumoured to have links to Putin), to disclose its ownership structure, he was blacklisted as a 'threat to national security' and barred from Russia. Hermitage's Moscow offices were raided in June the following year by – Hermitage claims – corrupt law-enforcement officers who used the tax documents and company seals they stole to perpetrate a spectacular theft from the Russian state budget. Magnitsky's investigations revealed that organised criminals working with corrupt officials used the stolen documents to fraudulently reclaim $230 million of taxes paid by three Hermitage subsidiaries. When Magnitsky officially accused the policemen who had raided the Hermitage offices of fraud, those same policemen at once arrested him and threw him into Butyrka prison, where he was held without trial for 11 months in squalid conditions. He fell seriously ill, was denied treatment and died on 16 November 2009. There is no medical record for the last hour of his life, and relatives found that he had broken fingers and bruises on his body. According to a report by President Medvedev's Council on Human Rights, in his final hours, when he was in need of immediate medical care, Magnitsky was handcuffed and taken to a small room by eight officers, where he was beaten and then left alone for over an hour until he died, while an ambulance team waiting outside was refused entry.[15]

The story is a Kafkaesque nightmare of an individual

destroyed by a ruthless and impenetrable system, in which the people who should have been upholding the law were breaking it, and the alleged criminals were able to persecute the man who accused them. Hermitage has since carried out detailed investigations into the case and compiled an impressive dossier of evidence. They discovered colossal sums of money in foreign bank accounts belonging to one Vladlen Stepanov, the husband of Olga Stepanova, who, as head of Moscow Tax Inspectorate No. 28, had authorised the 'tax refund' to dummy companies. The Stepanovs' fortune is estimated at $39 million (one thousand times greater than their declared joint income). They have luxury villas on the Persian Gulf and the Adriatic and one in the Moscow region worth $20 million. Not bad for a mere state tax official. Their alleged accomplices in the tax office and police also have fabulous fortunes. Hermitage has located assets worth $3 million, for example, acquired by the family of Lieutenant Colonel Artyom Kuznetsov (official salary $10,200) in the years after he arrested Magnitsky.[16]

In Russia, Hermitage's accusations have gone unexplored. Following the report by his Council on Human Rights, President Medvedev called Magnitsky's death a 'crime'. Several senior prison officers were fired, and two prison doctors eventually charged with negligence. But the report also found fundamental flaws in the prosecution of Magnitsky (including the fact that he was investigated by precisely the people against whom he had testified), yet those who allegedly committed the enormous fraud and then framed Magnitsky have gone unpunished. Indeed some of the investigators were rewarded and promoted for their services. The tax inspector accused by Hermitage, Olga Stepanova, now works at Rosoboronpostavka, the procurement agency of the Ministry of Defence, whose minister, Anatoly Serdyukov, happens to be a former head of the federal tax office.

In July 2011 the US State Department announced a visa ban for Russian state officials it believes are linked to Magnitsky's death. Rather than investigate the case uncovered by Hermitage, however, the Kremlin announced it would retaliate by blacklisting certain US citizens.

How high does the trail of Russia's sleaze, which is so blatant at lower and middle levels of the state, lead? There are simply no verifiable facts about corruption at the very top, only a wealth of speculation, gossip, accusations and circumstantial evidence. Putin, it is true, does not mind sporting luxury wristwatches that suggest an income far in excess of his government salary. Neither does Dmitry Medvedev. Several websites show photographs of the men wearing watches that cost as much as they earn in a year.

The allegedly well-connected commentator Stanislav Belkovsky famously claimed that he had 'evidence' that Vladimir Putin's assets amounted to $40 billion. According to Belkovsky, Putin controlled 37 per cent of the shares of the oil extraction company, Surgutneftegaz, owned 4.5 per cent of Gazprom and held at least 75 per cent of a secretive Swiss-based oil-trading company, Gunvor, founded by a friend, Gennady Timchenko.[17] There is simply no way of verifying such claims, and Belkovsky is something of a self-publicist. Putin himself described the allegations as 'just rubbish, picked out of someone's nose and smeared on bits of paper'. A prominent Russian businessman, acquainted with both Putin and Timchenko, told me the figures were nonsense and that Putin does not even need such huge sums of money because, like a mafia boss, he can simply *have* anything he desires. It is not ownership but control, and the network of acquaintances, that counts.

It is certainly undeniable that a clique of businessmen close to Putin made immense fortunes during his presidency.[18] It would be surprising if his friends did not feel indebted to him.

According to a list of Russia's richest people published by *Finans* magazine in February 2011, Gennady Timchenko, with a personal wealth of $8.9 billion, is in 17th place. His company, Gunvor, has become the world's third-largest oil trader, shipping one-third of Russia's exports, including those of the biggest state companies, Rosneft and Gazprom Neft. Timchenko and Putin have links that go back to the latter's days working in the mayor's office in St Petersburg. According to the *Financial Times*, corporate records show that the two men participated in the early 1990s in a company known as Golden Gates, which was established to build an oil terminal at St Petersburg's port, but foundered in a clash with organised crime. Local parliament records show that a Timchenko company was also 'a beneficiary of a large export quota under a scandal-tainted oil-for-food scheme set up by Putin when he worked as head of the city administration's foreign economic relations committee in 1991'. Timchenko is also said to have close ties with Surgutneftegaz, the Kremlin-loyal oil company whose ownership is undisclosed.[19]

Arkady and Boris Rotenberg, Putin's judo partners in his youth, each have assets worth $1.75 billion. One of Arkady's companies was awarded major contracts in the preparations for the Sochi Winter Olympics in 2014, another is involved in the construction of the Nord Stream gas pipeline under the Baltic Sea. Together with Gennady Timchenko, the Rotenberg brothers founded the Yavara-Neva judo club, of which Putin is honorary president (and whose trustees, incidentally, include first deputy prime minister Viktor Zubkov).

Yuri Kovalchuk, Putin's neighbour in the Ozero dacha cooperative back in the 1990s, is the majority owner of Bank Rossiya and the National Media Group, and owns assets worth an estimated $970 million. In February 2011 his media group, which already controlled two national television channels, RenTV and Channel Five, bought a 25 per cent stake in Russia's most popular station, Channel One, from Roman Abramovich for just $150 million. According to an opposition report on corruption, Bank Rossiya's assets soared from $236 million at the beginning of 2004 to $8.2 billion in October

2010, mainly through its acquisition, at knock-down prices, of key assets of Gazprom.[20]

Nikolai Shamalov, another dacha neighbour and co-owner of Bank Rossiya, is worth $590 million. His name surfaced at the end of 2010 in connection with sensational rumours that a 'palace' was allegedly being built for Putin in the south of Russia, at a place called Gelendzhik, near Sochi. Websites printed photographs of a Versailles-style palace; aerial photographs showed its position, at the end of a secluded road close to the Black Sea coast. Shamalov turned out to be the nominal owner of the 'villa'. However, one of his former business partners, Sergei Kolesnikov, claimed to have proof that the palace was in fact commissioned by the Kremlin property department in 2005 when Putin was president, and was intended for his personal use. *Novaya gazeta* later printed what it said was an authenticated copy of the original contract for the palace, signed by Vladimir Kozhin, the Kremlin's property manager. When investigative reporters tried to visit it they were turned away by government security men, even though the site was allegedly Shamalov's personal property. The whole story emerged after Kolesnikov wrote an open letter to President Medvedev asking him to investigate his claims. He said he had been personally involved in the project until 2009 when he was removed for raising concerns about corruption. He claimed a state construction company was building the palace and that state funds had been illegally diverted to the project. The claims were naturally denied by the Kremlin and by Putin's spokesman. In March, apparently to try to put a lid on the scandal, Shamalov sold the palace to another businessman, Alexander Ponomarenko – a partner of Arkady Rotenberg but not closely connected to Putin.

The network of corruption that gobbles up so much of the country's wealth touches almost every Russian's life – from the driver who bribes a traffic cop, or the small shop owner who passes cash to a public health official for a specious hygiene certificate, to the Kremlin bureaucrat who extorts millions from a foreign trading company.

A Spanish prosecutor, Judge José Grinda Gonzalez, who led a long investigation into Russian organised crime in Spain, resulting in 60 arrests, came to the conclusion that it was impossible to differentiate between the activities of the government and organised crime groups. According to a cable released by the Wikileaks website, he told American diplomats that Russia had become a virtual 'mafia state' and that there were 'proven ties between the Russian political parties, organised crime and arms trafficking'. He said that the authorities used organised crime groups to carry out operations it could not 'acceptably do as a government', such as sales of arms to the Kurds to destabilise Turkey. Any crimelords who defied the FSB could be 'eliminated' either by killing them or 'putting them behind bars to eliminate them as a competitor for influence'.[21]

Corruption is not just an impediment to investment and a destroyer of the economy, it is also politically explosive. The opposition has successfully branded Vladimir Putin's United Russia party as 'the party of crooks and thieves' – a slogan now recognised, I am sure, by most Russians, all the more so since United Russia tried to sue its originator, Alexei Navalny, for slander.

Navalny, in his mid-30s, is a lawyer, businessman and political agitator, who has made it his mission to scrape away layers of filth from the sleazy world of Russian corporate business. He is the most popular blogger in the Russian internet, and has uncovered corruption of fabulous proportions. Navalny bought shares in state-run companies such as Gazprom, Rosneft and Transneft (which runs the government's oil pipelines), and began investigating their finances. Some of his findings have spawned criminal investigations, as well as the ire of the authorities. In one case, he found that Gazprom was buying gas from a small company, Novatek, through an intermediary, Transinvestgas, though it could have bought it directly for 70 per cent less. The intermediary channelled at least $10 million of the difference to a fraudulent consulting company. In another case, VTB, a major state bank, bought 30 oil rigs from China – again at a vastly inflated price through an intermediary, which kept the difference, $150 million. His most sensational claim is that Transneft embezzled 'at least $4 billion' during the construction of a 4,000-kilometre oil pipeline from East Siberia to the Pacific Ocean.[22]

Navalny publishes his findings on a Russian blog site, Live Journal, and has a large following on Twitter. He recently founded a new website, RosPil.info, 'to fight against bureaucrats who use the system of state procurements for their own enrichment'. The site exploits an early decision by President Medvedev to post all state requests for tender online. Navalny asks readers to send in any that arouse suspicion ('for example, a 5 million rouble contract to design a government website, with a one-week deadline for applications'), so that experts can analyse them and follow them up. Faced with such exposure, dozens of dodgy calls to tender have already been cancelled: the website claimed in August 2011 to have thwarted corrupt contracts worth 7 billion roubles.[23] Examples include a regional governor's request to buy 30 gold-and-diamond wristwatches ('as gifts to honour teachers'), an interior ministry order for a hand-carved, gilded bed made of rare wood, and an order from St Petersburg authorities for 2 million roubles' worth of mink for 700 patients in a psychiatric institution.[24]

13

TANDEMOLOGY

A bicycle built for two

Ever since Medvedev became president, and Putin his prime minister, Russians and foreigners alike have searched for signs of differences between the two halves of what has become known as the ruling 'tandem'. Perhaps it is done more in hope than expectation, for the dissimilarities are more of style than substance. So elusive is the search that it has given rise to the modern equivalent of Kremlinology, analysing pictures and parsing sentences in the hope of discerning what is going on in the dark recesses of the Kremlin (or of Putin's and Medvedev's minds). It might be called 'tandemology'.

The differences between the two men are often played down because of the lack of real change since Medvedev became president – but, of course, lack of results does not in itself mean that change was not desired. I would argue that while in foreign policy, as we have seen, there was scarcely any discernible difference between the two men, the evidence suggests that they did have differing views on the economy and on human rights – even though actual progress in these areas was negligible. The differences, moreover, grew more pronounced in the second half of Medvedev's presidency, as a certain rivalry grew between them, and both appeared to be manoeuvring to become the 'establishment' candidate for president in the 2012 election. What is certain is that the two men developed separate constituencies of supporters, something that would not have happened if their views were identical. They could, in fact, have become the nuclei of separate political parties, offering alternative solutions for Russia's future. The reason this did not happen is because Putin had a firm grip on the handlebars, and rarely turned round to hear Medvedev's protests that they might want to take a different path, or get a better bike. The evidence suggests that Medvedev grew increasingly frustrated on the back seat, and was determined to stand for a second term as president. But the two agreed early on that they would not run against each other, and Medvedev knew that if Putin decided to return to the Kremlin, he would do it. This time, the prize was bigger than ever: at the end of 2008 Medvedev had extended the presidential term from four to six years.

Medvedev's most symbolic early act of defiance was to receive the editor of the opposition newspaper *Novaya gazeta* in January 2009, ten days after one of its journalists was shot by a contract killer. To feel the significance of this, you would have to hear – as I have done – members of Putin's team fulminating against the newspaper, which they consider beyond the pale. This is the paper that used to publish Anna Politkovskaya's full-blooded attacks on the Putin system. I have heard the prime minister's men use obscene language about it, and they told me Putin feels the same way. Owned by former Soviet president Mikhail Gorbachev and the proprietor of the London *Evening Standard* and *Independent* newspapers, Alexander Lebedev, *Novaya gazeta* is a small but strident campaigner against corruption and authoritarian rule. One of its young reporters, Anastasia Baburova, was walking down a Moscow street with a human rights lawyer, Stanislav Markelov, when they were both shot dead. Markelov, who defended victims of Russian atrocities in Chechnya and anti-fascist activists, worked closely with the newspaper. He was thought to have been the gunman's main target, while Baburova was killed as a witness.

After the shooting – in a move that contrasted vividly with Putin's brush-off of Politkovskaya's death – President Medvedev called Dmitry Muratov, the newspaper's editor. Muratov recalls: 'He invited Gorbachev and myself to the Kremlin to discuss the situation. I didn't expect that. At the meeting he expressed his condolences, and even mentioned Anastasia's parents' names without looking at any notes.' Muratov says he found Medvedev totally sincere, and reminded me: 'When Anna Politkovskaya was killed, Putin said that her death did more harm to the country than her life!' Muratov points out that, in contrast to Politkovskaya's killers, the murderers of Baburova and Markelov – members of a neo-Nazi group – were tracked down and sent to jail for life.[1]

When Muratov admitted that the murders of four of his journalists since 2000 had made him wonder whether to close the paper down, Medvedev replied: 'Thank God the newspaper exists.' He even agreed to give his first ever Russian press interview as president to *Novaya gazeta*, Putin's most hated newspaper, and told Muratov: 'You know why? Because you never sucked up to anybody.' In the interview, carried out three months later, Medvedev openly distanced himself from the Putinite idea of a 'social contract', whereby the state offered its citizens stability and a measure of prosperity in exchange for political docility. You could not counterpoise democracy and well-being, he said. He could offer Russia both freedom *and* prosperity.

On the same day as the interview was published, 15 April, Medvedev held an extraordinary session of the Presidential Council on Human Rights. The meeting lasted for many hours, but as it began Medvedev ordered his staff to start publishing the proceedings in instalments on his website – an unprecedented idea that ensured full publicity for his own words and whatever the human rights activists wished to say.

He criticised officials who interfered with the right to demonstrate, or who persecuted NGOs, and admitted that 'our government machine' was 'steeped in corruption'. Part of the discussion concerned the official portrayal of Russian history, at a time when democrats were worried by a growing tendency to underplay the enormity of Stalinism. One speaker, Irina Yasina, formerly vice-president of Mikhail Khodorkovsky's Open Russia Foundation, was blunt about the communist legacy: 'Our country has inherited a terrible legacy. Throughout the entire twentieth century the value of human life was negated, and human rights were trampled underfoot, to put it mildly. And now we, the children and grandchildren of those who lived through that century, must try to change this situation somehow.'

Medvedev replied: 'I have to agree with Ms Yasina that the entire twentieth century was one of denial of the value of human life.'

Six months later, in a video-blog posted on Remembrance Day for the Victims of Political Repression, President Medvedev appeared to lay into the authors of new schoolbooks, which attempted to whitewash Stalin. He said: 'Let's just think about it: millions of people died as a result of terror and false accusations – millions. They were deprived of all rights, even the right to a decent human burial; for years their names were simply erased from history. But even today you can still hear voices claiming that those innumerable victims were justified for some higher national purpose. I believe that no national progress, successes or ambitions can develop at the price of human misery and loss. Nothing can take precedence over the value of human life. And there is no excuse for repression.'

Contrast that with Putin, who as president reinstated the old Soviet national anthem, called for the reintroduction of

Soviet-era basic military training in schools and allowed the publication of a manual for history teachers which described Stalin as an 'efficient manager'. The book argued that one of the reasons for Stalin's repressions, in which millions were incarcerated or murdered, was 'his goal of ensuring maximum efficiency of the management apparatus, while the Great Terror of the 1930s had achieved 'the creation of a new management class suited to the tasks of modernisation under the conditions of scarce resources'.

It was not just 'liberal talk' on Medvedev's part. He also took small but real steps that gave heart to the democrats. In January 2009, for example, he quietly scuttled a draft law backed by Putin, that would have expanded the definition of treason to include almost any criticism of the government or contact with foreigners, and said he had been influenced by the outcry in the media and society against the proposed change.

He also took measures to defend the right to demonstrate. Since July opposition activists had begun holding unauthorised rallies on the last day of any month with 31 days, to draw attention to Article 31 of the constitution, which guarantees the right of assembly. The rallies were invariably broken up within minutes by riot police, and protestors arrested. The Duma then passed a bill to restrict street protests even further, but in November Medvedev vetoed it. Putin's view of protests, by contrast, is that it is normal for police to 'beat demonstrators about the head with a baton if they're in the wrong place'.

In June 2010 a Duma bill broadened the functions of the security services to 'fight extremism'. The law would have allowed the FSB to issue warnings to people it believed were 'about to' commit a crime, and threaten, fine or even arrest them for up to 15 days for disobeying its orders. After his Human Rights Council complained that the bill 'revived the worst practices of the totalitarian state', however, President Medvedev watered it down – and insisted: 'I want you to know that this has been done on my personal orders.'

Putin and Medvedev never, at this stage, openly contradicted each other. But a battle of ideas was being waged by their proxies. A liberal think-tank, the Institute of Contemporary Development (INSOR), was set up just after Medvedev was elected president, and he became chairman of its Board of Trustees. The institute's chairman, Igor Yurgens, says the president agrees with 'some but not all' of his views, but over the few years of its existence Medvedev has in fact veered more and more towards INSOR's ideas. In February 2010 it published a long report titled 'Russia in the 21st Century: Vision for the Future', which suggested undoing many of Putin's political reforms. It envisaged a Western-style two-party system, a media free of state interference, independent courts, directly elected regional governors and a scaled-back security service. The report was at once denounced by Putin's spin doctor, Vladislav Surkov, who declared: 'You can't create democracy in three days, you can't turn a child into an adult just like that.'

But in November Medvedev himself turned his guns on Putin's much vaunted 'stability'. He used words reminiscent of Gorbachev's, who branded the period of communist government just before he came to power as years of 'stagnation'. In a video blog Medvedev appeared to condemn the *de facto* one-party rule of Putin's United Russia party: 'It is no secret that for some time now signs of stagnation have begun to appear in our political life and stability has threatened to turn into stagnation. And such stagnation is equally damaging for both the ruling party and opposition forces. If the opposition has no chance at all of winning a fair fight it degrades and becomes marginal. If the ruling party never loses a single election, it is just coasting. Ultimately, it too degrades, like any living organism which remains static. For these reasons it has become necessary to raise the degree of political competition.'

Despite Medvedev's apparent encouragement to the media

to take risks, the Kremlin maintained its total control of the central television channels. At the end of November the popular presenter Vladimir Pozner had his closing remarks on his weekly show censored when he referred to the death in prison of Sergei Magnitsky. Another respected television journalist, Leonid Parfyonov, used an award ceremony to launch a stinging attack on how television news was controlled – mostly by the very people sitting at the tables at the ceremony. He said news bulletins had come to resemble Soviet propaganda, with no room for critical, sceptical or ironic commentary about the prime minister or president. 'The correspondent is ... not a journalist but a bureaucrat, following the service and logic of obedience,' he said.

The irony was that Medvedev himself, as recently as September, had used his control over state television – resorting to black propaganda techniques straight from the Communist Party handbook – to discredit and then oust the corrupt mayor of Moscow, Yuri Luzhkov. Here, there was no hint of Medvedev's democratic inclinations. Since Putin had abolished mayoral elections, there was no question of getting rid of Luzhkov through the ballot box. It had to be done by presidential decree – but you couldn't just do that, with no good reason, certainly not with a mayor as powerful as Luzhkov. His corruptness was just about as blatant as it could possibly be: everyone knew his wife had become Russia's richest woman principally by securing the vast majority of Moscow's most lucrative building contracts for her own company. But he was part of the Kremlin furniture, in office since Yeltsin's days, and still popular; he had transformed Moscow into a glittering showcase of post-communist revival; and he had Putin's support. But Medvedev wanted rid of him, and the last straw was Luzhkov's public criticism of the president's decision to halt construction of a controversial highway being built through an ancient forest north of Moscow. At a meeting with newspaper editors in St Petersburg, Medvedev adopted Putin-like language when he accused Luzhkov of 'rattling his balls', a quaint Russian expression meaning to talk nonsense.

Medvedev cranked up the old propaganda machine, and the journalist 'bureaucrats' described by Parfyonov were asked to oblige their masters. All three main television channels aired documentaries that blackened Luzhkov's character. They criticised his policy of 'reconstructing' Moscow's architectural heritage by allowing developers to retain only the facades of eighteenth-century buildings, while demolishing everything within. They blamed him for the city's traffic jams and described his wife's fabulous wealth. And they derided Luzhkov for spending the scorching summer of 2010, when Moscow was engulfed by poisonous smog from peat fires, on holiday abroad or tending to his bee-hives instead of helping Muscovites survive.

On 17 September Luzhkov was summoned to the Kremlin and asked by Medvedev's chief of staff to 'go quietly'. But he didn't go quietly. He went on holiday to Austria for a week, and then, on 27 September, wrote a letter to Medvedev, in which he laid into Medvedev's pretensions to be a democrat, accusing him of unleashing an 'unprecedented defamation campaign', designed to get rid of a mayor who was 'too independent and too awkward'. Luzhkov demanded that mayoral elections be reinstated. And he suggested that Medvedev's only motive for wanting rid of him was to move one of his own allies into the mayor's seat to boost his own chances in a future presidential election. 'You have two options,' Luzhkov wrote: 'fire me, if you have weighty reasons, or else publicly distance yourself from those who have done you this favour [the black propaganda campaign].' The next morning, Medvedev sacked the mayor, citing 'loss of trust'.

It took another fortnight for a new mayor to be appointed, however – a sign that Putin and Medvedev could not agree on a candidate. The choice finally fell on Putin's right-hand man, Sergei Sobyanin. He was Putin's chief of staff and owed his entire career to him (and, incidentally, knew little about the capital he was about to run, having lived there for only five years – during which he had observed the notorious traffic jams only through the darkened windows of his government limousine as it sped down the special lane reserved for the elite). If Luzhkov was right to suspect that Medvedev had wanted to install one of his own supporters, then this was an important battle he had lost to Putin. He was about to lose more.

Since the start of his presidency, Medvedev's attempt to project a liberal image had been undermined by the continuing imprisonment of the oil magnate Mikhail Khodorkovsky. His jail sentence was due to end in 2011, but his enemies (Khodorkovsky specifically names deputy prime minister Igor Sechin) were determined to keep him behind bars for longer. They certainly did not want him released just before parliamentary and presidential elections. And so a second trial was launched in February 2009. The fresh case against him was implausible. The first trial had already found him guilty of fraud and tax evasion. This time the prosecutors wanted to prove that he and his co-defendant, Platon Lebedev, had embezzled the total amount of oil that Yukos produced from 1998 to 2003 – oil that prosecutors had previously argued Yukos had sold, while failing to pay the correct taxes. How could Khodorkovsky have 'stolen' the oil if it was previously accepted that he had 'sold' it?

His defence appeared to gain a boost when the industry minister, Viktor Khristenko, and the former economics minister, German Gref, both appeared in court as witnesses, and cast doubt on the charges. If embezzlement had been discovered, I would have been made aware of it,' said Gref. Khristenko admitted he was unaware of millions of barrels of oil having disappeared.

Any hopes Khodorkovsky's lawyers had were short-lived, however. The judge was due to deliver his verdict on 15 December, but reporters turning up at the courthouse that morning found a note pinned to the door announcing, without explanation, that it was postponed until the 27th. Perhaps there was an explanation: the next day, the 16th, the prime minister was due to take part in his annual television phone-in, and he would have surely faced questions about the trial. That might have been awkward – and certainly too late for Putin to influence the verdict. By having the verdict delayed, he was able to use the phone-in to interfere quite brazenly in the course of justice. Asked about the case, Putin said, 'a thief should sit in jail'. It sounded like a direct order to Judge Danilkin, who was at that moment considering his options. Even President Medvedev took exception to such blatant interference. He said in a television interview: 'No official has the right to express their position on a case before the court announces its verdict.' It was the first time Medvedev had gone further than merely expressing views that differed a little from Putin's; this was, in effect, a public reprimand.

It made no difference to the outcome of the show trial, however. Judge Danilkin found Khodorkovsky guilty, as the *siloviki* desired, and sentenced him to 14 years behind bars, to run concurrently with his first sentence and backdated to his arrest in 2003. He would not be free until 2017.

If 2009 and 2010 saw President Medvedev speaking a lot about democracy and human rights, and occasionally taking action to support them, his prime minister's response became more and more bizarre. It was during this period that Vladimir Putin began to find more and more time in his busy schedule for publicity stunts – extravagant displays of virility that appeared designed to demonstrate that, despite being 13 years older than Medvedev, he was fitter and stronger.

In August 2009 Putin bared his chest and swam butterfly stroke in an icy Siberian river. Kremlin cameras clicked furiously as he went fishing and horse-riding. In 2010 scarcely a month went by without a photo-shoot. He put a tracking collar on a polar bear. He rode a Harley Davidson at a bikers' rally.

He sprayed wildfires with water from an aeroplane. He fired a dart from a crossbow at a whale in a stormy sea. He drove a Formula One car at 240 kilometres an hour. In October the press was full of speculation that he had gone one step too far to rejuvenate his image. He appeared in Kiev with his face looking puffy and bruised, and heavily made-up. 'There are no bruises there,' said his spokesman. 'He was just really tired after several flights and extra meetings. Also, the light may have fallen on him in an unfortunate manner.' But the press wondered if he had had a facelift, or botox injections, like his friend, the ever youthful Silvio Berlusconi.

Medvedev did not try to match Putin's strongman appearances – though he did begin to walk with an exaggerated swagger and to talk with rather aggressive mouth movements, not unlike Putin's. But for the most part, his props were not fast cars and wild animals but iPads and tweets.

Image was crucial to both men. They were appealing to different constituencies. By the end of 2010, with just a year to go before the coming parliamentary and presidential elections, two things were becoming crystal clear: that both men wanted to be the next president of Russia, and that it would be Putin who would decide which of them would go forward. Ultimately, the tandem was more of a penny-farthing.

2011: Paralysis again – the phoney campaign

In a sense the whole of Medvedev's presidency was a slow-burning campaign for the next election. But as the final year began, paralysis once again afflicted the president's Kremlin and the prime minister's White House – just as it had done prior to the last election. The agreed line was that the two men would 'decide together' which of them would be the candidate in 2012, and they would announce their decision when the time was ripe. Officials in both camps began manoeuvring, uncertain of how the dice would fall. At the top levels,

Medvedev's and Putin's spokespeople weighed every word like a raw diamond that could tip the scales. At lower levels, bureaucrats positioned themselves to jump ship if necessary when the situation became clear. At every level, officials were afraid of saying anything that might be a hostage to fortune.

Mikhail Dvorkovich (the brother of Arkady, the president's economic adviser) wrote in his blog: 'Ministers, not knowing who is their real boss, are tripping up, trying to carry out often contradictory instructions. It's no joke, having to choose between two people, either of whom could become president in 2012. One mistake and in a year you're a "political corpse".'

At the end of February, Peskov told me to expect 'hysteria' around the world in a few months' time. I took it to mean that Putin was going to announce his intention to run for re-election. But nothing was made public and the uncertainty continued.

Both 'candidates' began an undeclared campaign, starting with a farcical argument over the choice of mascot for the Sochi Winter Olympics. Putin decided to demonstrate his ability to influence any decision in the country merely by expressing an opinion. Just as he had put the judge in the Khodorkovsky trial in an impossible position by declaring that 'a thief should sit in jail', so he casually opined that the snow leopard would make a fine Olympics mascot – just hours before a nationwide television vote on the matter. Naturally, the snow leopard was chosen. Medvedev was not happy. Two days later, talking about something completely different – the idea that possible designs for a new universal electronic ID card should be discussed on the internet – he added caustically: 'I hope it will be fairer than the discussion of the Olympic symbols.'

There were more serious spats to come. In March open disagreement broke out between the 'candidates' over the world's response to Colonel Gaddafi's crackdown on dissenters in Libya. At the United Nations, Russia abstained on Resolution 1973, which authorised the use of air strikes against Gaddafi's forces. Russia's position was a compromise: Medvedev had wanted to back the Western stance, his foreign ministry was against it. But Putin was outraged by it, and said so publicly. Visiting a ballistic missile factory in the republic of Udmurtia, he likened the UN resolution to a 'medieval call to crusade'. He said he was concerned by the 'ease with which decisions to use force are taken in international affairs'. He saw it as a continuation of a tendency in US policy: 'During the Clinton era they bombed Belgrade, Bush sent forces into Afghanistan and then under an invented, false pretext they sent forces into Iraq. Now it is Libya's turn, under the pretext of protecting the peaceful population. But in air strikes it is precisely the civilian population that gets killed. Where is the logic and the conscience?'

When Medvedev heard Putin's words – a direct criticism of his own decision to allow the Western air strikes to go ahead – he hit the roof. Foreign policy was his domain, not the prime minister's. Within a couple of hours he called a handful of Russian journalists to his dacha, and emerged into the garden to deliver a stern and lengthy rebuttal of his prime minister's remarks. He looked nervous, swallowing hard and jerking his shoulders, as he called Putin's remarks 'unacceptable'. Talking about 'crusades', he said, could lead to a clash of civilisations. 'Let us not forget,' he went on, 'what motivated the Security Council resolutions in the first place. These resolutions were passed in response to the Libyan authorities' actions. This was why we took these decisions. I think these are balanced decisions that were very carefully thought through. We gave our support to the first Security Council resolution and abstained on the second. We made these decisions consciously with the aim of preventing an escalation of violence ... It would be wrong for us to start flapping about now and say that we didn't know what we were doing. This was a conscious decision on our part. Such were the instructions I gave to the foreign ministry, and they were carried out.'

For only the second time (after the Khodorkovsky incident), President Medvedev had put Prime Minister Putin firmly in his place. It came as no surprise when, a week or so later, Medvedev's press secretary, Timakova, made urgent calls to all the television stations, banning them from showing footage of Putin driving Medvedev around in an new experimental car. The phoney campaign was now in full swing: there would be no more images of Putin in the driving seat.

It was a surreal battle: the only people who really had to be convinced were Putin and Medvedev themselves – it was they who would decide which of them would run. (As one commentator put it, the only election going on was the one inside Putin's head.) But Medvedev decided to take his pitch to the people, perhaps hoping to gather support in the press and put pressure on Putin to allow him to remain as president. On 3 March he used a speech commemorating the 150th anniversary of Tsar Alexander II's emancipation of the serfs in Russia to set out his ideological platform, arguing that 'freedom cannot be postponed'. A few months later, not to be outdone, Putin chose his own historical role model – not the 'Tsar Liberator' but Pyotr Stolypin, the reformist but repressive prime minister of the last tsar, Nicholas II. Stolypin carried out liberal agrarian reforms but had so many dissenters executed that the hangman's noose became known as 'Stolypin's necktie'. Putin praised him in terms he could have used for himself, and called for a monument to Stolypin to be erected in front of the government White House.

Medvedev followed up his call for freedom with his economic pitch. In a speech in Magnitogorsk he listed ten priorities to improve the investment climate. Sensationally, he demanded that government ministers who held directorships of state companies should give them up. They included Putin's closest ally, Igor Sechin, the chairman of Rosneft. Medvedev (who himself used to be both deputy prime minister and chairman of Gazprom) said it could no longer be the case that 'government leaders who answer for the rules and regulations in a certain industry also sit on the board of directors of competitive companies'. The newspaper *Kommersant* called the proposal to replace the state officials with independent directors revolutionary: 'Dmitry Medvedev essentially demanded the liquidation of state capitalism.'

Arkady Dvorkovich says it was a 'difficult step' for the *government* (that is, Putin) to agree to.[2] Olga Kryshtanovskaya, a sociologist who specialises in studying the composition of the elite, says the move was part of a trend, however, which has seen the presence of *siloviki* in state structures weakened since Medvedev became president. At their height, in 2007, officials from the security services and military accounted for 47 per cent of the government elite, whereas by the summer of 2007 the figure had shrunk to 22 per cent. That does not mean Putin has forfeited his powers of patronage to the new president, however. Kryshtanovskaya says that of 75 'key figures', all but two remain 'Putin's men'.[3]

Significantly, the country's biggest state-controlled company, Gazprom – with its web of political, business and media connections – turned out to be exempt from the new requirement for government ministers to leave their directorships (just as it survived the reformers' attempts to demonopolise it a decade earlier). It was revealed at the end of August that first deputy prime minister Viktor Zubkov would remain chairman of Gazprom (though he had given up all his other directorships). Zubkov was Putin's former financial crime-buster, and also a St Petersburg friend and trustee of his judo club. Dvorkovich explained that Gazprom directors had access to a great deal of 'secret information', which made the appointment of independent directors 'complicated'.[4] The news seemed to confirm Gazprom's untouchable status at the very hub of the Putin system, used to control the media, to exert pressure on foreign states and to fill the pockets of a network of cronies.

Putin responded to Medvedev's 'manifesto speech' in Magnitogorsk with his own long speech to the Duma on 20 April, in which he warned against 'jerks or rash experiments based on liberalism' in the economy. It was beginning to look as if Putin no longer entirely trusted his protégé to stick to the right path.

For a while in the spring it looked as if Putin – and possibly Medvedev – were casting around for alternative political solutions. An official attempt was made to boost, and apparently co-opt, a small centre-right party called Right Cause, perhaps as an approved liberal 'opposition'. The first deputy prime minister Igor Shuvalov and the finance minister Alexei Kudrin were initially courted as potential leaders of the party, but after a week or so of intrigue both turned the offer down. Then one of the country's richest men, the oligarch Mikhail Prokhorov, became leader. But he pledged to turn the party into a real alternative to United Russia, and began fiercely criticising the Kremlin. This was not at all the 'loyal' opposition that was intended, and at a farcical party conference in September Prokhorov was ousted. He accused the Kremlin's 'puppeteer', Vladislav Surkov, of 'privatising the political system'.

Finally, on 6 May, came an announcement so redolent of the Soviet past that it seemed that all pretence at democracy had at last been dropped. Without any public consultation or prior discussion, Putin announced, during a speech in Volgograd, that he was setting up a new organisation, the All-Russia People's Front. At its heart would be his United Russia Party, but 'non-party supporters' – organisations and individuals – were welcome to join. By the very next day the People's Front already had a 'Coordination Council', which met at Putin's dacha to plan its election campaign. Over the next weeks, thousands of individuals and organisations were recruited. Whole streets joined, as did factories and offices, youth groups and war veterans, associations of music producers and reindeer herders. Trade unions signed up – often without even consulting their members. Some refused to be corralled in this way. The Union of Architects later voted to overturn the decision taken on its behalf. Individual members of the Composers' Union protested loudly, insisting they would not help Putin to stage 'sham elections'.[5]

Ostensibly the People's Front was formed to help United Russia fight the coming Duma election in December. The party's poll ratings were collapsing so dramatically that this might be the only way to ensure victory. But Putin's spokesman, Dmitry Peskov, revealed its true purpose. The Front would 'operate above the party, it's not based on the party,' he told reporters. 'It would more likely be based around Putin, who came up with the idea.'

Putin's initiative seemed to make a mockery of Russia's already emasculated party system. Instead of having normal political parties, representing different sectors of the political spectrum, Putin now envisaged United Russia as an amorphous mass organisation, representing all groups. It is worth recalling that the Communist Party of the Soviet Union also did not 'fight' elections alone but as part of 'the indestructible bloc of communists and non-party people' – claiming, in other words, to represent everybody.

Here is how Putin introduced his idea in his speech to United Russia members in Volgograd:

I have some suggestions. I will explain them now to you. I want to note that selections to the State Duma candidate pool must be completed before August. We then need to discuss the candidates, so that the electoral list can be finalised in September at the party congress. The selection procedure should not only involve party members, but non-affiliated United Russia supporters, trade union members, members of women's and youth organisations, public associations, citizens who take the initiative, who are actively engaged. In short, all those willing to have a direct influence on government policy through United Russia in the State Duma.

What am I suggesting and how do I propose we do this? Essentially, I propose creating what in political practice is called a broad popular front.
[Applause]
Thank you very much for that reaction, for your support.

This approach to consolidating the efforts of a broad range of political forces ahead of major political events has been taken in the past and is still practised in various countries at various points by a variety of political forces: by those on the left, and by what we know here as right-wing liberal, nationalist and patriotic forces.

How it is called is not the issue. The issue is how we conceptualise it and what we want to achieve. This is a tool for bringing together like-minded political forces.

And I would very much like United Russia and other political parties, trade unions, women's organisations, youth organisations, for example, veterans' organisations, including World War II veterans and Afghan war veterans – everyone who is united in their common desire to strengthen our country, united by the idea of finding optimal solutions to the challenges before us – to benefit from this single platform, let's call it, say, the 'All-Russia Popular Front', because ahead of May 9 and at Stalingrad, this kind of rhetoric is in the air, and the name 'All-Russian Popular Front' seems quite apt ...
[Applause]
Thank you.

I suspect that this was the event that Peskov predicted to me would cause 'hysteria', because it appeared to be so obviously aimed at further side-lining President Medvedev and positioning Putin as 'national leader' – head not just of a declining party but of a ubiquitous People's Front. The coming Duma elections would be dominated by People's Front posters and

Putin's image.

Medvedev at first reacted coolly – describing the idea merely as 'legitimate' – and then hostilely: a week after the prime minister's announcement, he told a group of 'young parliamentarians' from various parties: 'Attempts to tailor the political system to one specific individual are dangerous ... Excessive concentration of power is definitely a dangerous thing that has happened repeatedly in our country ... As a general rule, it led to stagnation or civil war.'

By the summer, Medvedev was beginning to sound defeatist. In an interview with the *Financial Times* he admitted for the first time that he did want to stand for re-election: 'I think that any leader who occupies such a post as president, simply must want to run. Another question is whether he is going to take that decision for himself or not. The decision is somewhat different from his desire to run.'[6] It was a humiliating admission that no president fully in charge of his country would ever make: I *want* to stand for re-election but it's not my decision, or not mine alone.

Medvedev still 'campaigned'. At a huge Putin-like press conference he showed his liberal side: Khodorkovsky, if released from jail, would be 'absolutely no danger to society at all', he said. In an interview to mark the third anniversary of the war against Georgia he showed he was just as tough as Putin, insisting that he alone took the decision to invade Georgia. At the St Petersburg Economic Forum he declared that Putin's reforms, though necessary, had run their course: 'Yes, we had a stage of development that is associated with an increased state role in the economy. It was important to stabilise the situation after the chaos of the 1990s. But now the potential of this path has been exhausted ... Such an economic model is dangerous for the country's future.' At a closed meeting with business leaders he reportedly appealed to them to support *his* economic policies, rather than his predecessor's. And he told leaders of political parties that he wanted to roll back several of Putin's political reforms: lowering the threshold to enter the Duma from 7 to 5 per cent, 'decentralising' power, and promising other, unspecified changes.

Some commentators suggested that Medvedev and Putin were in fact still working in tandem: one out front pushing for reform, the other calling for caution to stop the process from spinning out of control.[7] But that ignored the one indisputable fact: that an election was approaching and only one of them would be the ruling elite's candidate. Neither man was indifferent as to who that candidate would be.

It seemed that Medvedev was approaching an ignominious moment, when he would – in the words of the veteran Kremlin adviser Gleb Pavlovsky – 'tiptoe out of the Kremlin', confirming to the entire world that he had only ever been a stand-in for Putin. His four years as president would look like a farce, designed to keep the constitution formally intact while actually entrenching Putin's autocratic rule.

In August, Putin went scuba-diving in the Black Sea, over an ancient archaeological site, and emerged from the water clutching two Grecian urns that were conveniently lying on the sea bed, having escaped the attentions of thousands of other divers over the centuries. There seemed to be no end to his wizardry. Returning to the presidency would surely be no harder for him.

14

PUTIN MARK III

The king, the rook and the pawns

On the morning of Saturday 24 September 2011 thousands of people streamed out of the Sportivnaya metro station in Moscow's Luzhniki district. Mounted police officers, many of them women, shepherded them along the pathways towards the Palace of Sport. Others arrived in black limousines with blue flashing lights. Some 11,000 delegates from across Russia were heading for the 12th Congress of the United Russia party.

The agenda included discussion of the party's programme for the coming Duma elections and approval of the party's list of 600 candidates. The 'main intrigue', according to Boris Gryzlov, chairman of the Duma and day-to-day leader of the party, was 'who exactly will be on the list of candidates'. But it turned out there was a much bigger intrigue. President Medvedev and Prime Minister Putin (formally United Russia's leader) had been 'invited' to address the congress and were about to reveal an astonishing secret.

Putin strode towards the podium first, so eager to spill the beans that he forgot that the national anthem had to be played first. He stopped in his tracks as the old Soviet hymn boomed out and television cameras swooped over the vast crowd of delegates, as patriotic, powerless and obedient as at any Communist Party congress in the past.

He then coolly revealed that, contrary to the claims of the past year that he and Medvedev would decide which of them would stand for president 'when the time was right', they had in fact decided 'long ago'. The stonewalling had all been an elaborate pretence.

'I'll tell you straight,' said Putin with a little laugh. 'We agreed about what to do, about which posts we would hold in the future, long ago ... several years ago.' The audience applauded, but cautiously, still not certain just what the agreement was. Putin and Medvedev had choreographed their announcement carefully, to ensure maximum suspense. Putin first proposed that Medvedev should head the United Russia candidates' list. Medvedev then proposed that Putin should be the party's candidate for the presidency – and confirmed that this scenario had been 'discussed' (though not 'decided', as Putin had put it) four years earlier. Putin then returned to the podium to say that if he became president he would invite Medvedev to be his prime minister.

The decision itself was no surprise – yet still, because of its implications and the manner of its announcement, it came as a thudding shock. After all Medvedev's talk of political and economic stagnation and the need for reforms, Russia faced the possibility of another two terms – 12 years – of Putin. The dreams of Medvedev's 'Go, Russia!' article had vanished. The smile, stretched across the stand-in president's face as he proposed Putin's candidacy, could not hide his humiliation.

The audience, of course, jumped to their feet and applauded. But they were as shocked as anyone in the country. Dmitry Peskov, Putin's spokesman – the man who one might expect to have prepared a strategy to handle or spin such a dramatic announcement – admitted he heard the news the same time as everyone else. It seems possible – indeed probable – that no one at all apart from Putin and Medvedev themselves knew in advance of the announcement.

So what led to the president's dramatic capitulation? In a television interview, a few days after the United Russia congress, Medvedev appeared to confirm that his timid campaigning throughout 2011 had been aimed at raising his ratings in opinion polls to the level where he might have been able to challenge Putin's assumption that he would return to the presidency. 'Prime minister Putin is undoubtedly the most authoritative politician in our country at the moment, and his ratings are a little higher than mine,' he said. But if his ratings had risen above Putin's then, maybe, the choice would have fallen on him instead. 'Everything can change in this life. Yes, it's true that we had ideas about how to configure [the leadership] ... and we spoke about this at the congress. But on the other hand, life could have changed things in some completely different, paradoxical way. What if people's electoral preferences had changed for some reason?'

That was what Medvedev had been trying to do throughout 2011 – change the opinion polls to give him the right to challenge Putin. Even in late July, in conversations with finance minister Alexei Kudrin and others, Medvedev had still been insisting that he wanted to stand for a second term. But Medvedev's popularity did not rise, and when he met Putin in Sochi in August, he had no arguments with which to counter the strongman's arm-twisting.

Medvedev tried to pretend the situation was similar to America, where he said Barack Obama and Hillary Clinton took a decision on which of them would run for president 'based on who could get better results. This was how we also made our decision.' This of course glossed over the fact that Obama and Clinton campaigned against each other, openly and publicly, in Democrat primaries, before one of them was fairly elected over the other. By contrast, the Russian leaders had opted for secretive decision-making, and thrown away the chance to turn Russia into a democracy. There is no doubt that there were sufficient differences between the two for them to stand against one another, just as Obama and Clinton had done. It would not have brought down the system, but it would have given people a choice in how it was run.

Putin's early prime minister, Mikhail Kasyanov, noted that the president had organised his return as if it were a *spetsoperatsiya* – a top-secret, KGB-style 'special operation'. It appears that neither Putin nor Medvedev understood how arrogant their announcement to the United Russia congress would appear, or what repercussions it would have. This was a moment of monumental hubris – the moment when millions of Russians realised their powerlessness, their irrelevance to the political process. A chess-loving nation, they derisively described their leaders' manoeuvre as *rokirovka* – 'castling', whereby the king and the rook switch positions in order to protect the former. The pawns do not get consulted ... but they would soon demand to be heard.

The people find their voice

The first person to protest was Alexei Kudrin, Putin's trusted finance minister. In Washington, on the day his bosses announced their plans, he immediately declared that he would refuse to serve in a cabinet led by Medvedev. It was an open secret that Kudrin himself had hoped to become prime minister under a re-elected President Putin, but in Washington he framed his disagreement with Medvedev in policy terms, noting in particular that he disagreed with the president's push for a $65 billion increase in defence spending.

Kudrin then flew back to Russia to take part in a conference on modernisation, chaired by an incandescent President Medvedev. Twitching with indignation and spitting sarcasm, Medvedev began by noting that 'certain categories of citizens' like to go abroad to make important statements. 'Alexei Kudrin delivered the joyous news that he doesn't plan to work in the new government and that he has serious practical differences with the current president on, among other things, military spending.' Acting suddenly as though empowered by his new status as an officially lame-duck president, Medvedev (reading from notes on his iPad) reminded Kudrin that cabinet discipline and subordination had not been abolished, and that 'if you disagree with the president's course, you have only one option – to resign'.

Kudrin listened to the tirade with pursed lips, then quietly replied: 'I do indeed have disagreements with you. I will take a decision regarding your suggestion after consulting the prime minister [Putin].'

Medvedev could hardly speak with fury at this ultimate insult, which implied he was a total wimp, no longer even nominally in charge. 'You can consult whoever you like, including the prime minister,' he shot back, 'but so long as I am president, it's me that takes these decisions.' By evening, Kudrin was gone.

His was a rare display of defiance. Most members of the elite kept their heads down. Medvedev's liberal economic adviser, Arkady Dvorkovich (who had spoken publicly about his boss's desire to remain president), watched the astonishing announcements at the United Russia congress on television and immediately sent out not very cryptic messages on Twitter: 'Yes, nothing to be joyful about', and 'Time to switch to the sports channel'. After that he took to tweeting pictures of his breakfast, as though politics was too painful to talk about.

But soon things began to happen that seemed to indicate that some Russians were not at all happy about being treated with contempt by their leaders. Putin must have assumed he was among his most loyal supporters when he attended a martial arts event on 21 November: macho man at a macho sport. But when he climbed into the ring to congratulate the victor, he was booed by the crowd so loudly that he struggled to make himself heard.

Instead of taking note of the changing mood, the Kremlin proceeded at full tilt with preparations to ensure the Duma elections on 4 December would produce a resounding victory for United Russia – even if that required brazenly falsifying the result. Election day began ominously, with cyber attacks on the websites of *Kommersant* newspaper, Ekho Moskvy radio and Golos, an election monitoring organisation partly funded by the US government. Independent monitors witnessed many instances of 'carousel' voting, whereby groups of voters were taken by bus from one polling station to another to vote many times for United Russia candidates, using fake absentee ballot papers. Most damningly, videos were posted on the internet that showed blatant ballot rigging. It took many forms. In some cases, election officials were filmed simply filling in multiple voting papers with crosses against the United Russia candidates. In others, completed papers were found in the ballot boxes before the polls even opened.

Dmitry Finikov, a member of the electoral commission at polling station number 6 in Moscow's Arbat district, witnessed massive fraud, which he documented with photographs and video.[1] Throughout the day, voting progressed without incident. When the polls closed the ballots were separated into piles according to party, counted, and sealed in envelopes, with the total written on the outside. These figures were also entered on the polling station's official protocol. The result was as follows: total ballots cast 679; for the Communist Party 202 votes, Yabloko 134 votes, United Russia 128 votes, A Fair Russia 113 votes, followed by others. Putin's party, in other words, came a poor third, with 18.9 per cent of the vote. The chairman of the commission then left the building, taking the only two copies of the protocol (which the observer, however, had photographed), having locked the sealed envelopes containing the ballot papers in a safe. Early next morning an official accompanied by two police officers removed the envelopes from the safe and took them to the district electoral commission, where officials calmly – in front of a rolling video camera – put them into black garbage bags. The camera then turns to the protocol of the result pinned to the wall. Here the 'official' result for polling station number 6 had been transformed: United Russia 515 votes, A Fair Russia 83, Communist Party 29, Yabloko 4.

In the neighbouring polling station, number 9, United Russia's vote leapt, en route from the polling station to the official record, from 208 votes to 888. In Chechnya 99.5 per cent voted for United Russia. Regional governors had been set targets for the number of votes they should deliver for the party, and all delivered.

Despite all these efforts to secure victory, even the official results gave United Russia only 49.32 per cent of the vote, which translated into a small majority of seats in the Duma – 238 out of 450. (Four years earlier they had received 64.3 per cent and 315 seats.) Election monitors said the real figures could have been some 15–20 points lower.

The evidence of mass falsification, without which United Russia might easily have failed to secure a majority in the Duma, compounded the sense of impotence already felt by many Russians because of the Putin-Medvedev *rokirovka*. It triggered the deepest political crisis of the Putin years.

On the evening of 5 December, as the cynical manipulation of the election became clear, 5,000 protestors came out onto the streets of Moscow. Riot police were deployed, there were clashes, and 300 demonstrators were arrested. The blogger and opposition leader Alexei Navalny was jailed for 15 days. The next day 2,000 protestors were again brutally dispersed. Troops blocked off the main squares in the city centre.

But then, as tens of thousands pledged on social networks to turn out for a demonstration the following Saturday, 10 December, the Kremlin suddenly backed away from further confrontation, apparently afraid of provoking even greater protests. Why there was a change of heart has been the subject of much speculation, but the consensus view is that it was President Medvedev and his team, rather than Putin, who took the decision. Formally, it was the mayor of Moscow, Sergei Sobyanin, who authorised the rally. But one opposition leader says she was in the office of Medvedev's deputy chief of staff, Vladislav Surkov, when he took a call from the deputy mayor asking for advice about the demonstrations. Surkov (once regarded as Putin's chief ideologue, now Medvedev's) said the protests showed there was a need to open up the political system, to include 'a mass liberal party' which should 'represent the annoyed urban communities'. President Medvedev is said to have asked the Moscow police chief Vladimir Kolokoltsev to ensure the rally passed off peacefully.

And so it was that on 10 December an unprecedented protest – of some 50,000 people – took place on Bolotnaya Square in central Moscow, just south of the Kremlin. Wearing white ribbons and carrying placards demanding Putin's resignation and a re-run of the elections, it was by far the biggest display of discontent in Russia since the 1990s. It was as if something had snapped inside for a seething, resentful stratum of society who had hitherto bottled up their disgust at Putin's politics and gone into what in communist days used to be called 'internal opposition' – not apathy, but a deliberate turning away from politics. Now the disenfranchised middle class and liberal intelligentsia found their voice and a common purpose. 'The crowd was electric,' said one participant. 'There was a buzz, a feeling that everyone here shared the same views, the same feelings ... it was fantastic.'

Many of the protesters were people who had been encouraged by the vague promise of reform under Medvedev, disappointed by his failure to deliver and dismayed by his pusillanimous surrender of power. So it was not surprising, perhaps, that Medvedev and Putin reacted to the demonstrations in very different ways.

Putin showed himself to be out of touch with the new mood, as though he had finally lost his instinctive feel for society – or was taken aback by the very existence of a powerful group which for ten years he had ignored. First he had fixed his return to the Kremlin, then he had fixed the Duma elections, now – in a four-and-a-half-hour telethon, answering questions from around the country – he dismissed the demonstrators in shocking terms.

He did, it is true, make a gesture towards the protestors by proposing that web cameras be installed in all polling stations for the presidential election in March, to prevent fraud. And he acknowledged their right to protest, even claiming this as an achievement of the 'Putin regime'. But at the same time he sneered at them, with a traditional crude Putinism, joking that when he first saw the white ribbons pinned to their chests he thought they were condoms, adding with a smirk: 'I just couldn't understand why they had unrolled them.' In an earlier speech he had accused the United States, and in particular the secretary of state, Hillary Clinton, of standing behind the protests, saying she had 'set the tone for some opposition activists' and even 'given them a signal'. Now he went further, speaking of 'people who carry the passport of a citizen of the Russian Federation but act in the interests of a foreign state and with foreign money'. Trying to find a common language with such people was often, he said, 'hopeless or impossible'.

Finally, most tellingly, he described the demonstrators as 'Bandar-log' – the name of the 'monkey-folk' in Kipling's *The Jungle Book*. This was no unrehearsed line. The Bandar-log are not just monkeys: Kipling describes them as undisciplined, leaderless, chattering, full of fine ideas but unable to carry anything through to a conclusion – exactly how Putin regards the opposition. He remarked, 'I have loved Kipling since I was a boy', but I suspect that like most Russians he knows the Bandar-log scene mostly from a Soviet-era animated cartoon. In it the monkeys are rioting, and only the giant python Kaa is able to calm them – by mesmerising them and calling on them to step closer to him ... so he can consume them for his supper. Kipling writes:

> 'Bandar-log,' said the voice of Kaa at last, 'can ye stir foot or
>   hand without my order? Speak!'
> 'Without thy order we cannot stir foot or hand, O Kaa!'
> 'Good! Come all one pace nearer to me.'
> The lines of the monkeys swayed forward helplessly.
> 'Nearer!' hissed Kaa, and they all moved again.

In his television appearance, Putin quoted Kaa's words, with a wry smile on his lips: 'Come to me, Bandar-log!' It was as if he really believed he had the rioting 'monkeys' fully under his control.

But Moscow's 'chattering classes' were convinced that Russia's political scene had changed dramatically. And so was President Medvedev. In his first comments on the situation, he told parliament that he planned to carry out political reforms in his last months as president, because 'I hear those who speak of the need for change and I understand them.' He proposed reintroducing direct elections of regional governors (something I once heard him rule out 'for a hundred years'). The registration of political parties was to be simplified. It would no longer be necessary to collect signatures in order to qualify as a candidate in elections. There would be changes to the electoral system and the discredited Central Electoral Commission.

His declarations did nothing to stem the tide of dissent. Two days later, on 24 December, a second authorised (and peaceful) rally took place, on Sakharov Avenue – this time attracting as many as 80,000 protestors. Sensing the power of such a crowd, the anti-corruption blogger Alexei Navalny took the stage and observed: 'I can see that there are enough people here to seize the Kremlin. We are a peaceful force and will not do it now. But if these crooks and thieves try to go on cheating us, if they continue telling lies and stealing from us, we will take what belongs to us with our own hands.'

The protest attracted people from all walks of life, and the speakers included not just the traditional protest leaders but writers such as Boris Akunin and Dmitry Bykov, the shaven-headed neo-communist Sergei Udaltsov, and the glamorous socialite and TV hostess Kseniya Sobchak (daughter of Putin's former mentor, the mayor St Petersburg, Anatoly Sobchak). The ousted finance minister, Alexei Kudrin, supported demands for a re-run of the Duma elections and the resignation of Vladimir Churov, the head of the Electoral Commission. But he also called for dialogue between the protestors and the authorities, to achieve an 'evolution' towards a new leadership.

Kudrin then delivered the same message directly to Putin. In a series of private meetings, he urged the prime minister to begin a dialogue with the protestors. But, he said later in an interview, 'Putin doesn't understand who these protestors are, and he is deeply suspicious of that group that tries to present itself as representing them.'[2] In other words Putin did not trust the protest leaders – neither the former mainstream politicians such as Mikhail Kasyanov, Vladimir Ryzhkov and Boris Nemtsov, nor the newcomers such as Navalny and Udaltsov. Kudrin explained to Putin that the people attending the demonstrations were the nascent new middle class, partly from business, partly from a new creative segment of society, and that the authorities had to work with them, by finding representatives of the movement with whom they could start an immediate dialogue.

The Kremlin's *éminence grise*, Vladislav Surkov, was saying the same things out loud. In an interview with *Izvestiya* just before the Sakharov Avenue rally, the man who had once rationalised the Putin system as 'sovereign democracy' now admitted that it was 'strongly disliked' by many people, whom he described as 'the best, most productive part of our society'.[3]

A few days later he was sacked as the Kremlin's chief ideologue. An insider said, 'Putin won't work with Surkov.' Surkov portrayed himself sardonically as a victim of the system he had helped create: 'Stabilisation is eating its children.'

The protests continued to grow. On 4 February 2012, despite temperatures of -20C, up to 100,000 gathered on Bolotnaya Square. Simultaneously, an even bigger rally of pro-Putin demonstrators gathered elsewhere in Moscow and voiced their opposition to an 'orange revolution' in Russia. Accusations flew in both directions about how these protests were organised. Anti-Putin protestors claimed that the government had bussed in and paid thousands to take part in the pro-Putin rally; Kremlin supporters said the Bolotnaya protest was orchestrated by the United States.

In this period, between the Duma election and the presidential election, people spoke of a political thaw in Russia, a new epoch. Opposition leaders – banned from central television for years – began to appear as guests on talk shows. Kseniya Sobchak, routinely described as Russia's 'it girl' or 'Paris Hilton' thanks to her raunchy earlier career, used her own talk show – and celebrity status – to criticise the Kremlin and interview politicians from across the political spectrum.

Once again, a gap seemed to open up between Medvedev and Putin. The authorities' dialogue with the opposition, such as it was, took place only with the president, who invited protest leaders to the Kremlin and flirted with journalism students at Moscow University, saying the demonstrators included people who wished he had stood for re-election. Putin, by contrast, looked ever more isolated. He scarcely campaigned for re-election, preferring to publish a series of long articles in which he appropriated some of Medvedev's talk about democratisation and modernisation – without ever mentioning his protégé by name.

The central television channels made no pretence at

balanced coverage for all the presidential candidates. On 23 February, when Putin made his only major public appearance, at an almost American-style campaign rally in the huge Luzhniki football stadium, the evening news on Channel One devoted nine minutes to covering the event and just four minutes for the four other candidates put together. Putin's speech was super-patriotic, slamming 'traitors', and urging his supporters not to give in to foreign powers who wanted to 'impose their will' on Russia. On the eve of polling day, viewers were treated to a long, hagiographic documentary about the man who had 'saved Russia' from internal chaos and external foes. There was never any doubt that the election would deliver victory. And there was also little doubt that once back in the Kremlin, Putin would prove as pugnacious and uncompromising as he was in his only campaign speech.

The strongman returns

The web cameras deployed at polling stations for the election on 4 March 2012 had an unexpected effect. As well as reducing the possibilities of fraud, they also increased Putin's vote because many voters, especially older people, apparently assumed the cameras were spying on them as they marked their ballot papers. Election monitors again witnessed carousel voting and other violations, but to a lesser degree than in December. Putin's share of the vote collapsed from 72 per cent in 2004 to 64 per cent, and in Moscow, the locus of so much middle-class dissent, even the official figures gave him less than 50 per cent. The billionaire businessman Mikhail Prokhorov won a creditable 20 per cent in Moscow, attracting the support of many of the winter's protestors.

Nonetheless, opposition leaders accepted that Putin had won, and probably would have done so even without the violations on election day itself. The unfair coverage on television – and the lack of an effective alternative opposition candidate

– made sure of that.

So although 20,000 protestors turned out the following Saturday for a rally on Moscow's central Novy Arbat avenue, there was a sense of defeat and exhaustion about it. The euphoria of the winter was replaced by weariness, and dread that the re-elected Putin would crack down on further protests.

Most of the main opposition leaders stayed away from the rally, allegedly to give the floor to the election monitors who had heroically worked to prevent a repeat of the December fiasco. But tactically this was a mistake. Speakers banged on about things like carousel voting and ballot-stuffing, when in fact the real obstacle the opposition faced was the monolithic support of the state media for Putin. The election had been won long before polling day. They would have been better off venting their anger at central television than at the Electoral Commission.

The election also showed up the opposition's own weaknesses. Apart from their shared hatred of Putin, there was little to unite people like the groomed and pompous Kasyanov, the skinhead rabble-rouser Udaltsov and the nationalistic Navalny – no common programme, nothing that could really be presented as a practical alternative. Ever since the collapse of communism Russia's politicians had struggled to combine forces, each preferring to head his own little party, and it was no different now. If they were ever going to bring down Putinism, I reflected as I watched the disheartened faces on Novy Arbat that Saturday afternoon, they would need, first, to choose a single charismatic leader – a Yeltsin or a Sakharov – and, second, to break down the ruling elite's monopoly on state television. Neither goal looked remotely achievable at that moment.

In the meantime it was the *siloviki*, not the reformers, who now gained the upper hand inside the Kremlin. Proof of that came on 6 May, the day before Putin's inauguration. Although permission was granted for what the opposition optimistically termed a 'march of the millions', the softly-softly approach of the winter months was now gone. Around 20,000 protestors gathered on Bolotnaya Square, but this time violent scuffles broke out with riot police, who arrested about 650 people. Dozens of demonstrators and 30 policemen were injured. Overnight and throughout the next day, Moscow was emptied of protestors. Anyone wearing a white ribbon was detained, police raided cafés to hunt down suspects, and escorted any young men who resisted to military draft offices. Asked by a Duma deputy whether the police had been too violent, Putin's spokesman, Dmitry Peskov, replied that they had been too soft, and added, 'Protestors who hurt riot police should have their livers smeared on the pavement.' Perhaps this was just a loyal spokesman brilliantly emulating his boss's notoriously crude sense of humour, but I couldn't help thinking that he had wiped out – at a stroke – any benefit that might have been gained from the tens of millions of dollars spent in previous years on Western consultants to help him 'improve Russia's image'.

As a result of the crackdown, Putin's third inauguration took place in a surreal Moscow – his armoured motorcade swept into the Kremlin along roads emptied of people and eerily quiet, every junction guarded by police. Inside the Kremlin a pompous ceremony was followed by a sumptuous banquet, while outside police played cat and mouse with protestors. Over the next week a novel form of dissent evolved – 'roving protests' that popped up, moved around and melted away to avoid police persecution. Writers and artists led thousands on 'strolls' around the city centre. A sit-in around the statue of a Kazakh poet, Abay Kunanbayev, became known – after Occupy Wall Street – as 'Occupy Abay'. It lasted eight days before being broken up.

It took two weeks for President Putin and Prime Minister Medvedev to agree on a cabinet reshuffle, and in the end much of it seemed designed to allow each man to keep his own most trusted lieutenants. Medvedev retained a liberal economics team – minus the arch-*silovik* Igor Sechin, whom he loathed. Surprisingly, Sechin was given no job in the presidential administration either, but appeared destined to keep his grip on energy policy as head of a new 'presidential commission' on energy and as CEO of the state oil company Rosneft.

Sergei Ivanov – the former KGB man who had been passed over four years earlier as Putin's successor – had already been moved in December to the influential post of presidential chief of staff, to prepare for Putin's return to the Kremlin. Now he would play a key role as Putin's enforcer, meeting United Russia parliamentarians every Monday to ensure discipline in the Duma and arrange the passage of a raft of new laws designed to begin the long-feared crackdown on dissent.

Over the summer the Duma rushed through four repressive bills. One recriminalised defamation (libel or slander), which had been decriminalised by Medvedev. A second obliged NGOs that received foreign funding and carried out political work to register themselves as 'foreign agents' – a phrase with the same sinister connotation in Russian as in English – and to submit reports on their activities. A third imposed massive fines for organising unauthorised demonstrations resulting in public disorder – of up to $9,000 for individuals and $32,000 for organisations. Putin said the law was no tougher than analogous legislation in other countries. A fourth law enabled the authorities to ban certain websites. Although amended to refer specifically to sites containing child pornography, suicide instructions and drug propaganda, human rights groups feared its scope could be widened.

On 11 June, the eve of a planned protest to mark Russia's national day, police raided the homes of several leading opposition figures, including Navalny, Udaltsov, Nemtsov and Sobchak, and confiscated documents, computers and cash on the pretext of investigating disorders at the protest on 6 May. In all, 18 people were arrested and charged with rioting and other offences on the eve of Putin's inauguration. The first to be sentenced – a young man who had pleaded guilty and apologised for his actions – was jailed in November for four and a half years. Several leaders of the opposition, including Navalny and Udaltsov, were also charged with crimes that could entail long prison sentences if they were found guilty.

The raids were ordered by Alexander Bastrykin, a former university classmate of Putin, and now chief of the Investigation Committee, Russia's equivalent of the FBI. His state of mind as he launched Putin's witch-hunt may be divined from his bizarre behaviour the previous week. A journalist with the newspaper *Novaya gazeta*, Sergei Sokolov, had written an article implicitly accusing Bastrykin of protecting a criminal who was a regional United Russia deputy. Bastrykin invited Sokolov to a security conference in the southern city of Nalchik, where Sokolov apologised but repeated his view that the investigators were scoundrels. Bastrykin can be seen on film swearing at him and throwing him out of the room. On their return to Moscow, Sokolov was allegedly driven into a forest and left alone with Bastrykin, who threatened to have him murdered and 'joked' that he himself would be in charge of the investigation. After the whole incident became public knowledge, the two men apologised to each other and the matter was considered 'settled'. Bastrykin's actions, and the whole chilling episode, were simply swept under the carpet. In Putin's Russia a chief law enforcement officer can threaten a journalist with murder and not even face an inquiry.

When Putin first came to power he promised to bring in 'dictatorship of the law' – a Stalinist-sounding phrase that nonetheless was supposed to mean 'rule of law'. Medvedev phrased it differently: he would put an end to 'legal nihilism'. But in the summer of 2012 the law became a tool of political repression.

At the end of July Alexei Navalny was charged – not with political crimes, but with the embezzlement of timber while he had been working as an unpaid adviser to a regional governor. This happened a few days after he accused Bastrykin of illegally owning property in the Czech Republic.

At the same time, Moscow's Khamovniki district court opened its doors for what was condemned around the world as a political show trial – even though the defendants (and their activities) were a far cry from the well-trodden Russian tradition of 'dissidence'. Nadezhda Tolokonnikova, Maria Alyokhina and Yekaterina Samutsevich were members of what they called a feminist punk-rock band named Pussy Riot, which emerged in the autumn of 2011, shortly after Putin and Medvedev announced their proposed job-swap. They set out to be highly provocative, wearing lurid tights and clashing dresses, and balaclavas with slits for their eyes and mouths, and performing raucous songs with screeching vocals and vulgar, politically charged lyrics. In a newspaper interview they described their ideology: 'We are united by feminism, opposition to Putin's regime and his vertical power, by anti-authoritarianism and leftist ideas. Some of us are anarchists, some have leftist liberal positions.'[4] Their performances were usually brief, but filmed and placed on the internet. Few of them attracted attention until January 2012, when the band stood on a snow-covered wall in Red Square, facing the Kremlin, screaming out a song called 'Riot in Russia – Putin's pissed himself'. The performance featured purple smoke bombs and crunching guitar riffs, and ended with the women's arrest and small fines for insignificant 'administrative offences'.

But it was their next performance, on 21 February, that brought the full force of the law down on them – not because it was more vulgar or more critical of Putin, but because it was performed in Moscow's main cathedral, the Church of Christ the Saviour, and was – according to the indictment – blasphemous and intended to insult believers. The church and state in Russia are separate, but in this instance the court saw fit to judge the women solely on religious grounds.

The actual performance – in an almost empty cathedral – lasted only about a minute, and consisted of the women jumping about, pretending to play guitar and miming words. They later added a soundtrack and more footage from a similar performance filmed in another church two days earlier to create a video clip which was posted on the internet. The song was intended to ridicule the church for its support of Putin in the coming election. The Patriarch, Kirill, had described Putin's rule as a 'miracle from God'. Pussy Riot's song, or 'punk prayer', titled 'Mother of God, drive Putin out', alluded to the closeness of the church and the KGB – 'black robes, golden epaulettes' – and included the refrain: 'Shit, shit, holy shit'.

Three of the women involved were arrested and, after five months in jail, tried on charges of 'hooliganism motivated by religious hatred', a crime punishable by up to seven years in prison. Opinions were divided in Russia and around the world. Supporters championed the women as heroines of democracy, claiming the case was patently political and the proposed sentence out of proportion to their misdemeanour, which was presented as little more than a prank – tasteless, perhaps, or even offensive, but nonetheless a peaceful protest in which no property or person was damaged. Others saw their behaviour as outrageous and said their actions would have caused serious offence in most countries.

During a week-long trial that often bordered on farce, the judge, Marina Syrova, was intent on proving that their motives had been religious, not political. She cut them off in mid-sentence, overruled inappropriate questions and led witnesses towards the required testimony. The witnesses (or 'victims') included an elderly lady who sold candles in the church, another who worked as a concierge, and an altar-boy, all of whom said they were traumatised by the actions of the young women. (Their written testimonies contained identical phrases, apparently cut and pasted from the prosecution's charge sheet.)

Did the women 'cross themselves as all citizens do', the judge asked, like some medieval inquisitor. Could they in fact be possessed by the devil? Well, said a witness, they flailed their arms about and kicked their legs high in the air as if possessed. (The official charge was that they 'started to satanically jerk around, jump, run, kick their legs up, and twirl their heads while they shouted very insulting, blasphemous words'.)

But how could the witness be sure that Tolokonnikova was really one of the three who had desecrated the church? She was, after all, wearing a balaclava. 'You could identify her,' said the witness, 'by the structure of her calf muscles!'

Many people wondered why the authorities insisted on proceeding with the trial, which brought day after day of mockery and condemnation in the world's press. Had the women been given a small fine, the bad publicity would have been avoided. Some speculated it was the church's doing, with the court willingly playing along to 'please' Putin. Others said Putin himself was directly behind it, using a 'show trial' as a warning to the growing protest movement. At one point (in London, addressing foreigners) Putin suggested the women 'should not be judged too harshly', but after Judge Syrova handed down a two-year sentence (later suspended for one of the women), he said they had got what they deserved.

The iconic image of three young women gazing angelically from behind bars in the courtroom endeared them to the world's media. Politicians across the world, and celebrities including Sting, Paul McCartney and Madonna, called for their freedom. But in Russia the reaction was very different. Even some opposition leaders, who condemned the trial as politically motivated, felt queasy about the women's performance. Alexei Navalny opposed the verdict, but described the women as 'fools who committed petty crimes for the sake of publicity'.

Millions of ordinary Russians who had never been exposed

to Western performance art or punk rock considered it disgusting and blasphemous. The authorities highlighted the previous activities of two of the women, who had been members of a radical art collective known as Voina (War), which had posted videos of themselves performing group sex in a museum and lewd acts with a frozen chicken. To many, this looked more like exhibitionism than political protest.

The Pussy Riot trial once again exposed differences between Putin and Medvedev, who said several times he thought the women should not be imprisoned. As usual, it was Putin who was more in tune with domestic opinion and Medvedev who reflected liberal Western views.

But the former president's opinion counted for little, as the country entered what the commentator Gleb Pavlovsky termed a period of 'de-Medvedevisation'. The decision to restore elected regional governors was watered down by the introduction of a 'presidential filter' to approve candidates. The retirement age for officials, reduced by Medvedev to 60 (or 65 in special cases), was raised to 70. Bluntly contradicting Medvedev's version of how he had handled the Georgia war in 2008, taking all major decisions alone, Putin said that he had telephoned him twice from Beijing at the start of the military operation. Putin even cast doubt on the wisdom of Medvedev's decision to tamper with Russia's time zones, moving permanently to summer time.

The opposition's brief honeymoon was now over. NTV ran a series of Soviet-style documentaries purporting to expose protestors as puppets of the West. Following the Pussy Riot trial, the Duma now proposed to criminalise blasphemy.

In the West, governments wondered: would the 'reset' be the next casualty?

Russia and the West

Russians have always had contradictory attitudes towards the West. In the decades of communism, though enveloped in a mist of propaganda about Western poverty and backwardness, young Russians would nonetheless pester foreign visitors for the forbidden fruits of capitalism – anything from chewing gum to blue jeans. Today they sit in McDonald's or Starbucks wearing the latest Nike shoes and fingering an iPhone, while telling you with total conviction that 9/11 was a CIA plot or that the USA is bent on world domination. The common theme? That the West – in particular the USA – is prosperous and successful, but also evil.

It is a way of thinking that chimes well with Vladimir Putin's world view. The Russian security analyst Andrei Solda-tov says that more than a decade under Putin and his former KGB colleagues has changed the political culture of Russia into something more closed and suspicious than it has been since the days of Mikhail Gorbachev's *glasnost*. But he adds, 'Most surprising of all, the middle classes in large, cosmopoli-tan cities like St Petersburg and Moscow, which were praised for the recent democratic protests, actually share many of the Kremlin's prejudices about America. Very simply, Russia is awash with misinformation, and the supposed authoritarian-ism of President Vladimir Putin is only partly to blame.'

The view that Putin was most keen to propagate (and exag-gerate, to rally support for his anti-Western stance) was that the West did not merely support the opposition with words or even advice, but actually financed and directed it in order to foment a 'coloured revolution' which would impose a US-style system and allow multinationals to devour Russia's resources. While Medvedev had tried to harness the positive potential of American influence, the evidence from the beginning of Putin's third term suggested that he intended to build a picket-fence of laws around Russia to keep out the evil.

To ward off pernicious 'democracy promotion' the Duma had already decreed that all NGOs receiving funding from abroad must register as 'foreign agents'. (On the day that law came into force, zealots spray-painted the doors of such organisations with the words 'foreign agent'.) In the meantime the Kremlin abruptly ended the work of USAID, an American government agency which had supported public health and environmental projects, as well as civil society groups, for two decades. It financed almost the entire budgets of such organisations as Memorial, which documents the atrocities of the communist period, Transparency International, which monitors corruption, and Golos, the biggest independent election monitoring group. Deprived of almost $50 million of funding, these groups would struggle to keep going.

Then the noose was tightened further, when Putin signed an FSB-sponsored law on treason (previously shelved by Medvedev) which significantly widened the definition of traitor to embrace almost anyone possessing information that could be deemed secret and who came into contact with foreigners. Providing advice to an international organisation could be deemed as espionage or treason, punishable by up to 20 years in prison.

All of this cast doubt on the viability of President Obama's Russia policy. The 'reset' had produced results only with the support of President Medvedev, who understood that his pet modernisation projects such as the innovation centre at Skolkovo depended on a free exchange of ideas – and people – with the West. The spirit of give and take implied by the reset had allowed the New Start treaty to be hammered out, but with Putin back at the tandem's handlebars Russia's objections to the US missile defence system were likely to become more intransigent – and even less likely to be taken into account. When Medvedev met Obama in Seoul in March 2012, microphones picked up the American quietly telling his partner that he would have 'more flexibility' on the missile defence issue once he was re-elected later in the year. Medvedev's reply was: 'I will transmit this to Vladimir' – a blunt reminder to Obama that he, Medvedev, no longer had any say in Russian foreign policy.

Putin-III and Obama-II both had to consider whether the reset had run its course or should continue. The policy was largely the brainchild of Obama's Russia adviser, Michael McFaul, who became ambassador to Moscow in January 2012. An academic rather than a career diplomat, his approach to the job was innovative – and not at all understood in the stuffy smoke-stained corridors of the Russian foreign ministry. McFaul was breezy and casual, tweeting constantly, meeting opposition groups as well as diplomats, and engaging in a kind of public diplomacy unheard of in Moscow. A speech to Russian students contained jokes and asides that were taken with deadly seriousness by the foreign ministry, earning McFaul a stern rebuke. Russian television accused him of trying to foment revolution. Even well-disposed Russian commentators began to suggest he would be better to 'sacrifice his personal fame' and stick to 'classical diplomacy'.[5]

In short, McFaul became a symbol of precisely what the Russians did not like about the reset – a 'dual-track' approach that envisaged engaging both the Russian government and Russian society, without linking unrelated issues. The Kremlin had no problem with the first part, which meant looking for common goals and mutually acceptable outcomes. They saw this as a big improvement on the Bush administration's headstrong approach. But the second half – 'engagement with Russian society' – presumed to give American politicians the right to lecture Russia about human rights, while the Kremlin had little opportunity to 'engage' American society, or at least not in any credible way.

Although the attacks on McFaul ended after about half a year, the initial rough welcome given to him looked like a warning not to 'meddle', and when I met him at the end of

2012 the ambassador looked shocked and puzzled by the level of harassment he had been subjected to. His predecessor had also engaged with opposition figures, and indeed President Obama had met them on his first trip to Moscow – and that had not been an issue for the Kremlin. But that was before the opposition grew into a mass protest movement.

In the view of the analyst Dmitry Trenin, governments are best at dealing with other governments, and societies with other societies. 'American society is already present in Russia in myriad ways. But US government support for Russian society – when it touches on political issues – is controversial not just for the Kremlin but for the more conservative, communist-leaning or nationalistic parts of Russian society.'[6]

Arguments swirled about whether the reset had achieved much anyway. Each side could draw up very different balance sheets. American gains included the New Start treaty, a new transit base in central Russia to supply troops in Afghanistan, and Russia's tougher approach to Iran (including its cancellation of a $1 billion contract for the supply of an air defence system). On the other hand, the reset did not persuade Russia to reduce its support for Bashar al-Assad's regime in Syria, leaving the international community wringing its hands impotently as government troops massacred civilians. Believing that the Kremlin's objections to intervention were due to worries about its military interests in Syria, Washington secretly offered to guarantee the survival of Russia's base there. But Russia had more fundamental objections: its principled stand (for obvious reasons) against regime change and interference in other countries' internal affairs, and its belief that revolution in Syria would lead to chaos and possibly bring to power a dangerous fundamentalist Islamist regime – something it expects to be the ultimate result of the Arab Spring generally.

From the Kremlin's point of view the reset helped it in its negotiations with the WTO (which it finally joined in August 2012), and earned it *de facto* recognition of what it liked to call its 'privileged interests' in its own backyard, particularly Ukraine. On the other hand, the reset saw America continue to 'meddle', as Russia saw it, in its internal affairs. So while there was relief at the end of 2012 that Congress finally abolished the Jackson-Vanik amendment, this was offset by fury that it was done only in conjunction with the passing of the so-called Magnitsky Act. This created a blacklist of Russian human-rights abusers, including those implicated in the prison death of Sergei Magnitsky (see pp 288–291), who would have their assets frozen and be denied US visas.

In some ways the passing of the Magnitsky Act sounded the death-knell of the reset policy. It was an initiative of Congress and was initially opposed by the Obama administration. A senior US official admitted to me that the administration had qualms about publishing a list of alleged criminals, since it effectively meant meting out an extrajudicial punishment on people who – however sound the reasons for suspecting them – had not undergone due legal process or trial. Secondly, he said, any government had the discretion to ban whomever it wished, without a legislative act, and indeed Obama himself had already issued a proclamation in August 2011 banning entry to the US of suspected human rights violators – including the 60 on a (secret) Magnitsky list. Others noted that the Act discriminated against Russia, while taking no action against countries with even worse human rights records.

If American legislators expected the law to help bring Magnitsky's killers to justice, they were deluding themselves. Russian prosecutors promptly withdrew charges against the only person facing trial in connection with the lawyer's death and ploughed on with the macabre and absurd posthumous prosecution of Magnitsky himself for alleged tax evasion. The Act provoked a frenzy of anti-Americanism in the Duma and the Kremlin, resulting in a 'retaliatory' law that banned American adoptions of Russian children. It was dubbed the 'Dima Yakovlev Law' after a Russian toddler who died of heatstroke in July 2009 after his American adoptive father left him in a parked vehicle for nine hours. The father was acquitted of involuntary manslaughter. About 60,000 Russian children, many of them with special needs, have been adopted by American families in the last 20 years, and the vast majority enjoy normal, happy lives, yet in his zeal to punish Washington for the Magnitsky Act, Putin signed off on a law so ill-conceived that its only real victims would be thousands of abandoned and disabled children, many of whom might now be condemned to lives in Russian orphanages, where conditions are often dire.

It had been hoped in Washington that the reset would lead to strong Kremlin cooperation on a broad range of international issues. Opponents said it had failed and it was now time to 'stand up' to Putin. In Russia opponents also said the reset had failed, not just because of the human rights component but because Obama was pursuing a missile defence plan it regarded as little different from Bush's.

The Kremlin continued to present missile defence as a vital threat to its security. In May 2012 General Nikolai Makarov, Russia's military chief of staff, presented NATO officials with a detailed analysis which claimed that the Western system – despite Obama's modifications, and the continued insistence that it was intended to guard against an Iranian threat – would have the potential to intercept Russian strategic ballistic missiles by 2017–18. He said that in a hypothetical future period of heightened tension with the West, Russia would make a pre-emptive strike against the system's components in Poland and Romania. Moscow's conditions for accepting the system were joint control and a binding NATO guarantee that it would not be used against Russian missiles. NATO balked at both demands. 'We don't trust them,' a senior official told me, 'and what's the point of written "guarantees"? Who's going to remember them if an ICBM is heading for Washington?' The alliance ceremonially launched the first stage of the system at a summit in Chicago in May 2012.

Obama had promised 'flexibility' if re-elected, but it seemed highly unlikely that he would ever be in a position to satisfy Moscow's concerns. As we saw in Chapter 9, when Robert Gates offered the Russians sufficient flexibility to allay their fears, his concessions were instantly shot down by the military establishment back in Washington. As for flexibility on the Kremlin's part, that also seemed unlikely.

Readers with a sense of history will remember that we have been here before. In 1986 at a summit meeting in Reykjavik the Soviet leader Mikhail Gorbachev and President Ronald Reagan agreed on sweeping arms reductions that could have *eliminated* nuclear weapons entirely. This epoch-making deal foundered on just one thing – Reagan's insistence on developing a missile defence shield (then known as the Strategic Defence Initiative, or 'Star Wars'), and Gorbachev's refusal to countenance it.

I pointed out earlier in this book that Russian foreign policy tends to be reactive: it took the advent of Obama, with a less confrontational attitude than George W. Bush, to tease a positive response out of the Kremlin. But it also depends on who is doing the reacting. Medvedev saw the benefit of the reset and felt that it produced tangible results. But as Obama returned for his second presidency, it was Putin, not Medvedev, who was settling in to a new six-year term in the Kremlin. Russia looked to be on track for greater isolation, and the reset was all but dead.

CONCLUSION

I concluded the first edition of this book by quoting, approvingly, Sir Rodric Braithwaite, a former British ambassador to the Soviet Union, whose affection for the country and understanding of its people led him to a rare understanding of Russia's situation. 'There are many flaws in the Putin system,' he wrote. 'But it has restored Russian self respect, and laid the ground for future prosperity and reform. As the process goes forward, the rest of us are better employed in keeping our mouths shut, rather than offering advice which is sometimes arrogant and insulting, and often irrelevant or useless.'[1]

Within a few months, I found myself breaking my own rule by publicly offering advice that probably deserved all of those adjectives! I will tell the story because the Kremlin's reaction to my intervention serves as a useful lesson, which fully backs up my original view.

It was in April 2012, and I had just visited Moscow and witnessed the disheartened protest rally that followed Putin's re-election as president. The opposition, it seemed to me, was too divided and leaderless to mount a serious challenge. But the root cause of its failure was the Kremlin's total control of central television, which had silenced opposition politicians for years and ensured absurdly one-sided coverage for Putin during the campaign. President Medvedev had already launched a proposal to create a new 'public' television channel, and I decided to contribute to the debate by publishing an open letter to Dmitry Peskov – Putin's spokesman, for whom I had worked as a consultant – in the *Kommersant* newspaper. The paper published it, together with Peskov's reaction.[2]

The thrust of my article was that uncensored television was an inalienable part of any real democracy. Putin's view of television was the same as the old Communist Party's – that it existed merely to 'explain the government's plans' rather than to debate and criticise proposals before they became policy decisions. There was no place in a democracy at all, I wrote, for 'state' television. Governments should not have their own TV channels. Even Medvedev's idea of an extra 'public' channel was wholly inadequate because it 'would still leave three state channels pumping out government propaganda. Such a system exists only in a dictatorship, not in a democracy.' I described how the BBC works and suggested that lessons could be taken from that. Kremlin censorship should be entirely abolished; Russian TV should be used for the presentation of opposing views, for discussion and analysis, rather than the promulgation of decisions; and they should restore satirical programmes, because in a democracy people also need to laugh at their leaders.

Peskov was incensed and called my letter 'absurd'. The paper quoted him as saying that he had nothing to do with public television (even though within a month or so Putin would appoint its head), and – this is the important point – Peskov fulminated that 'a foreigner ... has no right to use words like "should" do this or "should" do that.'

In other words I had done exactly what I had advised Westerners against doing and got exactly the reaction I should have predicted – not thanks for my help, but indignation that I had dared to give it. It is a lesson that could usefully be learned by all outsiders who try to lecture Russia about how to behave. It makes us feel better – but if it has any effect at all, it tends to be precisely the opposite of what we want.

So how should the West deal with Russia? And does Western pressure actually have any effect on Kremlin politics? This book has recorded the successes and failures of several different strategies over recent decades.

In Chapter 1, we saw how President Clinton's approach, though well-meaning, failed; the West threw away a chance to bring Russia in from the cold by failing to understand its fears and aspirations following the collapse of communism. There was certainly more freedom in the 1990s than ever before, but the Yeltsin the West praised was scarcely more democratic than Putin: he fiddled elections shamelessly, used the army to shell his own parliament and committed wholesale atrocities in Chechnya. The US praised his domestic policies, which were inflicting turmoil on Russia, but refused to treat Yeltsin as a serious global player, thereby adding to the sense of humiliation felt by many in the country.

The main part of the book charted the advent of a new Cold War in the 2000s, arguing that it was due as much to the insensitivity of George W. Bush's administration to Russia's security concerns as it was to Putin's stridency in pursuing the perfectly legitimate goal of restoring Russian pride and status. At the same time, Putin failed to grasp that his rollback of democracy made the West afraid and less likely to take him seriously as a partner.

The modest gains of the 'reset' after 2009 were the result of the *lowering* of tension and confrontation. Its subsequent failure was due not to the West being 'too soft', but to Russia's perception that the US was again raising the stakes – with its insistence on building a missile shield without including Russia, and unwelcome 'democracy promotion'.

In fact, the only time relations have ever improved significantly between Russia and the West was in the period preceding the events covered in this book – under Mikhail Gorbachev in the late 1980s. That came about precisely as part of a package – lessened tension between East and West coupled with the loosening of controls inside the Soviet Union.

As for the relationship between external pressure and liberalisation at home, the evidence, as shown by the historian Archie Brown, is that 'throughout the post-war period, the icier the Cold War became, the stronger was the position of hard-liners inside the Soviet Union'.[3] The West's fierce opposition to communism did not in any way improve human rights under Leonid Brezhnev and his hard-line successors throughout the 1960s, 1970s and 1980s. The Jackson-Vanik amendment, introduced in 1974, did not persuade the USSR to let Jews emigrate freely (in fact emigration fell dramatically for several years) or to release dissidents from prison.[4] That only happened when Gorbachev came along, and it coincided with a period of rapprochement, not confrontation.

Indeed, in the last 60 years progressive or liberalising reforms in Russia have always emerged from within the establishment, not from the streets – and certainly not under Western pressure. Khrushchev was a Communist Party man through and through, but it was he who dismantled the worst of Stalinism. Gorbachev rose through the party ranks and as general secretary cajoled and sometimes hoodwinked his reactionary colleagues into accepting his *perestroika* agenda. He was helped, to be sure, by public pressure – but even that (the pro-democracy rallies, the newly unchained press and public organisations) was made possible only by his own reforms. It was not the dissidents or any other outsiders who brought about the collapse of the system. The final assault on the system was led by Boris Yeltsin, who had also emerged from the ranks of the communist establishment.

So is it realistic now to expect the disparate forces leading the anti-Putin protests to bring him down? Or will change once again have to come from within? And if so, who will be its instigator? Dmitry Medvedev sometimes struck me as a Gorbachev figure, who really wanted to reform from within, but was too weak and lacklustre to achieve much. Unlike Gorbachev he never became the paramount leader – Putin remained that – and for this reason never had the upper hand. Similarly, Medvedev failed to replace reactionaries in the leadership with like-minded reformers and never built up a critical mass of popular support either. That meant it was easy for Putin to return to the presidency and start undoing even the modest reforms of the Medvedev period. His failure is a grim reminder of the stranglehold that Putin has on the Russian system, through his network of KGB men, business associates and cronies.

It remains the case, though, that change in Russia is more likely to emerge from within the establishment than from without. It is likely to be prompted not by political protest on the streets but by a future economic crisis, perhaps a slump in oil prices, making the case for reform unassailable. Could the key figure be Alexei Kudrin, the former finance minister? He is an insider, a close colleague of Putin's, but enjoys the respect of the opposition. Or Mikhail Prokhorov, the billionaire who has challenged Putin but managed so far to escape repression – though he is not exactly an insider? Or could it fall to an emboldened Medvedev a second time around? Or to some other figure, as yet unrecognised as a reformer, in Putin's entourage?

While arguing that it is impossible (not to mention presumptuous) for the West to change Russia's internal policies or leaders, I would also argue that *until* Russia changes, East–West relations will not improve. As the Soviet-era dissident Andrei Sakharov put it, 'A country that does not respect the rights of its own people will not respect the rights of its neighbours.' Again, there is a historical parallel. It was Gorbachev's sweeping reforms in the late 1980s that persuaded the arch anti-communist Ronald Reagan to take him seriously and to embark on a close relationship that led to arms-control agreements and – in effect – the end of the Cold War. During my spell as a media consultant to the Kremlin, Dmitry Medvedev – just weeks into his presidency – unveiled a sweeping proposal to reform Europe's security structures. I sent his advisers a memo (recalling 'Gorbymania' and the reasons behind it) arguing that Medvedev's initiatives would not be taken seriously unless he demonstrated *first* that he was a democrat at home. Needless to say, my memo was ignored.

In short, the West needs to stop thinking it can influence Russian internal affairs, and the Russians should stop imagining that they will be accepted as equal partners globally so long as they trample on human rights. The 'reset' may have tried to delink these two matters, but in everyone's minds they are inextricably bound together.

To be sure, the picture of Russia that has emerged in this book is dire – not at all the one I hoped for 20 years ago when the country emerged from communism.[5]

After a positive start, when he wooed the West and took steps to stimulate the economy, Vladimir Putin presided over the smothering of media freedoms and democracy, and developed a personality cult that exploited all the modern means of communication. The economy remains almost entirely dependent on exports of raw materials, with no modern manufacturing base to speak of. Putin's pledge to crack down on the oligarchs applied only to those who opposed him politically, while the country's wealth was amassed in the hands of fabulously rich tycoons and state bureaucrats. A land of limitless human and natural resources, freed two decades ago from the grip of totalitarianism, failed to burst into bloom. Some 40 per cent of young people, according to a poll, would rather live somewhere else.[6] Russian businessmen also prefer to take their money elsewhere: capital flight reached around $57 billion in

2012, after $80 billion left the country in 2011, according to the Central Bank. Corruption is by the government's own admission overwhelming and growing – the glue that holds together a mafia-like state dominated by a clique of Putin's friends and colleagues, from the KGB, St Petersburg and even his dacha cooperative. An unexpected fresh assault on high-level corruption in late 2012 resulted in the sacking of the defence minister, Anatoly Serdyukov, the arrests of several high-level officials, and revelations of tens of billions of roubles of bribes and kickbacks. As this book went to press it was too early to say whether this was the start of a meaningful crackdown, at a level never tackled until now, or a brief campaign designed to steal the thunder of the opposition.

Yet despite the mountain of problems that can be laid at his door, Putin remains, even 12 years after coming to power, relatively popular in Russia. Polls by the Levada Centre show that his approval rating has been steadily dropping since a high point of 88 per cent in 2008 – but it still stood at 63 per cent in November 2012.[7] A different polling group, FOM, showed 'trust' in Putin falling during the same period from 70 per cent to 41 per cent.[8] Yet these are levels most Western politicians can only dream of.

For part of the answer to this conundrum, read again his favourite song which I translated at the end of Chapter 10. It may sound maudlin and cheesy to Westerners, and it might be scorned by the sophisticated and cynical Russian intellectuals who loathe Putin and everything he stands for. But you could go into millions of Russian homes and find people going watery-eyed over Soviet-era classics. It doesn't mean they are all old communists! The chord that Putin strikes among millions of Russians is one of nostalgia – for simpler days, for 'equality', for comradeship, unity, the wartime spirit that lasted so much longer in Russia than anywhere else. These things are real. Alien perhaps to most Westerners, but real.

The mass of the Russian public is not generally the same

as 'average' Westerners. In a television contest in 2008 to find 'the greatest Russian', Stalin came third – and, it is thought, would have come first if the authorities had not rigged the result to avoid complete embarrassment. Putin's support is lowest among the intellectual and middle classes of Moscow and St Petersburg, and highest among the larger swathes of society in the provinces, the working classes and state administration.

In Chapter 1 I pointed to the mistaken Western (especially American) belief that Russia was just a Western country waiting to be freed. Putin plays to that part of the Russian mind that rebels, instinctively, against that. He speaks for those who want to have a Western economy, and enjoy all the benefits of it, but who want to find their own path towards that future, and recoil from some of the West's failings. He speaks for those who want Russia to be respected in the world – and for those millions who mistakenly confuse respect with fear. And he speaks for those who simply love Russia and savour its uniqueness – those who infuriate Westerners like myself, who genuinely endeavour to 'understand' it, by smirking at us, saying, 'You'll never understand the Russian soul.'

If only Putin had combined his intuition with an instinct for democracy and trust in the people's choice he would have been a great leader. But Putin does not really understand democracy. As we have seen, he believes that American presidents can have pesky newscasters removed from their jobs. He falls for conspiracy theories (the Georgia war was started to help Senator McCain) and believes nonsense served to him by his intelligence service (America has separate poultry factories producing substandard chickens to sell to Russia). He has created a system where (he believes) nothing will happen properly if he does not personally supervise it: after the outbreak of wildfires in the summer of 2010 he even had CCTV cameras installed in damaged villages so that he could monitor the progress of reconstruction work from his own office.

His style of leadership includes publicly berating officials on television, sometimes forcing them to change their policies on the spot, because the cameras are whirring. An example:

Vladimir Putin: I want to understand how many Russian airplanes Aeroflot is going to buy. Otherwise the situation is that you want to dominate the domestic market, but don't want to buy domestic equipment. That's no good.

Vitaly Savelyev (Director General of Aeroflot): But we are buying Russian-built planes ...

Vladimir Putin: Not enough of them.

Vitaly Savelyev: All right, we will draw up plans. I will report back.

Vladimir Putin: Good.

Putin instituted a tradition of having the opening of every cabinet meeting recorded and shown on television news, apparently in the belief that this demonstrates openness and democracy. In fact, it means that government sessions turn into shows. Instead of a natural, and perhaps difficult, discussion in the privacy of the cabinet room, there is a speech by Putin and, at best, a stilted dialogue with ministers. No Western government televises its cabinet sessions and no one would expect this to happen, because difficult decisions can only be taken in private. Putin has thus taken a superficially 'democratic' idea – televising the decision-makers – and turned it into an instrument of dictatorship.

For all the iniquities of the Putin system, however, it is not 'like the Soviet Union', as is so often glibly stated. I was struck by ex-President Bill Clinton's sarcastic comment to Putin after the latter's homily about how to reform the capitalist economy in Davos in January 2009: 'I'm glad to hear Prime Minister Putin come out for free enterprise. I hope it works for him.' The *Baltimore Sun* ran an article in 2011 about the Russians' love of fast-food restaurants under the headline: 'We're lovin' it, comrade.' Comrade! It's 20 years since Russians were 'comrades' – but it seems they are lumbered with the stigma of communism.

You only need to see the queues of excited families at Moscow airport, heading for holidays abroad, or visit the Gulag Museum with its displays from Stalin's camps, or go to a theatre production of Solzhenitsyn's *One Day in the Life of Ivan Denisovich* (which is also taught in schools), or look at Russian websites and blogs, or simply eat and shop in Moscow today, to understand that communism is well and truly buried. It does the victims of Stalinism and Brezhnevism, who were murdered or languished in labour camps and psychiatric hospitals, a terrible disservice to equate today's Russia with those awful days. The freedoms enjoyed today are incomparable. There is no ubiquitous Communist Party ruling *every* aspect of people's lives (United Russia is a tool of the regime, but it does not have cells at every workplace, taking all decisions); there is no centralised, command economy; some protests may be broken up, and state television may be controlled and vicious, but every Russian citizen can access opposition and foreign sources of information through newspapers, radio and the internet.

Above all, there is no 'Russian ideology': wishing to have a say in world affairs is a far cry from the Soviet ambition to spread communism around the globe. Yet as we have seen throughout this book, both sides fall too easily into stereotyped thinking, rooted in an era when two ideologies fought for world domination. Cold War thinking and frictions remain on both sides, each winding the other up instead of trying to understand the other's fears.

There are many commentators who argue that because Putin is undemocratic the West must 'biff' him. But confrontation alone – without offering some incentive for him to cooperate – would mean throwing away all hope of improvement in relations for the next six years (at least), because, like it or not, it is Putin the West must deal with. I have argued that Putin, with his Soviet-era, KGB mindset, is paranoid about the West's intentions, and would suggest that it makes sense to treat a paranoid man with caution, not threats.

Of course we want Putin to change and Russia to become democratic. The question is: will we promote that aim by antagonising him, or by pragmatic, constructive engagement? Or are our efforts pointless anyway? As I have argued above, the evidence of history suggests that pragmatic engagement is the only chance of success, but that in the end Russia will reform from within, not under outside pressure.

As for gaining Russia's cooperation in international affairs, it is nonsensical to imagine that the Kremlin will support the West over Syria, for example, while the West is confronting Russia over its key concerns such as missile defence. Seen from Moscow, these things are a package. If the West wants them to cooperate it needs to draw them into global decision making rather than excluding them.

Anyone who cares about democracy is right, indeed duty-bound, to criticise Russia over its human rights record and increasing authoritarianism. As a senior Western diplomat put it to me, 'If you don't speak out about egregious behaviour you send a signal that you approve.' But I would suggest that while criticising, we should be aware of our limitations.

First, we would be more convincing if we ourselves were paragons of virtue. Many Russians do not see why they should take lessons from governments that themselves invade, torture, and trample on human rights. How would we take it if any other country – even the most democratic one – lectured us about who should be our leader or how we should run things? Why does anyone think Russians should react otherwise?

Secondly, our interventions are sometimes of debatable value. The West applauds a rag-bag of Russian opposition figures – nationalists, communists, showbiz stars and punk musicians – who would be scarcely plausible in most Western countries.

Thirdly, our protests arguably do more to make us feel better ourselves than to change anything in Russia. That does not mean we should not protest. The killers of Sergei Magnitsky, for example, must be brought to justice, and the US Magnitsky Act is certainly a strong way of expressing concern and outrage. Hopefully, unlike Jackson-Vanik, which had no demonstrable effect on improving human rights in the USSR, it will at least stop a few criminals spending their ill-gotten fortunes at Bloomingdale's. But overall – if we are realistic – the law is unlikely to restrain murderers and embezzlers protected by the Russian state. At best such protests serve as a constant reminder to the Kremlin that 'we care'. In the 1980s the street in Washington housing the Soviet embassy was renamed 'Andrei Sakharov Place' – which probably annoyed the diplomats, until they got used to it, but it certainly cannot be said to have brought about the dissident's freedom: he was released from exile only when a new leader, Mikhail Gorbachev, who saw Sakharov's plight as an abomination, became strong enough to overrule his hard-line colleagues.

And a final thought. Even when Russia eventually gets a democratic leader – as it no doubt will – that leader will be no more happy to take lectures and lessons from abroad than Putin is. However democratic he is (no doubt it will be a 'he'), however much the West approves of him, he will not be a patsy. Russian leaders will always put their own country's interests first. For Russia is not the West, it is Russia.

NOTES

Chapter 1. The Secret Policeman's Ball

1. Strobe Talbott, *The Russia Hand* (New York: Random House, 2002), p 416.
2. Interview with Konstantin Kosachev, 16 December 2009.
3. Talbott, p 397.
4. Stephen F. Cohen, *Failed Crusade: America and the Tragedy of Post-Communist Russia* (New York: W.W.Norton & Co, 2000), p xii.
5. Interview with Toby Gati, RIA Novosti, 22 March 2011.
6. Vladimir Putin, *Ot pervogo litsa* (http://archive.kremlin.ru/articles/bookchapter3.shtml – last accessed 7 September 2011).
7. For a good account of this part of Putin's career, see Peter Baker and Susan Glasser, *Kremlin Rising: Vladimir Putin's Russia and the End of Revolution* (New York: Lisa Drew, 2005), pp 47ff.
8. *Ibid.*, p 53.

Chapter 2. Courting the West

1. Interview with George Robertson, 9 March 2011.
2. Interview with Jonathan Powell, 9 March 2011.
3. *Guardian*, 18 April 2000.
4. Interview with Mikhail Margelov, 29 April 2010.
5. Interview with Condoleezza Rice, 14 April 2011.

6. Interview with Stephen Hadley, 24 January 2011.
7. Interview with Colin Powell, 3 March 2011.
8. Interview with Igor Ivanov, 11 December 2010.
9. Interview with Sergei Ivanov, 29 October 2010.
10. Yelena Tregubova, *Bayki kremlevskogo diggera* (Moscow: Ad Marginem, 2003), pp 160ff.
11. Bob Woodward, *Bush at War* (New York: Simon & Schuster, 2002), p 119.
12. Interview with Colin Powell, 3 March 2011.
13. Interview with Condoleezza Rice, 20 June 2011.
14. Bolton interview with Peter Baker and Susan Glasser, quoted in *Kremlin Rising*, p 131.
15. Interview with Sergei Ivanov, 29 October 2010.
16. White House translation, quoted in Woodward, *Bush at War*, p 118.
17. In 2009 the Russians finally tried to force the Kyrgyz government to eject the Americans from Manas by offering loans worth $2 billion. The price paid by the US to be allowed to stay was a quadrupling in the rent and the renaming of the air base into a less permanent-sounding 'Transit Centre'.
18. John Bolton, *Surrender is not an Option* (New York: Threshold Editions, 2007), p 71.
19. Interview with Gerhard Schröder, 8 June 2011.
20. Interview with George Robertson, 9 March 2011.
21. Interview with Sergei Prikhodko, 30 June 2011.
22. Interview with George Robertson, 9 March 2011.
23. Interview with Colin Powell, 17 May 2011.
24. Interview with Stephen Hadley, 24 January 2011.
25. Interview with Igor Ivanov, 11 December 2010.
26. Interview with Colin Powell, 17 May 2011.
27. Interview with Sergei Ivanov, 29 October 2010.
28. Interview with Condoleezza Rice, 20 June 2011.

Chapter 3. The Battle for Economic Reform

1. Interview with Alexei Kudrin, 14 December 2010.
2. Interview with German Gref, 7 December 2010.
3. Interview with Andrei Illarionov, 27 January 2011.
4. Interview with German Gref, 7 December 2010.

5. Mikhail Kasyanov, *Bez Putina* (Moscow: Novaya gazeta, 2009), p 216.
6. Interview with Mikhail Kasyanov, 16 February 2011.
7. See Marshall Goldman, *Petrostate* (New York: OUP, 2008), chapter 5.
8. Interview with Vladimir Milov, 16 February 2011.

Chapter 4. The Darker Side

1. Interview with Viktor Shenderovich, 14 December 2010.
2. *Komsomolskaya Pravda*, 11 February 2000.
3. *Novaya gazeta*, 27 March 2000, reprinted in Anna Politkovskaya, *Nothing but the Truth* (London: Harvill Secker, 2010).
4. Mikhail Kasyanov, *Bez Putina* (Moscow: Novaya gazeta, 2009), p 217.
5. Interview with German Gref, 7 December 2010.
6. David E. Hoffman, *The Oligarchs* (Oxford, Public Affairs Ltd, 2002), p 449.
7. John Browne, *Beyond Business* (London: Weidenfeld & Nicolson, 2010), p 145.
8. Interview with German Gref, 7 December 2010.
9. Martin Sixsmith, *Putin's Oil* (London: Continuum, 2010), p 52.
10. Interview with Mikhail Kasyanov, 16 February 2011.
11. My account of this meeting is based on interviews with those present, on (edited) video of the event and on the versions given by Sixsmith, *Putin's Oil*, and Andrei Kolesnikov in *Kommersant*, 20 February 2003.
12. Interview with Leonid Nevzlin, 14 May 2011.
13. Interview with Andrei Illarionov, 27 January 2011.
14. Interview with Mikhail Kasyanov, 16 February 2011.
15. Kasyanov, *Bez Putina*, pp 199ff.
16. Quoted in Sixsmith, *Putin's Oil*, p 153.
17. *Observer*, 2 November 2003.

Chapter 5. New Europe, Old Europe

1. Interview with George Robertson, 9 March 2011.
2. Interview with Jonathan Powell, 9 March 2011.
3. Interview with Dan Fried, 27 January 2011.

4. Interview with Nicholas Burns, 15 July 2010.
5. Interview with Nicholas Burns, 21 January 2011.
6. Interview with Maurice Gourdault-Montagne, 20 June 2011.
7. *Die Zeit*, 5 April 2001.
8. Interview with Gerhard Schröder, 8 June 2011.
9. Interview with Alexander Kwaśniewski, 24 November 2010.
10. Interview with Igor Ivanov, 11 December 2010.
11. Interview with Nicholas Burns, 21 January 2011.
12. Interview with Sergei Ivanov, 29 October 2010.
13. Interview with Maurice Gourdault-Montagne, 20 June 2011.
14. Interview with Condoleezza Rice, 14 April 2011.

Chapter 6. Putin Mark II

1. Interview with Igor Ivanov, 11 December 2010.
2. Interview with Nino Burjanadze, 29 March 2011.
3. Interview with Mikheil Saakashvili, 9 May 2005.
4. See Thomas de Waal, *The Caucasus: An Introduction* (Oxford: Oxford University Press, 2010), pp 194–5.
5. Interview with Colin Powell, 3 March 2011.
6. de Waal, *The Caucasus*, p 197.
7. Interview with Mikheil Saakashvili, 31 March 2011.
8. *Wall Street Journal*, 30 August 2008, *Daily Telegraph*, 23 August 2008.
9. de Waal, *The Caucasus*, p 199.
10. Interview with Eduard Kokoity, 4 April 2011.
11. The cause of the fire, which left only the outer walls intact, has never been fully established. The destruction of the historic building (erected after the Napoleonic fire of 1812) provided an excuse for its total reconstruction, which was criticised by conservationists for distorting the original architectural vision.
12. *Komsomolskaya Pravda*, 28 September 2004.
13. Surkov on Chechen television, 8 July 2011, quoted by Interfax and Reuters.
14. Dmitry Trenin, '*Moscow the Muscular': The Loneliness of an Aspiring Power Center* (Moscow: Carnegie Moscow Center Briefing, volume 11, issue 1, January 2009).

Chapter 7. Enemies Everywhere

1. Interview with Leonid Kuchma, 22 March 2011.
2. Interview with John E. Herbst, 16 May 2011.
3. Interview with Gleb Pavlovsky, 18 February 2011.
4. Interview with Sergei Markov, 30 June 2011.
5. Interview with Oleh Rybachuk, 28 November 2010.
6. Interview with Viktor Yushchenko, 29 November 2010.
7. Interview with Alexander Kwaśniewski, 24 November 2010.
8. Interview with Leonid Kuchma, 22 March 2011.
9. Interview with Alexander Kwaśniewski, 24 November 2010.
10. *Washington Post*, 9 February 2010.
11. Gleb Pavlovsky, *Nezavisimaya gazeta*, 7 December 2004.
12. *Nezavisimaya gazeta*, 7 December 2004.
13. Interview with Tony Brenton, 5 April 2011.
14. *ICNL (The International Journal of Not-for-Profit Law)*, volume 9, issue 1, December 2006.
15. Interview with Lyudmila Alexeyeva, 23 February 2011.
16. Interview with Jonathan Powell, 9 March 2011.
17. Interview with Mikhail Kasyanov, 16 February 2011.
18. Interview with Viktor Yushchenko, 29 November 2010.
19. Interview with Damon Wilson, 2 March 2011.
20. Interview with Oleh Rybachuk, 28 November 2010.
21. Interview with John E. Herbst, 16 May 2011.

Chapter 8. A New Cold War

1. Interview with Stephen Hadley, 24 January 2011.
2. Rather was at the centre of a controversy after publicising documents critical of President Bush's military service during the 2004 presidential campaign. The documents' authenticity was later disputed, and in November Rather announced he would retire the following March, but there was never any suggestion that Bush had put pressure on CBS to fire him.
3. Interview with Damon Wilson, 2 March 2011.
4. Interviews with Nicholas Burns, 21 January 2011, and Condoleezza Rice, 20 June 2011.
5. Wikileaks cable in the *Guardian*, 1 December 2010.
6. Interview with Oleg Mitvol, 14 April 2010.

7. These events are reconstructed from interviews with Condoleezza Rice, Bill Burns, Sergei Ivanov, Igor Ivanov, Sergei Lavrov and others.

8. Some of Litvinenko's colleagues later 'returned' to the FSB fold and accused him of having tricked them into making this appearance. For an excellent account of all the conspiracy theories and intrigues surrounding the case, see Martin Sixsmith, *The Litvinenko File* (London: Macmillan, 2007).

9. Yelena Tregubova, http://viperson.ru/wind.php?ID=413357& soch=1 (last accessed 7 September 2011).

10. Interview with David Miliband, 7 July 2011.

11. Interview with Sergei Lavrov, 25 October 2010.

12. Sixsmith, *The Litvinenko File*, pp 303ff.

Chapter 9. Media, Missiles, Medvedev

1. Dmitry Peskov, interviewed on Dozhd television, 4 October 2011.

2. US companies are obliged to declare fees received from foreign principals for 'political activities'. For the period January to June 2008, the fee declared by Ketchum and its partner The Washington Group for work done in North America and Japan on behalf of the Russian Federation was $2,436,600. GPlus received a similar sum for its work in Europe, making a total of almost $5 million for that six-month period. The initial contract for the G8 year has been rolled over year by year, with the fees for each new contract varying somewhat.

3. Dmitry Peskov, interviewed on Dozhd television, 4 October 2011.

4. See, for example, *The New Times*, 16 March 2009.

5. See Luke Harding, *Mafia State* (London: Guardian Books, 2011).

6. Lilia Shevtsova, *Lonely Power* (Moscow: Carnegie Endowment, 2010), pp 98ff.

7. Interviews with Dan Fata, 1 March 2011, and Eric Edelman, 4 March 2011.

8. Dmitri Trenin, 'Moscow the Muscular': The Loneliness of an Aspiring Power Center (Moscow: Carnegie Moscow Center Briefing, volume 11, issue 1, January 2009).

9. Interview with Sergei Prikhodko, 30 June 2011.
10. Off-the-record interview with senior Russian official.
11. Interview with Condoleezza Rice, 30 June 2011.
12. Interview with Stephen Hadley, 24 January 2011.
13. Interview with Eric Edelman, 4 March 2011.
14. Interview with Robert Gates, 16 May 2011.
15. Interview with Sergei Lavrov, 25 October 2010.
16. Interview with Anatoly Antonov, 2 April 2011.
17. Boris Nemtsov and Vladimir Milov, *Putin: Itogi* (Moscow: Novaya gazeta, 2008).
18. Michael McFaul and Kathryn Stoner-Weiss, 'The Myth of the Authoritarian Model', *Foreign Affairs*, volume 87, number 1, January/February 2008.

Chapter 10. The Descent into War

1. Interview with Damon Wilson, 2 March 2011.
2. Interview with Mikheil Saakashvili, 31 March 2011.
3. Interview with Jean-David Levitte, 12 March 2011.
4. Interview with Robert Gates, 16 May 2011.
5. Interview with Stephen Hadley, 24 January 2011.
6. Interview with Radoslaw Sikorski, 25 November 2010.
7. Interview with Condoleezza Rice, 20 June 2011.
8. Interview with Frank-Walter Steinmeier, 20 June 2011.
9. Angus Roxburgh, 'Georgia Fights for Nationhood', *National Geographic*, volume 181, number 5, May 1992.
10. Quoted in Thomas de Waal, *The Caucasus: An Introduction* (New York: Oxford University Press, 2010), p 208.
11. Interview with Damon Wilson, 2 March 2011.
12. http://www.rferl.org/content/Did_Russia_Plan_Its_War_In_Georgia __/1191460.html (last accessed 7 September 2011).
13. Interview with Giorgi Bokeria, 30 March 2011.
14. Interview with Batu Kutelia, 29 March 2011.
15. Interview with Nino Burjanadze, 29 March 2011.
16. Interview with Mikheil Saakashvili, 31 March 2011.
17. Interview with Sergei Prikhodko, 30 June 2011.
18. I do not regard Saakashvili as a particularly reliable witness. His interview for the TV series contained at least two 'memories' that are verifiably false. He has a clear tendency to embellish

stories to his own advantage.

19. Interview on Ekho Moskvy, published 7 August 2011.
20. Medvedev interview with Russia Today, PIK-TV and Ekho Moskvy, published 5 August 2011.
21. Interview with Condoleezza Rice, 20 June 2011.
22. Interview with Radoslaw Sikorski, 25 November 2010.
23. I accept that this is an oversimplification. The ethnic balance of Abkhazia changed hugely over the decades: the Abkhaz were once the majority ethnic group, and huge numbers of Georgians and Russians were brought into the region during the Soviet period – a deliberate Georgian policy, the Abkhaz say, to turn them into a minority.
24. Interview with Jean-David Levitte, 12 March 2011.
25. Medvedev interview with Russia Today, etc, 5 August 2011.
26. Interview with Condoleezza Rice, 14 April 2011.
27. Interview with Sergei Lavrov, 25 October 2010.
28. Interview with Mikheil Saakashvili, 31 March 2011.
29. Interview with Robert Gates, 16 May 2011.
30. Interview with Stephen Hadley, 24 January 2011.
31. In a live television phone-in programme on 4 December 2008 Putin was asked by a viewer, 'Is it true that you promised to hang Saakashvili by "one place"?' Putin paused for a moment, smiled, and replied: 'Why by "one"?'

Chapter 11. Resetting Relations with the West

1. Interview with Michael McFaul, 15 April 2011.
2. Interview with Sergei Ryabkov, 27 October 2010.
3. Interview with Sergei Prikhodko, 30 June 2011.
4. Interview with James Jones, 4 March 2011.

Chapter 12. The Strongman and His Friends

1. Interview with Alexei Kudrin, 14 December 2010.
2. Interview with German Gref, 7 December 2010.
3. Sergei Guriev and Aleh Tsyvinski, 'Challenges Facing the Russian Economy after the Crisis', in Sergei Guriev, Anders Aslund and Andrew Kuchins (eds), *Russia After the Global*

Economic Crisis (The Peterson Institute for International Economics, 2010), p 21.

4. Interview with Arkady Dvorkovich, 29 June 2011.
5. *Kommersant*, No. 124, 13 July 2010.
6. Currently available only in Russian and Swedish.
7. http://www.doingbusiness.org/rankings (last accessed 7 September 2011). The top ten countries for ease of doing business are, in order: Singapore, Hong Kong, New Zealand, UK, USA, Denmark, Canada, Norway, Ireland, Australia.
8. http://www.gazeta.ru/politics/2011/05/24_a_3627341.shtml (last accessed 7 September 2011).
9. http://news.kremlin.ru/transcripts/9368 (last accessed 7 September 2011).
10. Report by INDEM foundation, quoted in V. Milov, B. Nemtsov, V. Ryzhkov and O. Shorina (eds), *Putin. Korruptsiya. Nezavisimyy ekspertnyy doklad* (Moscow, 2011).
11. http:// eng.kremlin.ru/news/752 (last accessed 7 September 2011).
12. http://www.vedomosti.ru/politics/news/1247042/skandal_s_ zakupkami_tomografov (last accessed 7 September 2011).
13. http:// ria.ru/trend/belevitin_case_02062011/ (last accessed 7 September 2011).
14. *Financial Times*, 12 November 2010.
15. http://en.rian.ru/russia/20110706/165063309.html (last accessed 8 September 2011).
16. See http://russian-untouchables.com/eng/ (last accessed 7 September 2011).
17. *Guardian*, 21 December 2007. In a different interview, with *Die Welt*, Belkovsky put Putin's stake in Gunvor at 50 rather than 7 per cent.
18. Putin's own website reprints an article from the opposition newspaper *Novaya gazeta* about the prime minister's network of business friends and interests: http://premier.gov.ru/pda/eng/ premier/press/ru/4558/ (last accessed 7 September 2011).
19. *Financial Times*, 15 May 2008.
20. Milov, Nemtsov, Ryzhkov and Shorina (eds), *Putin. Korruptsiya. Nezavisimyy ekspertnyy doklad.*
21. *Guardian*, 1 December 2010.

22. http:// navalny.livejournal.com/526563.html.
23. http:// rospil.info/results.
24. See Julia Joffe's excellent account of Navalny's work in *The New Yorker*, 4 April 2011.

Chapter 13. Tandemology

1. Interview with Dimitry Muratov, 14 December 2010.
2. Interview with Arkady Dvorkovich, 29 June 2011.
3. Interview with Olga Kryshtanovskaya in *Svobodnaya pressa*, 8 February 2011, svpressa.ru/politic/article/38451 (last accessed 7 September 2011).
4. http://www.bfm.ru/news/2011/08/29/dvorkovich-zubkov-ne-ujdet-iz-gazproma-do-1-oktjabrja.html (last accessed 7 September 2011).
5. *Guardian*, 1 July 2011.
6. *Financial Times*, 20 June 2011.
7. http://www.rferl.org/content/medvedev_talks_reform_in_st_petersburg/24238558.html (last accessed 7 September 2011).

Chapter 14. Putin Mark III

1. http://vyrodok.livejournal.com/1600.html (last accessed 18 November 2012).
2. http://www.kommersant.ru/doc/1856438 (last accessed 20 November 2012).
3. http://izvestia.ru/news/510564 (last accessed 20 November 2012).
4. http://www.webcitation.org/mainframe.php (last accessed 21 November 2012).
5. Fyodor Lukyanov, 'What's the Problem with the US Ambassador?' Russia Today, 6 April 2012.
6. Interview with Dmitry Trenin, 25 November 2012.

Conclusion

1. http://valdaiclub.com/history/29960.html, 18 August 2011 (last accessed 7 September 2011).
2. http://www.kommersant.ru/doc/1921892 (last accessed 1

December 2012).

3. Archie Brown, *The Rise and Fall of Communism* (London: Vintage Books, 2010), p 602.

4. There is no correlation at all between the passing of the Jackson-Vanik amendment and the numbers of visas issued to Soviet Jews. In 1973 34,733 visas were issued, and in 1974 20,628; in 1975 (the first full year of Jackson-Vanik) the number fell to 13,221. It recovered to pre-Jackson-Vanik levels only in 1978 (28,865), reached a peak in 1979 (51,320), then slumped to less than a thousand a year in the early 1980s. Visa restrictions were lifted only under Gorbachev in 1989, leading to the emigration of hundreds of thousands in the early 1990s.

5. I notice that my book about the Gorbachev years ended very hopefully. See Angus Roxburgh, *The Second Russian Revolution* (London: BBC Books, 1991).

6. *Sunday Times*, 14 August 2011.

7. http://www.levada.ru/indeksy (last accessed 1 December 2012).

8. http://bd.fom.ru/pdf/d47ind12.pdf (last accessed 3 December 2012).

INDEX